Stories
That

Make
History

Mexico through
Elena Poniatowska's
Crónicas

Stories That Make History

Lynn Stephen

Duke University Press
Durham and London 2021

© 2021 Duke University Press
Designed by Aimee C. Harrison
Typeset in Adobe Caslon Pro and ITC Usherwood by Westchester

Library of Congress Cataloging-in-Publication Data
Names: Stephen, Lynn, author.
Title: Stories that make history : Mexico through Elena Poniatowska's
crónicas / Lynn Stephen.
Description: Durham : Duke University Press, 2021. | Includes
bibliographical references and index.
Identifiers: LCCN 2021001842 (print) | LCCN 2021001843 (ebook) ISBN
9781478013716 (hardcover)
ISBN 9781478014645 (paperback)
ISBN 9781478021940 (ebook)
Subjects: LCSH: Poniatowska, Elena. | Women authors,
Mexican—20th century—Biography. | Authors, Mexican—
20th century—Biography. | Politicalactivists— Mexico—Biography.|
Social movements—Mexico—History—20th century. | Mexico—
History—20th century. | BISAC: SOCIAL SCIENCE / Anthropology /
Cultural & Social | HISTORY / Latin America / Mexico Classification:
LCC PQ7297.P63 Z85 2021 (print) | LCC PQ7297.P63
(ebook) | DDC 868/.6409 [B]—dc23
LC recordavailableathttps:// lccn.loc.gov/2021001842
LC ebookrec ordavailableathttps:// lccn.loc.gov/2021001843

ISBN 978-1-4780-9266-7 (ebook other)

Cover art: Elena Poniatowska at her typewriter with a copy of *La noche de
Tlatelolco* on her desk, c. 1971. Courtesy of the Fundación Elena
Poniatowska Amor, Mexico City, Mexico.

Contents

Abbreviations

AMLO	Andrés Manuel López Obrador (president of Mexico)
CND	Convención Nacional Democrático (National Democratic Convention)
CNH	Consejo Nacional de Huelga (National Strike Council)
Comité ¡Eureka!	Comité Pro-Defensa de Presos Perseguidos, Desaparecidos y Exiliados Políticos de México (Committee for the Defense of Political Prisoners, Disappeared and Political Exiles of Mexico)
CUD	Coordinadora Única de Damnificados (United Coordinator of Earthquake Victims)
EZLN	Ejército Zapatista de Liberación Nacional (Zapatista Army of National Liberation)
IACHR	Inter-American Commission on Human Rights
IGIE	Interdisciplinary Group of Independent Experts
INI	Instituto Nacional Indigenista (National Indigenist Institute)
IPN	Instituto Politécnico Nacional (National Polytechnic Institute)
MLN	Movimiento de Liberación Nacional (Movement of National Liberation)
MESA	Mecanismo Especial de Seguimiento del asunto Ayotzinapa (Special Follow-Up Mechanism for the Ayotzinapa Case)
MORENA	Movimiento Regeneración Nacional (National Regeneration Movement)
NAFTA	North American Free Trade Agreement

PAN	Partido Acción Nacional (National Action Party)
PRD	Partido de la Revolución Democrática (Party of the Democratic Revolution)
PRI	Partido Revolucionario Institucional (Institutional Revolutionary Party)
TRIFE	Tribunal Federal Electoral (Federal Electoral Tribunal)
UNAM	Universidad Autónomo de México (National Autonomous University of Mexico)

Acknowledgments

This book emerged as an idea after a visit from Elena Poniatowska to the University of Oregon in May 2010. She delivered the Bartolomé de Las Casas Lecture in Latin American Studies. First, of course, I thank Elena for coming to Eugene, Oregon, but most of all I am thankful for our beautiful and ever-deepening friendship that accompanied the process of writing this book over the past ten years. I have greatly enjoyed my trips to Mexico City to visit with Elena and her family and to continue our conversations in Chimalstac over meals, tea, and more.

I want to also thank Carlos Aguirre, professor of history at the University of Oregon, who was the director of Latin American studies who brought Elena to be the Las Casas lecturer. Carlos has also been an amazing colleague and friend during the time this book was written and was one of the first people to really encourage me to go forward with the project.

After Elena's visit to Eugene, I taught a class, Seminario de Migración e Inmigración Indígena," at the Instituto de Estudios Antropológicos at the National Autonomous University of Mexico. There I was generously hosted by anthropologist Hernán Salas. It was during this time that I first visited Elena in her home and broached the idea of a book to her. Hernán was encouraging of this project since its beginning.

The summer before beginning a sabbatical in the fall of 2011, I went to Mexico City in late July and August to record my initial long interview with Elena over several days. My colleague and friend Gabriela Martínez, professor of journalism and communications at the University of Oregon, accompanied me for part of that visit and also helped with some video recordings in Elena's home. I thank Gabriela for this initial work together and our friendship and long history of collaboration in teaching, research, and documentary filmmaking.

That initial interview with Elena generated a transcript in Spanish that was about two hundred double-spaced pages. My then graduate student, Ivan Sandoval Cervantes, did a superb job of transcribing that long interview. I thank Ivan for his amazing work with me on this project. Other shorter transcriptions were done by another graduate student, Darien Combs, who is pursuing a PhD in counseling psychology. I appreciate her work with me on this project and other projects we share.

I want to thank friends and colleagues Rachel Sieder, Aída Hernández Castillo, and Teresa Sierra for lodging, great dinners, fun, and support during trips I took to Mexico City to move this project forward over the past nine years.

A major milestone in my writing of this book was a fellowship I received in the fall of 2015 from the Oregon Humanities Center (OHC), which allowed me to draft the introduction and one of the chapters of this manuscript. I thank Paul Peppis, director of OHC; Melissa Gustafson, OHC program coordinator; Peg Gearhart, communications coordinator of OHC; and Julia Heydon, former associate director of OHC. My time there and public talk provided valuable feedback and support for this project. I thank the Oregon Humanities Center and the College of Arts and Sciences at the University of Oregon for funds that supported the indexing of this book.

A second important stepping stone to the book manuscript was a session at the Latin American Studies Association (LASA) Congress in Lima, Peru, in 2017 organized by Morna Macleod and Natalia De Marinis centered on the Colombian anthropologist Myriam Jimeno's concept of emotional community. Titled "Comunidades Emocionales: Memoria y Justicia en América Latina," the double session provided me with an opportunity to develop the concept of strategic emotional political communities used in the framing of this book. I am extremely grateful for the critical feedback I received from Natalia De Marinis, Morna Macleod, and discussant Rachel Seider. My paper subsequently became a chapter in a book edited by Macleod and De Marinis. I am grateful to Palgrave Macmillan for permission to republish parts of that chapter, "Testimony, Social Memory, and Strategic/Emotional Political Communities in Elena Poniatowska's Crónicas," from *Resisting Violence: Emotional Communities in Latin America* (Cham, Switzerland: Palgrave Macmillan, 2018), 53–76.

A source of very significant support for this project has been a fellowship from the Center for U.S.-Mexican Studies at the University of California, San

Diego (UCSD), during the 2018–19 academic year while I was on sabbatical. It is there where I finished the book manuscript. This was my fourth stint at the Center for U.S.-Mexican Studies as a fellow and the fourth book I have completed there. I have a special place in my heart for the center and for San Diego. There, director Rafael Fernández de Castro provided a warm welcome and with Greg Mallinger, an old friend and coordinator of the fellowship program, put together a wonderful group of fellows. I thank my colleagues who were fellows with me for their warm reception, political engagement, and wonderful ideas and feedback on the book. They include Kevan Antonio Aguilar, Helga Baitenmann, Daniela Barba-Sánchez, Angie M. Bautista-Chavez, José Bucheli, James Daria, Silvia López Estrada, Cecilia Farfán-Méndez, Kevin Middlebrook, Sergio Miranda Pacheco, Francisco José Paoli Bolio, Jorge Ramirez, Tesalia Rizzo, Teresita Rocha-Jimenez, Melissa Rogers, Brian Stevenson, Abigail Thornton, and Carolina Valdivia. I also want to give a very special thanks to Matthew Vitz, from the Department of History at UCSD, who not only served as a fantastic discussant at a public talk I gave about the book project but generously read five draft chapters and provided bibliography and detailed feedback. Shannon Speed was a wonderful friend and colleague while we worked on a different book project.

Local friends Nancy Postery and Jeff Harkness provided wonderful dinners, great local outings, and fun times. Joyce Quaqundah, Steve Wallace, and their kids were wonderful friends and provided great meals, a warm place to hang out, and many nights of fun playing music and singing together. They kept my bass chops alive. Joyce and I took an amazing trip together to Baja to see whales that provided a much-needed break and adventure in February 2019 as I was in the last throes of completing the first draft of the manuscript.

For part of March 2019, I was in residence at Stanford University as the Latin American Perspectives Lecturer. There, Alberto Díaz Cayeros, director; Elizabeth Ackeron, associate director; Sara Clemente Vázquez, events and communications officer; and Perla Garcia Miranda, academic and student services administrator, all provided a very warm environment and helped me with many parts of my visit. I thank Alberto Díaz Cayeros; visiting faculty member Cristina Rivera-Garza; and Adan Griego, curator for Latin American, Iberian and Mexican American Collections at the Stanford Libraries, for their helpful suggestions on the book project.

Colleagues at the University of Oregon provided ongoing support and encouragement for this project and others while I was slowly completing the manuscript. They include Erin Beck, the late Sandi Morgen, Lamia Karim, Frances White, Ana Maurine Lara, Michael Hames García, Ernesto Martínez, Gabriela Martínez, Alai Reyes-Santos, Laura Pulido, Michelle McKinley, Margaret Hallock, Pedro García Caro, Alice Evans, Eli Meyers, and Feather Crawford, all of whom provided encouragement and support for this project at various stages. Robert Long provided important support and editing for project proposals while he was at the University of Oregon. The UO Dreamers Working Group was a joy to work with and provided an ongoing source of meaningful work through our ally trainings and more.

Christine Sherk provided important editorial assistance while I was writing the manuscript. I thank Sylvia Escarcega for her great translation work from Spanish to English of quotes from my interviews and untranslated works of Elena Poniatowska and other sources in Spanish in chapters 1, 2, 5, and 6. She has also been an important friend and support during different phases of this project. Translations in the introduction, chapters 3 and 4 and the conclusions were done by me. Exceptional editing on the second draft of the manuscript was provided by Anitra Grisales. I also thank Annalise Gardella for a final read-through and corrections. I am grateful to Brandon Larsen for the two maps he created for the book.

This project benefited from funds from the Phillip H. Knight Chair I hold, which I was able to use to partially support my sabbatical in 2018–19. The University of Oregon also provided generous support for my sabbatical year during 2011 and 2012, which allowed me to make significant progress on this manuscript. I want to thank former College of Arts and Sciences (CAS) dean Andrew Marcus, acting CAS dean Bruce Blonigan, and social science dean of CAS Phillip Scher, for their support during my sabbatical and before.

I truly appreciate the many letters of support that Patricia Zavella and Jean Jackson wrote for me while I was pursuing this project. I thank Beth Jorgenson and Deborah Castillo for their encouragement and letters in support of this project. I want to extend my deep appreciation to my editor, Gisela Fosada at Duke University Press. This is my fourth book with Duke, and Gisela has been behind this project since its inception and different incarnations. I appreciate her faith in me and the project and patience in waiting for me to complete it. I also want to recognize and remember Duke editor Valerie Millholland, who passed away in 2017. It was Valerie who first discussed this project with me and encouraged me to write this book and several others. ¡Valerie presente! I also thank the two anonymous reviewers for Duke University Press for their many useful and insightful ideas for how to improve the book. It is a much better book for their creativity and guidance.

I thank Alejandro de Avila for his ongoing interest and support of this project, for faithfully clipping Elena Poniatowska's columns out of *La Jornada* for me for many years, and for his ongoing friendship and for being a part of my family. To my mother, Suzanne Brown, I thank you for your lifelong support. It has been wonderful to have you close by during the past four years in Eugene and a pleasure to share time with your husband, Bill Rodgers. To my brother, Bruce, your visits and presence during important times is something I treasure and appreciate. To Gabriel and José, my sons, who are now grown young men, I thank you for all your love and our experiences together during this project and beyond. I am so proud of both of you. To my spouse, Ellen Herman, every day in every way, you have been my life partner. Our journey together continues now past its third decade, and I look forward to our walk together into the future. Through this book and so much more, you are the one.

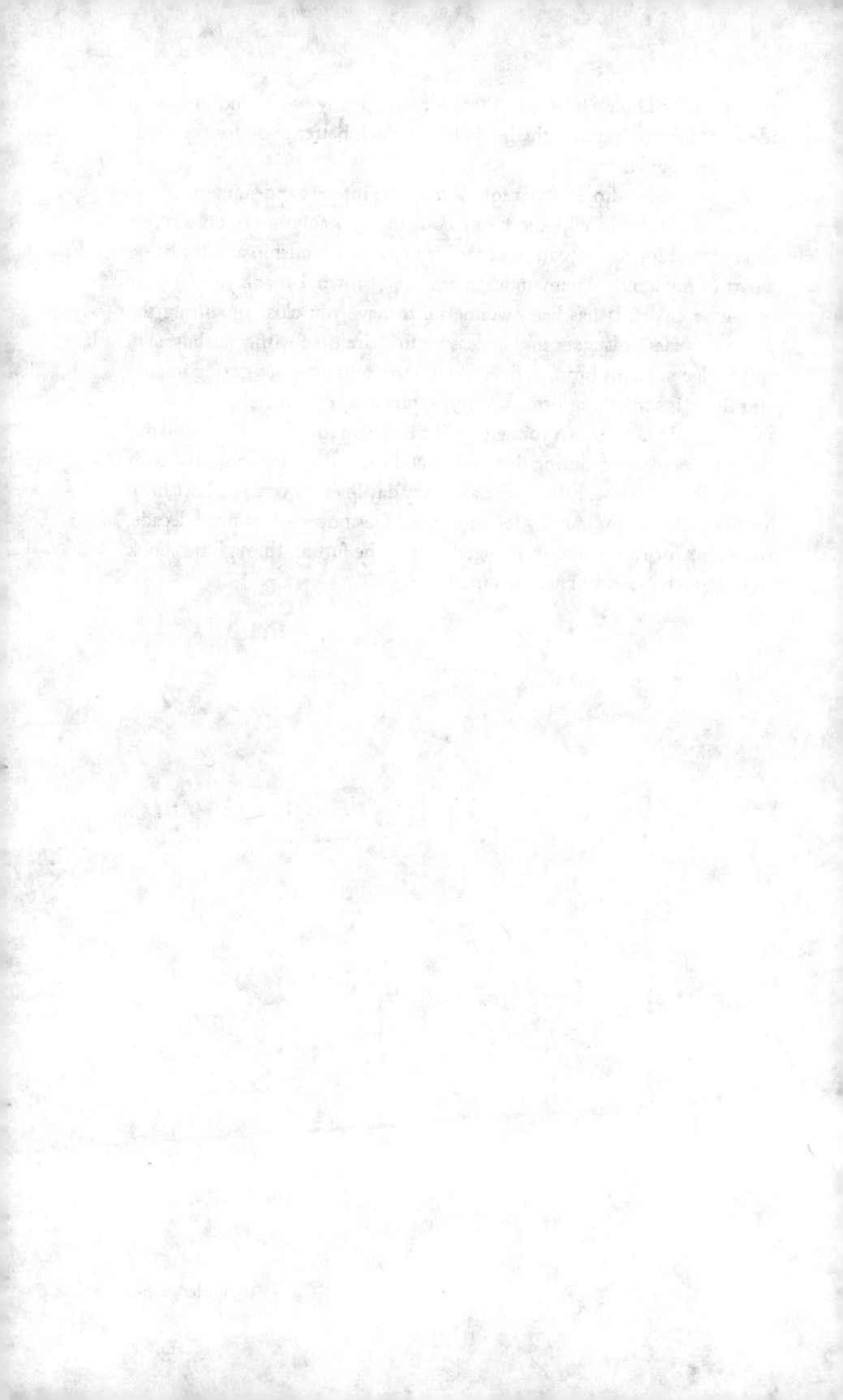

Introduction

On Testimony, Social Memory, and
Strategic Emotional Political Communities
in Elena Poniatowska's Crónicas

TO TRAVEL ACROSS THE ZÓCALO in Mexico City with Elena Poniatowska is to see her connected to her readers and public. In July 2012, I spent an afternoon with Poniatowska as she participated in a rally for Andrés Manuel López Obrador (AMLO), following national elections in which he ran for president a second time (the third time ended up being the charm). The rally took place in the midst of a large annual book fair, the Feria Internacional del Libro del Zócalo (International Book Fair of the Zócalo).

Ostensibly, we were crossing the Zócalo to look for a particular book Poniatowska was interested in. Instead, we spent at least an hour inching across this large public square as Poniatowska signed her books, primarily her crónicas, for dozens of people. In contemporary Mexico, the term *crónica* can refer to shorter essays written as reports for newspapers or to longer journalistic pieces written in a polished literary style, sometimes described as testimonial narratives. From thirteen-year-olds to people her own age to entire families, people commented again and again about how much they loved her books. Most mentioned *La noche de Tlatelolco* and *Nada, nadie: Las voces del temblor*. People had purchased these books and others, and they wanted her to inscribe them, which she did with unfailing

Figure I.1 Elena Poniatowska at the International Book Fair in the Zócalo, July 2012. Photograph by author.

patience, writing personalized inscriptions for each fan and agreeing to be photographed with most of them (figure I.1).

"This one is for my grandmother," who lived in Tlatelolco, said a young man with a small child in tow. "What is her name?" asked Poniatowska. "It is María de la Luz," he answered. Poniatowska slowly opened the front cover of a copy of *La noche de Tlatelolco*, gently folded it back, and carefully inscribed the book, dedicating it to María de la Luz. She often decorates such dedications with a drawing of flowers or hearts. She writes them in a careful script, with fat cursive letters and emphatic punctuation that exudes enthusiasm.

The people who stopped her were from all walks of Mexican society and many appeared to be working class, from what are called "las clases populares." Throughout this hour, I realized I was watching Poniatowska literally wading into her public. This book explores the power of Elena Poniatowska's crónicas and her public presence in creating what I call "strategic emotional political community" and influencing the historical memory of many Mexicans. As her interactions at the book fair illustrate, Poniatowska has forged a strong connection to her readers. One of the ways she has done this is by questioning the stance of the distanced and objective observer in her crónica writings and public persona. She has progressively pushed against the assumed divide between journalism and activism, between observation and participation. While her first book-length crónica, *La noche de Tlatelolco*, is explicitly written by someone who was not a direct participant in the student movement and is based on interviews prior to and after the 1968 massacre of students—from her reporting on Mexico's "Dirty War" of the 1970s when she was an advocate for the rights of political prisoners and the disappeared, to her account of the 1985 earthquake when she became an activist supporting one of the organizations that came out of the quake, to her crónica of the 2006 occupation of the Zócalo by Andrés Manuel López Obrador and the Partido de la Revolución Democrática (PRD, Party of the Democratic Revolution)—she documents her own participation in the occupation as well as her observations about the thousands of men and women who sustained it. In her journalistic crónicas with the Zapatistas in the 1990s, she becomes an ardent supporter of the Ejército Zapatista de Liberación Nacional (EZLN, Zapatista Army of National Liberation) and a public fan of Subcomandante Marcos and his writing. More recently, in her engagements with the movement seeking forty-three disappeared students from Ayotzinapa in 2014, Poniatowska not only writes and talks about the disappeared and their families but uses public spaces such as the Feria Internacional del Libro (International Book Fair) in Guadalajara to help the families gain access to news media and the public.

Elena Poniatowska at a book fair in Mexico City, surrounded by a multigenerational crowd of enthusiastic readers who call her name, talk to her, take photographs with her, and ask her to sign copies of books: this is just a snapshot of the interconnected stories this book tells about Poniatowska, her mastery of the crónica, and her and their roles in Mexican politics, culture, and memory. These stories include how Poniatowska has used the crónica along with public performances and dialogues as political tools; how her evolution as a writer and journalist defied the division between observation and participation; and how through time, based on her chronicling of crisis events, she helped shape an influential narrative of contemporary Mexican history.

In building narratives of history, we are always confronted by the fact of multiple and complex truths and the stakes and consequences of particular episodes and events. We also have to consider how these narratives are connected to individuals and communities of people. How do they make their way into a critical public formed by different kinds of people? How do particular versions of events come to take hold in print media? How are they shared, memorialized, and reproduced through time? What role does the writing style through which events are captured in print media have in engaging readers? How do writers engage in different kinds of public performances and dialogues that may augment the force of their writing and their personas in the eyes of their publics? How does engaged writing influence politics? Taking a close look at Elena Poniatowska as a public figure and chronicler of Mexico can help us answer these questions.

Her singular approach has made her deeply significant to many Mexicans and kept her relevant on the Mexican political and cultural stage for more than sixty years. If we look at Poniatowska's writing career through time, we can clearly see how her method urges us to dig deep in our quest to understand the truth, how different truths emerge, and how we can engage with what may ultimately be the unknowability of history. We can also see how, through her crónicas, Poniatowska has built a multistory house of collective memory.

Her writing as public engagement with Mexican politics along with her performative politics in multiple venues contributes to the consolidation of Poniatowska as a significant Mexican political figure. She is perhaps the Mexican writer who has had the greatest impact on oppositional politics during the past four decades. She has done this through the power of words, emotional expression, personal writing, and stories in a style very different from masculine writing of the same period. Through respect and a deep probing of her characters' emotions, she connects them to her readers across class, ethnicity, race, and generations. Through telling the stories of those left on the outside looking in, of the poor and working classes who are the builders of popular culture, Poniatowska widened and deepened who is visible and heard in Mexican history. One of her most important vehicles for doing this is through the crónica.

On Telling Stories. Whose, How, and Why

The crónica is a major genre in Mexican letters that is malleable in nature and can be tied to earlier narrative forms such as "The History of the Indies of New Spain and Islands of the Mainland" by Diego Durán, commonly referred to as the Durán Codex, published around 1579. In Mexico, the crónica is a literary genre that serves as the major bridge between politics and culture. Poniatowska has excelled in both short and long forms of crónicas; analysts of her early career (when she was a journalist specializing in interviews) even credit her with inventing a particular Mexican crónica style and a unique style of fiction built on real-life characters and situations, along with writer Carlos Monsiváis.[1] Her longer crónicas are known for their gripping narratives, such as the layered stories that help us see, smell, hear, and feel the tragedy of the earthquake in Mexico City that registered 8.0 on the Richter scale, as documented in *Nada, nadie*. Testimonies shared orally and told into a tape recorder or written up in detailed notes and translated into a text are the building blocks in her crónicas.

In Mexico, historians Eugenia Meyer and Alicia Olivera de Bonfil published a seminal article in 1970, "La historia oral: Origen, metodología, desarrollo y perspectivas" (Oral history: origin, methods, development and perspective). As part of the research team that founded the Departamento de Investigaciones Históricas (Department of Historical Investigations) at the government-funded Instituto Nacional de Antropología e Historia (National Institute of Anthropology and History), they worked with others, including Winberto Jiménez Moreno, to organize a sound (oral history) archive in 1959, "with the objective of retrieving and preserving live testimonies from distinguished people from political and military life during the Mexican Revolution of 1910."[2] In 1968 they concentrated their oral history project on all kinds of survivors of the Mexican Revolution, whose stories were deemed of urgent importance because of their advanced age. In 1985 Olivera de Bonfil published *Mi pueblo durante la Revolución* (My town during the Revolution), which highlighted testimonies of the revolution from the oral history archive at the Instituto Nacional de Antropología e Historia. Meyer published accounts of socialist education in Mexico under President Lázaro Cárdenas (1934–40), exiles from the Spanish Civil War in Mexico (who arrived during the Cárdenas presidency), exiles from other Latin American countries, and other topics—all based on oral histories.

In their article, Meyer and Olivera de Bonfil lay out guidelines for how to conduct oral histories and note that "humble people, less culturally evolved, are more accessible for interviews."[3] While today we would clearly question the idea of people being "more or less culturally evolved," the importance of Meyer and Olivera de Bonfil's project at the time was to validate a wide range of perspectives on the Mexican Revolution and other historical events and to affirm the role of oral accounts in the construction of historical narratives. The fact that this movement happened in Mexico City at the same time that journalists were pursuing interviews and using oral testimonies in their newspaper and supplement stories is no coincidence. The use of tape recorders, transcriptions of what people said, and then their editing and publication was a growing practice in Mexico in the 1960s and 1970s. Elena Poniatowska's use of testimonials she collected, previously published testimonies and narratives, and newspaper articles in her first book-length crónica, *La noche de Tlatelolco* (1971), is consistent with the legitimization of oral histories and narratives in the Mexican academy through the work of Meyer, Olivera de Bonfil, and others.

Oral testimony refers to a person's account of an event or experience as delivered from their lips. It is an oral recounting of a person's perception of a past event through sight, sound, smell, and other sensory information. It signifies witnessing and is often performative and public.[4] The practice of oral testimony has been broadly defined as a form of retrospective public witnessing of historical events that are "essentially not over" and are "in some sense brought into being by the process (itself interminable) of testimonial witnessing."[5] In this way, oral testimony can become a vehicle for broadening historical truth by opening up who legitimately speaks, and is heard, in a given society.

There is a robust literature on the role of *testimonio* (testimony) in Latin American social movements and politics, and in determining what kinds of "truths" are captured through testimonies.[6] Spurred by David Stoll's book *Rigoberta Menchú and the Story of All Poor Guatemalans* (1999), which questions the objective "truth" of *I, Rigoberta Menchú: An Indian Woman in Guatemala* (1983), an Indigenous Guatemalan's published testimony about the violence and genocide perpetrated against her family and other Indigenous peoples, the debate has taken many different directions. In my 2013 book on the role of testimony in a Oaxacan social movement that displaced the state for several months, I take the position of the film critic José Rabasa: all "forms of collecting testimony are by definition forms of engaged dissemination of the truth."[7]

Poniatowska's crónicas and other writings have been crucial in broadening Mexican historical truths and perspectives. Poniatowska's friend and fellow chronicler, Carlos Monsiváis (1938–2010), pointed to Poniatowska's *La noche de Tlatelolco* and *Fuerte es el silencio* (1980 crónica of political prisoners, the disappeared, and victims of Mexico's Dirty War of the 1970s) as seminal contributions to the contemporary genre of Mexican chronicles.[8] Beth Jörgensen, a longtime analyst of Poniatowska's work, writes that the contemporary Mexican chronicle, which is "perched on the threshold between literature and advocacy, narrative and essay, document and figure, elite and popular culture, and investigation and advocacy . . . makes a contribution to democratizing culture and to imagining a more inclusive and authentic democracy."[9] While Poniatowska's crónicas do all of this, they also do something more. They forge direct emotional connections between the oral testimonies of the people whose stories she tells and readers. Channeling her ability to create complex and rich characters in her novels, Poniatowska uses this same technique to communicate the full humanity of those whose stories she shares and links them to larger political, economic, and social relationships and structures. One of the main conduits of communication is human emotion. In order to develop the concept of emotional strategic political community, I am particularly interested in how testimony forges emotional connection. How do people giving public testimony on repression and traumatic events and those listening become emotionally connected to each other? Can they, through this connection, act together to denounce, document, and create political impact? Are they part of emotional communities tying speakers and listeners together through shared emotional connections linked to difficult and tragic events? As I explain later in this introduction, the concept of "emotional community" is proposed by Colombian anthropologist Myriam Jimeno as a way of positing how it is that people can become connected through traumatic events.[10] The oral narratives in crónicas and in public performances by writers such as Poniatowska bring listeners and readers into community with those whose stories are shared. The transfer of what are told as oral testimonies onto the written, textualized page and their dissemination can play an important role in whose voices are heard, and by whom. Testimonies collected and widely disseminated through crónicas and in other forms can influence the way that historical events are remembered and canonized.

Poniatowska has challenged the idea that she "gives voice" to the people whose stories she records, transcribes, and publishes: "I always believed that the people had a strong voice. When they say that 'the people don't have a voice,' I say that, on the contrary, they have a very powerful voice. The voice of the people is much stronger than the conventional voices that we are used to hearing."[11] But a voice captured on an audio recorder and then filed away and never transcribed or played back does not resonate beyond the moment of telling. If, however, the recording of a voice is transcribed and included in a newspaper article that is read by thousands, it is "heard" by many. In the case of the 1985 Mexico City earthquake, as I explore in chapter 3, Poniatowska first tape recorded narratives of survivors on a daily basis, wrote them up, and published them in *La Jornada*. Later, in 1988, they were published as a book titled *Nada, nadie: Las voces del temblor*.[12] The daily publication of the narratives in 1985 helped bring survivors' experiences to the entire country. As a published writer of crónicas, Poniatowska has a critical role in amplifying what she says are already strong voices.

The key, then, to the effectiveness of crónicas, like the oral histories Meyer and Olivera de Bonfil published, is the amplification of voices that are often silenced, actively delegitimized, or confined to family and neighborhood conversations. Poniatowska agrees that this is a legitimate focus for her work: "Rather than give voice, what I have been doing is to gather voices that have not been heard before. This has been a fascinating process for me because it opened up a world for me that was very creative and that I learned so much from. I learned a great deal from the people I encountered in the street. And I keep on learning."[13]

Why Crónicas?

Poniatowska credits her self-taught training in journalism, which began in the 1950s, with giving her the tools to solicit testimonies and craft them into the narratives of crónicas. Poniatowska joined the *Excélsior* newspaper in 1953 to write for the "society" column. Since that time, what has remained of central importance to her is the question of "¿para qué?" (what for?). What are the stakes in journalism and publishing crónicas? What are the consequences of bringing forward particular points of view and getting them into the public record? How can writing and publication be political tools? When I asked her to define the genre of the "crónica," Poniatowska highlighted these questions through her emphasis on the "¿para qué?"

> I think that you have to respond to the crónica with the four or five fundamental, basic questions of journalism, which are: how, where, when, why, and then you always add another question, which is *para qué*, what for? Why does it matter? These are the fundamentals they teach to any journalist when they start their career.... But for me, you always have to add, why. Why are you telling something? I believe that the crónica is an event that you observe and you try to be the most objective possible, but you are always limited by who you are as a person.[14]

While she mentions trying to be "objective," she tempers this by acknowledging that how a writer observes and captures an event on the page is always linked to who the writer is. In this sense, a writer's politics will likely influence how they document and interpret particular events.

In discussing the genre of the crónica in relation to other literary genres in Mexico, Poniatowska believes that the Mexican public is more interested in crónicas than novels.

The material of real life is so amazing that it forms the basis for stories that are far superior to anything that could be plucked from a writer's imagination. In the case of the crónicas in Mexico, the great chroniclers [cronistas] really have been more important than novelists. You could think about the case of Monsiváis, who is an extraordinary chronicler. . . . A fabulous crónica goes so much further than any novel. For example, you have the case of one year, 1994, which includes the assassination of Luis Donaldo Colosio, presidential candidate of the PRI [Partido Revolucionario Institucional (Institutional Revolutionary Party)]. The same year Subcomandante Marcos and the EZLN burst on the scene in Chiapas. And that very same year, the wife of Luis Donaldo Colosio, Diana Laura—who was a lovely woman—dies of cancer. Before she dies, she refuses to take the arm of Carlos Salinas de Gortari [who was the actual president of Mexico at the time] when he offers it. You couldn't find a greater amount of Shakespearean tragedy than this.[15]

Mexico provides ample dramatic material for crónicas and that has been the case since their start. Poniatowska places contemporary Mexican crónicas and cronistas in a genealogy beginning with Bernal Díaz del Castillo, originally a foot soldier in the army of Hernán Cortés in the conquest of Mexico and later the governor of Santiago de los Caballeros de Guatemala, present-day Antigua, Guatemala. His chronicle, *Historia verdadera de la conquista de la Nueva España* (The true history of the conquest of New Spain), was completed in 1568. As she explains, "Mexico is a country linked to the Chronicles of the Indies, from Bernal Díaz del Castillo and from others who sent their chronicles to Spain. We have cronistas who go much further than novelists and they cover an entire epoch. The important thing in a country as big as Mexico is to document the country."[16] She identifies in some ways with chronicler Díaz del Castillo as he moved through Mexico for the first time, chronicling what he saw, informed by his foreign Spanish background. Poniatowska felt a powerful sense of discovery as her own writing developed and she came to know the many different Mexicos that existed in parallel to her life as a child in an upper-class family with many privileges. When she came to Mexico City from France at age ten, everything was new and interesting to her: "I remember arriving in Mexico.

In contrast with France where I came from, when I looked at the map of Mexico, I saw zones that were yellow and it said, 'zona por descubrir,' zone still to be discovered. That was fascinating to me."[17] The zones "of discovery" on the map Poniatowska saw as a child erased Indigenous precolonial crónicas. Ethnohistorians of Mexico point to the importance of Indigenous codices in the genealogy of crónicas, which begins long before the conquest. The largest collection of preconquest Indigenous documents are Mixtec Codices, which contain genealogies, biographies of particular individuals, mythologies, and accounts of ceremonies and important events.[18] The history of crónicas has deep roots in Mexico, a perspective Poniatowska endorses in general and in relation to her own work.

Heralded writer and chronicler Carlos Monsiváis also discusses crónicas in relation to the era of conquest in Mexico. In the prologue to his edited book, *A ustedes les consta: Antología de la crónica en México* (You will make known: anthology of the chronicle in Mexico), Monsiváis begins with an epitaph that links the past and present through the written form of the chronicle: "And the Aztecs arrived from Aztlán unto Lake Tenochtitlán, and observed the signs as prophesied, and there with the nopal, eagle, and serpent, a crowd of reporters and chroniclers awaited them."[19] This passage subtly suggests how time travels through chroniclers, linking the Spanish chroniclers and seemingly present-day reporters to the arrival of the Aztecs from Aztlán to Lake Tenochtitlán. While splashed with Monsiváis's ironic sense of humor, the epitaph is quite serious in relation to what Monsiváis identifies as key to the definition of a chronicle: "a literary reconstruction of historically verifiable events, characters, and atmospheres in which attention to language and form prevails over the immediate demands of reporting information."[20]

Crónicas and Gender

While historically many chroniclers have been male, recent scholarship on colonial women writers has also analyzed those who wrote letters, inquisitorial transcripts, and wills and testaments as part of the genre. Valeria Añón suggests that although women's writing was often relegated to the "private sphere," if we look carefully at the colonial written record, we can find forms of chronicle that women wrote that were directed to public authorities.[21] For example, a letter from Isabel de Guevara to Governess Princess Juana, written in Asunción in 1556, narrates the conquest of Río de la Plata while highlighting the role of women in that process.[22] Other documents such as wills and testaments reflect women's direct voices and articulate their desires. Isabel Moctezuma (Mexico, 1510–1550) and Francisca Pizarro (Cusco, 1534–Madrid, 1598) are examples of women who left such documents.[23]

Michelle McKinley's pathbreaking book, *Fractional Freedoms: Slavery, Intimacy, and Legal Mobilization in Colonial Lima, 1600–1700*, uses legal and ecclesiastical archives to highlight hidden sources of women's testimony, suggesting that they serve as a kind of crónica. For example, slave women used *censuras hasta anathema* (censures until damned)—publicly stated demands issued from the pulpit during Mass "requiring those with knowledge of an event or action to provide truthful testimony or suffer the consequences of excommunication" or ultimately damnation—to gain a forum.[24] McKinley's original use of religious archives and her skill in highlighting the testimonies of enslaved women as legal and everyday protagonists who occupied multiple identities and fought for their own and their children's freedom have added much to our understanding of how colonial women saw their world and worked to have their experiences chronicled and documented. While discussions of contemporary crónicas often emphasize their hybrid nature and connection to orality, if we are able to expand our notion of varied "discursive forms and other traditions in which the importance of orality ... takes center stage," we can successfully include many more women as chroniclers of the colonial period in Latin America.[25] While that is not my primary focus here, I feel it is important to recognize the current work being done to broaden the analysis of crónicas throughout Latin America history, particularly those written by women.

Historically, women's crónicas have not received the same attention as men's have in Mexico. The "premier" urban chronicler of Mexico City is usually considered to be Salvador Novo (1904–1974). In fact, Novo was named the official chronicler of Mexico City in 1965 by President Gustavo Díaz Ordaz. Novo launched his writing career in the early 1920s and became a poet, essayist, journalist, and member of an avant-garde "non group-group" of writers. While known for his writing, he also became a figure of popular culture himself, frequently photographed and appearing on radio and television. Writing thousands of articles on Mexico City that painted the city in vibrant terms, he cultivated a "provocative public persona, conspicuously exploring frivolous or banal themes precisely at the time when intellectuals were expected to act as solemn guides for a nation that was emerging from ten years of civil war."[26] Doing little to hide his homosexuality, Novo celebrated the boom in popular culture through newspapers, magazines, radio, and cinema, bringing them to the attention of urban Mexicans. Closely linked to official government circles—and supporting the official version of events in the 1968 student massacre in Tlatelolco—Novo had a consistent conservative tone to his writing. He later was of interest to a broader public because of his pioneering role as an "out" gay writer in Mexico.[27]

At the same time that Novo was writing in Mexico City, so was Cube Bonifant. In fact, her first column was for *El Universal Ilustrado* magazine in 1921, the same publication that would become a stepping-stone for Salvador Novo. Writing what was ostensibly an advice column for women, she offered "sharp social and political criticism that would undoubtedly have been censured in more serious sections of newspapers."[28] She went on to write film criticism for the next twenty years, providing both historical context about films and comments on trends and genres. She acted as well, and became a public persona. Known for her acerbic wit and confrontational style, she pioneered a kind, ironic humor and contentious writing that other chroniclers later followed. Because she was female, Bonifant was expected to write for an audience of women. As Viviane Mahieux, who analyzes the writing of Bonifant and other female urban chroniclers in Latin America, notes, "rarely could a female chronicler walk out of the feminine page to other sections of a publication without an anxious editor pointing out the unique status of her gender."[29] Bonifant began to write for the daily *El Mundo* in 1922 in a column called "Solo para ustedes" (Only for you). But the name was later changed to "Solo para vosotras" (Only for you women).[30] In writing about radio in a different publication, she simply signed her initials. By writing about film for much of her later career, she was able to escape the gender straitjacket to some degree, but open coverage of news and politics in the mainstream sections of newspapers was not an option for her or other women writers. They had to fit their critical commentaries into other spaces.

Bonifant's early career writing for women in some ways foreshadows that of Poniatowska, who first wrote for the society section and stuck to the interview format. She also wrote often about Mexican literature, film, and culture. If seen from a gendered point of view, the form of the crónica that Poniatowska became known for, beginning with her book *La noche de Tlatelolco*, could be seen as a skillful adaptation, innovation, and reinvention of the spaces to which female journalists were confined. The style she developed in writing shorter essays about everyday Mexicans, in interviews, and in observations that were published in supplements and parts of the newspapers not formally defined as "news" is consistent with the kind of limits put on women's writing. By publishing her 1968 crónicas in book form in 1971, she was able to break out of the gendered spaces of newspapers and cultural supplements. As the formats and number of newspapers, magazines, and other print media grew from the 1960s on, the options for where and how to publish also grew. Poniatowska's commitment to focusing on women in her newspaper and book crónicas have helped her forge a connection with female readers and to profile women as participants in history in ways that were often overlooked by other reporters.

While male writers such as Monsiváis, a close friend of Poniatowska's, use wit and keen intellectual insight to engage with politics and popular culture, they do not use emotional expression or engage with the emotions and feelings of those they portray to connect with readers. Poniatowska does, and that, I suggest, is an important part of the power of her writing. At a larger level, Poniatowska has also made the sentiments, experiences, and insights of a wide range of different kinds of Mexican women legible and legitimized in Mexican society. Her crónicas, in particular, have emphasized the participation of women in a wide range of social movements and have illustrated the importance of their activism. As a woman writer who has elevated women in her writing for five decades, she has also participated in widening the participation of women and others in the Mexican polity.

The Power of the Crónica

In his 1987 essay "De la Santa Doctrina al Espíritu Público (Sobre las funciones de la crónica en México)"—often known as his complaint about why not enough attention is paid to crónica writing—Monsiváis outlines some key functions of the crónicas in Mexico: "Why has the crónica been situated in such a marginal position in our literary history? Neither the enormous prestige of poetry, nor the omnipresent seduction of the novel are sufficient explanations for the almost absolute disdain for a genre that is so central to the relationships between literature and society, between history and daily life, between the reader and the formation of literary taste, between information and amenity, between testimony and the primary material of fiction, between journalism and the project of nation-building."[31]

Discussed by literary analysts as a hybrid text or "liminal genre," the chronicle sits at the intersection of fiction and nonfiction.[32] As Jörgensen notes, in Mexico "literature is not systematically divided into fiction and nonfiction texts," providing the opening for genres like the crónica, which straddles both categories.[33] She goes on to examine how the role of language itself and postmodern theorizing about language and discourse offer tools for helping us see how "skepticism toward what we know about the world and how we know it increasingly pervades literary writing, historiography, journalism, anthropology, and ethnography."[34] Jörgensen suggests that if histories of events are understood not as "what actually happened" but as discourses "not in the service of truth, but of power," then this produces an instability in textual categories.[35] Jörgensen's insight that histories and narratives of events should be taken as discourses in the service of power is important. What I hope to document in this book is how Poniatowska's crónicas—through their narration of historical events from multiple perspectives, often highlighting the voices of those who are not in power—push back on power. Discourse cannot be taken as "the truth" but as a part of the human experience of events. Thus, the versions of events we find in Poniatowska's crónicas should be seen as broadening history. She is telling stories that make history, as the title of this book suggests.

Jörgensen further argues that beyond making a case for "reality" in nonfiction (which one can question based on language as constitutive and not reflective of human perception, memory, and communication), there is little else that "separates nonfiction and fiction as verbal texts."[36] There are, in fact, more similarities than differences between the two:

> all manner of linguistic registers, narrative structures, and rhetorical devices are common in all modes of storytelling. Most importantly, the story itself, whether it be characterized as historically based in nonfiction or hypothetical in fiction, is equally employed in both forms, and the strategies of emplotment construct a meaning that exists only in the narrative, and not, even for nonfiction, in some preexisting, original form that writing has somehow retrieved. Here is where the distinction threatens to blur. In the recognition that the plot or nonfictional narrative shapes or composes its thematic "content" and does not simply transmit a meaning already contained in real-life events, nonfiction seems to cut loose from its moorings to the referent and edge toward fiction.[37]

Many of the conventions of storytelling are common between fiction and nonfiction, blurring the distinction. In crónicas, the nonfictional narrative shapes the interpretation of the oral testimonies. In *Nada, nadie*, for example, each individual oral narrative achieves its meaning not in isolation but because of the larger narrative structure it is a part of. The power of crónicas comes from their storytelling conventions and the ways in which individual experiences are interpreted as part of a wider, collective experience. In the case of Poniatowska's crónica *Nada, nadie*, for example, the testimony of Judith García, "My Family Was Not Killed by the Earthquake; What Killed Them Was the Fraud and Corruption Fostered by the Government," achieves its power both through García's individual experience and the emotional communication of her raw fear and terror— "I thought, 'I'm going to die; I'm on the fifth floor, I'm going to die.'...I knew I was being ejected. It occurred to me to look for the window frame, and I thought that by falling from the fifth floor I was going to be the one killed"—and its connection to a larger interpretive frame.[38] After detailing how her family died and by some miracle she survived, García continues, "I want to state that the people who died didn't die because of the earthquake; that is a lie. People died because of poor construction, because of fraud, because of the criminal incapacity and the inefficiency of a corrupt government that doesn't give a damn about people living and working in buildings that can collapse."[39] This oral testimony coexists within the larger structure of the book, which builds layer after layer of similar stories, and then oral testimonies from social movement activists who point to a long history of poor construction, fraud, and government ineptitude.

While Jörgensen places crónicas within the set of overlapping conventions that characterize fiction and nonfiction, Linda Egan proposes what she calls "an Indigenous theory of the chronicle," which arises "out of the works themselves."[40] Her analysis is based on the work of Monsiváis as a journalist and theorist.[41] She suggests that a crónica does the following:

- Includes history . . . and [because it translates local and national experiences into literature, is the incomparable ally and accomplice of history], but itself is not history;[42]
- Belongs to the field of journalism but exceeds the brief length of both straight news reportage and opinion-page essay;
- Enjoys close kinship with the essay, but stretches and ultimately overwrites that form's staid boundaries;
- May contain the testimony of witnesses or others . . . without becoming what is understood today in Latin America as *testimonio*; and
- Ostentatiously helps itself to the same narrative tools used by the short story and the novel, and thus may, at least in part and some of the time, resemble fictional discourse.[43]

These characteristics that Egan identifies underscore Jörgensen's point about the fuzzy line between fiction and nonfiction. My primary concern here is to explore the power of the crónica in using cultural forms to transform politics and how we remember historical events. In this project, its hybridity and mixing of genres within the space of a storytelling narrative is precisely the secret to its transformative power. Crónicas, perhaps more than other literary forms, have the potential to reach a broader audience, and therein lies their power.

Encountering Reality through Storytelling

Why do people in Mexico like to read crónicas? Due to their specific form, Jörgensen suggests, crónicas permit an encounter with reality and combine "the power of storytelling with the power of critical commentary and analysis within the authorizing frame of nonfiction discourse."[44] Several other characteristics, Jörgensen highlights, contribute to the appeal of crónicas to a broad audience. The crónica "seamlessly blends fact with fiction and the urgency of on-location reporting with a more literary attention to style and aesthetics. . . . It freely borrows characteristics of the short story, the essay, and the ethnographic narrative in offering a perspective that frequently runs counter to official or authorized versions of events."[45] By drawing on the drama of real life, blending it with the aesthetics of storytelling and striking photographs, invoking a prominent orality of language and testimony—that is, retelling what happened from multivocal perspectives—the crónica draws readers into intense emotions and often crisis situations.

In her discussion of what she terms crisis chronicles, Jörgensen comments on how both Monsiváis in *"No sin nosotros": Los días del terremoto, 1985–2005* ("Not without us": Days of the earthquake) and Poniatowska in *Nada, nadie* not only document the tragedies that thousands of people suffered in the earthquake but also "delve into existing structural factors that cause or exacerbate catastrophic events and the potential for a constructive challenge to the status quo."[46] In the case of Poniatowska, I would build on Jörgensen's observation to say this is a fundamental characteristic of all her crónicas, and is part of the ways in which her written works as well as her very public persona have contributed to a powerful narrative of Mexican history and politics.

Egan suggests that cronistas such as Monsiváis and Poniatowska deliberately position themselves to report on sites of struggle and social movements—an observation with which many would agree. She suggests that crónicas can be understood as critical mirrors of society: "The crónica positions itself in a public space to hold up a critical mirror to society caught in the act of re-inventing itself. . . . But the cronista, practicing what has aptly been called transformational journalism, will choose to report on thematic sites where struggles over power implicitly contain the greatest potential for change."[47] Thinking of crónicas as critical mirrors makes a great deal of sense, particularly in their ability to reveal structural causes of inequality and injustice through a literary form that uses storytelling to convey this information. The movement between the first-person voice of the author and the third-person voice of others telling what happened to them is one of the conventions that makes this possible.

Unlike newspaper stories that in the past could be thrown away and thus were somewhat disposable (at least until the advent of the digital archiving of newspaper stories, which may give them eternal, if not a very long, life), the compiling of individual stories and testimonies in books gave that form of crónica perhaps a different purpose. Documentation of testimonies at a particular point in time—as Poniatowska does in her crónicas—does not freeze the meaning or significance of those testimonies in the moment. Each time they are recited, read, and remembered, they acquire new meaning in a new context. And it is also the emotion embedded in such public testimonies that allows them to transcend specific historical contexts. In this way, social memory can be thought of as having ever-changing and distinct relationships with time.

The models of time that many Indigenous peoples work with can provide us with important insights here. Rather than assume that time is linear and that we as humans exist on one plane marked by a distinct past, present, and future, the knowledge systems of Native peoples—such as the Nahua, the Maya, the Nasa, the Mixtec, and the Kahnawake Mohawks—can link the past, present, and future through one event, through one feature of the landscape that marks a significant occurrence, or through a ritual, a song, a prayer, or a map.[48] If we think of a testimony or collections of testimonies on the written pages of crónicas as symbolic objects, like a prayer or genealogy that has emotional force through its telling and reproduction, then we can see it as a continual generator of emotion and memory.

Crónicas and Strategic Emotional Political Communities

Poniatowska's crónicas—often containing firsthand testimonies of intense suffering, trauma, and resilience—result in the construction of what Myriam Jimeno has called "emotional community."[49] I build on Jimeno's concept to explore how textualized oral testimony can spark emotional and political connections, often across economic and social difference. This is not to deny the often-entrenched racial, ethnic, socioeconomic, and gender hierarchies that permeate the network of people who provide and listen to someone's testimony about a traumatic event. Rather, it is to suggest how emotion—such as the fear felt in looking for disappeared loved ones after an earthquake or after detention by police—can serve as a link across difference to forge strategic emotional political communities that, in turn, can have an impact on how tragic events are remembered and, through historical memory, forge paths for current political action. In most cases, this network of testifiers and readers, what I call a *strategic emotional political community*, are brought together in a shared political ethic.

Here I would like to briefly unpack the four components of this concept and their individual and mutually constituted meanings. *Strategic* may recall for some the concept of "strategic essentialism," coined by postcolonial theorist Gayatri Chakravorty Spivak to describe how marginalized and minoritized groups mobilize around a shared identity to represent themselves. Much discussed in anthropology and ultimately disavowed by Spivak herself because of the way the concept was used by nationalists, my intention here is not to channel the original Spivakian sense of the word.[50] The word *strategic* here refers to the ways in which flexible and differentiated communities have both been documented by writers such as Poniatowska in particular political junctures in order to move forward a particular political agenda but also in terms of the kinds of choices involving intentionality and selectivity that is part of how Poniatowska and any writer or chronicler gives meaning to a particular event. Tragic and dramatic events like earthquakes, massacres, and, as I write today, pandemics tend to magnify existing inequalities and injustices. Often social movements and other forces for change emerge out of these moments, and in that sense, they work strategically in the space created by the rupture of the "normal" or status quo. Strategic in the sense that I am using it here in relation to emotional political communities has to do with when, how, and with what means an event, a group of people, a social movement, or other phenomena are represented by an author. Politically strategic means that an author like

Poniatowska aims to create a community and intends for it to have a political dimension, such as pushing the government to reform. At the same time, politically strategic refers to the intention to build a sector of critical and politicized readers and actors, usually in concert with others.

Emotional in this concept has to do with the embodied, affective dimensions of connection that are wrought in life through shared participation in events and how such connection is crafted on the page by a writer such as Poniatowska. One of the distinguishing characteristics of Poniatowska's writing is her unique ability to capture the personalities, feelings, and affective dimensions of those she writes about and connect them to larger events but also to readers. I say much more on this in the pages ahead and also in relation to the concept of emotional communities coined by Jimeno.

Political refers here not only to institutional and electoral politics but in relation to the ways that Poniatowska and other writers work in crafting their political participation and performances to include informal politics such as activism, media campaigns, theater, rallies, and now social media. Poniatowska has been one of the major Mexican figures over the past four or five decades who has helped redefine what counts as politics in Mexico. In the case of Poniatowska, this redefinition has come not only through her writing and coverage of other forms of politics but also how she herself has functioned as a political actor, often but not always outside institutional and electoral politics.

The term *community* has a long and complex history in anthropology, history, and other social sciences. In 1983 historian and political scientist Benedict Anderson published his book *Imagined Communities*, in which he explains how people came to perceive themselves as connected in imagined communities called nations after the Industrial Revolution, primarily through the means of print capitalism. A nation, he wrote, "is imagined because the members of even the smallest nation will never know most of their fellow-members, meet them, or even hear of them, yet in the minds of each lives the image of their communion."[51] The nation is imagined as a community because, despite inequality and exploitation, "the nation is always conceived as a deep, horizontal comradeship."[52] The imagined community, Anderson suggests, exists between people who feel connected but don't actually know one another. Anderson's suggestion that part of what defines a community comes primarily through imagination is problematic here. The strategic and political aspects of the communities Poniatowska documents and is a part of actively creating involve serious effort—the crafting of writing, its dissemination, and connections with readers but also the building of active networks and the creation of meaning. There is nothing imaginary about the work involved in creating these connections.

Assumptions about the coherence of imagined communities across differences, inequalities, tensions, and conflict also need to be troubled. Strategic emotional political communities are not static. They are flexible and people can move in and out of them at different points in their lives and in time. The emotional intensity that may come out of a particular experience such as the student movement of 1968 can change over time for those who were there. The ways that such experiences are captured and given meaning on the page and in political performances by actors such as Poniatowska and many others can and does work to preserve and expand what might be called a strategic left emotional political community through time, and render it as a touchstone for oppositional politics in Mexico. The creation of and work of keeping this strategic emotional political community functioning and connecting it to the making of history is at the heart of my discussion.

Beginning in the late 1970s, Poniatowska became a public activist at the same time that she documented social movements. She was a part of building strategic emotional political communities through participating in ongoing public protests in the late 1970s dedicated to pressuring the government to account for political prisoners and the disappeared, through being a public advocate for and organizer to support the labor union known as the Sindicato de Costureras "19 de Septiembre" (Nineteenth of September Garment Workers Union) that grew out of the 1985 earthquake, through advocating for the EZLN, and through using her public-speaking platforms to keep the forty-three students from Ayotzinapa disappeared in 2014 in the public eye. She also wrote crónicas as newspaper articles and books that continued to build relationships between readers and the people whose stories and social movements she documented. Wedding activism to writing permitted her to do this.

Jimeno suggests that people who have lived through and commemorate horrible events, such as the massacre of Naya carried out in Timba Cauca in 2001, create an emotional identity.[53] We can see that the identification process involved in creating emotional community does not center on concepts of identity such as ethnicity, class, race, or gender but on creating networks of connection through shared emotion. Such connections may eventually articulate into political action, and in that context result in shared identities, but the processes of identification involved in creating emotional community work somewhat differently than those linked to structural identity categories of difference. The concept of emotional community requires important discursive work, the creation of shared symbols, and the production of connection across difference—processes that work against compartmentalization and tensions that emanate from the production of opposing conflict-based identity categories.

The process of creating emotional community is centered in the act of one person narrating his or her experience of suffering to another so that it is not identified only with the victim "but is extended to other audiences who can identify with the experience and be moved by it."[54] It produces not just a moment of compassion but also a connection, sometimes political, that can be translated into concrete actions. This raises the question of whether we can separate emotional and political communities. My prior research on social movements would suggest that the answer is in the very way that people talk about and narrate their own experiences of repression, resilience, and action. There is no neat analytical way to separate emotions as experienced in the body (rapid heartbeat, tightening of the neck, tensing of the muscles, perhaps a rise in body temperature in the case of anger and fear), the description of events, and then the way an individual feels. Afterward, when people share an oral narrative about something that happened, the emotional experience is part of what they narrate. Take, for example, this testimonial from *La noche de Tlatelolco* by Diana Salmerón de Contreras:

> I was still clutching my brother's hand, despite the fact that there were other people between us and I tried to pull him closer to me. Some students were lying there on the ground between us, some of them dead and others wounded. There was a girl right next to me who had been hit square in the face with a dum-dum bullet [bullets designed to expand on impact]. It was ghastly! The entire left side of her face had been blown away.
>
> The shouts, the cries of pain, the weeping, the prayers and supplications, and the continuous deafening sound of gunfire made the Plaza de las Tres Culturas a scene straight out of Dante's *Inferno*.[55]

As a reader, I am drawn intensely into the text by the anguish and fear Diana felt—first in the moment of this experience but also as reflected in her telling of it. As a listener and reader, I am connected emotionally to her and indirectly to the scene and experiences of others she alludes to. Humans have used oral narrative as a mode of knowledge transmission for a very long time. If we want to truly understand the ways that emotions work in narrative, in the creation of memory, and in ethical-political viewpoints and strategic actions, it does not make sense to conceptualize them as separate.

The experiences of testifying, listening to, and reading others' testimonies are key to how political perspectives develop not only in individuals but also in how these individuals connect with others to analyze the world from a partially shared optic (often cognizant of difference at the same time), and in how groups of people can participate in shifting public political discourses and perceptions. Analyzing this process entails scaling down to document the pivotal, emotive experiences of individuals; scaling across to see how actors who experience a shared trauma connect with one another; scaling out to see the networks constructed through testifying, listening, and reading; and scaling up to see how this strategic network or emotional/political community can take on a larger ideological life in relation to other public discourses and ideologies. As suggested by the example of Diana's testimony and what happened on October 2, 1968, in Tlatelolco, the emotional connection her testimony brings connected her first to Poniatowska and then through the publication to other readers. The chapters that follow further develop how this process can involve politicization of readers and the building of political and emotional connections through public events that memorialize tragedies like the student massacres of 1968.

In a larger sense, we might think of different levels and kinds of participation in emotional communities. There are the emotional communities formed by those who share an immediate experience of suffering from the same event, and by those who share a similar experience in a different context. Emotional communities can also include those who are empathetic listeners; they may be not be suffering directly, but they are willing to act and to take risks to bring tragic and horrific events to light, and they will work to prevent their recurrence. Such listeners might be considered part of a strategic emotional political community.

Meeting Elena

In the mid-1980s, I lived in a Zapotec community in Oaxaca, Mexico, and frequently visited friends in Mexico City. Going from a small town of five thousand to the largest city in the world at that time was challenging but exciting. I got to know the city riding around on the Mexico City Metro, jostled together with thousands of other people as we wove our way underground through the city. Most exciting to me was the chance to read a wide variety of Mexican newspapers and visit bookstores. I first became familiar with Poniatowska's crónicas when I read *La noche de Tlatelolco*. I found her work in what is now known as the "old" Gandhi Bookstore in Mexico City, near the Miguel Ángel de Quevedo subway stop. I was living in Mexico when the 1985 earthquake occurred. I flew to Mexico City to try to help out with the organization of civil society and made it in time for the second aftershock. The aftermath of the earthquake and the Mexican citizens' amazing participation in recovery efforts made a lasting impression on me. Poniatowska's crónica about the earthquake, *Nada, nadie: Las voces del temblor*, was not published until 1988, when I was back in the United States and working at my first tenure-track job in anthropology at Northeastern University in Boston. The book was an important source for anyone trying to understand urban social movements in Mexico City and elsewhere.

In thinking about how my perspective on Mexican history was influenced by Poniatowska's crónicas as a graduate student, I came to wonder about how her work had affected other readers, in Mexico and the United States, and their ideas about Mexican history. As an anthropologist, I ended up documenting some of the same social movements as Poniatowska, including urban social movements that grew out of the organizing of civil society after the 1985 earthquake, as well as the story of the Zapatista uprising in the 1990s and its impact not only in Chiapas but elsewhere in Mexico, including Oaxaca.[56] I felt a kinship with her method, and perhaps with what I perceived to be her ends.

For the past two decades, I have framed my work as collaborative activist ethnographic research.[57] Collaboration implies cooperation, having a share or part in a process. Being an activist suggests that one is aligned with and committed to a particular sociopolitical process. Ethnography invokes the self, rich description, and interpretation as a means to knowing, while research suggests uncovering information and interpretations. Thus, as an activist anthropologist, one is open about one's political sympathies and alignment. Furthermore, through processes of collaboration in defining the questions to be studied, how to study them, and who participates, the division between "object of study" and the researcher is blurred. Participants in a study can include a wide range of people who participate not just as interviewees but also as intellectuals who conceptualize, analyze, and in some cases cowrite.[58] I see myself as an anthropologist who also identifies as a participant in a larger shared project with those whose lives I am documenting. Creating this sense of a shared project involves pushing against the distinction between observer and participant—something I felt was present in Poniatowska's work. This perspective also has a significant history in Latin American social science. For example, Colombian sociologist Orlando Fals Borda originated the concept of participatory action research, a method that "attempted to erase the distinction between researchers and researched, and to rewrite the history of the peasantry from below using novel formats."[59]

A further question of interest to me as I began to contemplate the role of testimony and emotion in social movements and politics was the role of readers and print media, particularly historical accounts that brought in multiple voices. In studying Poniatowska's crónicas and through my three decades as a researcher in Mexico, it became evident to me that her work was of crucial importance in shaping an influential narrative of Mexican history. When I had the chance to get to know Poniatowska on a visit she made to the University of Oregon in May 2010, and in subsequent conversations in Mexico City, I wanted to try to understand how this happened. Many people I spoke with about her work mentioned her novels, but the majority always talked about her crónicas. How, I wondered, did these crónicas contribute to understandings of Mexican history? Did they influence politics? Could we consider her a political as well as cultural actor in Mexico?

While the formal sphere of "politics" is so often relegated to elections, political parties, politicians, and the interpretation of political scientists—often but not exclusively men—I seek to broaden how we understand and remember Mexican history and politics. The actions and writing of figures such as Poniatowska are primarily interpreted as part of the literary cannon, which indeed they should be. However, because I personally have documented and written about Mexican history and politics as an anthropologist and ethnographer, I view Poniatowska's contributions through a different lens. Much like an ethnographer, through her crónicas, Poniatowska has captured the daily lives, opinions, and experiences of many people who are not in the circles of power. She has also captured the lives of the elite and famous in her novels and interviews. Poniatowska's published crónicas have reached a broad, critical public that has thrived in Mexico from the 1950s to the present—particularly through print media, as I discuss in chapter 1. The versions of historical events she has created by assembling a multitude of voices—along with many others' works—have helped influence how some people in Mexico remember these events. Part of their power is in their ability to harness a reader's emotions. I suggest that we consider readers a part of strategic emotional political communities that persist through time.

My interactions with Poniatowska began with several days of long interviews and exchanges on July 27–29, 2011, that produced about 200 pages of transcription. She also provided me with copies of many of her books, photographs, unpublished pieces, and other materials. After our initial long interview, I began to visit Poniatowska whenever I went to Mexico City, at least once or twice a year, beginning in 2011. We often talked, went to events together, or hung out at her house. I had the privilege of meeting her children, her grandchildren, and some of her friends. My project is based on more than a dozen lengthy interviews with Poniatowska from 2011 to 2019, analysis of key crónicas she has written, secondary sources, interviews with people who worked closely with her, and interviews with and observations of people who have engaged with her crónicas. At the readings, speeches, and public conversations that I had the chance to attend with her, I observed her interactions with a wide range of Mexicans—students, the urban poor, the Indigenous, social movement leaders and participants, and mainstream politicians. I also observed reactions to her work in the public spaces where it was presented; often I spoke with the people at these events and thus have an ethnographic record of public interpretations and reception of her work. I also explored exhibits where her work was featured, where I observed and recorded the reactions of museum visitors. The process of working with her on this book and getting to know her over the past ten years has been an enormous pleasure and gift.

Stories in This Book

I use the lens of Poniatowska's crónicas to explore how this cultural form contributes to history. At a broader level, I am interested in how testimony, writing, and the voices of public intellectuals such as Poniatowska enter the critical public sphere (as discussed in chapter 1), influence processes of democratization, and impact social memory. Specifically, I address how contemporary crónica writing and publishing intersect with key political events through the creation of emotional connections wrought not only through the act of narration but also through its extension to a wider public who can identify with the experience and are moved by it. Poniatowska's development as a writer, public intellectual, and activist is woven through the chapters that follow.

On a morning Metro ride through Mexico City, after riders are packed into a car with most standing, grabbing a pole for balance, the lucky few sit down and open up their newspapers, Mexican true crime comic series, novels, or cell phones. Throughout the city, readers are engaged with these sources and also often talking to each other about what they read and the news of the day. Chapter 1, "Mexico City's Growing Critical Public: News and Publishing, 1959–1985," outlines how a critical public sphere developed from 1959 through the mid-1980s through print media. Drawing on recent historiography of the Mexican press, this chapter highlights the importance of cultural supplements, crime news, and the small circulation of more radical publications in broadening Mexico's critical public sphere as well as engaging different kinds of readers. In Mexico City, the opening of the press followed its own dynamic. There, independent publishing houses and news outlets that grew in some cases out of more official publication venues were critical to the dissemination of Poniatowska's and others' work. In order to understand why people like to read crónicas and potentially how crónicas and their readers contribute to building strategic emotional political community, this chapter suggests how different forms of print media engaged with the public and the role they played in developing a historical narrative. Annual events such as rallies, public lectures, debates, and museum exhibits that memorialize events such as the student massacre in 1968 further solidify the place of these events in the public imagination. Through documenting such events, print media further contribute to etching them in larger historical narratives.

During the summer and fall of 1968, the student movement in Mexico City was the topic of reporting, governmental meetings, and talk on the street. Student activists from the Consejo Nacional de Huelga (CNH, National Strike Council) moved about the city in mobile brigades, setting up lightning meetings on street corners to dialogue with people in their neighborhoods on the way to work. A march of thousands of students and workers moved silently through the city, signaling the government's own silence and the movement's desire to communicate that it was a nonviolent, peaceful movement.

On the night of October 2, 1968, military officers and police fired on students marching into the Plaza de las Tres Culturas (Plaza of the Three Cultures) in Tlatelolco. Dozens, perhaps hundreds, were killed. Chapter 2, "The 1968 Student Movement and Massacre," discusses Poniatowska as a chronicler of the student movement and explores how Poniatowska's *La noche de Tlatelolco* has become a staple in historical narratives about that event and worked through multiple generations of readers to craft strategic emotional political community. Annual memorialization of the event and of Poniatowska's account of it reinforces and amplifies the power of this crónica and of Poniatowska herself as a writer and public intellectual. The story of what happened the night of the massacre in Tlatelolco has also served as a historical touchstone for other episodes of violence, such as the disappearance of forty-three student teachers in Iguala, Mexico, in 2014. Poniatowska's crónica about Tlatelolco and her ongoing activism defending the rights of the disappeared and of students continues to amplify the impact of this book and connect it to the present.

Following the 1968 massacre, some student activists went underground and others spread out across Mexico to organize peasants and the urban poor. Their optimism and desire to change the system were strongly opposed by the Mexican state, which initiated a period of repression, selective political killings, and disappearances known as the Dirty War. Poniatowska became a public activist for groups advocating for the poor and marginalized. In September 1985, when hundreds of Mexico City buildings were leveled in an instant, people were living on the streets, and the government was slow to respond, Poniatowska was there documenting what happened and the organized response of the people of Mexico City. Chapter 3, "A History We Cannot Forget: The 1985 Earthquake, Civil Society, and a New Political Future," analyzes Poniatowska's book *Nada, nadie* and follows its influence in building strategic emotional political community through the face-to-face organizing it documents and then through its replication, citation, and memorialization in the anniversaries of the earthquake.

By the 1990s, Poniatowska was a well-known writer and her texts *La noche de Tlatelolco* and *Nada, nadie* were widely read, particularly by those on the left, and taught in some schools. When the EZLN burst out of secrecy in January 1994, its charismatic spokesperson, Subcomandante Marcos, strategically reached out to public intellectuals and writers in an effort to harness their support. He let it be known that Poniatowska's crónica *La noche* was on his bookshelf and invited her to meet with him and the EZLN in Chiapas. Poniatowska accepted the invitation.

Chapter 4, "Engaging with the EZLN as a Writer and Public Intellectual," examines how Poniatowska's public dialogues with Subcomandante Marcos and other leaders of the EZLN used writing and publishing to broaden understanding and support for Indigenous rights and autonomy in the 1990s. The chapter also explores her engagement with Zapatista gender politics and the ways that her own personal experience as a young, single mother who suffered assault pushes her to engage across large differences with Zapatista women. Poniatowska's personal dedication, admiration, and advocacy for Zapatista women are seen through her care for Comandanta Ramona at her house, the use of her newspaper columns to publicize and promote the ideas of EZLN women, and her ongoing references in public performances to their accomplishments. Poniatowska, among many others, forged face-to-face strategic emotional political community with and for the Zapatistas (particularly the women) and used her public appearances and writing as a political tool for the EZLN and its ideas. The chapter draws on Poniatowska's 2019 novel, *El amante polaco* (The Polish lover), as a source to illuminate her personal experience with gender inequality, sexual assault, and the challenges for women raising children alone. For Poniatowska, this personal experience was foundational in pushing her to engage with many marginalized women, including those from the EZLN, and center them in many of her crónicas. The appearance of the EZLN in Mexico's Zócalo and Congress in March 2001 were events Poniatowska helped advocate for and document, along with other public intellectuals.

Mexico City's Zócalo could be known as La Plaza de Protesta (Protest Square). On any given day, its vast concrete expanse is host to two or three different groups of people working to engage the public to understand their issues. Banners protesting mining, signs advocating for Indigenous rights, and encampments of discontented peasants are part of the daily scenery. Without protest, the Zócalo looks naked.

When AMLO was declared the loser in the 2006 presidential elections, he organized a very large-scale and ongoing occupation of the Zócalo in protest. The occupation became a small city with participants from all corners of Mexico and an army of organized people to prepare food and provide education and entertainment, medical services, and more. For Poniatowska, who participated in the occupation and also documented it, there was a direct connection to the kind of civil-society organizing that emerged after the earthquake. Solidarity and collective connection were daily and widespread.

Chapter 5, "*Amanecer en el Zócalo*: Crónica, Diary, and Gendered Political Analysis," explores how Poniatowska positions herself as both activist and chronicler in López Obrador's 2006 campaign and the occupation. This chapter also highlights her participation in formal politics, her friendship with Jesusa Rodríguez, her portrayal of the *plantón* (sit-in) and its people, and her portrayal of AMLO. She also provides a critical analysis of formal political processes and at the end, of some of the forms of PRD organizing she observed. The chapter points to how, through this work, she has formally merged observation and participation in historical events and social movements. Her detailed descriptions of the people in the plantón and how they carried out political theater, dialogues, and events elsewhere in the city also suggest how the strategic emotional political community forged in the plantón was extended to other parts of the city. The harsh criticisms and even death threats she received for her political activism for López Obrador highlight the risks taken in combining activism with writing.

As suggested by the constant occupation of Mexico City's Zócalo, public activism is a normal part of the continuum of Mexican politics. Student activism is expected, and each year on the anniversary of the massacre of Tlatelolco, students organize events and marches to commemorate the student movement and the massacre. In order to prepare for such events, students sometimes jump onto public buses and ask the drivers to loan them the bus for a period of time to transport their fellow students to events. In late September 2014, several groups of student teachers departed from the town of Ayotzinapa to head to the larger city of Iguala. There they attempted to commandeer buses. What could have been a somewhat normal occurrence went horribly wrong on the night of September 26, 2014. Chapter 6, "¡Regrésenlos! The Forty-Three Disappeared Students from Ayotzinapa," explores Poniatowska's journalism and speeches as well as her advocacy surrounding the disappearance of forty-three students from the Ayotzinapa Rural Teachers' College in Iguala, Mexico, in 2014. Drawing from two examples of Poniatowska's public speeches and performances, the chapter suggests that Poniatowska, along with the missing students' parents and many other groups and individuals, helped keep the memory of the students alive and pushed the government to carry out a credible investigation of the disappearances. This last chapter is also a portal to the understanding of how repeated cycles of repression become compacted in Mexican social memory and can create new social movements with connections through time. The chapter describes how Poniatowska leveraged her status as a public figure and decades of accumulated networks and connections to bring attention to the disappeared students through using almost all her public appearances, lectures, and dialogues to advocate for justice for the disappeared students and their families. In doing so, she brought to bear the accumulated strategic emotional political community forged through her and others' activism and her writing.

As a public intellectual and writer, Poniatowska and many others have influenced public perceptions of historical events in Mexico, from the 1960s to the present. By mobilizing the hybrid form of the crónica, public dialogues, and performances as cultural and political tools, Poniatowska illustrates the importance of vibrant and accessible writing and speaking to shaping social and historical memory. At a larger level, when viewed collectively, Poniatowska's crónicas, activism, and performances can be seen as crucial building blocks in the forging of a multigenerational political community with others committed to achieving social justice for the marginalized and the silenced in Mexico.

1

Mexico City's
Growing Critical Public

News and Publishing, 1959–1985

ON OCTOBER 2, 2018—the fiftieth anniversary of the massacre of students in the Plaza de Tlatelolco—Elena Poniatowska spoke on CNN en Español about her book *La noche de Tlatelolco*. She was interviewed in Mexico City in the living room of her home, with shelves piled high with books behind her. Wearing elegant pearl earrings and her trademark red lipstick, she was relaxed and engaged with the interviewer, Rey Rodríguez. When he began by saying, "You have written many books," Poniatowska smiled. He continued, "One of the books that has most marked your career as a writer and journalist is *La noche de Tlatelolco*." Poniatowska leaned in toward Rodríquez and told him about the death of her younger brother, Jan Poniatowska, in 1968, which served in part as an inspiration for her to write the book. Rodríguez turned to her, stating, "Nobody had written anything like you did, with an investigation."[1] Poniatowska turned to face him and shared the story of how she found out about the massacre through two friends: "But I couldn't go at that moment because I had a baby in my arms. My son Felipe was breastfeeding. I went the next morning between one feeding and another at five in the morning. And I saw a landscape from after a battle. Tanks, soldiers, blood, shoes. They hadn't taken anything away. I saw everything."[2]

Later in the interview, Rodríguez asked her, "Did anything change afterward?" Poniatowska replied without hesitation, "Afterward, yes, it did change, I think . . . for the good. The government thought, here there are citizens. Here there are Mexicans. Here there are people with an opinion. A very critical press emerged afterward."[3] The 2018 interview forms part of an annual set of activities that mark the 1968 massacre in Tlatelolco—including marches, exhibits, and, often, an interview with Poniatowska.

Poniatowska's underlining of the emergence of a critical press after the 1968 massacre highlights the importance of the growth of a critical public sphere in Mexico. Historians have provided insights into the beginning of a critical public sphere not only through print media but also through radio, stage theater, movies, and comics. Through her biography of Mexican painter Pepe Zúñiga, for example, historian Mary Kay Vaughan suggests that in Mexico City "the media participated in the creation of publics and subjects."[4] Through her analysis of Mexico City life focused on youth in the 1950s until the 1980s, Vaughan writes that "the mass media, its messages and technologies suggest the formation of a more critical and demanding subjectivity and a new notion of rights."[5] Vaughan's work importantly underlines how more creative forms of expression (outside print media) generated a critical public of youth drawing on emotion, human empathy, and the insistence on rights to affection, protection, and freedom of expression. The role of print media in democracy and, more specifically, in creating access for a wider range of people to engage with politics and discuss cultural, political, and other themes is an important part of the story of how crónicas such as *La noche de Tlatelolco* and the reporting that preceded the book reached a broad Mexican audience. The emergence of a critical public in Mexico through the Cuban Revolution of 1959; the formation of a broad leftist movement known as the Movimiento de Liberación Nacional (MLN, Movement of National Liberation) that united major intellectuals, left politicians, and activists in favor of social justice; and the explosion of youth activism focused on the right to freedom and protesting adult authoritarianism and corruption all acted to consolidate a critical public in the 1960s. This critical public was significantly concentrated at the Universidad Autónomo de México (UNAM, National Autonomous University of Mexico), which was a significant source of new outlets for critical expression. The autonomy of UNAM was crucial to this capability for fostering new and independent media and other outlets of political and creative expression.[6]

While mainstream media before that time was largely controlled by the state with some exceptions, with the emergence of a strong critical public in the 1960s and subsequent pressuring by civil society for an opening of print and broadcast media and of political representation, government control of mainstream media decreased over time. This was in part because of some actions on the part of the government in the 1970s to open up politics and some parts of public media gradually. But other events, such as the 1985 earthquake and the strengthening of independent media and social movements as well as the state's own negligence and corruption over time, greatly expanded the critical public that first consolidated in the 1960s. For the period discussed here, from 1959 to about 1985, it is important to see the state's participation as enabling an opening under Luis Echeverría and José López Portillo in limited ways but also through negligence, corruption, and ineptness under the subsequent PRI regimes facilitating the consistent expansion of that critical public until 1985 and far beyond. In what follows, I seek to make this dynamic clear but also to highlight the importance of precursor spaces in print media prior to 1959 that also warmed up readers as part of an eventual critical public. I also suggest how print and other media were crucial to the building of strategic emotional political community through time and across generations through their roles in the annual memorialization of events linked to 1968 and other crucial events in Mexican history.

Historians who document the creation of a growing critical public sphere in Mexico from 1959 to the 1980s push back against the idea that a hegemonic Mexican state had a stranglehold on media and allowed no openings. Historian Vanessa Freije suggests that urban Mexicans, such as those who eventually consumed Poniatowska's crónicas, developed "a 'mediated citizenship' in which their political commitments and practices were forged through everyday interactions with mass media."[7] Focusing on what she calls *denuncia* journalism carried out by reporters who exposed (denounced) official wrongdoing, Freije offers a nuanced look at how journalism connected ordinary people with political elites and fostered public debate in the process. Her research and that of other historians detailed here make clear that denuncia, independent journalism, and political commentary flourished well before the mid-twentieth century and served an important function in facilitating critical media consumption and commentary skills among literate Mexicans. Building on other studies of cultural politics, historians of the Mexican press now point to the many ways in which the state permitted limited opposition journalism, how regional papers offered investigative journalism that took down public officials long before Mexico City papers did, and how crime news and other forms of popular publishing opened up venues for debate.[8] These dynamics are particularly important for looking at independence in the press in regions outside Mexico City, which had its own distinct dynamic.

The critical public sphere in Mexico City that these historians document revolved in important ways around UNAM and the Instituto Politécnico Nacional (IPN, National Polytechnic Institute). Intellectuals moved between the universities and institutions of the government, participating in political organizations as well as publishing books and essays that could be critical of the state. Eric Zolov's recent book, *The Last Good Neighbor: Mexico in the Global Sixties*, details the ways that Mexican president Lázaro Cárdenas (1934–40) participated in a broad leftist movement—the MLN, founded after the Cuban Revolution in 1959, acting as a kind of elder statesman of the left—with access to the state. When competing visions for a revolutionary utopia and how to get there splintered the MLN by 1962, the government of Adolfo López Mateos (1958–64) simultaneously repressed some members of the MLN, which was linked to the Communist Party, but also "cultivated and shielded" others, such as novelist and intellectual Carlos Fuentes.[9] When Gustavo Díaz Ordaz assumed the presidency from 1964 to 1970, the relationship between the office of the president and left-wing intellectuals frayed, according to Zolov.[10] Zolov's earlier work on countercultural aesthetics and influences on the Mexican student movements of the 1960s suggests the importance of the West and internationalism on a critical public sphere as well.[11] In other words, the ways in which Mexicans came together to engage in critical public debate on the page, face-to-face through political demonstrations, or in cultural means of expression such as theater were influenced not only by Mexican history and events but also by what was happening in the rest of the world, particularly in Latin America, Africa, and Europe. In sum, this historical work suggests the importance of a rich, critical public sphere that had widespread participation by a range of Mexicans. Mexico City was at the epicenter of this engaged public.

Coming of Age in the *Excélsior* Society Pages

In the 1950s, newspapers in Mexico, as elsewhere, had gendered geographies of writing. Even in the alternative cultural and small-scale presses, editors and most essayists and reporters were men. There were, however, sections of mainstream papers aimed at women. *Excélsior* was no exception. The "society section" featured discussions of high-society news such as dances and charity events, tips on raising babies, and coverage of famous celebrities. There were few female reporters at the paper, and those who were hired covered these "feminine" stories. It was difficult for women to transcend stories targeting female readers and to move into mainstream reporting.

Elena Poniatowska began her journalistic writing career with *Excélsior* in Mexico City in 1953, after returning from studying in the United States. Not only did she not have any experience writing for newspapers, but she had been educated in the sheltered environment of an elite Catholic girls' school, Eden Hall, Convent of the Sacred Heart Boarding School in Torresdale, Pennsylvania. Poniatowska's parents sent her there to study along with her sister Kitzia in the late 1940s. A memoir of Eden Hall written by V. V. Harrison and published in 1988 describes the experience of Sacred Heart as "not just a strict school" where life "closely aligned to a penal colony," but it also explains how the mission of the Society of the Sacred Heart instilled a sense of social justice in students.[12] The book also emphasizes the close attention that the nuns paid to their students. Barbara Boggs Sigmund, mayor of Princeton, Pennsylvania, from 1983 until her death from cancer in 1990, wrote a review of the book for the *New York Times*. A graduate of a different Sacred Heart school and of Manhattanville College, which Poniatowska had hoped to attend, Boggs wrote that "self-confidence was instilled in us, along with self-control."[13] Poniatowska recalled that the writing education she received as well as the daily discipline of Eden Hall both served her well. While Poniatowska wanted to remain in the United States after she completed high school to study medicine, the devalued peso made it impossible for her parents to afford college tuition. Instead, she returned home to Mexico City and studied shorthand and typing, as many young women did. The skills she attained at boarding school and her family connections got her recommended and hired for a job at the major Mexican newspaper, *Excélsior*, to write for the society pages.[14]

At age twenty-one, Poniatowska's first assignment was to interview an important political figure, the U.S. ambassador to Mexico, Francis White, who had recently arrived in Mexico City. "Un hombre optimista: El

Embajador Sr. White" (An optimistic man: The Ambassador Mr. White) was published in *Excélsior* on May 27, 1953, on the front page of Section B, "Sociedad y eventos varios" (Society and various events).[15] According to an article in *Excélsior* about Poniatowska's one-year stint with the newspaper, she conducted and wrote up 365 interviews—one a day. In his reflections on the history and role of the supplement in Mexico's print media, writer and editor Fernando Benítez stated, "Elena Poniatowska made the interview into an art."[16] She certainly got a lot of practice during her first year at *Excélsior*.

Elena leaned forward in her chair as she described to me how she began a journalism career: "I got myself into journalism, and I was conducting one interview daily. I didn't know my country at all; I didn't even know who the people I was interviewing were, and it was a huge learning curve for me." She paused, smiled, and continued with increased energy, her eyes sparkling. "Also, journalism is addictive. There's a saying ... when the snake bites, there is no remedy in the pharmacy—meaning once journalism piqued my interest, there was no turning back. And it was true. I then began conducting one interview daily, every day. I no longer thought much about studying." Beginning with Mr. White the ambassador, Elena was hooked on writing. The vast number of interviews she did during her first year made her a very efficient and disciplined writer. What is even more remarkable is that with her admitted lack of knowledge about the people she was interviewing, she was able to produce vivid and complex portraits of those she talked with. For example, in a 1953 interview with photographer Gertrudes Duby, a resident of San Cristóbal de las Casas, Chiapas, and wife of archaeologist and explorer Frans Blom, Poniatowska paints a picture of Duby as a powerful female figure proud of her age, physical strength, and knowledge. The interview, "Woman and Explorer: Tireless at 52," appeared on July 28, 1953, in *Excélsior*. She quotes Duby: "I can navigate rivers, swim across them, open paths with my machete, climb up and down mountains for ten or twelve hours, and ride on horseback for fifteen hours a day under a scorching sun, notwithstanding my fifty-two years."[17] Poniatowska asked Duby about what femininity meant to her. "In the first place, it is very difficult to analyze what femininity really is. If one understands by this concept that one must not reveal one's age (which I have just done) it just seems like a lot of nonsense," responded Duby.[18] Even at a young age, Poniatowska knew how to get people to open up to her. She interviewed actress Dolores del Río, writer Octavio Paz, sculptor Henry Moore, and other distinguished cultural figures.

Pleased at seeing her name in print every day, Poniatowska began to think about her public image and her name. Born as Hélène Elizabeth Louise Amélie Paula Dolores Poniatowska, she wanted to simplify her name to something readers could remember, pronounce, and relate to.

At first, I didn't want to write under my name because in the newspaper there was a young female reporter, well, very beautiful, whose name was Bambi—like the deer in Walt Disney's movie—so I said that I wanted to be named "Dumbo," because I really liked that little elephant that used to fly. So the editor of the section I was writing for, the Social Events Section, told me, "No, no, no, we are not going to have all Walt Disney's characters in here; you will use your own name." And for me, my name . . . I thought I had to explain it every time. . . . So, I used Elena Poniatowska, but I wrote many crónicas under the name *Hélène*, with an *H*, which means *Elena* but in French.

Reporting, interviewing, and traveling around the city opened up Poniatowska's life and her political consciousness. Her social class and family clearly provided her with support and independence that most other women her age did not have, something that she still keeps in mind: "My father bought me a car and a typewriter, so I was given all the tools I needed to work. I suppose that without a typewriter, I wouldn't have been able to become a journalist. So, my parents made it easy for me. And also, my social status allowed me access to people to interview—which surely I wouldn't have been able to do otherwise—for example, painters, writers, and also many French people, as my social circle included the French."

As she became accustomed to reporting and carrying out interviews, she also grew more socially conscious about the privilege she had, not just as a journalist but also as an upper-class Mexican in Mexico City: "There was vanity. And, well, people would tell my parents, 'I saw the article written by your girl,' so I liked that a lot, too. . . . I was kind of discovering life. I was young, and also journalism, being a journalist, allowed me to access many places, many houses, to participate in many activities I never thought I would have participated in had I not been a journalist. It opened a lot of doors for me." As we talked, I suggested to her that maybe having social status was not such a bad thing. She responded, "Social status gives you a certain impunity, because when you feel that you have a little bit . . . it is strange, but if you feel you are being impertinent, you feel you have the right to do everything, that you deserve everything, even if unconsciously, even if you are kind, but behind you there is a whole system that supports you."

"The whole system" that supported Poniatowska's early and later writing is a reference to the strategic emotional political community behind the ways that textualized oral narrative or testimony can spark emotional and political connections, often across economic and social difference. While Poniatowska's initial set of interviews for *Excélsior* were with more elite cultural figures, as she matured as a writer, she soon expanded her interviews and journalism to cover the poor, the Indigenous, and, as in her early career, women. New opportunities at other newspapers broadened her personal and print connections.

After a year at *Excélsior*, Poniatowska went on to write for another large Mexico City daily, *Novedades*, the paper where Fernando Benítez established the supplement "México en la Cultura." At that time, Rómulo O'Farrill owned *Novedades*. During the 1940s, O'Farrill established XHTV and broadcast Mexico's first television transmission.[19] His son, Rómulo O'Farrill Jr., took over *Novedades* in the late 1950s and ran it out of the television company's office. He was, according to historian Benjamin Smith, "a stalwart member of the business elite, branching out into air transport, sitting on the boards of U.S. banks, and helping to found the Mexican Council of Businessmen" (Consejo Mexicano de Hombres de Negocios).[20] Unlike *Novedades*, the other major nationals, *Excélsior* and *La Prensa*, were not privately owned but run by cooperatives, which had limited power under editors who maintained strong links to the state. Most press barons such as O'Farrill and the cooperatives promoted politics that supported their own business interests.[21]

Most of the journalists were middle-class men who would not work in "the kitchen of journalism," as the society pages were called.[22] Like Poniatowska, other female journalists interviewed the rich and famous as well as politicians, but they were not allowed to join the journalists' union.[23] And, as Smith suggests, many editors and journalists at the large Mexico City papers were on the political right. But there were important political openings, particularly through the lens of culture.

1950s Mexico City and Print Journalism

Mexico City in the 1950s was a cosmopolitan, vibrant, global urban center. A new critical youth public began to take shape in Mexico City at the end of the 1950s.[24] Multigenerational, it included art, politics, literature, music, poetry, theater, new architecture and buildings, counterculture, a movement in support of the Cuban Revolution, and a communicational and political opening. In the 1960s, UNAM's autonomous status was a launching pad for "critical thought, international exchange, and vanguards of all sorts," launching new publications, recordings of jazz and other music broadcast on its own radio station, art exhibits, cinema clubs, and experimental theater.[25] Cultural publications were important in opening critical public space in Mexico City, and one of the most important was published at UNAM. *La Revista de la Universidad de México* (The University of Mexico City Magazine) featured work in literature, critical social science, new areas of knowledge production, and "Marxism, existentialism, and psychoanalysis," according to its editor from 1953 to 1965, Juan García Ponce.[26] During this period, UNAM was itself likened to "free territory in a repressed and repressive Mexico" by chronicler Carlos Monsiváis, a contributor to *La Revista de la Universidad de México*, according to an essay summarizing the formative role of the publication in spawning a multitude of other cultural and political forums.[27]

Aside from independent publications such as *La Revista de la Universidad de México*, one of the most important kinds of publications that became venues for critical commentary were called "cultural supplements." These were usually weekend magazines inserted into mainstream newspapers. In addition to showcasing and commenting on Mexican writers, artists, and publishing houses, the supplements also encouraged writing beyond essays, poems, or short stories, such as interviews and chronicles.[28]

The career trajectory of journalist, writer, and editor Fernando Benítez is suggestive of the ways in which supplements inserted inside mainstream newspapers opened up critical cultural and political space for public dialogue, before mainstream papers themselves became consistently open to opposition viewpoints. Born in 1912 in Mexico City, Benítez had a passion for Mexican history, ethnography, and testimony as reflected in his many published works. In addition to being a prolific writer, Benítez was also the force behind a series of influential cultural supplements that were a part of mainstream newspapers, including the "Revista Mexicana de Cultura" in the newspaper *El Nacional* in 1947; "México en la Cultura," published in the newspaper *Novedades* (1949–61); "La Cultura en México," in the weekly publication *¡Siempre!* (1962–70); "Sábado," in the *Unomásuno* newspaper (1977–86); and "La Jornada Semanal" and "Libros," published in *La Jornada* newspaper. With these venues, Benítez opened up print spaces for some of Mexico's leading writers and intellectuals to publish political critiques and independent opinions despite significant state control over most mainstream newspapers in the capital. Newspapers had different sections with different readers, and sections labeled as "cultural" were likely to have greater autonomy and less scrutiny—but not total freedom. When Benítez published an article in defense of the Cuban Revolution in the supplement "Mexico en la Cultura" in 1961, O'Farrill fired him. Thirty of his collaborators left with him. In a retrospective essay about the history of supplements, Benítez described how "President Adolfo López Mateos sought me out and offered me enough money to start a new supplement."[29] He then founded "La Cultura en México" as a part of the newspaper ¡Siempre!, supported by the same team he worked with at Novedades and enriched by a younger generation of writers.

President López Mateos's support for Benítez's new supplement was short-lived. Benítez wrote: "Our contact [with López Mateos] was abruptly broken off in July of 1962 when . . . we published a report . . . where we described the assassination of Rubén Jaramillo and his pregnant wife in Xochicalco [Morelos]."[30] Jaramillo, who fought in the Mexican Revolution, was an ardent advocate for land redistribution for the landless, leading multiple armed uprisings against the Mexican government. When López Mateos was elected president, Jaramillo attempted to negotiate with him as thousands of his followers occupied land that had been redistributed to them after the revolution but was subsequently occupied by cattle ranchers. The army forcibly removed them before Jaramillo and his family were murdered. According to an essay by Gabriel Zaid as discussed by John King, López Mateos tried to shut down Benítez's supplement after the report on Jaramillo's assassination was published.[31] The attempt was unsuccessful. Poniatowska, alongside a host of other distinguished writers, published in Benítez's supplemental in ¡Siempre!, particularly on the student movement and massacre of 1968. Benítez then went on to form two other weekly supplements, one of which continues to this day in La Jornada newspaper. Benítez died in 2000 in Mexico City.

In addition to the supplements, Mexico City news venues viewed as more marginal or those that had small circulations also offered spaces for public debate. As Freije notes, "Political magazines and newspapers with smaller readerships such as El Día, Política, and Siempre! were among the first Mexico City publications to discuss the problems of landlessness, poverty and corruption" as well as to attack leading power brokers in the early 1960s.[32] The existence of alternative news and publication spaces in the 1950s and 1960s suggests holes in the state's attempts to control print journalism and underlines the kind of porous relationships that existed between reporters and those in power.

While the Mexican state did hold significant power over print media and publishing in Mexico City by controlling what was published, the purchasing and distribution of newsprint and advertising, loans, and the indirect management of the authorities who oversaw newspaper cooperatives and unions, it was not uniform or absolute. The relationship that existed between mainstream Mexico City newspapers and the Mexican government after 1920 was one of "productive reciprocity," as historian Pablo Piccato has noted.[33] And under López Portillo (for example), his secretary of the interior, Jesús Reyes Heroles, designed a political electoral reform that opened up the system to limited opposition and played a role in working with the press to expose corruption. As Freije's work highlights, this could involve journalists strategically exposing scandals when there were disagreements among those in power, or guarding secrets. Gossip columns, crime pages, radio, comics, and flyers were also spaces for critical dialogue and exchange—much before the 1960s.[34]

As Piccato writes, newspapers—even the large postrevolutionary dailies—could not be described as "solely targeted at elites."[35] The ideal reader for the national daily paper *Excélsior*, for example, would be "probably a slightly conservative middle-class person interested in public affairs and in socially integrative modern consumer culture."[36] However, to capture a maximum number of readers of all economic means and interests, papers published "different sections with different styles and their own visual and written languages, addressing multiple parallel audiences."[37] Newspapers in Mexico, like elsewhere, offered sections on national and foreign politics, high society, culture, sports, crime, entertainment, and showbusiness as well as many advertisements.[38] Newspapers also sponsored contests and events for readers. *Excélsior*, for example, promoted Mother's Day as a holiday in Mexico.[39] Thus one newspaper contained different sections that attracted different types of readers.

A Diverse Reading Public

Who were the readers of Mexico City? How did different reading publics develop in relation to different kinds of newspapers and magazines? In his discussion of the opening of Mexico's print media, Chappell H. Lawson suggests that newspapers mattered because of who read them and how they shaped politics and public opinion: "Newspapers and magazines are widely read by the nation's elite, including 'opinion leaders' and political decision makers. . . . Independent publications have played a crucial role in legitimizing civic activity, altering elite discourse about politics."[40] Beyond elites, however, other reading publics existed.

To understand the rise of newspaper readership and of books such as Poniatowska's crónicas, we also have to understand something much more basic: Who reads? Where do they live? What do they read? Smith states that as early as 1960, about 79 percent of urban men and 76 percent of urban women were literate.[41] Freije notes that national literacy rates climbed from 42 percent in 1940 to more than 76 percent by 1970, with even higher rates in Mexico City.[42] Smith correctly points to the expansion of state education as the primary cause for the rise, but as Freije notes, these rates must be taken with a grain of salt as they included those who could only write their names.[43] Ethnographic researchers such as U.S. anthropologist Oscar Lewis found that tabloid readership was common in the poorer sections of Mexico City.[44] Ever-increasing literacy rates were reflected in advertising (including film advertisements), posters, signage in the cities, and more— and in the proliferation of print media. Smith, for example, documents the rise in the number of new current-affairs and news publications in Mexico: there were 244 in 1940; thirty years later, in 1970, there were 1,249.[45] The number of daily newspapers grew from 44 in 1931 to 256 in 1974. As Smith suggests, this steep growth rate far outstripped the rise in population; from 1940 to 1970, Mexico's population increased by 165 percent, while the growth of publications increased by 250 percent.[46] But not all readers were reading the same publications or the same sections of daily newspapers.

Who was reading the major daily papers such as *Excélsior* and *El Universal*? They were concentrated in Mexico City, and, Smith suggests, most readers of these papers came from the upper and middle classes, echoing Lawson's findings.[47] According to an internal survey conducted by *Excélsior* in 1970, the paper was read "predominantly by people of the upper middle class, merchants, professionals, and industrialists."[48] But the supplements of papers, such as those Benítez created, may have attracted different readers from the newspapers that housed them.

Readership also was rapidly growing among the urban working class and the poor in Mexico City. They were just reading different kinds of publications. Books such as Oscar Lewis's ethnography *Five Families* document how poorer families read the tabloid press. Anthropologist Margarita Nolasco Armas notes in her book *Cuatro ciudades: El proceso de urbanización dependiente* how the poorer residents in Mexico City's outlying neighborhoods read "comics, photoromances, and sports sheets" or "the morbid magazine of the day."[49] When I lived in Mexico in the mid-1980s in the city of Oaxaca, and when I rode the metro in Mexico City, I regularly saw many people reading *nota roja* tabloids that focused on crime, theft, and the hardships of everyday people.

Piccato writes that "crime was a theme that allowed critical ideas about the government to be published with little or no censorship. . . . The *nota roja* encouraged the critical involvement of readers in public affairs, creating a shared sense of the reality of everyday life."[50] Piccato also demonstrates how the narratives assembled in notas rojas challenged "the legal truth" and used first-person testimonies in their narratives. And the explanations that came from these everyday voices, he suggests, often challenged formal legal explanations.[51] Crime news, Piccato states, "was the terrain on which civil society addressed the separation between truth and justice— the disjunction between people's knowledge about the reality of criminal acts and the state response to those acts."[52] Crime news also sold well. For example, Piccato notes, "in the 1960s, *Alarma!*, the most popular magazine of the genre, was said to sell half a million copies during the development of a famous case of multiple homicides in a brothel in Guanajuato."[53] The reading public of *Alarma!* was clearly different from that of *Excélsior*.

Nota roja narratives were conveyed with strong emotional force in stories and headlines such as "Tres señoras fueron ayer acribilladas a navajazos, ¿quién es el troglodita?" (Three women were riddled with razor slashes, who is the troglodyte?), which punctuated the front page of *La Prensa* on April 24, 1934.[54] This strong emotional language was "part of an interaction between newspaper, authorities and readers intended not only to stir the latter's feelings but also to incite their participation in the resolution of cases."[55] When readers engaged with the stories in nota roja tabloids, they were encouraged to "get involved in the pursuit of truth through the use of critical reason."[56] For example, many letters to the editor of the publication *La Prensa* were written to denounce "policemen who were thieves, *murderers*, kidnappers or extortionists."[57]

In his 2017 book, *A History of Infamy: Crime, Truth, and Justice in Mexico*, Piccato provides a detailed history of the nota roja genre and makes a compelling case for how crime news "nurtured a broad and engaged public."[58] Piccato demonstrates how this genre of news was central to the development of Mexico's critical public sphere. He cites the newspaper *La Prensa*, founded in 1928, as the most successful and influential example of a newspaper built on crime news. The contents of short stories, readers' letters, and columns in the paper revealed its critical edge. As he notes, "While the editorial page could be conservative and pro-government, smaller news articles conveyed a populist outrage that could only be interpreted as critical of the government. . . . Strong sales driven by crime stories insulated the newsroom from management interference and allowed for sharp reporting on the corruption and brutality of the police and local authorities. . . . Readers' letters and daily columns . . . persistently complained about urban governance and security."[59]

Piccato's analysis also captures important characteristics of the reading public as intelligent, interested in everyday life, and drawn to testimony and emotional narrative. He underlines the importance of working and poor urban readers who found outlets for challenging the state's version of events and its exclusive right to judge and administer punishment. In addition, Piccato's research strongly suggests the ways in which the emotional narratives and testimonies (for example, in the genre of the criminal confession) consistently worked in the same way that literary analysts have characterized crónicas—they walk the line between fiction and nonfiction, rely on real people and events developed as characters, and engage with dramatic story-telling elements. The papers also made extensive use of photography from crime scenes often mixed with female nudes. Magazines such as *Por Qué?*, Piccato notes, followed the visual and journalistic conventions of nota roja publications but combined them with "open attacks of President Gustavo Díaz Ordaz." He suggests that *Por Qué?* was "probably the only popular journal to publish photos of the victims of the October 2, 1968 massacre of Tlatelolco."[60] Poniatowska's crónica about the massacre contains an extensive photo section that includes inspired students marching through the streets, arm in arm, in hopeful anticipation. This is followed by shots of armed soldiers with their guns raised, students lined up against a wall with their hands up, shoes scattered in the plaza, dead and bloodied students stretched on metal shelves inside a detention facility or on the pavement, and student leaders in jail.

Those who analyze the emergence of independent newspapers such as *Unomásuno* and *La Jornada* connect them to the nota roja genre in terms of their tabloid format, focus on social movements, coverage of traumatic events and politics, and use of photojournalism to illustrate stories.[61] They are also connected to the weekly newspaper supplements. The use of interviews, testimonials, and flash polls engaged readers' emotions. Piccato summarizes the genre's contribution as creating a public that could agree on "a basic fact of Mexican life: impunity."[62] He also suggests that the genre offered a "persuasive depiction of reality that incorporated multiple voices" and "engaged readers as citizens whose opinions and experience could help solve a case—and pressure authorities to investigate."[63] Crime news engaged readers in a deliberative process of truth seeking from multiple angles.

Readers of crónicas such as *La noche de Tlatelolco* faced a similar task in negotiating multiple perspectives on the massacre, including student leaders, their parents, professors, army officials, news reporters, and state officials. The testimonials readers confront are laced with emotion: the absolute euphoria of students in the march of silence as throngs greeted them, the extreme grief and anger of parents who lost their children, the outrage of jailed student leaders, the confusion of a soldier following orders, the arrogance of government officials. The harnessing of readers' emotions connects them to the testimonies and to a desire to find out more and seek a truth to explain what happened. Such truth seeking can also extend to political action and reaction, both in the form of more traditional social movements or through creating more independent publishing venues.

The Creation of Independent Leftist Publishing Houses in Mexico City

Just as the number of news publications grew from the 1930s to the 1970s, so did publishing houses. Adding another dimension to the complex relationship between the Mexican state and the emergence of a critical public sphere is the importance of two left-leaning independent presses that sprang out of a government-sponsored publisher founded in the 1930s. Intellectuals and universities were linked to the Mexican government in multiple ways, including through publishing houses that were partially state sponsored. In 1934 Daniel Cosío Villegas founded the Fondo de Cultura Económica or "El Fondo" (hereafter the Fondo) publishing group with partial funding from the Mexican government under the presidency of Cárdenas. Originally, the Fondo was created to provide specialized books in Spanish for students at the Escuela Nacional de Economía (National School of Economics). In the following years, the Fondo expanded to include humanities, literature, science, children's books, and, eventually, history and social science.[64]

Over time, the Fondo expanded its offices to other parts of Latin America and Europe. In 1945 a branch opened in Buenos Aires and Arnaldo Orfila Reynal became publisher. He moved to Mexico City in 1948 as head publisher for the Fondo's main office.[65] In 1961 the Fondo published C. Wright Mills's *Escucha yanqui: La revolución en Cuba* (first published in English as

Listen Yankee: The Revolution in Cuba [1960]), establishing its willingness to engage with the Cuban Revolution—a position that also found some support in the administration of López Mateos, at least initially.[66] Under Orfila Reynal, the Fondo published cultural critiques of modern Mexico such as Carlos Fuentes's novel *La región más transparente* (1958). In a story that centers Mexico City as the primary protagonist, the book exposes the hollow promises of the Mexican Revolution through its representation of the Mexican social and political system. It is a harsh critique of Mexico's upper classes in a nonlinear narrative style that builds the text out of a series of encounters. As Freije describes, while books like these stirred debate, "public officials publicly discounted these creative pieces as interpretive works of art."[67] The same could not be said for the state's response to critical social science during the first year of Gustavo Díaz Ordaz's presidency. He confronted left-wing intellectuals and, for the first time since the Mexican Revolution ended in 1920, ruptured the linkage "between the intelligentsia and the presidency . . . thus laying the groundwork for the breakdown of legitimacy that culminated in the 1968 protests and brutal government response."[68]

In 1965 the Fondo published *Los hijos de Sánchez* by Oscar Lewis (first published in English as *The Children of Sánchez* in 1961), which exposed the poverty, violence, and ongoing uncertainty many people living in Mexico's urban *vecindades* (neighborhoods) experienced. *Los hijos de Sánchez* is narrated by two brothers and two sisters, Jesús Sánchez's children. After their mother died, they were raised in the neighborhood of Mexico City known as Tepito. The Fondo's Spanish publication of Lewis's book in Mexico caused a scandal; Díaz Ordaz's cabinet intervened, as did the Sociedad Mexicana de Geografía y Estadística (Mexican Society for Geography and Statistics). They demanded that the Fondo recall all copies of the book and that Orfila Reynal resign, citing his profile as a subversive Argentine. When he refused to resign, he was fired.

Lewis's book not only contained abundant ethnographic descriptions of poverty, gender inequality, and violence in Mexico but also critiqued Mexico's political system and the PRI. Fidel Castro declared it a "revolutionary text."[69] In the United States, reactions to the book focused more on Lewis's thesis about the "culture of poverty," and it was cited as a basis for policy intervention. In Mexico, it broke through as a critique of the modern Mexican miracle, a narrative emphasizing Mexico's steady economic growth from 1940 to 1970, with the economy growing an average of

4 percent per year and industrial manufacturing increasing steadily. Lewis told the story of those left behind. As historian Louise Walker states, "The so-called Mexican Miracle was miraculous for a privileged few. Its darker side included economic desolation and political repression."[70] As Walker writes, what is significant in the 1960s and early 1970s is not the accuracy of the miracle narrative "but rather the fact that PRI functionaries, and others, believed it. . . . In this belief, the middle classes came to represent the modern, developed Mexico, symbolizing the goal toward which all Mexicans ought to strive."[71] *Los hijos de Sánchez,* published by the Fondo under Orfila Reynal's leadership, seriously questioned that narrative.

In his preface to the 2012 Fondo edition of *Los hijos de Sánchez/Una muerte en la familia Sánchez,* anthropologist Claudio Lomnitz writes, "In this book, 'Sánchez' children' showed the world that the modern, prosperous and optimist Mexico of those times, the Mexico of the 'Mexican Miracle,' was only one face of the national coin, and the place inhabited by the authors of this autobiography was the other face."[72] A further point of anxiety the Mexican government felt about the text, according to Lomnitz, came from the fact that the four Sánchez siblings were intelligent, eloquent, and very explicit in their narratives, causing many to doubt the truth of the book. This resulted in charges that Lewis had fabricated the Sánchez family and their stories.[73] More than five hundred intellectuals declared their support for the book and for Orfila Reynal. Legal charges were filed against Lewis and the Fondo, but they were ultimately dismissed. Orfila Reynal, however, was still fired. Lomnitz suggests it was because he was a foreigner.[74]

Freije documents in detail the efforts to defend Oscar Lewis's academic credentials by a range of intellectuals as well as middle-class Mexico City residents and activists who wrote letters in *El Día.* According to Freije, members of a youth labor and peasant organization sent a letter asserting that what was truly offensive was "poverty, hunger, poor health, anguish, insecurity, and unemployment" itself rather than Lewis's account of it.[75] In March 1965, 1,500 people crowded into a roundtable on *Los hijos de Sánchez* sponsored by a leftist student organization in the auditorium of the Escuela Nacional de Economía, the institution the Fondo was first created to serve. *El Día*'s detailed account of the roundtable, as Freije describes it, makes it evident that those present wanted to add their voices to the national debate about the book. When Luis Cataño Morlet, judge in the Tribunal Superior de Justicia del Distrito Federal (Superior Court of Justice of Mexico City) and president of the Sociedad Mexicana de Geografía y Estadística, read the charges that had been filed against Lewis and Orfila Reynal as part of the roundtable—including that Lewis's informants had called the government "a gang of thieves"—the crowd of mostly students began to cheer.[76] The response of a society official present was to shout back at the students that they were "Pro-Yankee" and "wanted Mexico to become like South Vietnam, where the United States controlled a foreign government."[77] This exchange signaled growing tensions between government officials and the willingness of students to make public critiques.

The significant popular response in favor of Orfila Reynal as well as the critical public sphere that developed in the 1950s and 1960s harnessed a generation of young political and cultural writers who helped him form a new press in 1965. Scientists such as renowned Mexican astronomer Guillermo Haro, who later married Elena Poniatowska in 1968, also supported Orfila Reynal. Haro, born in Mexico City in 1913, first studied law and philosophy at UNAM and then worked as a reporter for *Excélsior*. After interviewing the prominent Mexican astronomer Luis Enrique Erro Soler, he dedicated himself to astronomy. After a residency at the Astronomy Observatory at Harvard, he returned to Mexico to work with a new and powerful camera in the Observatorio Astrofísico Nacional de Tonantzintla (National Astrophysics Observatory of Tonantzintla) in Puebla.[78] Haro helped develop the profession of astronomy in Mexico and brought Mexican astronomy to the attention of the world. He was also a strong political leftist who supported unionists, was sympathetic to the Cuban Revolution, and in 1959 went to China to lead a delegation of the Sociedad Mexicana de Amistad con China (Mexican Friendship Society with China). Mao personally received the delegation and shook hands with every member.[79]

What is important in this story, however, is Haro's relationship with Mexican intellectuals and writers. During the week, Haro lived in the town of Tonantzintla, close to the colonial city of Puebla and not far from the archaeological zone and town of Cholula. In her biography of Guillermo Haro, *El universo o nada*, published in 2013, Poniatowska writes about Haro's role in helping launch Orfila Reynal's new press, Siglo XXI. She describes how in 1964, Fernando Benítez, Carlos Fuentes, and other writers and cinematographers were in Tonantzintla and "brought life to Haro's bungalow."[80] Fuentes, basking in the success of his renowned book *La región más transparente* and a newer book, *La muerte de Artemio Cruz* (1962), went to Tonantzintla to write. He would go to the nearby pyramids that were part of the archaeological site in the town of Cholula to talk with the peasants there.[81]

In 1965 Haro organized a group of writers, publishers, and intellectuals who first expressed their indignation at the charges filed against Orfila Reynal and Lewis. Two weeks later, according to Poniatowska, three hundred men and women each paid one hundred pesos to get into an event at the Club Suizo in Mexico City. Guillermo Haro and Fernando Benítez were among the speakers. Haro offered Orfila Reynal the sum of 200,000 pesos that he had raised from the assembled group and announced that his new press, Siglo XXI, "already has a house, which was made possible by our beloved Elenita Poniatowska."[82]

Haro and Poniatowska had met some six years earlier when she first interviewed him as part of a series with Mexican scientists for the supplement "México en la Cultura." Poniatowska has written about that first interview in various places, most recently in her biography of Haro. She describes how in 1959 she first went to his office at UNAM, where he barely looked at her and told her to make up the answers to her questions from copies of articles he gave her. She then asked him if she could visit him at the observatory in Tonantzintla. Two or three weeks later, Poniatowska took the bus out to the observatory. When she showed up at his office there, Haro didn't remember her visit to UNAM. Once she got into his office, he warmed up and began to talk with her about his passion for the Instituto de Astronomía (Institute of Astronomy) at UNAM, the observatory, his colleagues, and his students. They spoke for an hour and then Haro offered to drop her off at the bus station so she could return to Mexico City. On the way, he offered, they could stop to eat in the city of Puebla.[83] Poniatowska accepted his invitation and they began a friendship that later developed into a more intimate relationship.

In November 1966, Siglo XXI, named after a magazine called *Siglo XXI* that Orfila also hoped to start, published its first novel and an anthology of poetry by some of Mexico's most distinguished writers. Orfila Reynal was interested in the history of ideas in Latin America, opening up a space for young writers, and providing an uncensored publication venue. Nearly thirty years later, in 1997, Monsiváis wrote an article in *Proceso* titled "El centenario de Arnaldo Orfila Reynal" (The one-hundredth birthday of Arnaldo Orfila Reynal). He described the kinds of publications that characterized Siglo XXI and how it signaled an important new publication venue not only for Mexicans but for all of Latin America.

In its first phase, Siglo XXI published some of the most notorious trends of the period marked by the Cuban Revolution, new Latin American thought, the narrative boom, the astonishment over "dependency theory," the zenith and tragic failure of the continental guerrilla, the emergence of Liberation Theology, new community education methods, Marxist revisionism. . . . Siglo XXI published . . . the Central American revolutionaries, the Marxist classics, Argentinian sociology. Orfila, a sympathizer of revolutionary movements, disseminated the critical views and versions, orthodox and heterodox, that would so influence the Latin American youth. For a decade, leftist groups and parties, grassroots ecclesiastical communities, social science students, revolutionary nationalists, those dissatisfied with the situations of misery and exploitation, turned to the Siglo XXI collection to get informed, to create their own horizon of revolutionary expectations, to define and redefine the meaning of their actions.[84]

Orfila Reynal died in Mexico at the age of one hundred in January 1998, about six months after Monsiváis's article was published. Although Poniatowska did not publish her own crónicas with Siglo XXI, she was an ardent supporter of the press.

Another leftist independent press, Ediciones Era, published at least twenty of Poniatowska's books.[85] Ediciones Era was founded in 1960 by a group of young Spanish exiles: Vicente Rojo; José Azorín; and Neus, Jordi, and Quico Espresate. They were part of the large number of Republicans who fled the Spanish Civil War and came to Mexico at the invitation of Cárdenas's government. Many Spanish exiles became influential in cultural fields and played a significant role in the development of the Fondo de Cultura Económica, "translating over a hundred titles from other languages in the fields of sociology, philosophy, history, and political thought."[86] They also helped create many small publishing houses, like the one that the Espresates, Rojo, and Azorín started in 1960, named after the abbreviation of their initials: ERA.[87] Ediciones Era's inaugural book was *La batalla de Cuba* (The battle of Cuba), a report written by Fernando Benítez. With this book, Era established its reputation as a leftist press with a willingness to publish topics that many others would not. As Monsiváis described it, "Era publishes what the official and the majority of the private publishing houses do not accept: topics such as Castroismo, the presence of transnational companies, and new colonialism. The impulse for transformation, where social sciences and sociology play an important part, generates a very broad field of credibility. [This arena] is well considered [by this press]."[88]

Editorial Planeta Mexicana, which has published seven of Poniatowska's books, including her most recent titles, also has ties to a Spanish exile. Joaquín Díez-Canedo, born in Madrid in 1917, came to Mexico in 1941 as a refugee after Francisco Franco assumed power at the end of the Spanish Civil War. He studied in the Facultad de Filosofía y Letras (Faculty of Philosophy and Letters) at UNAM and began his editorial career in the Fondo, under Orfila Reynal. In 1944 he founded La Editorial Joaquín Mortiz. The press published some of the best-known Mexican writers—including Carlos Fuentes, Octavio Paz, Elena Garo, and Rosario Castaneda—and some of the most important poets, critics, and narrators of the 1960s, 1970s, and 1980s, such as Carlos Monsiváis, Enrique Krauze, Juan Villoro, Julieta Campos, Alejandro Rossi, Marco Antonio Montes de Oca, and others.[89] In 1985 Joaquín Mortiz Press joined with Planeta. According to Planeta's website, during the Franco dictatorship, Joaquín Díez-Canedo "signed letters sent to his mother in Madrid as Joaquín M. Ortiz and on occasion the surname and initial merged and gave rise to the name Joaquín Mortiz, which he would subsequently use to name the publishing company."[90]

Era, Siglo XXI, and Joaquín Mortiz (later part of Planeta) were important pioneers in independent book publishing in Mexico and emerged as part of the critical public sphere. At the same time that these independent leftist presses were getting established in Mexico, Poniatowska was going through a personal transformation in terms of her perspectives about the world and regarding the kinds of people she wanted to interview and write about. She began to go to Lecumberri Prison, known as El Palacio Negro or the Black Palace. Built in 1900, Lecumberri was Mexico City's primary penitentiary. Though built for eight hundred prisoners, by the 1970s it held up to four thousand inmates, including many political prisoners who were kept in isolated dormitories. Eventually closed in 1976 for being outdated, Lecumberri now serves as the site of Mexico's Archivo General de la Nación (General Archive of the Nation).

A Widening Social View

Prior to her visits to the prison, beginning in 1957, Poniatowska had begun to document the Sunday activities of ordinary Mexicans for the Sunday magazine in *Novedades*. She worked together with illustrator Alberto

Beltrán, a talented graphic artist specializing in depictions of ordinary Mexicans and political cartoons. He illustrated many well-known books and participated in the Taller de Gráfica Popular (People's Graphic Workshop), of which he became a leading member. Through her work with Beltrán, Poniatowska became increasingly attuned to the rhythm of life for working Mexicans. She became aware of the masses of people commuting to and from work, early in the morning and late at night, and the precariousness of their lives.

> I could see how most people live. . . . You can see those who suffer, the lines they have to be in for hours; how full metro and bus transportation is; how there are people who spend two and a half hours on [public] transportation just to go back home; sometimes, they can spend three hours or four hours in the morning getting to work in order to start at nine. They have to wake up at five a.m. That's a very difficult life, very hard. Seeing this makes you ask the question, what kind of life are our leaders providing for ordinary Mexicans?

Beltrán's background was very different from hers. Born in the working-class neighborhood of Tepito, Beltrán only completed primary school before entering the Escuela Libre de Arte y Publicidad (Free School for Art and Advertising), where he studied drawing. In 1943, at age twenty, he enrolled in Mexico's Escuela Nacional de Artes Plásticas (National School of Plastic Arts, part of UNAM), where he studied engraving. From there he went on to the Taller de Gráfica Popular and began his career illustrating for newspapers and books while also helping start the Mexico City daily *El Día* in 1962. Poniatowska fondly described Beltrán as a "very important" person to her, a tour guide to real life in the city: "He was a poor man, an engraver, a graphic artist [printmaker], a socialist. His mother was a domestic worker or cook at someone else's home; his father was a tailor. And he showed me all around Mexico." Six years after Poniatowska and Beltrán published their weekly articles in "México en la Cultura," edited by Benítez, they were collected into the book *Todo empezó el domingo*, published in 1963 by the Fondo.

A few years earlier, in 1961, Era had published Poniatowska's first book, *Palabras cruzadas*, a collection of her most successful interviews, including conversations with painter Diego Rivera; artist David Alfaro Siqueiros; writer, screenwriter, and photographer Juan Rulfo; filmmaker Luis Buñuel; and former Mexican president Lázaro Cárdenas, among others. Poniatowska interviewed Siqueiros in Lecumberri Prison in 1960, where he was incarcerated until 1964. Siqueiros was an ardent defender of Demetrio Vallejo, the Secretary General of the Sindicato de Trabajadores Ferrocarrileros de la República Mexicana (Railroad Workers Union of the Republic of Mexico). In 1959 Vallejo and eight hundred railroad workers were imprisoned after López Mateos fired ten thousand of the workers and nationalized the railroad. Vallejo was in Lecumberri from 1960 until 1970. Siqueiros painted the mass arrest of railroad workers in 1959 as part of a mural in the Jorge Negrete theater. Afterward, the Mexican government sentenced Siqueiros to five years in jail for supporting the union.

Poniatowska began going to Lecumberri two or three times a week to interview the railroad strikers in 1959 and 1960.[91] Speaking at a public event at UNAM in 2009 to commemorate the fiftieth anniversary of the 1959 railroad workers movement, Poniatowska recounted how she was introduced to the prison: "Luis Buñuel went with me there because an inmate had written to ask me to come see the play 'Licenciado no te apures' [Counselor/lawyer, don't worry], inspired by an attorney who would always tell his clients, 'don't worry,' without ever solving anything. Once I made it inside the prison, I was never able to interview Vallejo, but I did interview Mutis [a Colombian poet known for writing *The Diary of Lecumberri*], Siqueiros, and other inmates."[92]

In the late 1950s and into the 1960s, Poniatowska's writing and personal life were transformed through her prison visits and work with Beltrán but also through the friendship she developed with the real person who was the model for the main character in one of her best-known novels. In 1964 she met Josefina Bórquez, who became the protagonist of *Hasta no verte, Jesús mío* (published in 1969 in Spanish and in 2001 in English as *Here's to You, Jesusa!*). Poniatowska visited Bórquez every Wednesday between 4 and 6 p.m., the only time Bórquez was available, in one of Mexico City's poor vecindades (figure 1.1). As Poniatowska describes in the preface to the English translation, "On Wednesday afternoon, as the sun set and the blue sky changes to orange, in that semi-dark little room, in the midst of the shrieking of the children, the slamming door, the shouting, and the radio going full blast, another life emerged—that of Jesusa Palancares, the one that she relived as she told it."[93] Bórquez's vecindad was similar to the neighborhood that Lewis profiled in *Los hijos de Sánchez*, and although Poniatowska and Bórquez lived in the same city, their lives took place in

Figure 1.1
Elena
Poniatowska with
Josefina Bórquez
(known as Jesusa
Palancares in
*Hasta no verte,
Jesús mío*) in front
of Bórquez's
house in 1971.
Photograph by
Héctor García
Cobo. Used by
permission of
the Fundación
Elena Poniatow-
ska Amor, Mexico
City, Mexico.

parallel universes. Between the time the first Spanish edition was published in 1969 and its translation and first publication in the United States
in 2001, Poniatowska had thought much about the social and economic
distance between her life and that of Bórquez. In the English edition,
she included an extensive introduction that underscored the difficulties she
had in getting Josefina Bórquez/Jesusa Palancares to talk to her and her
own discomfort with the inequalities in their lives. "I went to see Jesusa on
Wednesday afternoons and when I got home I'd accompany my mother
to cocktail parties at one embassy or another. I always tried to maintain
a balance between the extreme poverty that I shared at Jesusa's tenement
and the splendor of the receptions."[94] According to her biographer Michael Schuessler, "The impact these interviews with her mentor Jesusa had
on Elena was so strong and so deep that it altered her personal if not her
genetic condition. Through Jesusa, Elena felt for the first time that something belonged to her: that her Mexican life took on, day by day, a special
meaning."[95]

Beltrán's tours and her engagement with Bórquez also changed the way
that Poniatowska viewed the city itself, seeing how displacement from one
place to another functioned in the lives of the poor. She observed up
close how the narrative of progressive improvement tied to the promise of
the Mexican Revolution (the Mexican miracle) was not borne out in the
lives of those she engaged with.

I interviewed people in poorer neighborhoods. I had gotten closer to them when I was writing the novel *Hasta no verte, Jesús mío*, which is about a woman who was a *soldadera* during the Mexican Revolution and to whom the revolution gave nothing in exchange; on the contrary, she became even poorer. As time passed, she lived under worsening conditions and moved farther away from the part of the city where the services were located, from what could be called civilization in the sense of having basic things available. . . . First, she lived downtown, but she ended up living—the city rejects people, pushes them away—closer to Pachuca, so far away from where she worked [in the city]. She used to work at a printing house where she would wash the workers' overalls. She would do the cleaning; everybody admired and loved her because she was a great character. But her living conditions, instead of being better than when she was younger, worsened. [They] were dreadful.[96]

With this work, she more closely follows the kinds of observations and critiques Fuentes makes in his novels and Lewis reveals in his sociological books.

When she and I talked about the period between 1957 and the mid-1960s, Poniatowska remembered it as a time of growth and exploration that clashed with her sheltered upbringing as a girl in an elite family in Mexico City: "My field of action got much bigger. I began interviewing different kinds of people. I began learning about politics. I began to grow indignant about the social divisions that exist in Mexico, that is, the abyss that exists between one social class and another." As a child, after she arrived with her family in 1942, Poniatowska had been struck by how poverty was expressed on the feet of women and children in Mexico City—something she had never seen in France. She explained, "I think that as a girl in Mexico, I was very shocked when I saw people barefoot in the street. Nowadays, you no longer see them, but back then you'd see kids, women, elderly people, completely barefoot. . . . It was very shocking and unacceptable in the long run. Maybe when I was a girl, I did not see it because you are a kid, you don't . . . but later on, yes, I thought it was intolerable that some people had shoes and others didn't."

Seeing the poorer side of Mexico with Alberto Beltrán and working with Josefina Bórquez prepared Poniatowska to dive into the interviews that became the basis for her crónica *La noche de Tlatelolco*. Her experiences in Lecumberri talking with "ordinary Mexicans" also solidified her commitment to social justice and her interest in representing the voices of those who were often invisible or unheard.

Mexico's Expanding Critical Public Sphere in the 1970s and 1980s

Independent left-oriented newspapers and magazines that surfaced in the 1970s and 1980s helped broaden the network of connected readers who consumed the journalism of Poniatowska and others who reported on issues of social justice and burgeoning social movements. Such publications were places that continued to engage the emotions of readers through testimonials and photojournalism of dramatic events and eventually through the print memorialization of notable events and dates.

In 1974 government agents raided the offices of the leftist independent magazine *Por Qué?*. They broke down the doors, arrested journalists and secretaries, and then kidnapped the editor Roger Menéndez the following day.[97] Those who were arrested were taken to Military Camp #1, where they were tortured and questioned for two days. According to Smith's analysis, the newspaper had "traced the evolution of student radicalism from the Mexico City streets to the Guerrero jungle and Chihuahua mountains"; had exposed "violent *cacicazgos* [territories controlled by political bosses, known as caciques], crony capitalism, and rigged elections of the provinces[;] and uncovered corruption, repression and even links to the CIA at the highest levels of the Mexican government."[98] Smith points out that while most of the mainstream media printed the government's version of the student movement, *Por Qué?* supported the student movement and its politics. After the Tlatelolco massacre, Smith suggests, the paper transformed in style to more of a nota roja tabloid, publishing, for example, graphic photographs documenting the violence against the students no other papers would print.[99] For a time, the magazine became the voice of Mexico's extreme left and also offered "a new template for Mexican journalism."[100]

Smith suggests that *Por Qué?* also influenced other journalists, notably Julio Scherer García, founder of the weekly *Proceso*.[101] Smith writes, "When he launched *Proceso* in 1976, the magazine adopted [*Por Qué?*'s] direct, accusatory style, the emphasis on investigative journalism, the focus on the links between crime and official corruption, and even the politicization of the *nota roja*."[102] From 1968, he directed the major daily *Excélsior*. According to Freije, under his leadership, while the newspaper's front page followed official lines, the editorial page became more and more critical of the government until 1976. President Luis Echeverría (1970–76) orchestrated a coup in the *Excélsior's* newspaper cooperative, resulting in the dismissal of Scherer García and his team.[103]

Sherer García's firing and his founding of *Proceso* are seen as a watershed moment. The memorialization of the *Excélsior* coup "united a public of intellectuals, journalists and informed readers who identified with a liberal democratic ideology of speech rights. This public shared both a critical understanding of the episode and a distrust of official information."[104] Those fired made a spectacle of their censorship (reported in the *New York Times*) and launched *Proceso* on November 6, 1976. *Proceso's* principal news story in its inaugural issue was "From *Excélsior* to *Proceso*: The Struggle for a Public Voice." One year later, the magazine and several other news publications memorialized the state's intervention and firing of Scherer García, "solidifying a public of readers united every year by the memorialization."[105]

In 1977 reporters Carlos Payán, Carmen Lira, and Manuel Becerra-Acosta, who also left *Excélsior*, started the newspaper *Unomásuno*. The paper featured investigative journalism and photojournalism, building on the legacy of the nota roja tabloids and *Por Qué?*. According to Lawson, growing dissension over Becerra-Acosta's management during 1983–84 spurred Payán and Lira to inspire ninety people to resign and form a rival daily, *La Jornada*. Appearing in September 1984, *La Jornada* "soon became the voice of Mexico's anti-regime left."[106] People who worked at *La Jornada* went on to found more independent regional publications.[107] *Proceso* and *La Jornada*, Lawson suggests, "remain crucial pieces of Mexico's fourth estate," referring to the importance of the press as an independent political institution in the separation of executive, legislative, and judiciary powers.[108] *La Jornada* eventually surpassed *Unomásuno* in circulation.

Poniatowska was a founding member of *La Jornada* and has written columns and crónicas for the newspaper since 1985. Some of her most important pieces have appeared on its pages, including those covering the 1985 earthquake, the EZLN, and the Ayotzinapa students. Just as she was involved in helping found Siglo XXI by donating a house, she also participated with others in helping Scherer García get the weekly magazine off the ground. But her friendship with Scherer García went back to the 1950s. She first met him in 1953 at the *Excélsior* newspaper, but she remembers getting to know him more from a 1959 trip to Cuba, where he interviewed Fidel Castro.[109] Under Scherer García's leadership, during which Poniatowska and other chroniclers such as Carlos Monsiváis wrote for the newspaper, *Excélsior* was one of the few papers that covered the government massacre in Tlatelolco in detail.

The foundation of the magazine *Proceso* was important for me. I was friends with Julio Scherer García, and when Scherer and his followers were expelled from the newspaper *Excélsior*, then I worked [with them], I got together with them to help them create their magazine. . . .

Also, at that time many people in elite social circles and the government called me *rojilla* [red, meaning communist or socialist]. I was, in the end, persecuted a lot—if you will—because of my activities or social attitudes. They would tell me often that I was a traitor to my social class, that I was a communist, and I don't know what else. And that it wasn't my place. Well, there was a huge rejection.

Poniatowska consulted her file compiled by Mexico's Dirección Federal de Seguridad (DFS, Federal Security Directorate) for the first time in 2016. She later received a copy of it. She had no idea it existed nor that she was being spied upon, except for one incident. In a 2016 interview with *El País* newspaper, she stated that for two nights, in the late 1970s, there was a car parked outside her house with four men in it waiting for her to leave. She added, "I offered them coffee and then they rolled the window up. They thought I was completely out of my mind."[110] The dossier on Poniatowska, which covers the period from the 1960s through the 1980s, contains dozens of documents that label her as a communist and document her interactions with prisoners, feminists, intellectuals, and activists. She was characterized as "an affiliated communist," "who wrote for the magazine *Siempre*," and "who visited Lecumberri multiple times" in 1969.[111] The file also contains extensive documentation of the publishing house Siglo XXI, which Poniatowska helped found.

While Poniatowska would always face rejection because of her political perspectives, the 1976 rupture produced by Scherer García's firing opened up Mexican print media in ways that the state could not turn around. These new outlets, particularly *La Jornada*, provided a home where Poniatowska felt welcome, and they have broadened the ideological spectrum in Mexican print media. However, as Piccato reminds us, selling newspapers requires "a close relationship with readers."[112] Without a readership, these new publications would not have survived. *Proceso*, *Unomásuno*, and *La Jornada* were innovators in cultivating a culture of memorialization about their own beginnings and about events that foregrounded government repression, corruption, dysfunction, and tragedy, beginning in 1968. Through their ongoing memorialization, these print media also helped sustain and perhaps expand their reader base through multiple generations. They built upon the critical public sphere opened in 1959 and functioned as venues for constructing a critical narrative of Mexican history—often with the collaboration of chroniclers such as Poniatowska.

The 1968 Student
Movement and Massacre

My mind was a total blank. The tremendous crush of people screaming in panic made it hard for me to hear what he was saying. I thought later that if I'd known, if I'd realized that Julio was dying . . .

Later some of the soldiers who had been shooting at the buildings around the Plaza came over to us. The smell of gunpowder was unbearable. Little by little people made room for me so I could kneel down beside Julio.

"Julio, Julio, answer me, little brother," I said to him.

"He must be wounded," one woman said to me. "Loosen his belt."

When I loosened it, I could feel a great big wound. I found out later at the hospital that he had three bullet wounds: one in the stomach, one in the neck, and another in the leg. He was dying.

—DIANA SALMERÓN DE CONTRERAS, quoted in Poniatowska, *Massacre in Mexico*

We read the crónica [*La noche de Tlatelolco*] at the same time that we watched the film called *Red Dawn*, which portrayed what happened in 1968.[1] . . . It wasn't until I went to the university, however, that I really was able to understand the importance of the events of 1968 for the political life of the country. In this sense, I could say the book affected me in two different times of my life: in secondary school when I read it and it made me feel like an adult, and then when I revisited the events of 1968 when I was in the university and I understood their importance in the life of democracy (and its absence) in the country.

—THIRTY-YEAR-OLD LOURDES commenting on the impact of reading *La noche de Tlatelolco* in 2004, thirty-three years after the book was published

LA NOCHE DE TLATELOLCO, published in 1971 by Elena Poniatowska (translated by Helen R. Lane and first published in English in 1975), is based on dozens of eyewitness testimonies (which she either tape-recorded or took notes about), including those of student leaders and many others. The book also includes a wide range of excerpts from journalists who reported about the event. Drawing from a multivocal set of testimonies, the book reveals the complexity and contradictions of the student movement, its euphoria and energy, the students' insistence on having a voice, and their search for dialogue with the government. The Consejo Nacional de Huelga (CNH) circulated an official list of demands that included the release of political prisoners, the disbanding of the riot police, the dismissal of the city police chief and his assistant, compensation for police brutality against students, repeal of Article 145 of the Mexican Constitution (which sanctioned imprisonment of anyone attending meetings of three or more people, deemed to threaten public order), and no further invasions of educational institutions by police and armed forces, referred to as "the forces of law and order."[2] These demands were forged against a backdrop of what became a huge movement expressing a desire for liberty, nurtured locally and transnationally. The basic demand of youth in Mexico was to be heard and dialogue with the state, demanding accountability and basic freedoms from the government. Poniatowska's book makes visible the students' own creation and publication of their counternarrative, designed to challenge and offset that of the government. While the government controlled the media and attempted to control the narrative of the movement and the massacre that occurred, it was not able to entirely do so, as *La noche de Tlatelolco* (hereafter abbreviated as *La noche*) makes clear (figure 2.1).

The book then turns to the massacre itself, the resulting arrests and torture of those imprisoned, and the cover-up about the massacre, including,

Figure 2.1 Elena Poniatowska at her typewriter with a copy of *La noche de Tlatelolco* on her desk, c. 1971. Used by permission of the Fundación Elena Poniatowska Amor, Mexico City, Mexico.

literally, the cleansing of blood from the plaza. More than anything, *La noche* has stood the test of time and continues to be one of the most widely read and quoted books Poniatowska has written. It has influenced multiple generations of Mexicans and continues to be an accessible and moving account about a tragic event and an important social movement in Mexico's modern history. I suggest that its success is strongly based on the emotional connection Poniatowska builds with readers through the use of testimonies. It is the first of many texts, dialogues, and performances

Poniatowska has been involved in that help seed strategic emotional political community. The book also became an important political tool as a narrative of Mexican history that highlights government repression, the ongoing struggle for democracy, and the role of youth in that struggle. Poniatowska's book and 1968 give youth a clear vanguard role in Mexican politics, a role they have maintained since that time.

In this crónica, written when she was thirty-six years old and published three years later, Poniatowska was not a direct participant. While her world intersected with intellectuals and the university through the interviews she conducted and published, student activism was not one of her beats before 1968. At the time, she had been interviewing Josefina Bórquez and working on the novel *Hasta no verte, Jesús mío*, first published in 1969. She had friends in the movement, but, as she told me in 2011, the "social movement claims of the young people were not mine, like nothing that was linked to my reality or to what was happening to me."[3] Her second child, Felipe Haro Poniatowska, was born in June 1968 (figure 2.2).

He was just four months old she when she plunged into interviewing and documenting the story of the Tlatelolco massacre, spurred by two friends who came to tell her about what had happened on the night of October 2: "I heard about the massacre at 9 o'clock that night, when María Alicia Martínez Medrano and Mercedes Olivera [both active in Mexico's civil society] came to my house. . . . I thought they had gone mad. They told me that there was blood on the walls of the buildings, that the elevators were perforated with machine-gun bullets, that the glass windows of the shops were destroyed, that tanks were inside the plaza, that there was blood on the staircases of the buildings, that they could hear people shouting, moaning, and crying."[4]

The next morning, at 7 a.m., Poniatowska went to the plaza herself to look: "I saw the shoes of those who had been able to escape. I returned home and felt extremely indignant. . . . Then I began to gather testimonies."[5] The process of collecting the testimonies from those in the movement and their families, and then following them into prison, where many were held after the massacre, profoundly impacted her. The distance between observer and participant began to narrow for Poniatowska as she wrote this crónica.

La noche allows people to see the summer and fall of 1968 on an intimate, human scale rather than from the perspective of ideology or geopolitics. The book tells many stories within the larger story of the movement and massacre, such as the disbelief of the Mexican government at the time that

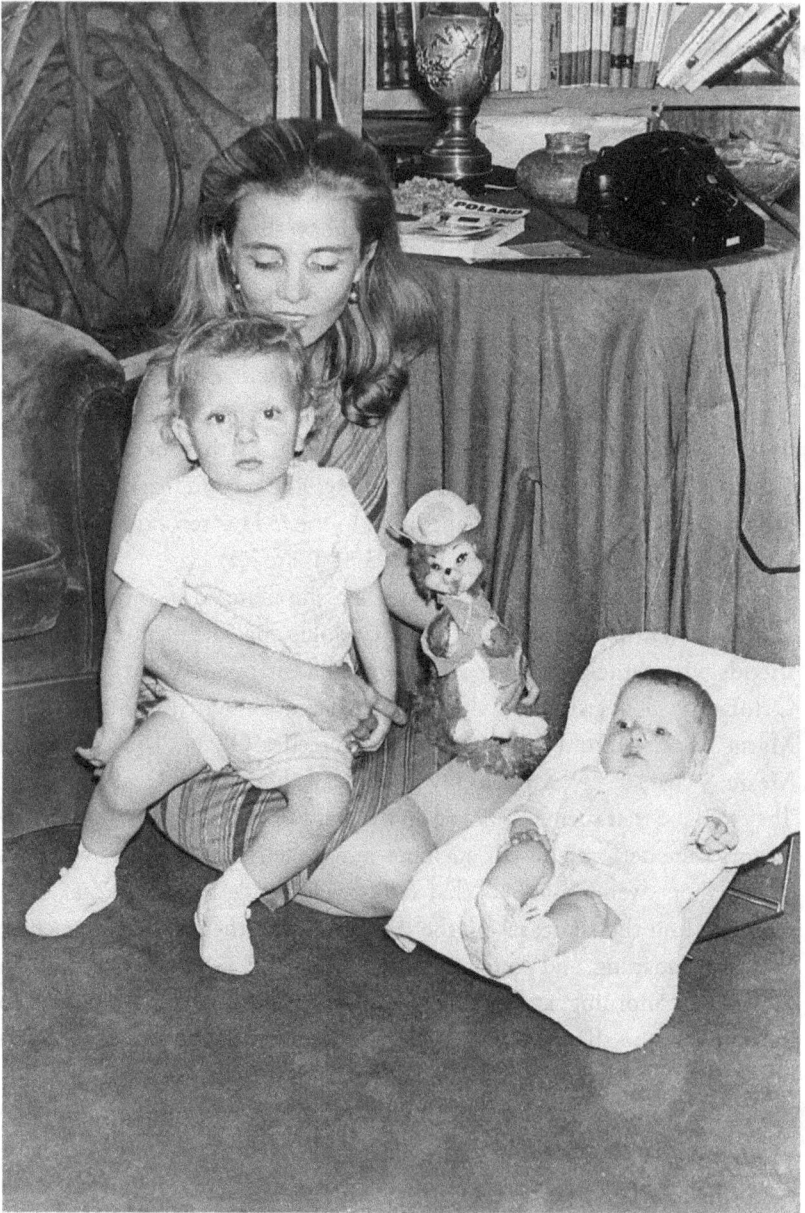

Figure 2.2 Elena Poniatowska with her son Felipe and daughter, Paula, December 1970. Photograph by Eduardo Iturbe. Used by permission of the Fundación Elena Poniatowska Amor, Mexico City, Mexico.

the student movement was autonomous.[6] The book underlines the complexity and differences within the student movement, providing a glimpse of a range of ideological and class positions held by student participants. It also highlights the intense euphoria and hope students felt in the spring and summer before the massacre. Like many of Poniatowska's crónicas, this one homes in on the role of women in the movement, including several key female leaders who have been overlooked in histories of the movement until fairly recently. Graphic testimonies about the massacre itself, and the detention and torture of student leaders in prison, are gripping and heart-wrenching. Accounts of a government cover-up provide a sobering look at a lack of state accountability for the tragedy. The book employs a compelling mix of photojournalism, testimonies, and juxtaposed accounts that draw readers into the events and characters woven through the book. This chapter serves as a historical bookend not only in the political life of Mexico but in Poniatowska's life as well; it was her first published crónica in book form and would set a standard in Mexico.

Student Movements

Student activism was a part of the growing critical public sphere in Mexico City in the 1950s and has important links to the 1968 student movement. In 1956 students from the Instituto Politécnico Nacional (IPN) challenged the authoritarian structure and corruption of their schools and opposed changes to the Mexican Constitution that would eliminate university autonomy and student participation. They organized a movement that "became national in scope and more than one hundred thousand students strong."[7] Demanding the dismissal of the director of the IPN and the implementation of a law that would guarantee student participation in governance and autonomy from the state, students organized information brigades to educate the public; held spontaneous "lightning" rallies to fundraise; took over classrooms, dormitories, and offices; and commandeered school buses—all tactics that the 1968 movement would use a decade later.[8] In response, the Mexican state used strategies of division, infiltration, media "smear" campaigns, paid provocateurs, militarized repression, arrest, and detention to undermine and dissolve the 1956 movement.[9]

While student movements continued from 1956, the government of Gustavo Díaz Ordaz seemed unprepared for the scale, intensity, and resonance of the student movement with other people in Mexico City in the summer of 1968. The loud critical public that took to the streets in growing numbers in July—until repression, a massacre, and mass arrests shut it down in the fall—marked the consolidation of an era of student activism and government repression.

As the movement expanded in the spring and summer of 1968, the PRI-led government tried traditional intimidation tactics to shut down the student movement as it grew.[10] It enforced an outdated article of the Constitution, Article 145, which outlawed gatherings and essentially equated public opposition to the government with treason.[11] Soldiers and police beat, shot, and wounded students. They raided offices, detaining and imprisoning student leaders. As the summer of 1968 wore on, student marches became larger and attracted more sympathizers. Mounting governmental repression emboldened the movement that proliferated in the late summer and early fall of 1968 to include more students and staff from many institutions of higher education, members of the few independent unions, and a variety of people in Mexico City from neighborhoods where the students were active; for all these people who were part of a burgeoning emotional strategic political community on the ground and later in texts, the movement transformed into a shared quest for justice and democracy. It included political theater, art, and music as well as more standard forms of protest. It was full of hope, energy, enthusiasm, and expansive intensity, like a multicolored hot air balloon filling up and slowly rising ever higher in the sky.

On the night of October 2, 1968, students and many other people had gathered to listen to speakers who were addressing the crowd from the fourth-floor balconies of the Chihuahua apartment building in the Plaza de las Tres Culturas in Tlatelolco. Green flares flashed, and snipers positioned at surrounding buildings began to shoot down into the crowd. Mexican army battalions and police officers, who had been transported and stationed around the plaza, returned fire. The crowd was confused and began to run for cover, trying to escape. As the army moved in on the plaza, many students and others were shot and wounded. Exits were blocked. Following the massacre, through its interrogations and torture of imprisoned student leaders and many others, the government suggested that the snipers who had begun shooting were armed students. Many years later, it was revealed that the government had likely planted the sharpshooters in an effort to discredit the movement and justify arresting the student leaders.

We now know more about what happened on the night of October 2, 1968, thanks to the release of significant government documents and film footage some three decades after the event. These came to light under the first non-PRI presidency, of Vicente Fox (2000–2006), and through the ongoing declassification work that Kate Doyle and others carried out at the National Security Archive in the United States and in Mexico.[12] But the exact number of people massacred is still unknown—as are some other details.

On the fiftieth anniversary of the massacre, in 2018, a wide range of articles was published, some attempting to estimate the number of deaths. The *New York Times* reported that Doyle and Susana Zavalla, a Mexican researcher, counted forty-four victims—thirty-four of them by name.[13] In Mexico, Televisa (a Mexican media conglomerate founded in 1955 that dominated Mexican television for decades) published a chronology of what happened that day, with commentary. Citing the government-run Instituto Nacional de Estudios Históricos de la Revolución Mexicana (National Institute of Historical Studies on the Mexican Revolution), Televisa wrote, "There were dozens of dead and wounded, but we still need a rigorous archival investigation and analysis to put names, faces, and voices to those who were assassinated."[14] The description goes on to note, "Nevertheless, it's important to acknowledge that the page where this history should be written is not blank. Among the first intellectuals who sought to tell this story, the name of Elena Poniatowska stands out." The text then introduces her book *La noche de Tlatelolco* and calls it a "documentary book that brings together different testimonial registers to tell a version of what happened in many voices."[15]

Five years earlier, in 2013, *Aristegui Noticias* (a news service run by Carmen Aristegui, a radio, TV, and social media journalist) published an article, "Los muertos de Tlatelolco, ¿cuántos fueron?" (The dead of Tlatelolco, how many were there?). The article begins with a quote from *La noche*: "'Who? Who were they? Nothing. The next day, nothing. At dawn, the plaza was swept clean.' As of now, there is no exact death toll for October 2, 1968, in the Plaza of Three Cultures of Tlatelolco."[16] The article goes through the conflicting sources. *El Día*, the newspaper of the student strike committee, reported no number the day after the massacre. On October 6, *El Día* published that up to that point, "about a hundred people" had died. The student strike committee then revised that number to 150 civilians and 40 military personnel.[17] The office of the president stated to the Mexican press that there were 26 deaths, 1,043 people detained, and 100 people wounded.[18] John Rodda, who was at the massacre, published the number of deaths at 500 in *The Guardian* on October 4, 1968.[19] In his book *Posdata* (1970), Mexican writer and then-ambassador to India, Octavio Paz, estimated 325 were killed.[20] Rather than postulate another number, Aristegui Noticias' article concludes with another quote from *La noche*: "As Elena Poniatowska wrote in *La noche de Tlatelolco*, 'The wound is still fresh; still feeling the blow to the head, Mexicans question themselves, stunned.' And the dead do not add up."[21]

Both the government-linked Televisa account of 2018 and the more left-oriented *Aristegui Noticias* news service share ambiguity about the number of dead. And they both turned to *La noche de Tlatelolco* as a source. Poniatowska's book never states it has "facts" or "the truth." In the first part, it focuses on stories filled with excitement, euphoria, and great optimism around the student movement. Then it shifts to narratives of horror, disbelief, terror, deep grief, and in some cases resilience in the descriptions of the massacre and its aftermath. The book's ability to capture emotion through testimonials makes it a source not only for news outlets at the far ends of the political spectrum like Televisa and *Aristegui Noticias* but for thousands and thousands of readers from multiple generations. In the preface to the second part of the book, Poniatowska writes, "Grief is a very personal thing. Putting it into words is almost unbearable; hence asking questions, digging for facts, borders on an invasion of people's privacy.... In these pages there echo the cries of those who died and the cries of those who lived on after them. These pages express their outrage and their protest: the mute cry that stuck in thousands of throats, the blind grief in thousands of horror-stricken eyes on October 2, 1968, the night of Tlatelolco."[22]

An Emotional Community of Readers

La noche and Poniatowska's other crónicas operate through a nexus of emotion and political connection, allowing readers to feel affinity with those people whose narratives they encounter on the page.[23] By juxtaposing the testimonies of victims, survivors, their families, academics, and newspaper reporters with press stories and headlines, Poniatowska strategically creates connections with readers. Her writing strategy of emotional connection is at the same time a political strategy that builds a network that we can conceptualize as a flexible community that readers can move in and out of. Her writing forges connections with readers at a personal level.

I didn't "join" the Student Movement; it had been an intimate part of my life for a long time.... I'm from Poli [IPN]. I live in a house there, that's where my pals, my neighbors, my work are. . . . My kids were born there. My wife is from Poli, too. The Movement has been very close to our hearts for many years. It's not a whim of the moment, or a joke or "good vibes," or anything like that. . . . It's a question of fighting for everything we believe in, for the things we've always fought for, things that our fathers and our fathers' fathers fought for before us. . . . We come from working-class families, people who have always worked hard for a living.[24]

La noche opens with this testimony from Raúl Álvarez Garín, a theoretical physicist and professor at the IPN, CNH delegate, and prisoner in Lecumberri. In one paragraph, we learn about his neighborhood, his home, wife, children, and family history linked to the student movement. A major leader who had been active in the Communist Party and with the Movimiento Revolucionario del Magisterio (Revolutionary Teachers Movement), Álvarez Garín was deeply engaged with the student movement and connects it to not only his own family but Mexican history, making indirect reference to the Mexican Revolution where his father's fathers fought. He identifies as working class and links that category to his family history. Later we learn about the history of leftism in his family. In one paragraph, we have a connection with Álvarez Garín and at the same time are linked to the larger story of the student movement. This passage does what so many of the testimonies in the book do. These personal narratives are woven into the larger story of the student movement, government repression, and student efforts to dialogue and push the state to create a truly democratic exchange and model of Mexican society. They provide an emotional connection for readers.

Writing on the intellectual history of the concept of emotional communities, coined by cultural anthropologist Myriam Jimeno, Morna Macleod and Natalia De Marinis argue that Jimeno believes there is "a clear link between cognitive processes of reasoning, memories, assessments and the role emotions play in experiences of violence."[25] Other cultural anthropologists have also written about the strong connections between emotions and memory.[26] Collective political and emotional experience, the staging or writing of traumatic events, and the relational nature between those who share a traumatic experience and those who listen or read about it are different dimensions I have built in to augment the concept of strategic emotional political communities, as outlined in the introduction.[27] According to Jimeno, "[Emotional communities] are created through the process of narrating to another, testifying lived suffering through a story, a narrative, to someone else, and succeeding in the other identifying with their pain."[28] The narrative may be performative or a statement. Jimeno suggests that this narrative acquires great currency when it creates emotional community, "that is, when the pain of the victim does not remain enclosed in the victim, but spreads to other audiences, who identify and are moved by the narrative. This creates a political bond, not simply a compassionate moment. This political link contributes to enhance actions that seek justice."[29] Thus Jimeno's notion of emotional community includes not only the emotions of victims or survivors, such as those whose narratives build *La noche*, but also emotions awakened in a wider audience—in this case readers.[30]

The social memory of the student movement and the massacre of Tlatelolco are not only held by those who lived at the time; it has become a major theme in the record of Mexican history. At almost every anniversary of Tlatelolco, there have been new inquiries and sometimes revelations. *La noche de Tlatelolco* has been published dozens of times in Spanish and has been read widely across Mexico, including as an assigned text in middle and high school. By 1991 *La noche* was in its fiftieth edition and 250,000 copies had been sold in Mexico.[31] In 2018, fifty years since the massacre, 500,000 copies of *La noche* had been sold.[32]

After conversing with dozens of people who had read *La noche de Tlatelolco*, I decided to informally survey some readers. I sent an invitation to twenty people who had attended school in different parts of Mexico between the 1960s and 2009. All have at least some university education. Among the fourteen who responded, ten had read *La noche de Tlatelolco*. One had read some of Poniatowska's other works, but not her account of the massacre. Six had read *La noche de Tlatelolco* in high school, two had read it in middle school, and two others had read it with their families or received it from friends to read. All identified the book as an important part of their historical and political education; for some it was a watershed moment.[33] While by no means the product of an exhaustive survey, the answers I received reflect the intergenerational effect of *La noche de Tlatelolco* on Mexicans who tended to read it as teenagers or young adults. As some of the narratives given here demonstrate, the book continued to be an important source of historical information and feelings, even when additional information and perspectives became available.[34]

Margarita, a fifty-seven-year-old woman educated in public schools in Torreón, Coahuila, read the book when she was in high school, about four years after it was published—not as part of an official curriculum but as a source given to her by high school friends—and she shared it with her siblings. The book made a strong impression on her in terms of her knowledge about historical events but also in relation to the importance of the pioneering political work that the student movement did in 1968.

> First of all, I was strongly affected after reading it, knowing that this had happened in my country. I was seven years old when the events of October 2, 1968, took place and I don't remember people in my family talking about it in those days. . . . Because of this crónica, I learned about what happened, the repression, and the violence directed against the students. It also made me aware of the importance of the political participation of youth at that time who fought for university autonomy and for the free expression of ideas, among other things.

Lourdes, about thirty years old, recalled reading Poniatowska's book in 2004 in her secondary school in Mexico City. As the epigraph to the chapter indicates, she credits the book with helping her to understand the student movement's importance to Mexican democracy.

She mentions, as did several other younger people, reading the book in conjunction with seeing the film *Rojo amanecer* (Red dawn), thirty-three years after it was first published. Initially finished in 1989 but not released until 1990, the fictional film portrays October 2, 1968, from the perspective of a middle-class family living in one of the apartment buildings on the Plaza de las Tres Culturas, where the massacre took place, and draws on some of the testimonies in *La noche*.

Maria, now in her midthirties, read the book in a public high school in the state of Oaxaca in 1989, almost twenty years after it was first published. She traveled about six hours every year from the regional public high school she attended in the town of Putla de Guerrero, in the Mixtec region in far western Oaxaca, to the state capital to participate in marches commemorating the 1968 massacre.

> I read *La noche de Tlatelolco* when I was in high school in 1989. I remember that it helped me understand the signs and graffiti in the streets of Oaxaca that said things like "We will never forget October 2!" It also provided insight into why the students from the state university of Oaxaca organized marches on this date as well. I came with people from my high school in Putla to some of these marches. I was just starting to understand the capital city of Oaxaca as an adolescent. This book was

definitely important in helping me formulate my ideas about government repression.

José, about thirty-five, read the book in his Catholic high school in Puebla in the mid-1990s, almost three decades after the events and twenty-five years after Poniatowska's book was first published. For him, the crónica style of *La noche de Tlatelolco* was initially confusing, but it opened an important new way of thinking for him.

I read the book in my first or second year of a Jesuit high school.... I remember that I wasn't completely clear on whether the book was fiction or history. I thought maybe it was a combination of both. I remember after reading it that I felt like I was discovering something new. Even though I read a lot as a high school student, I had not read a lot of women writers. I really felt like the book opened a new window for me. I remember that I talked about it with my friends. I had heard from some of them that there was a controversy about the book and about who had really written it.[35]

Even though the Zapatista rebellion had already happened when I started to read *La noche de Tlatelolco*, I had not made a connection between the rebellion and 1968. Poniatowska's book helped me connect them. I was a little informed about what happened in Tlatelolco, but it was based more on oral tradition passed on through family and friends. I had not read about it. I think reading the book also helped me to think differently about Mexico City. I wasn't familiar with Mexico City then, and the book gave me a lot of context and ideas for thinking more widely and more politically about what the city means.

These are instances of opinion among multiple generations of Mexicans who have read and discussed *La noche de Tlatelolco*. It has had a lasting effect, even in light of the many other sources of information about the massacre that have emerged over the decades. Thanks to the book's form—the combination and juxtaposition of photographs, poetry, and many different narratives—its narrative power endures.

The first public commemoration to mark the anniversary of Tlatelolco took place in 1978 in Mexico City, once the government forces lifted restrictions on access to the site.[36] Perhaps this initial access to the site for purposes of memorialization was linked to the electoral reform promulgated by José López Portillo (1976–82) that resulted in opening up the formal electoral process to small opposition parties. While the state provided this initial opening, the social position of the university students themselves is also a significant factor. As members of Mexico's elite, some of whom went on to become members of the print media, former students had a significant hand in processes of memorialization. The tenth anniversary received significant attention from the press. New publication venues, such as *Proceso* and *Nexos*, devoted their fall issues of that year to the views and perspectives of those involved in the 1968 movement.[37] Poniatowska published a piece in *Proceso* titled "Diez años después: El rumor de las manifestaciones" (Ten years later: The rumor of the protests). In that piece, she provided updates on the students who had been imprisoned and reflections on the state of politics and society ten years later. And of course, the place of the commemoration, the Plaza de Las Tres Culturas in Mexico City, has historical and symbolic power. This is further discussed in the next chapter.

Subsequent anniversaries of the Tlatelolco massacre have been memorialized in newspapers and magazines, on radio shows, in art installations, on film, and in television broadcasts (after 2000). For example, on October 1, 2018—fifty years after the massacre—hundreds of activists and students from UNAM were sprawled on the ground in positions of anguish with looks of pain on their faces. They were participating in a commemorative reenactment of the October 2, 1968, massacre. The following day, a large march wound its way from the site of the massacre in Tlatelolco through Mexico City, ending in the historic Zócalo. While the march included many young people walking with energy and enthusiasm, it also included people in wheelchairs who had reached advanced age since their days of activism in the 1960s. Among the marchers were survivors of the massacre, members of the student movement of 1968, students from many of Mexico City's universities, and family members of the forty-three disappeared student teachers from Ayotzinapa (see chapter 6).[38] Former member of the CNH, Víctor Guerra, spoke forcefully to the crowd assembled in front of him in the Zócalo: "Today, fifty years ago, genocide was committed in the Plaza of the Three Cultures. This genocide has been proven. It has been duly demonstrated in Mexico's legal institutions. Even so, no one has been punished for this genocide. That is why today we demand justice for our comrades [*compañeros*]." Fellow CNH member Félix Lucio Hernández Gamundi continued. "Here, nobody is backing down," he sternly stated while punctuating his words by pointing his finger in time with his speech. "That's why we were here. We are here fifty years later because on an afternoon like this, at this time of day, the government committed a massacre. The government wanted to extinguish the cry for liberty that rang through the streets of this city and many others in the interior of the Republic."[39] A moment of silence was held for the victims of the massacre in the Zócalo.

Poniatowska has been a part of many such commemorative events. Beyond annual interviews in October that ask her to repeat what she saw and how she came to write about the massacre, even the book she produced has been memorialized with anniversary celebrations of its publication date. For example, Carlos Monsiváis published an article about Poniatowska's book as part of a special issue of *La Jornada Semanal*, on October 13, 1991.[40] For the fiftieth anniversary of Tlatelolco in 2018, many interviews with Poniatowska or examples of her writing were published in Mexico, in Latin America, in Spain, and elsewhere.[41] In Mexico City, the Museo Universitario Arte Contemporáneo (University Museum of Contemporary Art), housed at UNAM, presented a graphic arts exhibit that referred to Poniatowska's book and highlighted posters and engravings from 1968. Poniatowska participated in at least one of a series of public events about 1968 that were hosted by UNAM. Televisa hosted an interview with her and posted a story online.[42] The online story links to a powerful short documentary.[43] These commemorative events have all contributed to building multigenerational links to the 1968 massacre, as has Poniatowska's book *La noche*.

Historian Diana Sorensen suggests that "for readers who in some way experienced the events in question, the book might help to locate shared memories and perhaps by an aggregated individual process contribute to the construction of collective memory of Tlatelolco and its power of resistance; for the rest it means confronting the powerful traces of a traumatic event that resists an integrated, unified narrative."[44] Sorensen's interpretation of the effect of *La noche de Tlatelolco* provides a strong opening for the argument I seek to make not only about this particular book but in relation to all of Poniatowska's crónicas. In assembling dozens of voices and offering a complex and multivocal version of history that differed from the Mexican state's official narrative for decades, Poniatowska's *La noche de Tlatelolco* provides a multivocal account of a national tragedy. It has been shared by the thousands of people and their families who were involved in the 1968 student movement, in the October 2 massacre, in the imprisonment and torture of student leaders and others, and through the systematic denial and cover-up of state repression. It has also been read by people who did not share the experience or have the same opinion or political view as those who participated directly in the student movement. When we consider how the book works in terms of forging strategic emotional political community, we have to define such a community as flexible in the moment and through time but also permitting a wide variety of different opinions to coexist on a broad political scale. Strategically, the book puts people in conversation with one another. But it is also a document in the archive of democracy and hope, as it captures the spirit of the 1968 student movement—its hopes, dreams, and belief in a different future as well as the different perspectives within and about the movement and that moment in time.[45]

Representing a Movement and Its Meaning

I can hear their voices, their footsteps, echoing as on the
day of the Silent Demonstration; I will hear those advancing footsteps all the rest of my life; girls in mini-skirts
with their tanned young legs, teachers with no neckties,
boys with sweaters knotted around their waists or their
necks; they come toward me, laughing, there are hundreds
of them, full of crazy joy walking together down this
street. . . . Father Jesús Pérez has set all the bells of the
cathedral ringing to welcome them, the entire Plaza de la
Constitución is illuminated. The youngsters are marching
up Cinco de Mayo, Júarez, the Reforma, the applause is
deafening, three hundred thousand people have come to
join them, of their own free will. . . . *Mé-xi-co, Li-ber-tad,*
Mé-xi-co, Li-ber-tad, Mé-xi-co, Li-ber-tad, Mé-xi-co, Li-
ber-tad, Mé-xi-co, Li-ber-tad.
—ELENA PONIATOWSKA, *Massacre in Mexico,* 4

These words bring us directly to the euphoria, joy, and wild hope felt by the young people who marched through the streets of Mexico City in 1968. Believing they were on the threshold of finding liberty for Mexico, their movement accelerated and was embraced by many.

Poniatowska and many others have commented on the importance of the Mexican student political engagement in the larger context of the 1960s, as a decade rife with student movements. Sorensen details the contradictory economic boom that fueled western economies and the rising expectations that ultimately could not be fully satisfied. As she explains it,

"An impatient longing for a transfigured world—stripped of the trammels of consumer society and the established regime of power—drew its energies from the very advanced capitalist economy that produced stunning urban growth, new markets, and new consumers."[46] Some theories of the New Left outlined a vision of more communal forms of life, politics, and economy, and the Cuban Revolution provided a Latin American model for how to create a successful socialist revolution. Vastly increased access to education through the expansion of university systems, including in Mexico, allowed middle-class youth to become enfranchised in a system that was "structured hierarchically as a system for the production and dissemination of knowledge" but also as "the purveyor of critical thinking that was to shake up existing structures of knowledge."[47]

While authority had previously rested with the wealthy and the old, youth emerged as a new category of consumer and political power. Zolov identifies several intersecting currents that profoundly affected leftist Mexican political culture and the university-age youth in 1960s Mexico. First were the influence of the Cuban Revolution, the reverence for Fidel Castro, and the ongoing defense of the revolution, particularly at UNAM and the IPN. Zolov discusses how the fracturing of the news magazine *Política*—a forum for left-wing intellectuals to critique the authoritarian PRI regime—reflected a broader split within the culture of the New Left into "those [who] came to embrace a 'heroic revolutionary' discourse that regarded a cultural manifestation derived from the First World as intrinsically 'imperialist' and those [who were] more open to the fluidity and increasing hybridity of cultural exchange."[48] Monsiváis, Fuentes, and Benítez were among those who left the news magazine. Campuses such as Puebla, Morelia, and Guadalajara, as noted in some of the testimonies in *La noche de Tlatelolco*, were sites of ideological and strategic battles to open up access to education and allow public universities more autonomy.

Zolov also analyzes the development of a youth counterculture in Mexico through music, art, and film.[49] Known as "La onda," the Mexican counterculture was part of a global youth movement that was exploring new languages, styles, and cultural sensibilities and was openly defiant of traditional authority and values. The student movement of the summer of 1968, Zolov states, "merged key tropes from the Cuban-inspired revolutionary experience (such as holding signs and slogans of Che Guevara) with that of La onda."[50] The protesters often "reflected the stylistic aspects of the youth movement internationally. Long hair, blue jeans, miniskirts, and a more casual look on both men and women more generally reflected shifting attitudes and assertions of individual aspirations.... Youth increasingly defined themselves as both activists and countercultural agents."[51] Zolov's analysis, with its emphasis on culture, captures some of the important aspects of "the meaning" of the events during the summer and fall of 1968. He identifies the staging of the 1968 Olympics in Mexico as balancing the need between "Mexican 'rootedness' (folklore) with a manifestation of Mexican 'modernity' (cosmopolitanism)."[52] Zolov argues that the tarnishing of this branding by the extreme levels of government-sponsored violence, and the government's narrative of foreign-directed student subversives intent on robbing Mexico of its long-deserved moment of international glory and modernity, revealed the real stakes of youth protest.[53] Government repression also brought to the surface the underlying political and cultural divides that permeated the student movement and the country before the massacre at Tlatelolco.

Cultural and political forms of protest were important elements of the student movement in Mexico, including gatherings, flash meetings, the incorporation of music and art into protest, and the exploration of new forms of creative and political expression.

We decided to do the only thing we know how to do: play-act.... Those of us in the group from the Theater of Fine Arts made up our minds from the start: "We can't stand on the sidelines with our arms folded. We have to help publicize the Movement." So we went to La Lagunilla, to the Merced, to Jamaica and all the other public markets, and we also organized brigades to visit public squares and parks.... We organized encounters—*happenings*, you know what I mean? ... I'd go up to a newspaper stand, for example, and ask for a newspaper, and just then a very "square," very middle-class matron, wearing earrings and a little pearl necklace ... would come by—another one of the Fine Arts actresses.

She'd buy a paper at the newsstand too, and then turn to me ... and say, "Those crazy students are born troublemakers. Just look at this, will you? When there are so many Mexicans like me, people who simply want to live in peace and quiet and not make trouble for anybody! What in the world do those students want? They just want to stir up a fuss, that's all! I'm certain they're Communists—they must be to act like that!"

I'd stand there in my boots and my mini-skirt listening to her, and then suddenly I'd turn to her and bust out, "Listen, *señora*, you're going to have to explain what you mean, because what you're saying is non-sense. What are you trying to insinuate?"

I'd say this very loudly, and the other actress would raise her voice too, till finally both of us would be shouting at the top of our lungs. A crowd would gather, because everyone's curious when they see two people having a violent argument, right? . . . Our audience wouldn't say anything at first, but then suddenly, without even realizing it, they'd begin to take sides. . . .

. . . The crowd would almost always end up siding with me and the "snob" would have to take to her heels.[54]

This passage illustrates in vivid detail the use of public theater to foster public discussions about the student movement. Margarita Isabel, the actress who narrated this passage to Poniatowska, explains that as people in the crowd started talking, bystanders who were politically aware would end up speaking and engaging in the scene. Afterward they would talk with those who seemed supportive and work to engage them further.[55] Street theater was an effective way of engaging people in public.

At the same time, the varied forms of print media that people consumed—supplements that featured interviews and photographs, tabloid crime news, and alternative papers—were also a part of the cultural mix, encouraging innovation and complexity. The city was awash in a spirit of experimentation, movement, and discussion—and sometimes confrontation—between generations about politics, public space, behavior, and culture.

The student movement evolved its own body of images that accompanied activists on marches and at events. The images were designed to have an impact in the critical public sphere. A 2018 exhibit of iconic posters from the 1968 movement suggests that the images were a "channel for the circulation of critical information or information that countered the dominant narrative."[56] A stark black close-up of a tank pointing directly at the viewer with a text reading "We don't understand this dialogue" or a side profile of a gorilla in a helmet with "Disappear the Police Corps" are examples of the blunt graphic style with brief but powerful messages that students deployed.[57]

Art schools such as the Academia San Carlos and La Esmeralda "began to produce graphics in the service of the movement. Similarly, students at the Centro Universitario de Estudios Cinematográficos (University Center for Cinematographic Studies) of the UNAM began to produce films documenting the events."[58] The production of graphic art and short films allowed students to circulate their demands and ideas about the movement through media they created. Independent artists also supported the student movement. A mural painted on the side of an UNAM building where many students and artists gathered on a daily basis was created in part by painters such as José Luis Cuevas and others who were important painters during the 1960s.[59] Images are an important part of *La noche*.

The quotations that accompany the photographic essay that is a part of *La noche de Tlatelolco* include the following: "They made us line up with our hands up, and took the ones with long hair aside. They made one kid kneel down and lopped off his hair with a bayonet." "'Here's a little farewell present for you.' And they started hitting us as though they were breaking *piñatas*." "Strewn about on the pavement, among the torn clothing and the plants trampled underfoot, were many shoes, most of them women's." "After the night at Tlatelolco, peopled gathered in many places all over the city seeking news of the dead and wounded. In the Third Police Precinct alone, we saw thirty bodies." "On the second of November, All Souls Day, we placed *cempazuchitl* flowers and candles on the Plaza de Las Tres Culturas. There were many Army troops on guard, but suddenly thousands of memorial candles were lighted and hundreds of people popped out from behind the trees and began to pray for their children who had been murdered at Tlatelolco on the second of October."[60] The book is an experimental work in terms of its use of photographs throughout, beginning on the inside cover flap, as a source of documentation of the event; its juxtaposition of newspaper stories and headlines reflecting different viewpoints; its deliberate positioning of different interpretations of the same event on the same page; and its use of multivocal sources and fragmentation of testimonies. Reading *La noche de Tlatelolco* is like viewing an experimental art installation that may include different film clips projected simultaneously on several walls, or sculptured objects with shifting faces speaking to viewers from video screens, or a nonlinear timeline reorganized as a spiral that names key events, or even an experimental film featuring multiple frames with rapidly shifting scenes and subjects but that then loops back to common elements.

Francisco, now in his early fifties, read the book in Mexico City during his first year of middle school (1978–79). He was particularly influenced by the photographs and student testimonies. Even though he has since read many other sources about the 1968 student massacre, Poniatowska's version of events has stayed with him to this day.

The photographs made a deep impression on me. Reading the testimonies of the students and leaders of the movement—what they were trying to accomplish and how the government responded—was very confusing to me. The students were right. This was the second time that I saw that the army can be really bad actors in history. The first time was their role in the coup in Chile. But this was the Mexican Army, and this all happened very close to my house. And it happened against students. The book forever changed my image of soldiers. I no longer saw them as the "good guys."

I read the book for a school project that I had to talk about in front of the class. At that time, there was not a lot of information about what happened, at least not information that I could get a hold of. When I read the book, it was like reading a prohibited book. Elena Poniatowska's version was the only truth for me about 1968 until many years later, when other books came out and more information was released about the events. Despite that, my point of view has not changed about what happened.

Luisa is an Indigenous teacher who grew up in the south of Oaxaca listening to her father talk about government atrocities, particularly in the state of Guerrero. She did not read Poniatowska's books in school, but her father had *La noche de Tlatelolco* in his library, and she read all his books. She said, "Reading *La noche de Tlatelolco* only reaffirmed the situation of repression in Mexico. I lived with histories of resistance and violence in my own state. . . . The parts of the book that impacted me the most were the photographs and the poetry." For this reader, the book resonated with the violence she experienced growing up as part of an activist Indigenous community in Oaxaca.

Her connection to the photographs and poetry in the book—Indigenous poetry and one poem from Rosario Castellano—suggest the multiple strategies the book undertakes to engage readers across visual and textual mediums and linking together aesthetics and politics.[61] Jörgensen pays special attention to the use of intertextual devices in Poniatowska's book, suggesting that these devices transform conventional narrative modes and cultural signs. Jörgensen is particularly interested in how the incorporated texts from *Visión de los vencidos: Testimonios indígenas de la Conquista* (Vision of the defeated: Indigenous testimonies of the Conquest) acquire unique status "through the discovery of extensive and at times uncanny connections between its depiction of ancient events and modern oral history."[62] This device, she argues, encourages readers to "break through the limits of a linear reading."[63] As stated by Sorensen, "The photographic representational system produces a kind of photographic memory. . . . and multiplies the ensuing *testimonios de historia oral* [oral history testimonies]."[64] Sorensen's and Jörgensen's comments about form and the relationship between the voice and image and about the disruption of linear time through directly connecting the massacre of students in Tlatelolco in 1968 with the massacre of the Mexica by the Spanish highlight the importance of key elements in the experimental form of *La noche de Tlatelolco.* Sorensen and Jörgensen also alert us to the intent of Poniatowska's book to follow traditional literary and cultural forms but also to disrupt the narrative of the Mexican state and offer a complex version of events.

Inside the Student Movement

Poniatowska interviewed students when they were imprisoned before and after the October 2 massacre. When read collectively, the narratives reveal a lot about how the CNH functioned, how marches were organized, the use of acting and political theater in public spaces to raise awareness, and details about the financial structure of the movement. Many of these student accounts also describe how police and other officials used torture to extract confessions from them.

Raúl Álvarez Garín, a member of the CNH, provides details about its process and internal politics.

> The CNH was terribly boring; lots of absurd things were discussed endlessly, but every once in a while there were fantastically funny moments. For example, the 210 or 240 delegates and the rank-and-file members spent hours and hours of time arguing as to whether the Student Movement was revolutionary or not—discussions provoked by Trotskyists and vague leftists. . . . The meetings dragged on so long that every once in a while the delegates would take time out to shout and whistle at the audience to wake them up. There were 210 to 240 delegates, so that no one political faction would predominate. Ten per cent of them were political militants and ninety per cent were independents, and this later contingent was the one responsible for the popular nature of the Committee, its originality, its strength.[65]

Poniatowska's ability to capture the ideological diversity within the movement provides readers with insight into the ways that unity was created across difference in the meetings. This suggests one of the important ways that strategic emotional political community was built within the movement through many hours of face-to-face meetings. By documenting this process, Poniatowska also provides readers with a link to how this community functioned.

Pablo Gómez, a student in the Escuela de Economía (School of Economics at the UNAM) and a member of Juventud Comunista (Communist Youth), describes how the CNH disrupted the vertical university-government hierarchies that excluded student participation. The CNH, he explains, "was all the students. They said so themselves. 'We are the CNH! We are the CNH!'"[66] It was "made up of untried young people with very little political experience, [and] despite the endless, repetitive meetings, the National Strike Committee came to be the one representative of all the students. . . . The CNH shattered all the old molds, all the patterns of organization that had existed previously."[67]

Most of the movement's activities were organized by student brigades, often based in particular schools. They were the basic building blocks for marches, demonstrations, and even the CNH's fundraising strategy. Salvador Martínez de la Roca of the UNAM Action Committee describes their reach: "The brigades were the very core of the Movement. People went to the demonstrations because of the brigades. . . . Because of the brigades, because before the demonstrations we handed out leaflets on the buses and trolleys, in the markets, the big department stores, the workshops, on the corners where we held 'lightning meetings,' scattering to the four winds the minute we smelled a *granadero* [riot policeman]."[68]

The brigades also did fundraising. Luis Cervantes Cabeza de Vaca, a member of the CNH, described in horrible detail the torture he endured in prison after the massacre as they tried to force him to reveal the CNH's money source. The government claimed that dissident politicians were financing the movement in an attempt to disrupt the PRI, and they were trying to get names. His narrative describes this process and the role of student leader Sócrates Amado Campos Lemus, who many believe was co-opted by the government when he worked inside the CNH as a leader.

> Then the torture started again; it was even worse this time though, and lasted longer. . . . I could hardly bear the pain in my testicles, in my stomach, in my legs; and I could scarcely draw breath. I was shaking from head to foot; my heart was pounding like crazy, and my mouth was dry as a bone.

I heard someone say, "The death squad. All set, chief." ...

Then they tied me to a post and said to me, "Sócrates is here."

I didn't see Sócrates; I just heard his voice saying, "Answer their questions, tell them the truth." ...

"I can't complain, Cabeza; they've been very decent to me. Look, there was money from the Biology Department at Poli [IPN] and the Faculty of Sciences at UNAM. Madrazo gave it to them to pass on to us."

"The only money I know anything about is the collections the brigades took up and the money all the delegates collected from the students in their schools and turned over to the CNH. A daily quota.[69]

A political science student at UNAM, Estrella Sámano, is quoted right after Cervantes: "When the brigades went out into the street with their collection boxes, people donated lots of money. What's more, the only things the schools had to spend money on were paper and ink and food for the brigades on guard duty."[70] Luis González de Alba describes the CNH's fundraising in detail: "Each school had a daily quota of a hundred pesos.... A hundred pesos from each of eighty schools add up to eight thousand pesos a day, and we needed only six thousand a week.... Did the schools usually make their daily quota? Sure, it was a cinch ... all we had to buy was paper and ink.... Food cost us a certain amount of money, of course, but it all came from the cafeterias, which stayed open all along and made a good profit during the time we ran them."[71]

Student leaders readily understood the Mexican government's suggestion that the student movement was really run by "subversive agents" and outsiders. Álvarez Garín says it was an old trick; the police were trying to discredit the movement by misrepresenting its goals and claiming that "subversive agents" were working for "hidden interests" behind the movement: "This time, however, the authorities couldn't claim that the whole thing was a 'Communist plot,' because the Movement was so broadly based that nobody would have believed them, so instead they suddenly came up with a new gimmick: they claimed that the brains behind the Movement were a group of 'sorehead politicians' who were trying to 'create problems for the administration' out of spite."[72] Álvarez Garín also reported that specific politicians were named in confessions "that a number of the people arrested had been forced to sign."[73] In addition to the government suggesting that these politicians were the source of financing for the movement, it also charged them with organizing a party to overthrow the government in power, according to Álvarez Garín. The forced confessions that some student leaders signed after torture were extracted after the massacre to reinforce the government narrative of who was behind the movement. As seen in the next section, the movement was accelerated by events taking place between different, sometimes rival, schools.

The Summer and Fall of 1968

Students in the movement learned to respond to the shifting terrain in Mexico City; in the past, events had proceeded unimpeded but now they were militarized through the presence of riot police first, and then the army. Most chronologies of the student movement begin on July 22, 1968, when a street fight broke out between two rival high schools, the Vocational School #2, which was affiliated with the IPN, and the Isaac Ochoterena Preparatoria, affiliated with UNAM. In a violent confrontation that continued for two days, police officers badly beat the students. They also arrested some students. After the beating and arrests, some students barricaded themselves inside one of the schools. The confrontations took place in downtown Mexico City.

On July 26, after a march by the Federación Nacional de Estudiantes Técnicos (National Federation of Technical Students) to protest police violence at the Vocational School #6, some IPN students decided to join another march being led by students sympathetic to the Communist Party to commemorate the Moncada assault that began the Cuban Revolution. As historian Jaime Pensado noted, while the IPN was a working-class institution in the 1940s and early 1950s, by the 1960s it had become more of a middle-class institution. While it had been a progressive student organization in the 1950s and was involved in leading a very large strike and movement, after the 1956 student movement was dismantled, the Federación de Estudiantes Técnicos became a "charro student federation"; in other words, it was aligned with the state.[74] Pensado notes that the group "could not hold its own in this conflict; it completely vanished from the IPN that same year [1968]."[75]

Over that weekend, student representatives from the IPN and UNAM met to discuss the possibility of organizing a strike, and they began to form a list of demands. On the day of the July 26 march, police officers invaded the headquarters of the Partido Comunista Mexicano (Mexican Communist Party), arresting and imprisoning several leaders. Students blocked access to the Preparatory 8 school, briefly held policemen hostage, hijacked public buses, and went on strike.

On July 30, the San Ildefonso Preparatory School was attacked. Bazooka rocket fire blew off the school's heavy oak door and wounded many students. Many were also arrested. The army moved in and took over the area. Following this event, students attending schools affiliated with the IPN and UNAM joined together and formed the CNH. On August 5 they published their demands, highlighted at the start of this chapter.

On August 1, before the formation of the CNH and the circulation of a list of demands, Díaz Ordaz had issued a warning: "Peace and calm must be restored in our county. A hand has been extended; it is up to Mexican citizens to decide whether to grasp this outstretched hand. I have been greatly pained by these deplorable and shameful incidents. Let us not widen the gap between us."[76] Following this response, the students called for the president to continue negotiations and consistently asked for public dialogue with the state. The government did not respond. This set the stage for growing massive marches, ongoing protests, and actions leading up to the October 2 massacre of students in Tlatelolco. While the number of protesters and people in crowds grew in the summer, after the military invasion of UNAM and the detention of students on September 18 and 19, 1968, crowd sizes began to diminish.

Two massive marches, one on August 13 and the other on August 27, ended in the Zócalo. The first demonstration drew at least 150,000 participants from a wide range of educational institutions and included people as young as fourteen. The second march drew anywhere from 300,000 to 500,000 people, depending on the source. Protesters marched from the Museo Nacional de Antropología (National Museum of Anthropology) to the Zócalo, and by showing images of Mexican national heroes such as Benito Juárez, Pancho Villa, Emiliano Zapata, and Miguel Hidalgo, they clearly intended to nationalize the movement.[77] Orders from the CNH insisted: "Don't carry placards of Che or Mao! From now on we're going to carry placards with the portraits of Hidalgo, Morelos, Zapata, to shut them up. They're our Heroes. *Viva Zapata! Viva!*"[78]

The deliberate use of Mexican national and revolutionary imagery and the decision to end the march on the Zócalo were punctuated by two specific acts that claimed public space and symbols of the Mexican Revolution for "the people," not the PRI—and they enraged the government of Díaz Ordaz. For one thing, parents, workers, teachers, nurses, vendors, and others joined the march as it swept through the area. Then, when the march ended, students ran a red-and-black flag up the flagpole where the Mexican national flag usually hung on important holidays. A few students climbed up the cathedral's tower and rang the bells. The pictures and captions in *La noche* portray the power and euphoria marchers felt. The left side of one spread features a photograph of the Angel de la Independencia with a long march winding around it. The caption reads: "Some fifteen thousand demonstrators took part in the marches in Mexico City. But six hundred thousand people, from every walk of life, and young people in particular, gathered to show their support."[79] On the opposite-facing page is a picture of two young men dressed in white, smiling from ear to ear while they tug a rope connected to the clapper of a giant church bell. Below is a picture of the Zócalo full of protesters and banners. The caption reads, "'We had to 'deconsecrate' the Zócalo—and we did, three times.' For the first time in forty years, an indignant crowd of Mexican citizens aware of their constitutional rights made its voice heard beneath the Presidential Balcony in the Plaza de la Constitución." González de Alba describes the emotional impact of ending the march in the Zócalo.

> Wherever you turned you could see a sea of heads, hands clapping, and people rushing to join the crowd.... Everyone had tears in their eyes.... And when we turned the corner to enter Cinco de Mayo [street], the best was waiting for us: the bells of the Cathedral tolling at full blast and all the lights turned on. We entered the Zócalo as if we were in a dream. The previous demonstration had been big, around a quarter million, and all of us together didn't fill even half of the enormous plaza that is the Zócalo; now, it was completely full, and half of the contingents were still to enter it.[80]

Accounts like this capture the emotional rush of the march and the weaving of community in the moment as the crowd occupies a space of deep historic importance in Mexico, resignifying it. As Zolov notes, these strategic actions are designed to "'poach' on government-ritualized domains in an effort to re-appropriate their meanings."[81] Transforming the Zócalo from "a regimented parade ground reserved for ceremonial design into a festive, declamatory, public meeting ground was profoundly symbolic in its implications."[82] González de Alba and hundreds of thousands of other marchers testify to the reshaping of the Zócalo into a public space claimed by the movement and the unity it represents.

One of the movement's other strategies also involved openly attacking the PRI and its claim to the revolution, as well as the Mexican president (Díaz Ordaz), through tactics such as rewriting a popular song to pressure him into engaging publicly with the movement.

Tell me, tell me, Gustavo,
Tell me why you're a coward,
Tell my why you've no mother,
Tell me, Gustavo, please tell me

Students chanted this parody of a well-known radio and television commercial during the August 27 demonstration.[83] The president's response came quickly in his annual message delivered on September 1, 1968, but it was not a call for public dialogue, as the students had hoped: "We would not like to find ourselves in a situation which would require measures that we do not wish to take, but we shall take such measures if necessary. Whatever our duty requires us to do, we will do. We will go as far as necessary."[84]

On September 13, a large silent march allowed students to hear for the first time the applause and enthusiasm of the spectating crowds, which were usually drowned out by the demonstrators' shouting. The march was the students' response to Díaz Ordaz's September 1 address, in which he called for peace and order but not public dialogue. The march invoked silence at multiple levels: "Many had their mouths taped over, placards, and a single loud speaker explained that their silence was in protest against the lack of public dialogue and to show their discipline in contrast to the violence of the *granaderos*."[85] González de Alba describes what it was like: "Since we had resolved not to shout or talk as we had during the other demonstrations, we were able to hear—for the first time—the applause and the shouts of approval from the dense crowds supporting us along the line of march, and thousands of hands were raised in the symbol that soon covered the entire city and was even seen at public functions, on television, at official ceremonies: the V of *Venceremos* ["We shall win"], formed with two fingers by young people.... Even after Tlatelolco, the V kept appearing."[86]

The students continued to feel confident and went ahead with their activities, organizing a fair on the UNAM campus, among other events. On September 18, army troops invaded and occupied UNAM, arresting some student leaders in the process. When the army then attempted to occupy the IPN, students carried out a strong campaign of resistance, throwing stones, Molotov cocktails, and firecrackers. Several died and others were wounded in the battle.[87] Many were arrested.[88] The CNH responded by continuing to organize, call out the repression, and demand accountability from the government. On October 1, the CNH announced that an important meeting would take place the following day at the Plaza de las Tres

Culturas in the Nonoalco-Tlatelolco Housing Unit. Student leaders prepared to speak from the fourth floor of the Chihuahua building in the complex.

Poniatowska's account not only shares a wide variety of stories from inside the movement as it is building but also includes outside perspectives and disapproval of the students' behavior. Pesero driver José Álvares Castañeda explains that he didn't receive any formal education because his parents couldn't afford it, "but if education nowadays is the sort that produces students like that, I'm glad I didn't go to school. I never in my life seen such disrespectful, vulgar, foul-tongued people."[89] Pedro Magaña Acuña, a restaurant owner, comments, "University students are the future solid middle class of the Mexican Republic. So what reason do they have to be doing all this?"[90] Some accounts hint at groups of young men who were dressed to look like students but who were engaged in destructive acts. "They stoned my window and shattered it to bits, but I'm not certain to this day whether it was students or policemen disguised as students," Marcelo Salcedo Peña recounts.[91] Others were sure and had harsh words. Margarita Mondado Lara, a librarian, describes an assault she suffered and the impunity some students seemed to enjoy: "One night, just for the fun of it, a gang of boys attacked me and ripped off half my clothes. Students are savages! They think they own the entire city; they've gotten it into their heads that they can do whatever they please, without fear or punishment."[92] Others indicate partial sympathy with police repression, but not the killing of students. "The students . . . often scandalized people, both by their rowdiness on public buses and by their unjustifiably bad behavior toward people on the streets around their schools. . . . These youngsters were warned on several occasions in the newspapers that the police could not be expected to tolerate indefinitely disturbances and attacks on citizens on the streets and aboard public conveyances. . . . All this in no way means that I condone what happened on October 2," says Marcos Valadez Capistrán, a civil engineer and teacher at José Vasconcelos Preparatory School.[93]

In her study of the mainstream newspaper *Excélsior*'s coverage of the student movement, Claire Brewster finds that it included "opinions for and against the protesters."[94] Like later work by historians of the press in Mexico, Brewster's analysis emphasizes the creative use of the opinion page. She also discusses the different points of view that sometimes appeared on the front page. For example, one reporter expressed alarm at the raising of the red-and-black flag in the Zócalo, but another, F. M. López

Naváez, pointed out that the silent march had been orderly.[95] In September, *Excélsior* published editorials that emphasized the need for conciliation and urged students to return to classes.[96] While the paper emphasized the government's conspiracy theory of foreign intervention in the student movement, the next day it "discussed the Army's duty to uphold democratic institutions without threatening the right to protest."[97] Julio Scherer García became the editor of the paper on September 1, 1968. He had held another post under the previous editor. Brewster suggests that because *Excélsior* did not have a specific stance on the student movement, "Scherer was committed to unbiased coverage."[98] Others, such as Monsiváis, did not agree.

La Cultura en México, a cultural supplement to the weekly magazine *¡Siempre!*, edited by Benítez and coordinated by Monsiváis, expressed outrage at the repression, supported the students, and used photographs to illustrate the army and police violence. Poniatowska wrote for *¡Siempre!* and focused her coverage on interviews with student movement leaders. She also used photographs in conjunction with her interviews, which is how she began collecting some of the materials that would be archived in *La noche de Tlatelolco*.[99]

Class and Gender in the Student Movement

The thousands of students marching through the streets in huge contingents carrying banners like "Education, Not Repression, the Students of Mexico," in a series of building protests in the summer and fall of 1968, were not all the same. Working-class and poor urban youth were marching next to young men and women from middle and elite families. Women marched and worked alongside men. Poniatowska's chronicle provides a rich array of evidence of this diversity and how young men and women from a wide range of backgrounds and experiences were able to work together. They also came from as many different ideological and political orientations.

While in the late 1940s and early 1950s, IPN students were viewed as predominantly from the working and lower class who would go on to work technical jobs, by 1968 this had changed.[100] Pensado writes that as the class position of IPN students changed, so did their demands. He suggests that their demands for a more democratic Mexico and the innovative repertoire of collective action they brought to the 1968 movement (including lightning meetings and informational brigades) were important resources.[101]

The UNAM students were primarily from the middle class and some elite families, and would often become professionals such as lawyers, doctors, engineers, writers, academics, and policy makers.

After riot police severely repressed a July 22 clash between students and affiliated youth gangs from each school, and after subsequent student marches drew further repression and arrests, members of the IPN and UNAM joined forces with students from other schools. According to historian Elaine Carey, these schools included the Universidad Autónoma Chapingo (National School of Agriculture at Chapingo) and schools specializing in education and teacher training. Other schools that joined the CNH included El Colegio de México (the College of Mexico) the Universidad Iberoamericana (Iberian-American University, a Jesuit school), the Universidad Autónoma de Puebla (Autonomous University of Puebla), the Universidad Autónoma de Chihuahua (Autonomous University of Chihuahua) and the Escuela Nacional de Antropología e Historia (National School of Anthropology and History).[102] The estimated 230 officials within the CNH came from a wide cross-section of social and economic groups, ideological currents, and educational experiences. Carey estimates that only 10 of the 230 official members were women.[103]

While some of the well-known leaders within the CNH were leftists from a variety of affiliates, a majority were not from the left. The CNH even included PRI sympathizers.[104] The organized left was a minority on the strike council, and diverse student voices and viewpoints were a part of it. As Carey explains, "For people to win seats, they had to be elected by their schools or departments. Thus, all members were elected democratically" from various institutions.[105] Beyond membership in the CNH, individual schools and sometimes departments had their own *comités de lucha* (action committees) that organized activities on their campuses and transmitted ideas and programs to the CNH. They also helped facilitate voting for representatives on the CNH.[106] Salvador Martínez de la Roca of the UNAM Action Committee stated, "All of us who just wanted to get something done were friends: Poli, UNAM, Chapingo. But in the CNH, it was a mess: the Maoists, the Trotskyists, the Spartacists, the Communists were all at each other's throats! I was just another activist."[107] Students like Martínez de la Roca were more interested in organizing concrete actions than engaging in leftist ideological debates.

Other students recognized the class distinctions reflected in the movement and their own place in the educational class structure of Mexico City—the diversity of the politicized students' views of the world. Carolina

Pérez Cicero, a student of the Facultad de Filosofía y Letras (Faculty of Philosophy and Letters) at UNAM, comments,

> Most of the girls studying at the Faculty of Philosophy and Letters came from petty-bourgeoisie families.... They're girls who've never had to worry about money.... Culture is simply a nice hobby to them. But during the Movement many of them who live in the fanciest neighborhoods—Pedregal, Las Lomas, Polanco—gave money, took part in demonstrations, passed out handbills on the streets, and lots of the students, both boys and girls, from *nouveau-riche* families enrolled at the Faculty of Philosophy and Letters—because that's one of the most *nouveau-riche* schools at the University—painted slogans on walls and worked just as hard as the others.... Since there was lots of talk about politics going on, they got a different view of the relations between the haves and the have-nots. The movement politicized many people.[108]

Pérez Cicero's experience captures how the movement served as a source of connection for female students from the most elite parts of the city to connect with working-class students. Isolated in their worlds of exclusive neighborhoods and prep schools, girls like Pérez Cicero learned how to build community and connect strategically and emotionally to people they had never been in contact with—the have-nots—and learn from them.

While women college students were still a minority at institutions such as UNAM in 1968, making up 22.84 percent of enrollments, they were a small but important part of the strike council.[109] Poniatowska profiles a number of the women leaders and student activists in *La noche de Tlatelolco*, including Roberta "La Tita" Avendaño, who represented the UNAM law school; Ana Ignacia Rodríguez Márquez, or "La Nacha," of the Action Committee of the UNAM law faculty; Margarita Isabel, a student, actress, and dancer; Carolina Pérez Cicero, a student at the Facultad de Filosofía y Letras, UNAM; Mercedes Olivera de Vázquez and Margarita Nolasco, both students at the Escuela Nacional de Antropología e Historia; as well as others. Avendaño, Rodríguez Márquez , Olivera de Vázquez, and Nolasco are quoted extensively throughout Poniatowska's book. Rodríguez Márquez and Avendaño were critical protagonists in the student movement, but their stories, like those of many women, were not highly visible. Poniatowska helps correct this by highlighting their testimonies.[110]

The importance of women in the movement is also recognized by male leader Eduardo Valle Espinoza, known as Owl-Eyes, of the CNH. In *La noche*, he characterizes women as "responsible for much of the Movement's fighting spirit."[111] His testimony mentions women from the Law School, Medicine, Nursing, Biological Sciences, and other departments. Thousands participated in the movement, according to his account: "The girl comrades from the School of Nursing were real heroines during the attack on the Santo Tomás campus. . . . They willingly risked their lives to care for our wounded, help get them off campus, and attend to their every need. Because of their courage and loyalty to the cause all our women comrades came to play a very important role in the Movement."[112]

Valle Espinoza told Poniatowska that one of his biggest regrets in the movement was a sexist comment he made during the last speech at the Silent Demonstration on September 11, 1968: "Let us not shed tears like women for what we were unable to defend like men."[113] The day after the demonstration, two brigades of women voiced their anger to him. As he described it, "I spent several hours trying to explain, amid angry shouts and quite justifiable protests on their part, that what I had said had merely been a figure of speech. They were finally kind enough to accept my apology."[114]

Tita Avendaño and Nacha Rodríguez deserve focused attention for their contributions not only as movement leaders but also as young women who demonstrate a consciousness about the key roles that women played and why. Avendaño is perhaps the most famous of the female student leaders. She was a teacher (*normalista*) who studied at the Escuela Normal de Maestros before she entered UNAM and earned a law degree. She was elected as a member of the CNH to represent the UNAM Law School. Avendaño appears to have developed a thick skin and strong consciousness about women's capacity to engage in the movement's leadership. Poniatowska quotes Avendaño sharing the following ditty, which one of the boys dedicated to her. While laudatory, it also points out her size.

> Our favorite among the gang of students was Tita,
> The woman the UNAM adored.
> She was so brave and of such ample proportions
> That even the director respected her
> And you could hear her fond friends all saying:
>
> If Tita disappeared from the Law School
> The law students would go to her, weeping:
> "Oh, Tita, in God's name I beg you,
> Please don't forget the Law School."[115]

While these lyrics suggest that Avendaño was extremely valued as a leader and member of the CNH, she recalled in an interview with the magazine *Nexos* in 1988 that when she was elected to be a member of the CNH, many thought that a male student should represent the UNAM Law School. She had to fight hard to obtain her leadership position: "I never thought that I was a leader of such a big, national, huge movement. Over time, I realized why I was being persecuted: the Law School had been ruled by the PRI; it entered into movements on the PRI side, with a lot of strength, with speakers. My classmates attacked me. They said that the School had to be represented by a man, by a speaker. But the rank and file supported me: I controlled the rank and file, not *grillos*; I was very blunt and they supported me that way."[116] Avendaño also credited her popularity with the movement's student base to her experience as a schoolteacher: "One of the good things about being a teacher was that it allows you to not lose the perspective of what it means to be young."[117]

Another well-known leader, Ana Ignacia "La Nacha" Rodríguez Márquez, became friends with Avendaño. Rodríguez Márquez was a student in the UNAM Law School. After she saw riot police assault her classmates during the violent July 26 march, she returned to UNAM and joined others in deciding to form a comité de lucha to protest the repression they had seen. Her classmates proposed that she be in charge of the finance committee in the law school. Occasionally she would go to the CNH assemblies with Tita Avendaño. In a 2013 interview, she recalled all the different ideological currents in the meetings and how difficult it was for the CNH to come to agreement. As the repression increased, however, the CNH became more unified, according to Rodríguez Márquez.

> At the CNH assemblies, my friend Roberta Avendaño Martínez "La Tita" was the representative of the Law School committee. Sometimes I would accompany her to the assemblies. There were Communists, Maoists, Trostkyists, free thinkers, from all different ideologies, and sometimes it was difficult to reach an agreement. They would deal with the issues at the assemblies, and then the representatives from each school would communicate what the CNH had covered to his/her local committee. It was a lot of work, too many people with different ways of thinking. When the repression increased, we unified even more.
>
> We talked a lot about the irrationality of the government; we sought public dialogue. In the mixed brigades or in women's-only brigades, we would inform our people about the mobilizations. We would do

fundraising on the streets and the people always supported us. Without the people, we wouldn't have been able to keep the movement going.[118]

Rodríguez Márquez was arrested and imprisoned three times for her activity with the student movement.[119] The first arrest was on September 18, when the Mexican Army occupied Ciudad Universitaria (University City), the main campus of UNAM. She was detained with forty-one other women and charged with being an agitator; several girlfriends who had nothing to do with the movement were swept up in the arrest: "They arrested anybody they pleased at CU, regardless of who they were. . . . They took forty-three of us women from the esplanade to Lecumberri and put us in the women's prison because the other jails were full. . . . Since there weren't any beds for us, they took us to the dining room and we had to sit there on the concrete tables until the next day—we almost froze to death. . . . Those days weren't bad—the bad part came later."[120]

Once released from prison, Rodríguez Márquez continued to work within the movement doing outreach to people in the city. On October 2, 1968, she was in the Plaza de Las Tres Culturas with Avendaño. Poniatowska devotes several pages to Rodríguez Márquez's and Avendaño's descriptions of the shooting and their subsequent imprisonment. Avendaño tells Poniatowska, "It never occurred to us that the government might attack us on October 2. . . . We thought that a sort of tacit truce had been arranged, since it looked as though the government was about to reach an agreement with the students. . . . We decided to cancel the march on the Santo Tomás campus, which had been occupied by Army troops, so we wouldn't be accused of stirring up more trouble. This was announced from the speakers' stand" on October 2. She continues, "I wasn't on the speakers' stand; I stayed down below on the esplanade with Nacha."[121] Avendaño and Rodríguez Márquez threw down a banner they held for the UNAM Law School and "leaped over those pre-Hispanic walls there and fell into a sort of ditch."[122] Rodríguez Márquez recalls, "We heard shouts and groans and cries of pain, and I realized then that the gunfire was getting heavier and heavier."[123] They crawled out and fled the scene. Students in a white Volkswagen called out to them, and they jumped into the car. Rodríguez Márquez later ran from the car and found herself in a Sanborn's Restaurant, where she saw an acquaintance, who accompanied her home.[124] Rodríguez Márquez escaped that day but was arrested the following day. She was in detention for two weeks and then released. They told her that if she didn't leave the city, she would be killed.[125]

Rodríguez Márquez left Mexico City to visit her family in Taxco, Guerrero, for Christmas. When she returned in early January 1969, she was detained for the third time. She was blindfolded, shoved into a car, and transported to a house. Eight men were present. They removed the blindfold and took mugshot photos. She was interrogated and accused of having been supplied with money and arms. The following day, she was taken to another house, where Avendaño, who had been detained the night before, was also being held.[126] Rodríguez Márquez was charged with ten crimes, including robbery, homicide, sedition, and incitement to rebellion. She was sentenced to sixteen years in prison and served almost two years at the Santa Marta Acatitla Prison for Women, from January 13, 1969, until December 24, 1970.[127] Avendaño was also sentenced to sixteen years and released after two.

Avendaño and Rodríguez Márquez both call attention to the treatment of female political prisoners during and after their confinement. As Avendaño reports, "There are lots of prisoners in here with me who can testify to the abuses they've been subjected to: women whose breasts were burned with lighted cigarettes during interrogation sessions, women suffering from cancer of the uterus because of the beatings they got, others who were raped, after being promised they'd be set free if they submitted."[128]

While twenty-three male activists were imprisoned together, with sentences ranging from three to seventeen years, only a few women were held together, including Rodríguez Márquez, Avendaño, and Adela Salazar de Castillejos (the mother of two students).[129] Unlike the men, they were not isolated with other political prisoners but instead were mixed with women who were labeled as "common criminals." Several women imprisoned with them were accused of being guerrillas.[130] Being held with prisoners who were not political prisoners made the women feel more isolated and limited what they could do to organize together inside prison. They also were much less visible than the male activist prisoners.

In an interview forty years after Tlatelolco, in October 2008, Rodríguez Márquez discussed the importance of women in the movement. Her observations and testimony reflect a significant part of what she told Poniatowska some thirty-eight years earlier while still in prison: "In 1968 women became political actors, the same as the men. They also went to plazas, markets, and factories; they stood on top of buses and trucks to inform people, since the press was a sellout. We suffered physical beatings, being chased, and being very frightened, just like the men. . . . The work in the brigades was also very important. Without them, the movement wouldn't have resonated the way it did. Nevertheless, some women, like the brigades, have remained invisible and, thus, have not been highlighted to the degree they deserve."[131]

In the fifty years since the Tlatelolco massacre, increasing attention has been paid to the women who were active in the movement, particularly from 1988 to the present, as women's movements have gained prominence in Mexico.[132] Poniatowska's crónica of Tlatelolco is unique in that it amply cites women and takes seriously their contributions and leadership roles. Her deliberate profiling of women leaders and others active in the movement set the baseline for future work about the women activists of 1968 and their continued involvement in a wide range of social movements in Mexico. Her detailed discussions of how women were crucial to weaving the movement together in many different ways also documents the role women had in creating community and joining emotion with politics.

The Massacre

Poniatowska introduces the second half of the book starkly: "These pages express their outrage and their protest: the mute cry that struck in thousands of throats, the blind grief in thousands of horror-stricken eyes on October 2, 1968."[133] Reading the layered accounts of the shooting—detailing the confusion, the blood, the wounded, and the bodies lying on the pavement—is an intense emotional experience. Shouting, shooting, blood, pain, terror, fear, confusion, and grief are channeled intensely through the eyewitness testimonies. While the testimonies in the first half of the book invoke emotions of hope, euphoria, and excitement as different people describe their participation in the movement—and in some cases anger against the students by those who oppose it—the narratives in the second half of the book center on horror, disbelief, and grief. The wide emotional register of the second part of the book dramatizes trauma on the page, making it extremely accessible to readers. Many of the testimonies capture corporal and expressive experiences. It is perhaps in this later section of the book where we can see the possibilities for the construction of emotional strategic political community between those who shared their stories and readers.

On October 2, 1968, in the early evening, students from the CNH were gathered on the fourth floor of the Chihuahua building in the Nonoalco housing complex on one side of the Plaza de las Tres Culturas. A green flash in the sky, likely a flare from a helicopter, appeared to signal to sharpshooters positioned on the roof and inside the building to start shooting into the crowd. Rodríguez Márquez recalled in a 2008 interview: "That day, October 2, I was with the Law School contingent, and we were even captured in one of the videos that was broadcast later on. We were carrying a banner with the word 'Freedom' on it and the name of the institution we came from. I remember there was a helicopter, and three lights/flashes descended from it. David Vega was the last speaker. We were in front of the Chihuahua building and all of a sudden, I saw a white-gloved arm covering Vega's mouth and dragging him backward. Then the hail of bullets began."[134]

Rodríguez Márquez, like Mercedes Olivera de Vázquez, Gilberto Guevara Niebla, and others whose testimony is highlighted in *La noche*, theorized what happened that evening. With fifty years of hindsight, film footage, and documents released by the Mexican government, along with the several detailed reports and dozens of documents assembled by Kate Doyle and others in the United States' National Security Archive, a somewhat clearer picture of the events has emerged. As Olivera de Vázquez explained to Poniatowska in 1968,

> I can assure you that the whole thing was obviously planned in advance; the authorities knew exactly what they were up to. They were trying to prevent any sort of demonstration or student disturbance before the Olympics and during the games. The flares were the signal to start shooting, and they began firing from all directions at once. As for the supposed "sharpshooters," I can assure you—because those of us who were there saw it with our own eyes and know it's true beyond the shadow of a doubt—that the sharpshooters were agents playing their part in the government's plan.[135]

Olivera de Vázquez's theory seems plausible. Other testimonies detail the presence of white-gloved men who detained students and blocked the exits. People were trapped in the plaza with no exit. Many were then caught in the line of army gunfire as the army advanced from two sides of the plaza. Claude Kiejman of *Le Monde* told Poniatowska about what another reporter friend had observed: "He was right there on the fourth floor, on the speakers' stand on the balcony, and he saw young people, very young kids, wearing white gloves and firing right at the crowd and shooting at people inside the Chihuahua building."[136] Poniatowska cites Jesús Mariano Bautista González, a sergeant second class, who made an official statement about the circumstances surrounding how he accidentally shot himself in the foot. The statement revealed that he had received orders to go to the Tlatelolco housing unit. There he "heard several bursts of gunfire coming from the tops of various buildings; they were firing at me and the other men in my unit, so one of my buddies and I started to run for cover in a zigzag pattern, but as I was running my rifle suddenly went off and wounded me in the right foot."[137]

These descriptions reflect the pain and horror felt by all in the Plaza de las Tres Culturas, echoing earlier horror with the arrival of the Spaniards in the same spot. Map 2.1 shows some of the contemporary landmarks in Tlatelolco, while map 2.2 depicts the same area as Tlatelolco and Mexica-Tenochitlán, ca. 1524.

Many of the testimonies in *La noche de Tlatelolco* describe the sense of panic and the experience of being surrounded. Gilberto Guevara Niebla of the CNH provides a detailed and compelling description in Poniatowska's account of what happened and how people reacted. He implicates a government helicopter, the army moving in around the plaza, and the takeover of the fourth floor where he and other members of the CNH were detained by the Olympia Battalion (a specialized military group trained as a security force for the 1968 Olympics).

> None of us there on the speakers' stand could see that the army troops below us were advancing across the Plaza. When they found themselves confronted by a wall of bayonets, the crowd halted and immediately drew back; then we saw a great wave of people running toward the other side of the Plaza; but there were army troops on the other side of the Plaza too. . . . That was the last thing we saw down below, for at that moment the fourth floor was taken over by the Olympia Battalion. . . . We were ordered to put our hands up and face the wall, and given strict orders not to turn around. . . . If we so much as moved a muscle, they hit us over the head or in the ribs with their rifle butts. Once the trap they had set snapped shut, the collective murder began.[138]

Daniel Esparza Lepe provides an intense description of the shooting on the plaza and the people desperately trying to flee.

> There was a general stampede then, because just after the first shot, all hell broke loose and a hail of bullets started raining down on us from all directions. I saw several comrades fall to the ground, and I tried to make my way over to help them, but the gunfire got heavier and heavier and there was nothing I could do but run for cover. There were several

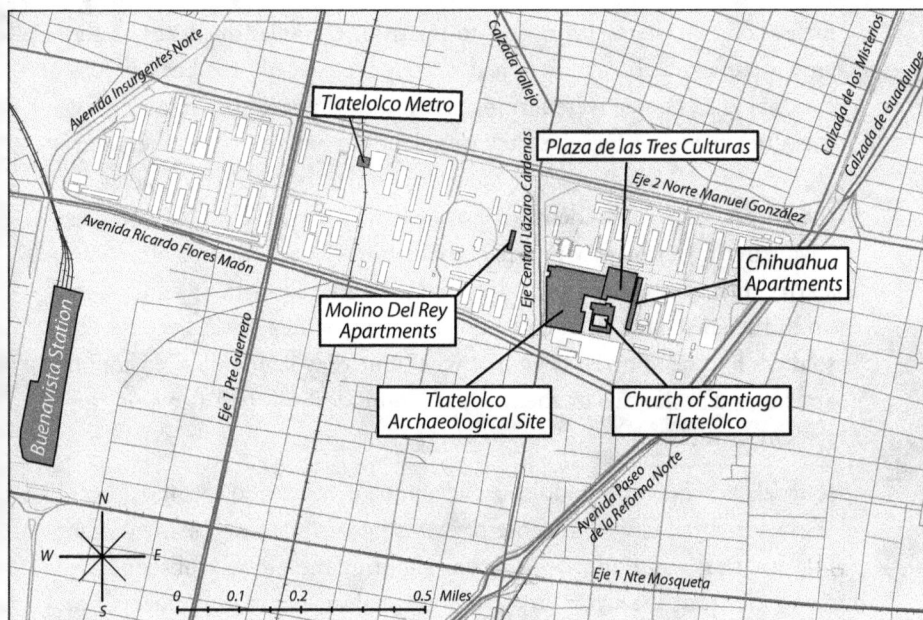

Map 2.1 Modern Tlatelolco and key buildings in the 1968 massacre.

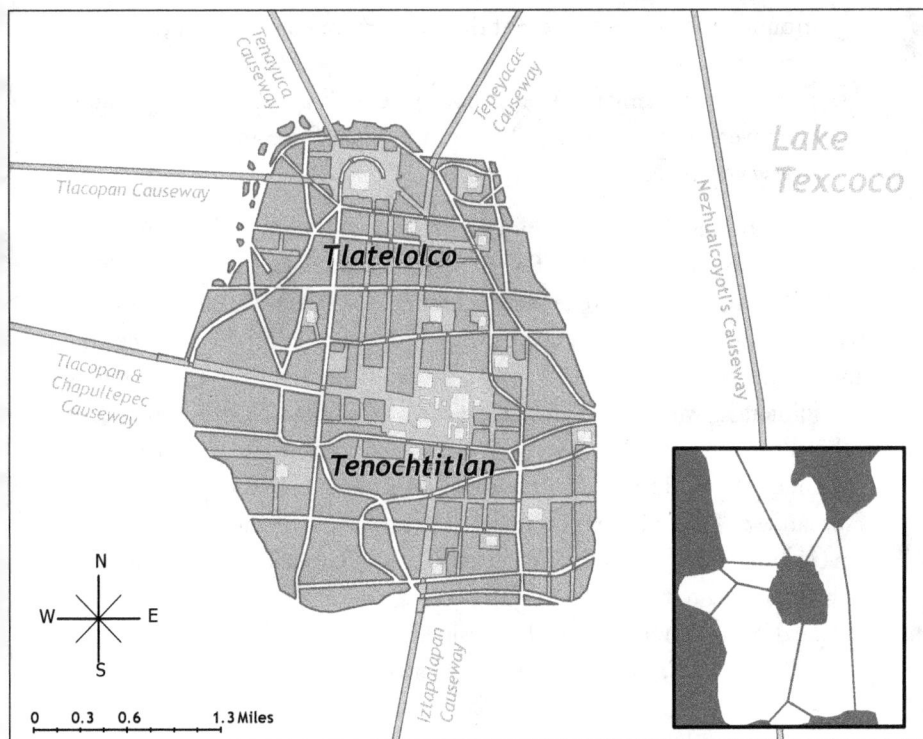

Map 2.2 Tlatelolco and Mexica-Tenochtitlán, c. 1524.

little kids that were either shot to death or trampled to death as the crowd panicked. The soldiers had already blocked off the back of Vocational 7. . . . People were leaping down into the pre-Hispanic ruins; it was utter madness, because they were landing one on top of the other; everyone was screaming and moaning—women with little babies in their arms, workers, students, railroad men, little kids. The soldiers were advancing towards us with fixed bayonets. . . . When the machine gun started firing, two comrades, a boy and a girl, raised their hands way up in the air to surrender and I don't know whether it was because the soldiers had been given drugs, or what, but they suddenly fired round after round at the two of them. Other comrades who had also seen this screamed in terror.[139]

Journalists present offered similar accounts of terror and surprise. Some of these accounts, as well as those of eyewitnesses, state that some of the people wearing white gloves began to shoot at the crowd, subsequently drawing fire from the army. One October 3 newspaper story Poniatowska cites describes the sharpshooters as shooting

women and children and innocent bystanders who had turned up at the meeting; they began to fire on the Army troops and the police who had surrounded the plaza to prevent the crowd from marching on the Santo Tomás campus.

As the first Army troops and police were hit and fell to the ground; orders were given to return the fire, and one of the most terrible gun battles ever to occur in our city began.[140]

Félix Lucio Hernández Gamundi of the CNH substantiated this account: "Hundreds of persons on the fourth floor of the Chihuahua building saw that after arresting the people they had found up there, the plainclothesmen wearing white gloves began firing on the crowd attending the meeting and also on the troops that were moving forward. Immediately thereafter, as the soldiers answered their fire, the agents in civilian clothes took cover behind the cement balustrade, their guns still aimed at the prisoners, who continued to stand there with their hands up, directly in the line of fire."[141] Hernández Gamundi went on to describe how some of the agents in civilian clothing talked to each other and tried to find a walkie-talkie to tell the army to stop shooting at them.[142]

The director of relations of the presidency was quoted in the headline of the mainstream *Excélsior* newspaper: "Serious Fights as Army Breaks up

Meeting of Strikers. 20 Dead, 75 Wounded and 400 Prisoners. Fernando M. Garza, Press Secretary of the President of the Republic."[143] According to an editorial inside the paper, "The presence of the Army who were ordered to disperse a meeting in the Plaza de las Tres Culturas left a horrible toll of blood and death there," and called for an investigation.[144] Poniatowska includes a range of headlines and how they captured the massacre, some of them blaming the students or implicating them in gunfire. *El Universal*'s headline read, "Tlatelolco a Battlefield. Serious Fighting for Hours Between Terrorists and Soldiers. 29 Dead and More Than 80 Wounded; Casualties on Both Sides; 1000 Arrested." Similarly, *La Prensa* reported, "Many Killed and Wounded According to García Barragán. Army and Students Exchange Gunfire." *El Día* reported, "Criminal Provocation at Tlatelolco Meeting Causes Terrible Bloodshed. Fight with Army at Tlatelolco Results in Many Dead and Wounded." *El Nacional*'s headline read, "Army Forced to Rout Sharpshooters," and *El Sol de México* wrote, "Foreign Interlopers Attempt to Damage Mexico's National Image. The Objective: Preventing the Nineteenth Olympic Games from Being Held."[145]

Rather than attempt to provide a definitive account of what happened in the plaza, Poniatowska builds a narrative out of many difference experiences and perceptions, including these newspaper headlines, that reflect the confusion people experienced at the massacre and in the range of theories that followed. The strong emotions and feelings that the account invokes, including confusion and lack of certainty about what happened, are at the core of the book. The intense narratives and confusion are unsettling but emotive, pulling readers in. The lasting impression left on the reader is of the chaotic scene that people witnessed and that the event was caused by embedded government sharpshooters.

The second half of Poniatowska's book also includes testimonies describing children being shot, of bodies lying on the pavement in the rain, and of people desperately trying to find relatives. Jesús Tovar García, a student, describes watching two children from a distance: "The two tiny bodies were left lying on the pavement there, one on top of the other. I saw the whole thing. I wanted to get the littlest one into the ditch where I was hiding. I called to him several times, but bullets were whizzing all over the place and I didn't dare go out there and get him. I just shouted several times, 'Come on down here, little boy!' but he was too busy trying to revive his friend to notice. Then the bullet hit him! I know I'm a coward, and I also now know now that the instinct to save your own neck is terribly selfish."[146] Salmerón de Contreras was searching for her young brother,

Julio, and finally found him involved in a grisly scene: "Now that I'd managed to get to Julio and we were together again, I could raise my head and look around. The very first thing I noticed was all the people lying on the ground; the entire Plaza was covered with the bodies of the living and the dead, all lying side by side. The second thing I noticed was that my kid brother had been riddled with bullets."[147] Another woman, Pilar Marín de Zepeda, describes what she saw: "The majority of the corpses were lying face down, swelling in the rain, but there were also some lying face up. They looked like trampled flowers, like the mud-spattered, crushed flowers planted around the Chihuahua building."[148]

These firsthand narratives are highly evocative and connect readers directly with the anguish and horror of Tovar García watching children die and Salmerón de Contreras finding her younger brother shot through with bullet holes. The corpses looking like "trampled flowers" bring readers right to grief. Such descriptions can bring "goosebumps to my skin," as one reader shared with me. The direct emotional connection forged from the testimony givers to readers by Poniatowska's form works in an entirely different way than journalistic summaries of what happened. These firsthand testimonies are the glue to the emotional strategic political community the book weaves with readers.

While the shooting was underway, hundreds of students and others were being arrested, including the CNH leadership on the fourth floor of the Chihuahua building. According to González de Alba and others quoted in La noche de Tlatelolco, the moment the flares went off, many agents stormed up to the fourth floor, onto the balcony, and then wrestled members of the CNH and others there to the floor. Everyone had to take off their shoes and shirts and drop their pants around their ankles. They were detained on the first floor when the shooting began, and then they were taken to Military Camp 1.[149]

Family members of the CNH and other people looking for missing children and relatives began to visit morgues. While the government eventually released a very low body count (24), the CNH initially reported 100 dead. Citing El Día, Poniatowska writes, "The final list of those killed and wounded in the Tlatelolco massacre has not yet been drawn up. Thus far we know of some 100 dead—those whose bodies were removed from the Plaza. There are thousands of wounded."[150] In her introduction to the second part of the book, Poniatowska writes, "Some thousand prisoners were taken to Military Camp 1. Around a thousand other persons arrested were taken to Santa Marta Acatitla Penitentiary, in Mexico City."[151] In early 1971, 165 were still imprisoned in Lecumberri. Later estimates suggested as many as 300 people had been killed.[152]

Testimonies of those who visited the morgues provide evidence of the number of bodies. One person testified about her husband's visit to the Third Precinct morgue, where he saw at least twenty bodies inside. He was looking for his son.[153] When Margarita Nolasco and others visited Military Camp 1, they were told that no prisoners were there.[154] Manuela Garín de Álvarez went to several places looking for Raúl, her son. She tells of other people who were looking as well and how they talked to each other.[155]

Cecilia Espinoza de Valle, the mother of Eduardo Valle Espinoza (Owl-Eyes), went to the morgue to look for him. She relates that she was shown a lot of young, male bodies, one whose face was blown off.[156] She eventually found her son in Lecumberri Prison. Her description of visiting him captures the torture and horrible treatment some of the CNH and other political prisoners received.

I saw Eduardo stumbling down the stairway from his cell block like a mole, clinging to the banisters, and only recognizing me because he could hear my voice as I shouted to him "Eduardo, over here! I'm over here."—well, it's something I'll never forget. He had to crawl downstairs like that, clutching the banister, because they'd beaten him within an inch of his life and he'd lost his glasses. All he had to guide him was my voice. He's had to wear glasses for the last four years and can hardly see without them; they're glasses with a very strong correction, with thick thick lenses—that's why everybody calls him Owl-Eyes.[157]

Espinoza de Valle, the mother of Owl-Eyes, makes a direct connection with readers. For anyone who wears glasses, they can't imagine being in such horrible circumstances without being able to see. The absolutely anguishing situation of looking for your son among the morgues and then finding him in an incredibly vulnerable situation in the prison speaks to everyone who has children. As a reader, this passage evokes a visceral response. The active roles of family members of the detained and dead who searched for their loved ones, visited them in prison, and testified about what they observed form some of the most compelling narratives in the book. The emotions generated from such testimonies build connections between readers and these individuals. At the same time, documentation of the process of parents searching for their children and sharing information also tells us how community was built even in this horrible process of discovery and grief by parents of students who were killed or detained and tortured.

Beyond suggesting that armed students in the Chihuahua apartment building initiated the October 2 shooting, the government engaged in a campaign to silence most of the press and erase evidence of the extent of the bloodshed. Some people in Poniatowska's chronicle suggest a theory that Sócrates Campos Lemus was co-opted by the government and police officials, most likely by force. In a public press conference on October 5, 1968, Campos Lemus substantiated many of the government's accusations against CNH leaders and other activists in the student movement. He detailed the CNH's structure and activities, and he confirmed that the movement had received support from specific politicians and public figures.[158] He also stated that part of the movement was armed.[159] Campos Lemus detailed a list of guns that were "found" and later shown to the press. He asserted that the students had been organizing armed groups and that there were armed students in Tlatelolco on October 2. Armed columns or groups, he said, were led by Guillermo and Jesús González Guardado, Sóstenes Torrecillas, Raúl Álvarez Garín, and Florencio López Asuna.[160] This information was used to imprison and sentence numerous people.[161]

Valle Espinoza discussed Campos Lemus's betrayal with Poniatowska: "Very very few people 'sang' to the cops like that stoolpigeon Sócrates. But what informers like that told the cops wasn't true at all—it was a pack of lies and false accusations, that whole business about 'fifth columns, arms, sorehead politicians plotting against the government.' In a word, it was all just muddle-headed personal opinions, coming from people who didn't know the first thing about politics, all merely to justify the Tlatelolco massacre and corroborate the government's version of what had happened."[162] Luis Tomás Cervantes Cabeza de Vaca makes similar accusations and describes being tortured and then identified by Campos Lemus.[163] Hernández Gamundi of the CNH provides a detailed description of the press conference with Campos Lemus and completely dismisses the idea of armed columns of CNH members who were instructed to fire at the granaderos or on the army troops. Hernández Gamundi runs through the ragtag list of weapons Campos Lemus had said the Chihuahua's School of Agriculture had provided to the movement. He concludes by saying, "Anybody with an ounce of common sense realizes that it would be ridiculous to try to fight the Army or the police with such an absurd arsenal."[164] According to Álvarez Garín, the only arms the students had were "our ideals . . . our fervent desires and ideas, which as the government sees it are much more dangerous than bullets."[165]

Silence? And Ongoing Questions

The Olympic Games, held on October 12–27, 1968, appeared to go off without a hitch just ten days after the massacre at Tlatelolco. The release of hundreds of doves marked the opening of the Olympic Games, which were presided over by Díaz Ordaz. The games were not without protest, however; Tommie Smith and John Carlos, respectively the gold and bronze medal winners of the two-hundred-meter run, raised black-gloved fists on the awards platform in front of a global television audience. In a nod to the Black Power movement, Smith and Carlos raised the political profile of the Olympics and signaled to the Mexican and global audience that despite the perceived unity at the games, there were many people struggling to achieve their rights and promote revolutionary social change.

Right after the massacre and as the Olympics played out, Octavio Paz was the only government official to resign. As ambassador to India, he submitted his resignation to the Mexican government in protest of its repression of the student movement and the government troops' role in the mass killings on October 2. Other politicians and public figures remained silent, as did most but not all of the Mexican press. Foreign journalists had managed to produce some news stories, and some photographs and film footage were saved and stored in secret locations by the Mexican and foreign press. Perhaps the most powerful quote in Poniatowska's book about the press after the massacre comes from Kiejman, writing in *Le Monde*: "What struck me most was that a week afterward, the Olympic Games began amid at least the outward appearance of perfect calm, as though nothing at all had happened. . . . What in any other country in the world would have been quite enough to unleash a civil war has resulted here in Mexico in nothing more than a few tense days immediately following the events of Tlatelolco."[166]

In 1968 it appeared to many people that what would prevail was the silence regarding the massacre and the majority's support of the government's version of what had happened. With time, however, more and more questions were raised. Many of the images of Tlatelolco—while removed from the public record by the government through both censorship and self-censorship of the Mexican press—remained in the minds of those who were there. A mother, Perla Vélez de Aguilera, recalls, "All the images, all the walls, all the curbs, all the stone benches stained with blood, all the traces of bodies bleeding to death in the corners—clean with our tears. But it is not true that images can be washed away with tears. They still linger in your memory."[167]

Strategic Emotional Political Community. From *La noche* to the Disappeared

La noche de Tlatelolco has served as a touchstone for generations of Mexicans in remembering the events of 1968. Over the years, more information about the October 2, 1968, massacre has come to light thanks to key documents made available by the National Security Archive, the Fox administration's decision to release military police and intelligence files in 2002, and Mexico's federal transparency law. But it was not until October 2018 that the Mexican government finally admitted that the massacre on October 2, 1968, was a state crime.[168] Representing the Mexican government through the Comisión Ejecutiva de Atención a Víctimas (Executive Commission for Attention to Victims), Jaime Rochín stated, "We should not forgive or forget." He also openly acknowledged that "the repression of students in Tlatelolco in 1968, and later on of social movements, gave rise to the ample use of executions, arbitrary arrests, torture and forced disappearances for the suppression of dissent."[169] At the time, Rochín also spoke about reparative justice. In addition to assuming state responsibility for the massacre, the government, he stated, would make available, through an open-access system, photographs, recordings, and documents that would allow for the reconstruction of what happened. In the meantime, he reported, an art project was being unveiled at the Centro Cultural Universitario Tlatelolco (Tlatelolco University Cultural Center), for which four hundred pairs of fingerprints were imprinted in public recognition of the victims. This is yet another new number. What remains to be seen is if new information will be released and, if so, how this may or may not influence how Mexicans remember the hopeful and tragic events of 1968.

In the fifty years since the movement and the massacre and since the publication of *La noche* in 1971, five generations of Mexicans have engaged with multiple versions and explanations of what happened. Through this time, *La noche* has remained a primary touchstone that continues to engage readers and is still cited today as a key source in relation to these historic events. Because the book captures many voices and perspectives and directly connects readers to the joy, hope, and euphoria of the movement and the intense terror, agony, suffering, and grief of the massacre and its aftermath through direct testimonies, it has endured. By deeply engaging readers through connecting emotion to politics, *La noche* has been an important part in building and maintaining, through time, a strategic emotional political community connected to the events of 1968 in Mexico. This community is simultaneously both specific and narrow for particular people but also wide and open, allowing for a variety of opinions and experiences on a broad political scale. Up to the present moment, *La noche* continues to perform important political work as a baseline for documenting and interpreting other moments of political crises and social movements.

In her private life, Poniatowska dedicated time to her children and took pleasure in weekends away and vacations (figure 2.3). But she continued to write, engaging with the movement of the disappeared.

In 1980 Poniatowska published her second crónica, *Fuerte es el silencio* (Strong is the silence), which focuses on the disappeared, imprisoned, and tortured in Mexico's Dirty War of the 1970s; the mothers and relatives of the disappeared in a hunger strike; and an agricultural cooperative in the state of Morelos where a charismatic figure nicknamed "El Güero" (the light-skinned guy, Florencio Madrano Mederos) led a group of armed peasants who took over land to escape persecution by local merchants. The book documents a polarized post-Tlatelolco Mexico. The state continues to use violence to silence opposition, and some of those who were in the student movement or sympathized with it have taken up arms as part of guerrilla movements. Poniatowska sympathizes with the mothers of the disappeared and profiles activist Rosario Ibarra de Piedra, who went on to become a personal friend of hers and one of the women she has profiled several times.

In 1980 Poniatowska herself became involved in the movement of those looking for the disappeared through her work with the Comité por la Vida de Alaíde Foppa (Committee for the Life of Alaíde Foppa). Alaíde Foppa came to Mexico in 1954 when she and her husband, Alfonso Solórzano, fled Guatemala after a CIA-backed coup forced the government of President Jacobo Arbenz into exile. Solórzano had been a member of the governments of both Arbenz and his predecessor, Juan José Arévalo Bermejo. Foppa was an advocate for women's rights and taught the first sociology class on women at UNAM, was a well-regarded and widely published poet, had a radio show broadcast on the UNAM channel called "Foro de la Mujer" (Women's Forum), and was the cofounder of *FEM* Magazine in Mexico in 1975.[170] Foppa had three children, who fought with

Figure 2.3 Emmanuel Haro Poniatowska, Felipe Haro Poniatowska, Guillermo Haro, Elena Poniatowska, and Paula Haro Poniatowska, c. 1973. Photograph by Rosa Nissan. Used by permission of the Fundación Elena Poniatowska Amor, Mexico City, Mexico.

and supported the Ejército Guerrillero de los Pobres (Guerrilla Army of the Poor) against the Guatemalan government in the late 1970s and 1980s. In June 1980, Foppa's son Juan was killed in Nebaj, Quiche, while fighting with the guerrillas. In December 1980, her husband was killed in Mexico City in a car accident. According to an interview with Foppa's oldest son, Julio, his mother disappeared on December 19, 1980, in Guatemala City.[171] Mario Solórzano, another son of Foppa's, died in combat in Guatemala City. He also was a part of the Ejército Guerrillero.[172]

Poniatowska, who was good friends with Foppa and knew her through feminist, literary, and artistic circles, joined with a friend, feminist intellectual Marta Lamas, and others to find out what happened to Foppa. She became part of a group of women who participated in demonstrations, meetings, visits to officials, and television programs to put pressure on the Guatemalan government to account for the life of Foppa. They also protested the ongoing campaign of genocide against Indigenous peoples and leftists that general Romeo Lucas García and his successors carried out in Guatemala. No one knows to this day what happened to Foppa, despite an ongoing campaign.

The interviews Poniatowska conducted with families of the disappeared in Mexico who were victims of the Dirty War in the 1970s and her involvement in the campaign to find out what happened to Foppa and others in Guatemala underline her shift from observer to public activist. While continuing her deep engagement of readers through the use of oral testimonies that bind emotion to politics, Poniatowska herself became a motor of building emotional strategic political community through her own activism. By the early 1980s, Poniatowska was simultaneously dedicating herself to activism and documenting it. By the time she wrote her next crónica, documenting the devastating earthquake in Mexico City in 1985, she was intensely involved in both supporting a group of women seamstresses who were the survivors of the earthquake and documenting the wide-ranging destruction, initial government indifference, and heroic organizing by the people of the city who led the rescue effort. She was both creating emotional strategic political community herself through her organizing and solidarity work and documenting it on the page.

A History
We Cannot Forget

The 1985 Earthquake, Civil Society,
and a New Political Future

July 28, 2015

I was sitting in the back seat of a car with Elena Poniatowska, two of her friends, and a representative of the Comité 19 de Septiembre de 1985 (September 19, 1985 Committee)—a community organization formed to commemorate the Mexico City earthquake of 1985. We were on our way to a public discussion being held by several organizations that had formed around the time of the earthquake. Some of the organizations have remained active and others have been reactivated. Poniatowska had been invited to share her thoughts about the upcoming thirtieth anniversary of the cataclysmic event. At eighty-three years old, she was the most prominent living figure of her generation of writers and chroniclers. Carlos Monsiváis and Carlos Fuentes, among others, had already passed away. The discussions would take place in the Museo de la Ciudad (City Museum), housed in the former palace of the Counts of Santiago de Calimaya, in the center of Mexico City.

We parked the car across from the museum and crossed Pino Suárez Street. The seventeenth-century *palacio* glowed a bright orange in the late afternoon sunlight. As we approached the building, a crowd converged

Figure 3.1 Elena Poniatowska with Cuauhtémoc Abarca in a public discussion commemorating the thirtieth anniversary of the 1985 Mexico City earthquake in the Museo de la Ciudad, October 2015. Photograph by author.

around Poniatowska. Selfie sticks came out, and she began to pose for pictures with a succession of young women. One of the event hosts kept Poniatowska moving forward into the central courtyard on the ground floor. Cuauhtémoc Abarca, an old friend of Poniatowska's, approached her. Abarca is the founder and representative of the Coordinadora de Residentes de Tlatelolco (Council of the Residents of Tlatelolco), formed in 1985 after the earthquake to bring together a wide range of neighborhood and residents' associations.[1] Poniatowska gave him a big hug and they sat down together in the courtyard (figure 3.1), joining a woman from the Comité 19 de Septiembre 1985 and Super Barrio, a costumed and masked superhero who represents the Assembly of Neighborhoods, formed in 1987, two years after the earthquake.[2]

The event moderator spoke: "We are going to get started. I would like to welcome Elena Poniatowska and the Nineteenth of September Committee in commemoration of the thirtieth anniversary of the earthquake. This is a history we cannot forget. It is a history that is present every day. Because of this we are profoundly grateful for the presence of Elena

Poniatowska, who is here to talk with us today." The audience greeted her with resounding applause.

In this chapter, I explore how Poniatowska's crónica *Nada, nadie: Las voces del temblor* (hereafter *Nada, nadie*), first published in Spanish in 1988, was crafted and used as a tool to confront and pressure the PRI government of Mexico to respond to the tragic consequences of the 1985 earthquake and engage with the widespread civil society organizing that followed. The book is politically strategic through pressuring the government to respond while also documenting a broadening of a critical public. While the crónica itself does not detail her immediate involvement in rescue efforts, psychological referrals for earthquake victims, and active support of a newly formed garment workers union (Sindicato Nacional de Trabajadores de la Industria de la Costura, Confección y del Vestido, Similares y Conexos 19 de Septiembre, known in short as the Sindicato de Costureras "19 de Septiembre" [Nineteenth of September Garment Workers Union]), her newspaper stories did, as did her interviews with others and with me.[3] What we also learn from those is that *Nada, nadie* emerged from an intense period of interviewing and writing that recorded the trauma and pain of earthquake survivors—trauma and pain that Poniatowska also felt while interviewing survivors.

In 1985 Poniatowska became an advocate for seamstresses who survived the earthquake, as did Monsiváis. An estimated one thousand garment workers lost their lives and about forty thousand were left unemployed.[4] Claire Brewster writes that both Poniatowska and Monsiváis "contributed the full strength of their skills and support as they chronicled the transformation of society . . . ensuring maximum coverage and working to encourage others to join and extend" the social movements that the tragedy spawned.[5] They "witnessed and broadcast" the social movements pushing for democracy as a basic right and demanding action from a corrupt and negligent government.[6]

By 1985 Poniatowska's crónicas were widely recognized, published, and read. She had become a consistent news item herself through her ongoing activism. As both a participant in strategic emotional political communities and a chronicler of such processes through emotive and detailed testimonies, Poniatowska demonstrated her ability to write a shared Mexican history. She continued this work with *Nada, nadie*. Through the use of powerful personal narratives of trauma and pain, Poniatowska connects readers to the protagonists in the book, creating an emotional bond between those sharing their testimonies and those listening and reading. Strategic emotional political community emerges from the page.

Nada, nadie is thematically connected with *La noche*, as well as *Fuerte es el silencio*, in its focus on social movements that question the Mexican government and highlight social and economic inequality, consequences of tragedy, and neglect for the poor. In this sense, the book suggests the expansion of the 1968 social movement. The moment of the earthquake reveals widespread economic inequality in Mexico linked to neoliberal structural adjustment policies (saps) that resulted in a withdrawal of social welfare support and a privatization of public resources. It is also a pivotal political moment in Mexico as political opposition began to consolidate not only through social movements but also through formal politics. José López Portillo promoted a political reform in 1977 that facilitated the legalization of several political parties, mostly on the left, expanding their representation in electoral politics. Poniatowska's account of the earthquake and aftermath stands out for its intimate, emotional engagement with readers; its use of personal testimony to share both individual experiences and a larger story; and its ability to harness the voices of those who lived through the earthquake as witnesses. Reflecting the voices of some of the poorest Mexicans—"los damnificados de siempre" (those who are always the victims)—Poniatowska's writing, in all its duplications and reproductions, citations and references, its reach well beyond Mexico, and its important role in keeping memories of the earthquake present, documents how Mexicans governed themselves from an ethic of mutual solidarity.[7] This solidarity emerged in a historical moment when the collapse of the economy took away the gain of a larger group of urban workers who had become accustomed to a somewhat comfortable lifestyle.

Economic Inequality and Structural Adjustment

From the 1940s through the 1970s, the model of import substitution industrialization, which replaces foreign production with domestic production, drove Mexico's economy. The economy grew at an average rate of about 6 percent per year, as measured in gross domestic product (GDP). While GDP measures overall growth, it does not indicate distribution of wealth and it leaves out parts of the economy. It thus should be used critically in relation to discussions of economic and social inequality in Mexico. As noted by political scientist Wayne Cornelius, "Inequality in personal income distribution worsened considerably during this period of so-called 'stabilizing development'; demographic pressures increased greatly; and the serious political disturbances in Mexico City in 1968 served to call attention to these deep-seated, structural problems."[8]

Economic growth expanded the urban middle class and working class, known as part of the popular urban sector.[9] The growth of these sectors is linked not only to employment but also to significant provisions for health care and, in some cases, retirement. Families from the *clases populares* (urban working classes) and middle classes supported the rich popular culture in Mexico City such as dance halls, restaurants, cafés, a wide range of markets, and different types of theaters. They were increasingly able to send their children to universities. The growing middle class expanded into white-collar positions in public administration, social services, education, finance, commerce, and manufacturing. Both sectors provided a reading public for a growing number of news and publishing outlets. Meanwhile, the poorest 10 percent of Mexicans in primarily rural areas lost income and saw their share of GDP drop significantly.[10]

During Mexico's "lost decade" of the 1980s, the economy (like others in Latin America) underwent a brutal transition as the value of oil plunged, the peso was devalued, and, in 1982, Mexico could not meet its interest payments on loans. The World Bank and the International Monetary Fund (IMF) provided Mexico with emergency loans to repay U.S. banks, but at a high cost. The loans required a series of SAPs that included privatizing public services, shrinking public expenditures, and slashing social services. Market-oriented policies opened up the country to foreign investment and eventually reoriented the agricultural sector toward exports instead of domestic food production. Unemployment increased, and the removal of import controls hurt formerly protected domestic enterprises. The quality and quantity of government services in basic areas such as health, education, and social security declined. Subsidies for basic foodstuffs fell.

As economic priorities shifted to export industries, wages dropped to make those exports competitive. The result was a significant deterioration of living conditions for all. There was a 60 percent drop in real minimum wages between 1982 and 1988 and a 30 percent drop in internal consumption of basic grains during the 1980s.[11] What the new popular and middle classes had gained before and during the 1970s was lost. And it got worse as the 1980s continued. According to one study, 52.5 percent of all Mexican households were considered poor in 1981. By 1988 that had risen to 62.5 percent.[12]

At the time of the economic crisis, more than 25 percent of Mexico's population was concentrated in Mexico City. Between 1960 and 1980, the city's population had almost doubled (from 4,870,876 to 8,831,079), and nearly 30 percent of the country's industries were concentrated there, along with many jobs.[13] The city was full of people who had migrated from elsewhere in the country, attracted by jobs, both formal and informal. It was estimated that in 1985, 38 percent of Mexico's GDP was generated by the informal sector, which included a wide range of small, unofficial businesses, from food stands to mechanic shops, transport, domestic work and childcare, artisans, and small-scale unregistered manufacturers.[14] The debt crises had a major impact on Mexico City, and the budget was one of the first things affected. Drastic cuts in public expenditures on transport, potable water, health services, and trash collection in addition to people living on untitled land created a crisis for many residents. As sociologist Diane Davis has documented, for three years beginning in 1984, prices for dietary staples in Mexico City rose 757 percent for beans, 480 percent for eggs, 340 percent for milk, and 276 percent for cornmeal.[15] This happened under the watch of Miguel de la Madrid (1982–88), who presided over the implementation of structural adjustment in Mexico. During his presidency, Mexico's economy grew a mere 0.18 percent.

Urban Social Movements, the Dirty War, and the Realignment of the Left

By the 1980s, the annual flow of migrants into Mexico City reached about 270,000 people per year.[16] Many arrived in areas without basic services or housing. If they did have housing, often it was located on land without clear title. Residents had to bargain with city and federal officials to receive basic services. Sociologist Vivienne Bennett suggests that urban popular movements in Mexico City, Monterrey, and other large cities emerged between 1979 and 1983, following a wave of repression called the "Dirty War" in the late 1960s and 1970s.[17] These included neighborhood organizations linked to land invasions and self-development projects—and in some cases the creation of whole new neighborhoods. As these urban movements formed, they coalesced into articulated regional and national coalitions.[18] In 1980 the first national congress of urban popular movements met in Monterrey with about twenty-one organizations, including from Mexico City.[19] A second congress convened in 1981 in Durango. At that meeting, the Coordinadora Nacional del Movimiento Urbano Popular (National

Council of the Urban Popular Movement) was formed; it embraced more than sixty organizations.[20] Demands focused on improving urban living conditions and democratizing Mexican society. The existence of the group and its Mexico City member organizations provided part of the backbone for further civil society organizing that emerged after the earthquake.

The 1970s were also marked by Mexico's Dirty War against leftist student activists and several guerrilla groups. Government forces carried out assassinations, disappearances, torture, and imprisonment. An estimated 1,200 people disappeared nationwide, hundreds in Guerrero, particularly those linked to the movement of Guerrero schoolteacher Lucio Cabañas and the Partido de los Pobres (Poor People's Party). Urban activists were targeted as well, such as Jesús Piedra Ibarra, who was disappeared in Monterrey in 1975, accused of being a member of the Liga Comunista 23 de Septiembre (LC23S, 23rd of September Communist League). His mother, Rosario Ibarra, formed the Comité Pro-Defensa de Presos Perseguidos, Desaparecidos y Exiliados Políticos de México (Committee for the Defense of Political Prisoners, Disappeared and Political Exiles of Mexico), which became known as the Comité ¡Eureka! (Eureka! Committee) in 1977 that worked with one hundred women to pressure the government to account for the disappeared and to liberate political prisoners. One of her hunger strikes is profiled in Poniatowska's 1980 crónica, *Fuerte es el silencio*, in the essay "Diario de una huelga de hambre" (Diary of a hunger strike). Poniatowska was one of a few intellectuals and journalists at the time to openly criticize the Echeverría government for its repressive actions against activists. In an interview about the role of the press during the Dirty War, she commented, "There were rumors but there was a lot of indifference. There were rumors that there were clandestine prisons, there were rumors that people were tortured, but you didn't know for sure. There was ignorance and indifference. There was a lot of pressure to keep quiet."[21] Ibarra credits Poniatowska with being an ardent supporter of Comité ¡Eureka! among journalists and intellectuals.[22]

Mexico's Dirty War rationalized state violence through rhetoric that often condemned those who were killed or disappeared as "terrorists," "subversives," "guerrilleros," or "agitators." These tactics went hand in hand with Echeverría's efforts to avoid conflict and promote an image of a more open, progressive government. In fact, Echeverría did provide funding for social programs, increase funding for universities, use leftist rhetoric, and appoint leading intellectual figures as Mexican ambassadors.[23] He also played a role in opening up the media, compared to the prior administration. For some who lived in Mexico City, there was a distinct and more open ambiance than in 1970.[24] The next president, José López Portillo (1976–82), legalized left-wing political parties in 1978—including the Partido Comunista Mexicano and the Partido Socialista de los Trabajadores de México (PST, Socialist Workers Party, dissolved in 1987)—allowing them to compete in elections. The reforms also increased the Mexican Congress to four hundred seats and set aside one hundred of them for opposition parties (to the PRI) on a proportional basis. Because López Portillo had been unopposed in his election, many people viewed the move to allow opposition as a way to bolster the PRI's legitimacy. What it also did, however, was open a door for the consolidation of the Mexican left, in this case through electoral politics. Fortified urban social movements and political organizing after the 1985 earthquake, along with a dissident current of the PRI, marked a shift in left politics that resulted in a coalition of small left-wing parties, the Frente Democrático Nacional (National Democratic Front), that supported Cuauhtémoc Cárdenas for president in the 1988 elections. Many believe he won. This was all part of the shaken landscape following the earthquake.

The Earthquake

On September 19 and 20, two powerful earthquakes—the first measuring as much as magnitude 8.1 on the Richter scale—shook Mexico City. While technically there were two earthquakes, they are usually referred to jointly as the (singular) earthquake (the primary event and its nearly-as-severe aftershock). Between ten thousand and forty thousand people died. Thousands of buildings collapsed. More than four thousand people were rescued. President Miguel de la Madrid waited for more than three days to respond to the crisis. After his first survey of the damage, he stated, "We are prepared to respond to this situation, and we do not need to request foreign assistance. Mexico has enough resources, and together people and government will overcome. We are grateful for the goodwill extended to us, but we are self-sufficient."[25] In the absence of any kind of government response, the people of Mexico took up the rescue effort. More conventional groups such as Boy Scout troops were among the first responders. The Salvation Army, priests, and nuns followed their lead. Neighbors, students, and people of all ages stopped their lives to dig for survivors, loan their cars for transport, and deliver medicine. Students formed brigades, and all kinds of volunteers joined in.

In the Zapotec Indigenous community of Teotitlán del Valle, Oaxaca, where I was living before arriving in Mexico City on the day of the second quake, the explanation for the earthquake was that the gods, angered by something, had sat up, causing the ground to buckle. The gods were not the only ones to sit up; in the midst of this tragedy, the people in Mexico City stood shoulder to shoulder to aid in the recovery. Amid the ruins, people discovered what was possible by autonomously organizing civil society (figure 3.2). Building on prior movements from the 1960s and 1970s, they created a sense of hope and the possibility for change.

The earthquake did not affect all areas of the city equally. In the southern zone where Poniatowska lived, many people did not feel it. Unaware of the destruction in other parts of the city as power outages knocked out television broadcasts, Poniatowska went into the center the following evening. According to an interview with Cynthia Steele published in 1989, she had been teaching a writing class that day and did not hear about the quake until about six or seven in the evening. When she found out, she gathered a pile of clothing and things from her house to donate and took them to her local city hall. She hosted some friends for dinner that night. By the next morning, she felt she had to go into the city: "I went with Paula [her daughter] and Angela, our maid, and we went to walk around the neighborhood of Alvaro Obregón. I remember that there was a building in pieces and there was a statue of a little Buddha on the edge of the window hanging in the air."[26] That night she helped excavate a building in the Colonia Roma. "They put me on removing rubble with a bucket. But I did it very badly because I loaded too much into the bucket and then I couldn't lift it. It was when I began to discover the solidarity of the people, because a boy said, 'Let's see,' and he helped me."[27] After that, she worked for days in two other devastated neighborhoods.

She then related in detail to Steele how she came to write about the earthquake.

One night, journalist Julio Scherer García of the magazine *Proceso* called me and said, "Hey, what are you doing, Elena?" "Well, I'm doing what everyone is doing." [She was helping]. [Scherer García] said, "I just talked with (Carlos) Monsiváis and he said, what, what is the best journalist in Mexico doing sitting in her house?" "Ay, well, I am not sitting in my house, but I can't write. What good is writing when we need to help with our hands?"

Figure 3.2 Carlos Monsiváis quote and photograph of civil society after the earthquake featured in the exhibit *19/09 1985 7:19: A 30 años del sismo* (September 19, 1985 7:19: 30 years after the earthquake), Museo de la Ciudad, Mexico City, October 2015. Photograph by author.

Then [Scherer García] said to me, "You have to do what you know how to do best, Elena, and don't go carrying buckets that other people can carry." Then Monsiváis called her and said, "Start writing."[28]

She did. Poniatowska immediately began recording earthquake survivors' testimonies, writing, and supporting survivors, particularly the group of seamstresses known as El Sindicato de Costureras "19 de Septiembre" in San Antonio Abad. She became close friends with union leader Evangelina Corona—their friendship continues to this day—and at feminist Marta Lamas's request, she served as treasurer of a group acting in solidarity with the Sindicato de Costureras. The seamstresses had suffered devastating losses as the factories they worked in crumbled on top of them. Survivors were without work, income, and support. Poniatowska wrote not only about the plight of the seamstresses and the many others whose lives the earthquake had turned upside down but also about government ineptness and corruption at a time when the incompetence of the PRI government was at a high point. Some of the most striking testimonials she collected pin the blame for the massive death toll on the government, not on the quake. For example, as Judith García testifies in *Nada, nadie*:

I want to state that the people who died didn't die because of the earthquake; that is a lie. People died because of poor construction, because of fraud, because of the criminal incapacity and the inefficiency of a corrupt government that doesn't give a damn about people living and working in buildings that can collapse. . . .

. . . This was not a seismic problem but a problem of having assassins in power who couldn't care less about the life of children, the life of what could have been a future for this country. Thousands of dead cannot be erased overnight.[29]

García voices the discontent and beliefs of many Mexicans who survived the earthquake, witnessed the lack of government accountability, and believed that a better political future lay ahead.

Hundreds of thousands of people organized to rescue survivors, then to help one another survive, and finally to create permanent organizations to hold the government responsible for its lack of action. Groups such as the Sindicato de Costureras, the Coordinadora de Residentes de Tlatelolco, the Coordinadora Única de Damnificados (CUD, United Coordinator of Earthquake Victims), and Amanecer el Barrio (Wake Up the Neighborhood) emerged in 1985, building on prior urban social movements. As thousands and thousands of people moved into the streets to help one another and organize to remove rubble, pull bodies out, and provide shelter and provisions for survivors, a new energy propelled the city. For some, it was the dawn of a hope for a new kind of democratic participation in Mexico.

In a special edition of the magazine *Proceso*, commemorating the thirtieth anniversary of the earthquake in 2015, Poniatowska wrote of 1985:

A revolution can erupt around each fallen building. It has been years since Mexicans mobilized in this way, it is a new phenomenon. They discover that before the government, it is they who save themselves. . . .

From the rubble emerges another city. Carlos Monsiváis contemplates this transformation and writes that democracy may be the appearance of a citizen who, from the window of his ruined building, refuses to descend to the street. Monsi cradles this thought that I repeat several times. In 1985, the term "civil society" acquired an unexpected credibility, since it was the poorest Mexicans who organized themselves and Mexico knew "the conversion of a people into government and official disorder into civil order. Democracies can also be the sudden importance of each person."[30]

Writing about the Earthquake

While de la Madrid initially forbade the Mexican Army from pitching in to help and rejected international aid, four days later, the government did an about-face and sought to impose order in Mexico City.[31] The attempted silencing of voices began with the government promoting a slogan of "normalization," according to Monsiváis.[32] The message came with increased military and government presence, and it discouraged volunteer efforts like those in operation. More than one million people who had organized strongly rejected the push for normalization.[33] In fact, just one week after the earthquake, on September 27, 1985, more than thirty thousand people marched in silence toward the presidential residency of Los Pinos to demand land, bank credits, a reconstruction program, the reinstallation of water and electrical services, and the acceptance and dispersal of international aid.[34]

The de la Madrid administration told reporters to "return to normal" and "not continue to report on these tragedies" (referring to the earthquake) because to do so was "depressing and counterproductive."[35] Like many, Poniatowska did not follow the order to normalize. She was working as a reporter when the earthquake struck, and she fully expected to be able to publish reports on the widespread devastation and amazing local response. Her employer, however, disagreed. As she recounted to me, "I was working for a newspaper whose owners had the Irish last name of O'Farrill. The paper was called *Novedades*. I worked there for many years, from 1955 to 1985, for thirty years without social security, vacations, or other benefits. . . . I left in 1985 when the newspaper *La Jornada* was founded, because at *Novedades* the O'Farrills told me that they could not publish a single article about the earthquake because it would demoralize people. . . . An order from the government said we should 'return to normality.'"[36]

After Monsiváis convinced her to write about the earthquake and *Novedades* rejected her articles, Poniatowska turned to the newly formed *La Jornada* newspaper. The editor and founder, Carlos Payán, immediately said, "Bring me a new article tomorrow," she recalled in a 2015 interview, "and that is how I wrote a series of articles every day, including on Sundays, for four months. . . . In the morning I would go to the sites of the earthquake damage, in the afternoon I wrote, and then I would deliver the article. The next day I did the same thing."[37] Poniatowska went to the encampments that were erected alongside the fallen buildings and would begin talking to the people trying to live outside who had been displaced from their ruined buildings. She also went to the Red Cross for information and interviews. "I spoke with everyone. . . . I would just arrive and I asked what happened. What did they need? Some people told me they were really hungry, so we would get a sandwich while we talked. It was all like this. While we were talking, I would interview."[38]

Poniatowska also conducted some interviews at an apartment occupied by various intellectuals where people gathered. She was concerned with people's mental health since she became aware of her own fragile state as she absorbed one tragic testimony after another. Monsiváis was an important support to her while she was interviewing a wide range of people. The place where they met was also a hub of intellectual emotional and political community. Poniatowska used it as a safe space to gather testimonies as well as to build community.

> During the earthquake [Monsiváis and I] worked a lot together. I did what you would call laying the groundwork of conducting interviews with families to collect their testimonies. Often we would run into each other at a center where people would gather, almost like a psychoanalytic center of catharsis in the Colonia Condesa. We gathered in an apartment that was called Peyton Place because so many things went on there. There were various intellectuals who lived there. And we would hear testimonies.[39]

Poniatowska worked tirelessly for months. Her daily routine of going out to a site and watching people search for loved ones, dig through the rubble with a pick or shovel, and cry for an irrevocable loss, yet also organize, eventually took a heavy toll on her. She told *Informador* in 2015, "I almost died from everything I had seen: all of the suffering, all the corruption, that Mexican engineers and architects built really poorly constructed buildings—they used a lot of gravel in the cement."[40] In May 2019, while talking with me about this time, she added, "I got horribly depressed and at the end I was taking an antidepressant prescribed by Dr. Javier Sepúlveda Amor, my cousin. It was a terrible time. . . . Hospitals and maternity units should never have fallen down, but they did. I remember those days as extremely painful."[41]

Part of the power of the earthquake testimonies that Poniatowska chronicled day in and day out in *La Jornada* stemmed from the survivors' emotional intensity and the widespread tragedies they revealed. Their testimonies also reflected the personal relationships Poniatowska developed with people as she accompanied them on errands and tried to help them get what they needed: "I couldn't just write, but I would go for the wheelchair, the bed, the rice people needed because they had to eat. These kinds of things are emotionally exhausting."[42] Her accompaniment of earthquake survivors and daily engagement with them forges a connection with their stories of tragedy, suffering, and persistence. As she explained during one of our interviews,

I write about people who are in extreme situations. An earthquake is an extreme situation, and people are more willing to talk. They are in pain, they are very emotive, and because of this they are more willing to tell what has happened to them, to complain, to share secrets that they would not share in everyday life. Outside of an emergency situation, people don't share this way. They don't have time or the emotional energy to do so. They are at work. But in this case, if I go to where people are looking at a building that fell down and where they lost their apartment or where a family member died, it is much easier for them to cry with me.[43]

As an active listener who could convey survivors' words on the pages of *La Jornada* on a daily basis, and then in her book, Poniatowska weaves strategic emotional political community between herself, those who testimonies she records, and those who read them. The way she selects, interprets, and gives meaning to the stories and episodes that together represent the pain of the earthquake for survivors and the power of the social movement unleashed in recovery by civil society is strategic. The writing and the activism she documents in *Nada, nadie* are meant to motivate political action. The people on the pages in *Nada, nadie* came to form part of Poniatowska's personal community and also were connected to one another through the ties they built in organizing and working together. Their testimonies in the book reflect the bonds they built with one another as well as with Poniatowska—suggesting the very hard and active work involved in building such networks and giving them meaning.

In some cases, Poniatowska has maintained and deepened the relationships she has built through the process of interviewing.

I have stayed in touch with a lot of people. We are friends. I have a great friendship with Evangelina Corona, who was the secretary of the seamstress' union and confronted Miguel de la Madrid, who was president of Mexico then. She said to him, "No, Mr. President. Things are not like you say they are. You have been telling lies." . . . She told him what she had been going through. And for the president, and above all for the people in his cabinet, it was impressive that a woman who came from the people [*del pueblo*] rose up and said, "No, Mr. President." She practically told him, "You, sir, are lying," or "You are very poorly informed."[44]

In documenting the exchange between Corona and the president in *Nada, nadie*, she is also helping publicize the performance, in which positions of power and hierarchy are reversed, with the working-class seamstress Corona telling the president that he is wrong. Poniatowska's portrayal of Corona as a woman who is fresh and smiling but also feisty and will stand up to a president partially inverts gender stereotypes of poor, working women as submissive. When she first introduces Corona, who shared her life story with her, she writes, "I don't know how she speaks in public; I imagine her freshness, her clean gaze, her smiling eyes, her lips over strong teeth, very white . . . teeth that reflect the luminous sparks of the day."[45] She consistently highlights women activists in her work and portrays them in their fullness as people and in their effectiveness in politics. The ways Poniatowska collected testimonials and then shared and talked them over with Monsiváis and other intellectuals suggested the importance of their collective conversations in their interpretations.

The testimonials that Poniatowska published in *Nada, nadie* were a group effort. Eighteen of her writing students helped Poniatowska assemble them. The writers are all recognized by name on a separate acknowledgment page and also within the text as subheadings of the section for which they were responsible. Their contributions complement Poniatowska's entries, which make up the majority of the book. In the process of collecting the testimonies, Poniatowska was actively building several intersecting networks, including with those whose testimonies she collected, interactions with her writing students, and her shared discussions with other intellectuals and writers such as Monsiváis. These intersecting networks can be seen together as a political community held together by the force of Poniatowska's writing, which gives meaning to the experiences of those included. The reproduction of the community she created on the pages of *Nada, nadie* extends to readers who connect with the narratives.

Contrast, Positioning, and Community

The structure of *Nada, nadie* is a patchwork that resembles people's experiences in Mexico City after the earthquake. Fragmented, crumpled, with chains of human ants working in the rubble, parts of the city were like war zones. In other places, such as Coyoacán in the south, not a blade of grass was out of place. Above ground in the city center, it looked like a jumbled, disordered mess. But underneath it were human networks and tunnels where people known as *topos* (moles) labored for days to pull out the living and then the dead. Families camped out for days and weeks hoping to be able to find the body of a loved one and bury them with respect instead of in a common grave. Hundreds of thousands of residents were displaced and living on the street, millions had no water, and more than a million children had no schools. In the rebuilding process, dozens of new organizations were formed, and neighborhoods pulled together to demand housing and basic infrastructure. They would not take "no" for an answer. Business did not go on as usual. In illustrating this, *Nada, nadie* reveals a world hidden from most of the press, from international visitors, and from the Mexican state. It highlights the amazing love, persistence, physical strength, endurance, and sacrifice that thousands of Mexicans demonstrated after the earthquake.

Poniatowska's strategic positioning of voices from across the class, race, gender, and ethnic spectrum of Mexico City ensures that many perspectives were heard and that themes previously forbidden in the press were exposed. In the short section "The Earthquake Cracked the Untouchables," she writes: "It used to be said that Mexican journalists always faced three taboos: the army, the Virgin de Guadalupe, and the President of the Republic with his family. We could not touch those subjects 'with the petal of a rose.' The earthquake also cracked those taboos. People know how to be critical. And their thoughts have been published."[46]

This breaking of the political taboos happens through a series of contrasts woven throughout Poniatowska's book. One of the most effective juxtapositions is Professor Antonio Lazcano Araujo's narrative, which describes his shift helping out at the Parque del Seguro Social (Social Security Park), where bodies were stored, disinfected, and prepared for burial, with Poniatowska's ethnographic description of the installation of the Comisión Nacional de Reconstrucción (National Reconstruction Commission) in the Museo Nacional de Antropología (National Museum of Anthropology).

Mexico City's Parque del Seguro Social (Social Security Park), a base-ball stadium also known popularly by its former name, Parque Delta, was converted into a giant morgue shortly after the earthquake. Unclaimed bodies and remains were stored there. Often, people who had survived the earthquake and had already searched in the rubble, in hospitals, and else-where would ultimately make their way to the stadium to try to find their loved ones. Hundreds of bodies in mounds were covered with *cal* (lime powder or calcium hydroxide) and ice, then covered with plastic. Rows and rows of coffins and the smell of decomposing bodies confronted all who entered the makeshift morgue. Some came as volunteers to help with identification and burial. Others came hoping to identify a missing rela-tive. From all walks of life, volunteers, public servants, and survivors met one another. In the space of this national morgue, humanity was stripped down to its essentials. It is here where Lazcano Araujo, an evolution-ary biologist who was teaching at UNAM, volunteered. He helped people find their unidentified relatives. He spoke with the dead and the living. They were all connected. Following is Poniatowska's passage on this scene, "What's the Deal on the Coffins" (in the voice of Lazcano Araujo):

When I turned my head to the left I saw a little girl with eyes wide open and the grimace of an interrupted smile, an eight-year-old: "Little girl, why on earth didn't you run? Why did the beam fall on you?" I insistently spoke to the cadavers to the point of rage, wrath, and hatred: "This isn't fair. It's not fair that in this country hospitals, schools, govern-ment buildings, and public buildings should collapse just like that." . . .

A small, skinny, brown guy appeared, the typical Mexican who has had to work very hard from birth, someone who probably lived in some lost tenement in some lost slum, with a sweater that was all too thin, Jesus! Really! Why are our people so unprotected? What helplessness, God! Really! It makes you mad to see people like that, with nothing. "And the coffins?" he asked, "What's the deal on the coffins?" He needed three of them. Three coffins. He wanted to know how much they were. And how would he have paid for them, the poor bastard?

"Have you identified your family?"

"Yes, they are there. But tell me how much do those caskets run?"

"No, the coffins are free; we'll give them to you right away. Are you here by yourself?"

He was there to claim his sister and two nieces, one fourteen, the other nine years old. . . .

... Then I asked the skinny man, "Listen, can we sprinkle limestone [*sic*, should be lime] on your relatives?"

"Yes."

The fourteen-year-old had to be transferred to an adult casket because she was too big for the other one. As I sprinkled her, I thought of Hamlet, when Ophelia, after losing her mind, drowns.... I had exactly the same sensation: "Girl, I am sprinkling limestone on you, so you'll go all whitened up, you who have not lived at all, fourteen-year-old girl."... I could only sprinkle limestone on her. Not a single flower, just a lot of white dust.

That's how she went.[47]

In the next section of the book, Poniatowska describes the initiation of the Comisión Nacional de Reconstrucción, first convened on October 9, 1985, on the patio of the Museo Nacional de Antropología. She writes it from the standpoint of a participant observer, with a clear political position. In his autobiography, de la Madrid describes the meeting, which included his entire cabinet and "1,000 guests who represented all the sectors and activities of Mexican society."[48] As one of the invited guests, Poniatowska arrived with a sense of urgency, thinking that she would hear from the survivors, the volunteers, the firemen, the residents of Tepito and of the neighborhood of Colonia Doctores, and other places where she had been collecting testimonies on a daily basis. When ushers passed around cards, she signed up to join the social assistance committee. The meeting did not turn out as she had expected. She writes about it in "Chronicle of a Disappointment."

There are nine speakers. Angel Olivo Solís, president of the Labor Congress, stitches together sentences that say nothing. Engineer Claudio González, president of the Entrepreneurial Council, warns that inflation will not be abated. Secretary General of the National Peasant Confederation ... Mario Hernández Posadas shouts his unshakable faith in the most dreadful clichés....

And nobody says what we are waiting to hear, in spite of the fact that we turn our tense eyes toward the presiding table. Some phrases attempt to take flight: "Mexico never shows its virtues better than when it faces adversity"; "With renewed faith we salute the commission and congratulate ourselves for the opportunity to become an integral part of it."... "Presidential leadership continues to be serene and firm"; "Nations and men can truly be known only in rough times."[49]

Those who were assembled on the podium with the president were freshly shaved, wearing suits straight from the cleaners. "Don't they know," she wrote, "that, at the moment of truth in the streets, the institutions they lead have proved their worthlessness to the Mexican people?"[50] She contrasts what was going on outside in the streets of Mexico City with the empty bureaucratic spectacle in the museum.

Five former Mexico City mayors were sitting next to superstar writer Octavio Paz, who at that time many people identified as aligned with the government. After he resigned as Mexico's ambassador to India in 1968, Paz was a visiting scholar at Cambridge University in England, Cornell, and Harvard, where he was awarded an honorary doctorate in 1980. A critic of human rights violations under Fidel Castro and an opponent of the 1979 Sandinista government that took power in Nicaragua, Paz had parted ways with the Mexican left; in 1984 an effigy of him was burned in front of the U.S. Embassy in Mexico City. He remained, however, a renowned writer and received the highest honor for literature in Spanish in 1981, winning the Miguel de Cervantes Prize to honor the lifetime achievement of an outstanding writer in the Spanish language. His presence at the meeting signaled its importance. Poniatowska wrote of those assembled on the podium on October 9, 1985: "Are they coming to talk about their own experience, while in the crumbled buildings some people are still searching for bodies? . . . Bathed in dust the rescue crews stop to drink water, but under the stone umbrella, time is the older time, the time of slow politics, rhetorical politics, anachronistic politics, tricky politics, egotistic politics, the politics of avarice."[51]

Poniatowska proceeds to express her disbelief about how the meeting was going. She raises the question of whether the assembled politicians, economists, and elites truly live in a parallel universe: "Does [Secretary of Labor] Arsenio Farell—up there on high behind his dark glasses—know that more than seventy thousand women work in clandestine sweatshops in Mexico City, without social security, without benefits, living in infamous hovels, and that eight hundred of them remained buried because their bosses preferred to recover their machinery?"[52]

When de la Madrid addressed the crowd, Poniatowska felt a spark of hope that the divide would be bridged between those who were inside the Museo Nacional de Antropología and those in the streets. She could see the pain on the president's face: "I think that the President of the Republic probably feels very bad, overwhelmed by the tragedy, hurt to the marrow of his bones. Not in vain did he see up close the ferocious helplessness of the people that he governs. He proposes a structural change."[53] Ponia-towska's words also suggest that de la Madrid recognized that recovering from the earthquake would require "transforming reality." She notes that, while these were not his exact words, "I feel that the president *is asking* for help."[54]

De la Madrid wrote in his autobiography that what the situation of the 1985 earthquake required "was something that I emphasized during my presidential campaign: participatory democracy."[55] This theme of participatory democracy was at the heart of the organizing that the earthquake inspired and went on to be an important component of the kind of political change many Mexicans hoped for then. The president's strategy for fostering participatory democracy was to "promote dialogue about all the themes that people were anguishing about" through the Comisión Nacional de Reconstrucción. He began this dialogue at that October 9 meeting at the Museo Nacional de Antropología. In his autobiography, de la Madrid reflected on this process. "We needed," he wrote, "to create enough forums so that anyone who wanted to would find an opportunity to participate, open channels so that society could have a catharsis."[56] The channels, it turned out, were a long list of committees, such as the one Poniatowska checked off on an index card that an usher handed her.

The Comité de Reconstrucción del Área Metropolitana (Committee for the Reconstruction of the Metropolitan Area [Mexico City]), Comité de Descentralización (Decentralization Committee), Comité de Asuntos Financieros (Committee for Financial Affairs), and Comité para Auxilio Social (Committee for Social Assistance) were tasked with coordinating efforts in health, education, employment, and housing. There were also the Comité para Auxilio Internacional (Committee for International Assistance) and Comité de Prevención de la Seguridad Civil (Committee for the Preparation of Civil Security). Through the formation of these committees under the umbrella of the Comisión Nacional de Reconstrucción, de la Madrid hoped to open up dialogue channels with the government as well as to "foment greater communication among members of society who, in fact, never talk among themselves."[57] De la Madrid wanted, in his words, "to take advantage of the political opening provoked by the earthquake."[58]

Perhaps de la Madrid was channeling some of these desires to his audience inside the Museo Nacional de Antropología. In her account, Poniatowska sees cracks in the "gray-suit uniformity of officialdom," in the president's speech that might mean that "we the citizens can get inside through them."[59] As de la Madrid asks, according to Poniatowska, "How are we going to improve the quality of life?" and "How are we going to transform suffering into an active process?" In *Nada, nadie*, Poniatowska shares the questions going through her mind while listening to the president speak: "Will the next working sessions include the sanitation workers of the Federal District, the nurses, the street kids from the gangs? . . . Is it possible that we can still believe in the efficacy of government when, at the crucial moment, *it was the people who did everything*?" Her description concludes with the hope that for all the people's struggling, a light has been cast through a curtain of doubt. Could this be the moment when Mexican politics as usual would change? "Are the insides of officials sufficiently shaken up? Do they have their own earthquake? At the moment, it is impossible not to notice the President's solicitousness."[60] In this section, Poniatowska positions herself also as an actor in the story, suggesting her move to activism from just observer and her role as a participant in civil society. She signals the wider strategic emotional political community she is both building and documenting. At this moment, she suggests the possibility of opening up that community to a broad critical public committed to participatory democracy and social transformation across different groups with a critical perspective.

Contrasting Accounts, Social Movements, and the Earthquake. Poniatowska and de la Madrid

Miguel de la Madrid wrote about what happened during and after the 1985 earthquake as part of his almost nine-hundred-page autobiography, *Cambio de rumbo: Testimonio de una presidencia, 1982–1988*, published in 2004, sixteen years after his presidency ended. Interestingly, he labels it as his "testimony." Most would call it an official autobiography of his presidency. It is his account. Written in his voice without the testimonies of others, the extensive section on the earthquake dovetails with many of the themes and even some of the people whose narratives are found in Poniatowska's *Nada, nadie*.

De la Madrid's account suggests just how much the social movements that emerged in 1985 worried him and his administration. "The groups that could become a political problem for the government were defining themselves," and he writes about them extensively in his book.[61] These potentially problematic groups included those who had lost their homes in the neighborhoods of Tepito and Tlatelolco, the doctors who were displaced by the collapse of the two major medical centers, and "the problem represented by the helplessness and demands of the seamstresses of San Antonio Abad."[62] These are precisely the people Poniatowska highlighted in many of her daily chronicles for *La Jornada* in the fall of 1985 and later in *Nada, nadie.*

Poniatowska was particularly moved by the plight of Mexico City's seamstresses, who labored in unspeakable conditions, and by the neighborhood organizations that came together to form larger federations. Poniatowska provides insights into two of the many organizations that became central in the efforts to change the living and working conditions of millions of poor urban Mexicans.

Evangelina Corona

Evangelina Corona emerged as a very effective spokesperson for the seamstresses who lost their jobs, livelihood, family members, and homes. Like peeling away the layers of an onion, Poniatowska revealed the plight of the seamstresses with each passing day—first in her daily *La Jornada* articles and then later in *Nada, nadie.*

Out of the factory ruins, Poniatowska raises up the figure of Corona: "Mothers, sisters, daughters, compañeras . . . they were dying. From this drowning in blood, rage was born. And from that rage a desire to change, a 'They have no right!' and now Evangelina Corona is a leader, she appears in public with a raised fist, microphone in hand."[63] Turning down what the bosses were offering them, the seamstresses formed a new union, the Sindicato de Costureras "19 de Septiembre." Their demands included three months' salary and twenty days per year for seniority, plus the wages they would have earned since the day of the earthquake until they were rehired.

Poniatowska portrays Corona as a leader but as someone who shares the fate and experiences of the other seamstresses. Her detailed life history of Corona traces her humble beginnings to the small farm community of San Antonio Cuajomulco, Tlaxcala. Her story of childhood poverty, migration to an urban area, work as a domestic servant for many years, raising two daughters as a single mother, and ultimately her employment in a garment factory highlight Corona's core life experiences. Corona recalls of her first days as a seamstress:

> When I started, I went directly into overlock work. I didn't even know the machine, but there I was, in charge of overlock. (She pronounces the word *overlock* with a great deal of respect.) They gave me a blouse to

which I had to attach a little bit of lace between pieces of fabric, with a little ornamental stitch, but I didn't know how to thread the machine, and the seams looked like jagged teeth. . . .

I had to redo two hundred blouses for being careless. After I got those two hundred blouses fixed, I never had a problem.[64]

Poniatowska notes in parentheses following this narrative from Corona that the overlock is done on a "high-speed machine that produces a locked stitch that is used for finishing a garment, reinforcing previously made seams. . . . The overlock specialist is the highest-paid seamstress."[65] Through Poniatowska's detailed description of how Corona learns to do the ornamental overlock stitch (the finishing lock stitch of a garment), the dignity of Corona's sewing emerges from the page.

Corona is depicted as a strong, independent, single mother but also as a political leader who was dead serious about the garment workers union.

We have signed up approximately seventy-two factories, and each day more are joining. . . .

The incorporation of the Nineteenth of September Union cost six hundred lives. . . .

The *patrón* [boss] fooled us blatantly. All the *patrones* did. They left us out on the street, literally. Thank God, we have registered our union, and the Supreme Being will not allow us to betray each other.[66]

Poniatowska signals Corona's importance and dedication in the ongoing political struggles that followed the earthquake but also the challenges she has in being a political leader: "I was always very docile in my job. . . . I never talked politics with the compañeros, and even now, it doesn't come easy. . . . It's hard for me; I say to the compañeras and also to the compañeros—because we also have men in the union—that the union belongs to all of us and all of us together are the union; but that we need to put our gumption in this and strengthen our organization, fighting with our heart."[67]

Poniatowska goes on to imagine what happened when Corona talked with President Miguel de la Madrid and Secretary of Labor Arsenio Farell Cubillas—which Corona actually did. Her portrayal of Corona here again partially romanticizes her according to feminine qualities but also evokes admiration for her political effectiveness and frankness.

I asked myself what President de la Madrid and Secretary of Labor Farell feel when they are before the clean face of Evangelina Corona, her skin of polished apple, her nose that wrinkles when she laughs, her hair braided at the nape of her neck. . . .

Evangelina speaks naturally; she answers without hiding anything. . . .

What does de la Madrid think before this fresh air, what does Farell think, when both are used to the courteous politeness of senators and representatives who earn hundreds of thousands of pesos a month, plus commissions?[68]

De la Madrid's autobiography also devotes several pages to the seamstresses and expresses sympathy for their plight. He describes the buildings where the garment industry was located as former housing units not made to hold machinery. The earthquake had a "devastating effect," he writes, and resulted in a high number of deaths among the workers. He describes in detail a confrontation that took place on September 24 when some of the garment factory owners arrived and tried to rescue their machinery and valuables from the rubble: "The surviving workers were afraid that if the owners took out all the things of value [i.e., the machines] that there would be nothing left as a basis for paying them what they were owed. . . . This produced a painful negotiation in front of the ruined factories. At the same time that the women workers were rescuing the remains of their fellow workers, they also tried to prevent the owners from taking out the machinery."[69] Remarkably, he does not seem to grasp the grief they felt for the loss of fellow workers and their incredulity that their bosses would care more about the machines than about them.

De la Madrid describes the difficult working conditions in which the women labored, which became apparent when the media revealed what their work lives had been like.

It was said that they worked shifts that were more than eight hours per day; that they were paid by the piece; that they were forced to complete very high quotas; that the sanctions for falling behind and below their quotas were severe; and that, due to the wide availability of labor, threats of being fired were frequent and the pay they received on many occasions was less than the minimum wage. It was also revealed that a lot of the owners only signed contracts for one week at a time so that they would not have to register their workers for social security.[70]

These problems led to a series of encounters and actions involving the seamstresses and various government entities that regulated labor. On October 11, when the Unión de Costureras en Lucha was formed (the earlier name of the Sindicato de Costureras "19 de Septiembre"), de la Madrid asked Hilda Anderson, the secretary general of the Federación Obrera de Organizaciones Femeniles (Workers' Federation of Women's Organizations) of the government-controlled Confederación de Trabajadores de México (Confederation of Mexican Workers), to manage the seamstresses' demands. According to de la Madrid, Anderson went to where the seamstresses were camped out, and they did not receive her well: "The only thing they wanted was an audience with me."[71]

On October 18 or 19 (depending on the account), the seamstresses marched to the presidential residence, Los Pinos, and talked with de la Madrid. According to two accounts, he received a delegation of approximately forty women.[72] Corona was among that group. On October 20, Farell formally registered the "Sindicato Nacional de Trabajadores de la Industria de la Costura, Confección y Vestido, Similares y Conexos 19 de Septiembre" (the formal name of the union). Corona was appointed secretary general of the newly formed union, which represented more than forty factories and eight thousand workers from the states of Mexico, Morelos, Coahuila, and Guanajuato.

De la Madrid's dates differ slightly in his account compared to that of Monsiváis and reporters who interviewed the seamstresses. His description of the meeting and his following actions walk a fine line between sympathy and political opportunism: "I listened to them, convinced by their candor, and I offered my support. The Secretary of Labor was in charge of defending their rights. I advised Farell about what had happened, and he promised to take up the issue immediately. . . . He was able to get each one of the owners to participate in the negotiation. In the end, in his hands, the problem was resolved with great skill."[73] De la Madrid notes that prior to Farell's efforts, Hilda Anderson's on the part of the official union had been unsuccessful. Nevertheless, he felt that it was important to take care of the seamstresses' issues because "the opposition political parties will try to gain ground here."[74] His words then suggest his motivation for agreeing to meet with the seamstresses: "The most important thing was to maintain an open dialogue and help to resolve their problems so that their organizations were not manipulated by those opposed to the State; in fact, their circumstances had converted them into a symbol of tragedy and injustice."[75]

Here de la Madrid expresses alarm at the kind of strategic emotional political community that the seamstresses had already built and their potential to connect their testimonies of trauma and organizing with other groups and continue to confront his government. Poniatowska's descriptions of Corona and the seamstresses capture their successful organizing and community building and their narratives of tragedy. De la Madrid's account recognizes their potential to disrupt his government, acknowledging not only their political power but also the force of their words as they testify about what happened to them. He sees their biggest danger in the fact that they have become a symbol of "tragedy and injustice." Poniatowska and de la Madrid also write about another powerful public figure who led a group of earthquake survivors and victims.

Cuauhtémoc Abarca

De la Madrid notes that the political ultraleft and the left were "trying to agitate," "supporting the needs of the earthquake victims," and "promoting the organization of those who sympathize with the earthquake victims."[76] The president expressed concern about leftist political leaders who were active in earthquake-victim organizations. The person he seemed most wary of was Cuauhtémoc Abarca, who, de la Madrid writes, directed the CUD. He notes, "He has a real base of people with valid demands," but he then dismisses Abarca because of his ties to opposition political parties (legal since 1978) and other leftist groups.

> The earthquake didn't change the rules of the political game, but it concentrated them into a short period of time. It also cost a great deal of wasted effort [un desgaste], a collective neurosis, and provoked a high level of political risk, which required that we establish a more flexible and open relationship with society. At the same time, we had to remain very alert to not allow a certain line of negotiation. For example, I could not permit Abarca to turn himself into the main leader of the earthquake survivors and from there contest the State. What I did was to engage with him at the same time that I took measures to undermine his basis of power.[77]

As with Corona, de la Madrid is recognizing the narrative power of Abarca as a public speaker and leader, hinting at Abarca's ability to build political community through his words and actions. He sees Abarca as so effective that he can threaten the power of the Mexican state. De la Madrid was not the only person who recognized Abarca's appeal to a critical public.

Poniatowska centers Abarca as one of several important narrators telling the Mexican public about the urgent needs of earthquake victims in the center of Mexico City. In *Nada, nadie* she first introduces Abarca as he is crying and pointing to the pit where the Nuevo León apartment building once stood. Two apartment complexes in Tlatelolco, the Unidad Habitacional Nonoalco-Tlatelolco and the Multifamiliares Juárez near Centro Médico, to the north of the historic center of Mexico City, suffered devastating damage in the earthquake. The Unidad Habitacional Nonoalco-Tlatelolco complex covered an area of two square kilometers and included 102 buildings as well as medical centers, schools, and hundreds of small businesses. About eighty thousand people lived there. Within this complex, two of three modules of the thirteen-story Nuevo León building completely collapsed in the earthquake. The other was severely damaged. At least three hundred bodies (other estimates say five hundred) were pulled from the ruins and many others were injured. In 1986 the Nuevo León building complex and others were demolished because of extensive earthquake damage.

Originally an island in Lake Texcoco, Tlatelolco was a city-state that had been incorporated into the Mexica empire centered in Tenochtitlán by the time the Spaniards arrived in 1519. Famous as a market, the site was later a huge rail yard for Ferrocarriles Nacionales de México. The Nonoalco-Tlatelolco apartment complex was built during the administration of Adolfo López Mateos, between 1960 and 1965. It was the largest apartment complex in Mexico and was created as a new model for urban development that emerged at the end of the 1950s—building neighborhoods vertically and making them all-inclusive, so that people would not have to leave to go to work, to shop, to play, or to attend school. The Plaza de las Tres Culturas where the Nuevo León was located contains a major Mexican archaeological site, the Church of Santiago de Tlatelolco, and the Nonoalco-Tlatelolco complex.

Against this backdrop of thousands of years of historic significance and the vivid memory of the 1968 massacre, this site, where hundreds of bodies were pulled from the ruins of the Nuevo León buildings in Tlatelolco in 1985, resonated strongly with the residents of the neighborhood. Abarca was a doctor who had been trained at UNAM. At the time of the earthquake, he was working as an academic administrator at the Instituto de Seguridad y Servicios Sociales de los Trabajadores del Estado (State Workers Social Security Institute).[78] On September 19, Abarca was warming up to go running with friends in preparation for the second Mexico City marathon. When the earthquake hit, he was standing outside between the Nuevo León building and another building, the Yucatán.

He recalled with Poniatowska as they stood in front of the Nuevo León: "This is full of memories, and I am saving them there, all of them. At the same time that I have witnessed the people's willingness to help, I have also seen the sad and lamentable ineptitude of the authorities."[79] With Poniatowska, Abarca made no bones about his dissatisfaction with the Mexican government. He also went into great detail about how international rescuers instructed him and others on how to rescue twenty-three people. He shared several accounts of rescue, including a boy with Down syndrome; a man who was pulled out but wanted to go back in to rescue his TV; a woman who would not come out until she put on lipstick; and two women, one forty-five, the other seventy, who each insisted the other be taken out first.[80]

Abarca and others who lived in or near the Nuevo León were not surprised that the buildings had collapsed. The Frente de Vecinos (Neighbors' Front) of Tlatelolco had complained in 1981 and 1983 about structural damage to the buildings. The contractor, Diseño Racional A.C., inspected the Nuevo León buildings and found that "the foundations were softened by constant water filtration . . . and the northern and central modules were in contact with each other."[81] This, explained Abarca in an interview in 2015, is why the buildings knocked against another and fell: "Six thousand tons against six thousand tons, there is no structure that can support that."[82]

While the dead were still being pulled out of the Nuevo León complexes in 1985, other people were very afraid that their buildings would collapse. Many rumors circulated. Abarca reported to Poniatowska in 1985:

We had to struggle fiercely against the rumors. All the people of Tlatelolco were waiting to see their building come down. . . . The news went from mouth to mouth, provoking sheer terror.

A man named Pacheco Alvarez, the investigator for SEDUE [Secretaría de Desarrollo Urbano y Ecología (Secretariat of Urban Development and Ecology)] here, . . . on the day that the people of the Nuevo León met with him for the first time, said at the public meeting, "Well, I'll be very happy to listen to your demands, but let me tell you, my specialty as an engineer is in load capacity, and I am afraid that there are so many of us in this office that the floor could cave in."

The residents of the Nuevo León stampeded out.[83]

When Poniatowska asked Abarca in the fall of 1985 if he thought that public officials were moved by the suffering of citizens, he responded, "No, man, of course they aren't. They are a bunch of cretins who were never able to listen to the way the residents articulated their problems. Now their biggest worry is how they will shield themselves from responsibility."[84]

Here Abarca suggests that the administration of de la Madrid is worried not about the pain and suffering of the victims and survivors of the earthquake but only about their own political survival. He more or less confirms what de la Madrid wrote almost twenty years after the event in his autobiography when he expressed deep concern that Abarca would be able to effectively confront his government. Abarca clearly understands the importance and power of articulating people's suffering in public, as does Poniatowska in her question.

After two days of meetings on September 22–23, Abarca and others formed the Coordinadora de Residentes de Tlatelolco. On October 24, after Abarca and leaders of other neighborhood-based organizations met with President de la Madrid to air their grievances, they formed the CUD, which, according to Abarca, eventually had forty-two neighborhood and earthquake victims' organizations affiliated with it.[85] On October 26, 1985, the CUD sent its demands to President de la Madrid regarding housing, infrastructure, social services, health, and employment; it also required that its organizations be respected and included in the reconstruction processes.[86] The letter concluded: "We believe, like you, that the participation of civil society is essential to the practices of a good government and to one that is capable of effective moral renewal, directed by criteria of social justice toward a more equal society. Therefore, we have no doubt that our petition will receive a favorable response and we will no longer encounter delays, coercion, or being ignored by the other levels of government."[87]

In an extended section about the CUD in *Nada, nadie*, Poniatowska describes the struggles Abarca, Lilia Mercado, and others went through in trying to get several government offices to listen to them. They also struggled to get reconstruction going and to help residents resist displacement and the privatization of their buildings.[88] They all experienced a lot of disrespect from government officials. "I believe," said Abarca, "that meeting the needs of the victims constitutes an elementary obligation for the President."[89] He described going from the Head of the Department of the Federal District to the Secretary of Labor and Social Protection, and then to the head of the Fondo Nacional de Habitaciones Populares (National Fund for Low Income Housing), who blocked a project to rebuild the Nuevo León building foundations. One of the CUD's demands called for the punishment of those who were liable for the Nuevo León's substandard construction. When Abarca tried to bring up this idea for liability in a public meeting, Gabino Fraga dismissed it. Fraga represented the government and was there along with representatives of the Instituto de Seguridad y Servicios Sociales de los Trabajadores del Estado, banks, and the Instituto del Fondo Nacional para la Vivienda de los Trabajadores (National Workers Housing Institute).

I told him, "First of all, we must establish who is responsible . . ."

Fraga retorted, "I want to leave that for later, because first of all I want to express my condolences [from] the Sr. Presidente, who has been deeply affected by what happened to you."

That was a detonator. The audience was furious. The public rose to its feet and a Tlatelolcan dared to say, "The only thing I want is for the SEP [Secretaría de Educación Pública (Department of Education)] to return the school certificates of my children. That's the only memory I'll have of them, because they died buried in the Nuevo León."

That's all the people needed. On their feet they began to shout, "Justice, assassins!"[90]

Someone then shouted "Beristáin," the name of an official, blaming him and another official for the Nuevo León tragedy. Beristáin had infamously stated that the Nuevo León was one of the safest buildings in Mexico. People were incensed, and one shouted that they would kill Beristáin if they could find him.[91] Fraga ended the meeting and left. Guillermo Carillo Arena, head of the Secretaría de Desarrollo Urbano y Ecología, was visibly enraged, according to Abarca. Poniatowska writes that Carillo Arena told those assembled:

"You are a bunch of professional agitators who have no business pressuring the President of the Republic. You are bad citizens with no moral conscience because you don't realize what kind of crises the country is in, and you simply want to be against the government." . . .

[Abarca responded:] "We are not intimidated, only small-minded people are afraid of a swine like that. Not us. In Mexico, anyone who stands up for his or her rights is called an agitator, a traitor to the homeland—or worse, a traitor in the service of a foreign power. . . . But I'll tell you who is a traitor. A traitor is the one who, while having the full power of an elected government and every opportunity to govern, doesn't lead in favor of the country and the Mexican people."[92]

Carillo Arena was later fired, and Manuel Camacho Solís, under the tutelage of future president Carlos Salinas de Gortari, became the new head of the Secretaría de Desarrollo Urbano y Ecología. Eager to build positive relations with earthquake victims as a possible future political base, Camacho Solís signed a Democratic Reconstruction Plan with the CUD and other groups. According to journalists Julia Preston and Sam Dillon, he listened to their petitions, incorporated many of their demands into his plans, and constructed "almost 50,000 dwellings for the homeless in one year."[93]

Abarca continued to work for the neighborhood of Tlatelolco. He went on to found a children's organization, and he traveled around the world to help victims of other earthquakes and catastrophes. He went to Haiti after a devastating earthquake in 2010 killed more than 230,000 people. Abarca told Poniatowska in a 2015 interview: "In Haiti I should have about 2,000 kids and teenagers who call me papa. There I was able to put on workshops for widows, orphans, and amputees so that they could put their lives back together. I have learned on these trips that we all suffer and we all laugh in the same language. . . . I believe that because of what we have lived through in Mexico and other countries, that the solidarity of the people is a balm [bálsamo] for the soul. I think that our worst enemy is forgetfulness (forgetting history)."[94]

Thirty years after the earthquake, Corona and Abarca were still important public figures in marking the anniversary of the earthquake in 2015. Corona went on to be elected to the Mexican legislature as a representative of the PRD and served as secretary of the environment of Mexico City from 2006 to 2012. In 2007 she published her own testimony, *Contar las cosas como fueron*—her version of the truth about the earthquake. Corona's book, Poniatowska wrote, "results in a freshness, a moving frankness, because Doña Eva (as she is called by her compañeras) reveals her intimate self without hiding anything, and she hands us everything so that we can drink it like a glass of pure water. . . . She doesn't paint herself as a victim or a martyr, she naturally tells of her life experiences and the changes in her life."[95] Poniatowska's description of the prose and tone of the book reinforces her original descriptions of Corona as fresh, pure, and natural—building an almost virginal picture of Corona while also validating her experiences and descriptions, which have, like those recorded by Poniatowska, become part of the national historical archive of the earthquake.

Abarca and Corona were two of the most compelling figures captured in *Nada, nadie*. Their testimonies detailed the powerful political, personal, and emotional networks and organizing that burst out of the tragedy of the earthquake. Poniatowska's use of extensive testimonies from them signaled the importance of the organizations they headed and their power to confront the state. De la Madrid's attention to both figures and the movements they represented also acknowledges the effectiveness of their public testimonies and leadership to motivate thousands of Mexicans to take to the streets and to confront the state in 1985. Their words and those of others Poniatowska captured in 1985 circulated not just in the press at the time but far and wide through many channels, and had a long afterlife.

Strategic Emotional Political Community during and after the Earthquake

Testimonials narrate history one experience at a time, but when dozens of testimonies are collected and shared and reproduced time and time again, they acquire a cumulative narrative power. Consider the words of Juana de la Rosa Osorno shortly after the earthquake.

> Seated on the sidewalk of Lorenzo Boturini Street is Juana de la Rosa Osorno, fifty-five, who works for Dimension Weld employed by Elías Serur:
> Now with this disaster, she says, putting her hands under her green and white checkered apron, we're here in the street waiting for people's charity to be able to eat. The boss is not a bad person; he's just fickle. He offers one thing, then another; he changes his mind; we can never come to an agreement. He first yelled at us, 'The machinery is yours with my compliments. I've lost it all, my life is buried here.'"
> His life is not buried there; if any lives are buried, it's those of the compañeras. The boss came running when he heard that the building had fallen down. . . . And the dead were here, bleeding among concrete and steel mesh. Elías did not suffer a scratch. So why would he say that his life had been buried here?[96]

According to activists at the Museo de la Ciudad on July 28, 2015, those words uttered into a tape recorder in October 1985 in the Mexico City neighborhood of San Antonio Abad appeared in print in the newspaper

La Jornada. The paper was photocopied and transported to Monterrey, Guadalajara, and other cities by activists who worked with the CUD. People in these cities read the newspaper aloud to their families, and they made more copies.

In 1988 the words appeared on pages 145–46 of *Nada, nadie.* In 1995 they were published on page 143 of *Nothing, Nobody,* the English translation. In September 2015, words from the same testimony were placed on the wall of the Museo de la Ciudad as part of an exhibit titled *19/09 1985 7:19: A 30 años del sismo* (September 19, 1985 7:19: 30 years after the earthquake) (figure 3.3). On October 11, 2015, I walked through the exhibit and listened to a fifteen-year-old girl marvel to her mother, "How could they leave so many people buried in those buildings? Could this happen now?" She stood in front of Juana de la Rosa Osorno's words and a series of photographs showing the utter destruction of the sweatshops where thousands of garment workers labored and hundreds died.

She was connected to the words uttered by Osorno in 1985, recorded by Poniatowska, and then published and spread by others. Through the emotional bond forged on the page, this testimony and others in *Nada, nadie* connected readers through time, loosely linking them together into the strategic emotional political community forged in and through the crónica. While carried in different moments in time and with different degrees of emotional and political engagement, we can see a thread of continuity between different readers and museumgoers. The memory building that *Nada, nadie* has performed through time and repetition is part of a strategic left emotional political community that Poniatowska and others have nourished for decades and that serves as a beacon for opposition politics, both formal and informal. Next I provide another example of how this memory making and connection through time work.

The fifteen-year-old museumgoer I observed related to the words and experience that Osorno articulated in 1985, long before the girl was born. Poniatowska's account of the earthquake was only one of many in the museum exhibit. It was part of a larger, multivocal historical narrative about the earthquake that included photographs, videos, newspaper accounts, radio and television coverage, and testimonies. The museum exhibit, with all its content connected directly to *Nada, nadie* and the people represented there, added a contemporary level to the emotional strategic political community the book built while it was being created and afterward. Ponia-

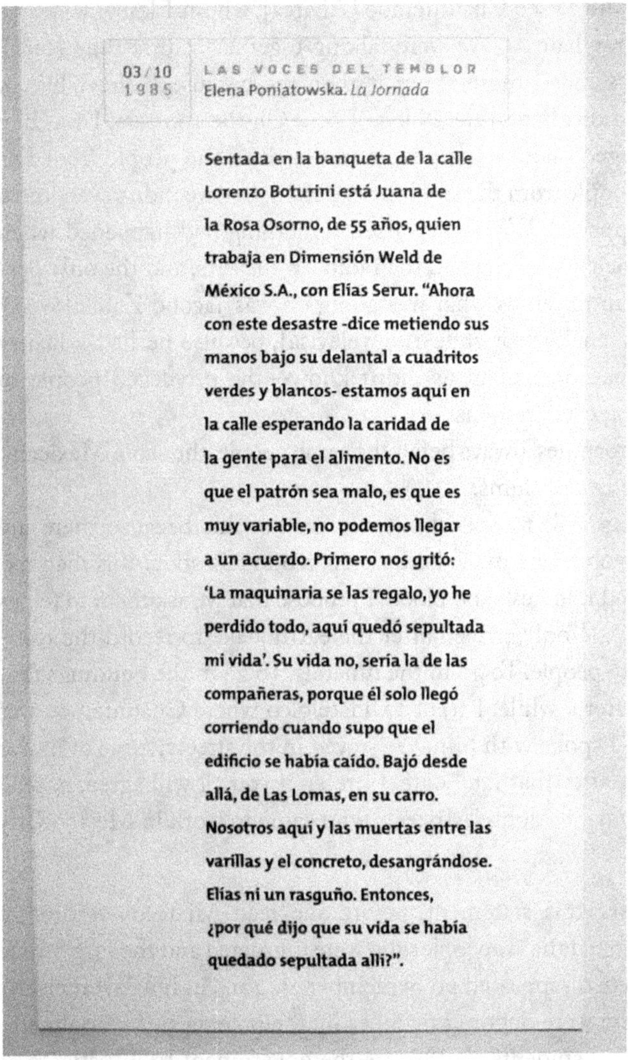

LAS VOCES DEL TEMBLOR
Elena Poniatowska. *La Jornada*

Sentada en la banqueta de la calle
Lorenzo Boturini está Juana de
la Rosa Osorno, de 55 años, quien
trabaja en Dimensión Weld de
México S.A., con Elías Serur. "Ahora
con este desastre -dice metiendo sus
manos bajo su delantal a cuadritos
verdes y blancos- estamos aquí en
la calle esperando la caridad de
la gente para el alimento. No es
que el patrón sea malo, es que es
muy variable, no podemos llegar
a un acuerdo. Primero nos gritó:
'La maquinaria se las regalo, yo he
perdido todo, aquí quedó sepultada
mi vida'. Su vida no, sería la de las
compañeras, porque él solo llegó
corriendo cuando supo que el
edificio se había caído. Bajó desde
allá, de Las Lomas, en su carro.
Nosotros aquí y las muertas entre las
varillas y el concreto, desangrándose.
Elías ni un rasguño. Entonces,
¿por qué dijo que su vida se había
quedado sepultada allí?".

Figure 3.3 Juana de la Rosa Osorno quote from Poniatowska's crónica *Nada, nadie* featured in the exhibit *19/09 1985 7:19: A 30 años del sismo* (September 19, 1985 7:19: 30 years after the earthquake), Museo de la Ciudad, Mexico City, October 2015. Photograph by author.

towska's talk at the Museo de la Ciudad that I described at the beginning of this chapter brought some of the members of that original community together, including at least half a dozen people whose testimonies appear in the book.

That day at the museum, the audience of about 150 people was sitting in a large circle on an open patio on black metal folding chairs with white plastic seats. The event was well underway. Poniatowska read two testimonies from her 1988 book and said:

What a pleasure to see Cuauhtémoc [Abarca], whom I knew when he didn't have gray hair. . . . We were talking together in that time [1985]. But he knows much more about it than me because I didn't live in Tlatelolco. I didn't live in the Nuevo León. On the contrary, I was one of the privileged ones. Some people in the city—the people from Las Lomas, the people from the south of the city . . . —we didn't even know what had happened. We only realized something had happened when we lost electricity. We only had the radios in the cars, and the only person who began to tell us what was going on was Jacobo Zabludowsky [longtime TV anchor for state-run Televisa], because he had a luxury radio in his car. So half of us didn't know—the privileged people to whom nothing ever happens.

Great misfortunes always befall the same people, the same Mexicans, the ones who live in slums.

Rather than talk to you about the earthquake, because there are many more people here much better prepared to talk about this than me, those who lived it in flesh and blood, I propose that we ask them to tell us their stories. . . . I only arrived after the earthquake to record the testimonials of the people. To go to the funerals. To go to the buildings that had fallen. After a while, I went to Tlatelolco where Cuauhtémoc was working, and I spoke with him. We stayed in the streets, some of us, for three months after that fatal date. I prefer, if you all will agree, to read you a testimony of Alonso Mixteco, who came to work in Mexico City from Guerrero.[97]

Immediately after this statement, before she read Mixteco's testimony, Poniatowska invoked the six people who were murdered and the forty-three students who were disappeared on September 26, 2014, in Iguala, Guerrero. At the time, there were ongoing marches by the parents and schoolmates of the disappeared students to pressure the government to investigate as well as widespread protest art about the disappearances. The students were from a teacher education college in Ayotzinapa, Guerrero. Poniatowska continued, "We all are wearing Ayotzinapa, Guerrero, like a brand that has been burned onto us with a hot iron." Connecting the experience of Alonso Mixteco in 1985 with the tragedy of the students who disappeared in 2014, Poniatowska built another layer of memory among the 150 people gathered at the museum.

The second testimony she read was of a university student who worked at the Parque del Seguro Social: "Now Parque Delta is a giant store, like Liverpool or Palacio de Hierro. . . . He tells about how he went to that park to fumigate bodies. . . . It was a stadium where all the seats were empty and people in the center of the arena were dead." After she read the second testimony, she concluded, "I hope that by reading these words to all of you, it will provide an understanding of the depth of terrible pain people experienced by the deaths of so many caused by the earthquake."

About forty minutes into the event, a bald man in his fifties, wearing fashionable dark-framed glasses and a suit and tie, raised his hand. He was clutching a yellowed copy of the *La Jornada* newspaper. The following example suggests how the process Poniatowska went through of collecting and publishing testimonies in 1985 built emotional strategic political community through time. In this case, the person speaking was the brother of a young man who died in the earthquake. He read Poniatowska's articles in *La Jornada* following the quake featuring the testimonies of family members of victims and survivors. He was so moved at the time that he called Poniatowska and asked her to record his testimony about his younger brother. She did and it was published. After this, he went on to do his own writing. During the conversation at the museum in 2015, he rose to speak to Poniatowska about how her recording of his testimony in 1985 inspired him to share his own longer testimony as a book that he now hopes to share with those assembled and the larger strategic emotional political community connected to her work. He stood, and then took the microphone to address the crowd.

> My name is Andrés. . . . Reading the testimonies that Elena Poniatowska recorded has fascinated me. On the nineteenth of September, something very difficult happened to me. On this day, my brother died in the collapse of building number 156 in Colonia Roma in Chihuahua. But thanks to God, I didn't feel as bad as I could have. I wanted to share my testimony by telephone. I contacted Señora Elena and she made an appointment for me to come to her house. It was thirty years ago, and I still had hair. I went to her house there in Chimalistac. I was very wound up and very nervous. I was feeling really bad, really bad, because I had lost my younger brother, who was like a son to me. He was twenty-six years old and I was thirty-three.
>
> Elena interviewed me, and to my surprise, two months after the earthquake happened, on November 28, La Señora Elena Poniatowska published my testimony.[98]

Andrés stopped there, holding up a copy of the *La Jornada* newspaper from November 28, 1985, and the crowd broke out in wild applause (figure 3.4). Andrés continued:

> This testimony impacted me in a big way. It motivated me to carry out further investigation, to study, and to take on another life. In 1989 I went to visit Señora Elena with my wife; on January 6, 1989, she gave us a copy of her book *Nada, nadie: Las voces del temblor*, which included my testimony on pages 246, 247, and 248.
>
> After this, I was motivated to do much more. I started attending workshops, working on my writing. All of this allowed me, although I am not a writer, to produce a book. . . . I know that you [addressing Elena] are a great writer, but thanks to God here is my book. I am going to write about this in an open letter to *La Jornada* this Sunday. I have the printed version for you here on a USB.
>
> And I tell you. I am an architect, not a writer, but I am a writing apprentice. The fact that you took my testimony and published it had a very big impact on me. On the basis of that published testimony, I have written my own book, called *Thirty Years after the Earthquake: The Workday of the Wolf, a Spiritual Awakening)*. Thank you.

Andrés's original testimony in *La Jornada* and in *Nada, nadie* was "El Lobo Would Never Get Mad: Those who want to cooperate, please plant a flower." Andrés's brother, Alejandro Escoto, died in a poorly constructed school, the University of Chapultepec, in Colonia Roma. Alejandro was buried "with other students, who like him studied tourism." Speaking about his brother, Andrés stated in his 1985 testimony, "I'm not going to place a tombstone or a memorial there. I am going to have a little garden, and whoever wants to cooperate can plant a flower. I don't know where Alejandro is, but I feel that I may be a little better as a person because I reflect something of my brother."[99] As Andrés spoke in the Museo de la Ciudad to some of the primary political actors and survivors at the time of the 1985 earthquake, the press took his picture and some (including me) recorded his words. His image, along with other pictures from that day, is on Facebook. By being there, he has participated in creating another layer of social memory regarding the 1985 earthquake that's linked to Poniatowska's account of that event. He also participated in continuing the memory making and historical strategic emotional political community tied to *Nada, nadie* that day through a face-to-face conversation in the museum. In the same space, a short time later, the exhibit featuring

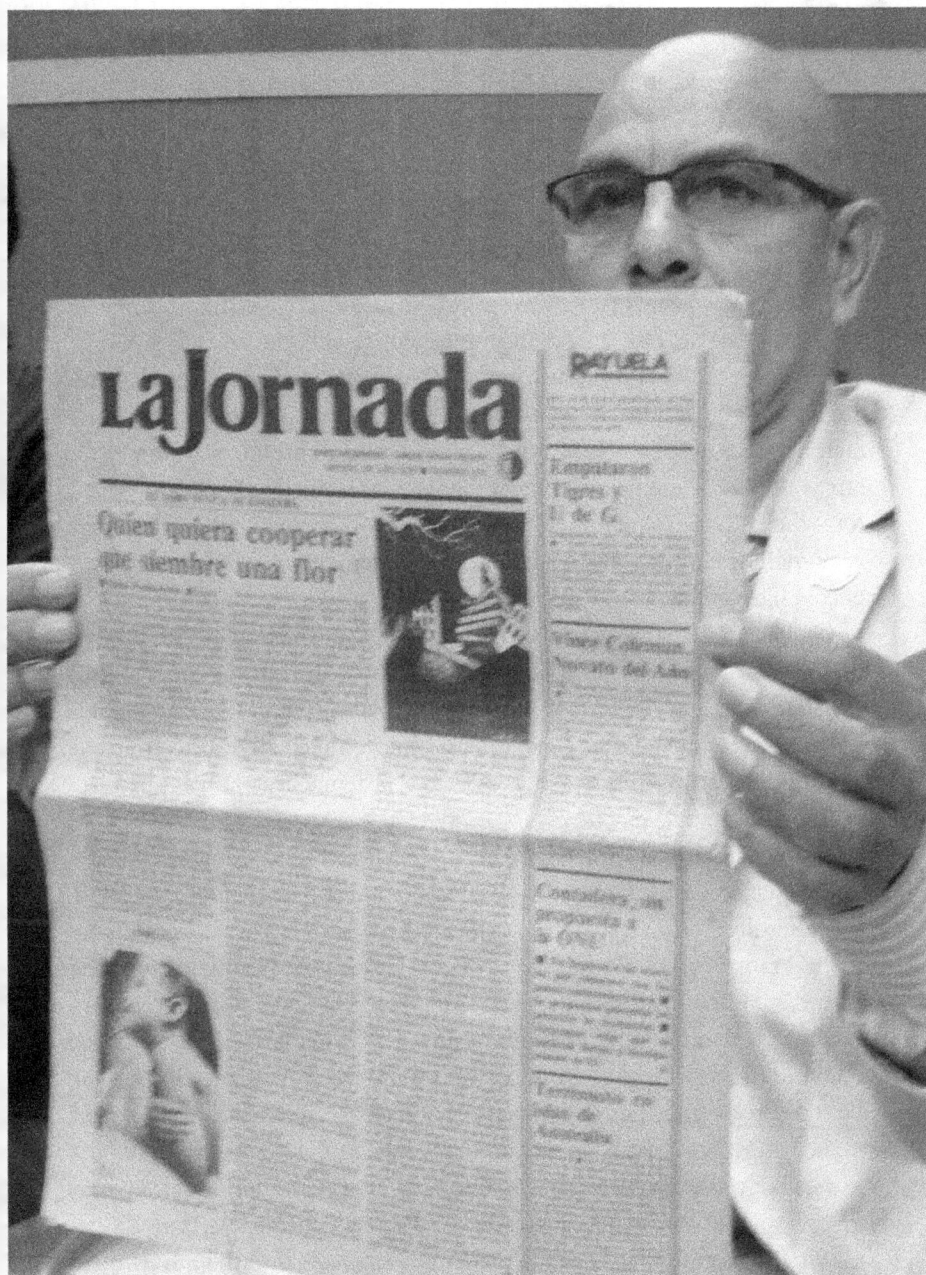

Figure 3.4 Andrés with the 1985 *La Jornada* article written about his brother by Elena Poniatowska, in discussion with her at Museo de la Ciudad, October 2015. Photograph by author.

pictures, testimonies in print—including quotations from *Nada, nadie* and many other sources—in video, and in art, continued telling the story of the earthquake in Mexico City, most likely influencing to some degree the thousands of people who saw it and their shifting ideas about the story of the 1985 earthquake.

From Physical to Political Earthquake

The earthquake spawned a wave of urban social activism that ultimately helped transform city governance and, along with the consolidation of left-wing political parties, affected national elections. In the 1988 presidential elections, opposition candidate Cuauhtémoc Cárdenas, a former member of the PRI and a son of Lázaro Cárdenas, president in the 1930s, ran as the candidate for the Frente Democrático Nacional. The PRI defectors who had been expelled from the PRI and other small left-wing groups were members of this party. Many social movements in Mexico City supported his candidacy.

On the day of the elections in July 1988, the government announced that the computer system used to count votes had shut down—"se cayó el sistema." When the system was restored, Carlos Salinas de Gortari was declared the winner. Later, Salinas de Gortari ordered all records from the election be destroyed. The saying "se cayó el sistema" became a euphemism for electoral fraud.

In his autobiography, former president Miguel de la Madrid provides the best evidence to date that the elections were rigged in favor of the PRI. Early results from Mexico City indicated that the PRI was losing badly. De la Madrid writes, "I felt like a bucket of ice water had been dumped on me, . . . I became afraid that the results were similar across the country and that the PRI would lose the presidency."[100] De la Madrid described becoming increasingly nervous as the results came in suggesting defeat. He then received a phone call from the head of the PRI. He and others told de la Madrid that he had to announce the PRI's victory—even though it was likely a lie. He was told by the head of the PRI and other advisers that the public was demanding to know the results of the election. Rather than tell the truth, de la Madrid's account suggests that the government lied and said that the computer system was broken. De la Madrid recounts what the PRI leader told him: "You must proclaim the triumph of the PRI. It is a tradition that we cannot break without causing great alarm among the citizens."[101] Cárdenas was preparing to declare himself the winner.

De la Madrid decided to preempt him and ordered the president of the PRI to declare Salinas de Gortari the winner—without any official vote count. "The electoral upset was a political earthquake for us," de la Madrid wrote. "As in any emergency, we had to act because the problems were rising fast. There was no time for great meditation, we needed to be agile in our response to consolidate the triumph of the PRI."[102]

Cuauhtémoc Cárdenas did not send his supporters out into the streets to protest the results. When I asked Poniatowska about this, she said, "Cárdenas, who I have always admired, didn't want to send the people into the street to start a revolution. He didn't think that it was the right moment to do that."[103] Cárdenas's political movement—broadly supported by urban activism that grew in power after the earthquake—did, however, spawn a political temblor in Mexico City. It transformed Mexico City's governance from the mid-1990s to the present, consolidating a leftist city government.

In 1996 a new government post was created, the *jefe de gobierno* (head of government) for the federal district of Mexico City. This post was a bit like a city mayor and a governor. Given the federal district's dense population and high number of voters, it has become and continues to be a crucial base of political power. Cárdenas was elected to the post in July 1997 with 47.7 percent of the popular vote. He resigned in 1999 to run for president. The PRD held this post until 2018, when Claudia Sheinbaum from the Movimiento Regeneración Nacional (MORENA, National Regeneration Movement) won it.

Poniatowska's ongoing relationships with some of the key actors who emerged from the tragic 1985 earthquake such as Corona and Abarca and the continued connection that Andrés felt to her through a thirty-year period based on the testimony he provided to her about his brother suggest the durability of the strategic emotional political community Poniatowska forged with others while recording and publishing the testimonies that became *Nada, nadie*. The book's continued publication in new editions and the reproduction of the testimonies in exhibits, anniversary publications, and through Poniatowska's public performances and speeches have extended the original community she created. Like *La noche de Tlatelolco*, *Nada, nadie* has a multigenerational community of readers. Annual memorials of the earthquake and Poniatowska's interviews every year close to the anniversary are part of the activities that keep this devastating event alive in Mexican history and memory.

Poniatowska's embrace of activism while documenting the quake and her continued public engagement with some of the key urban social movement activists who emerged in 1985 had become an integral part of how she worked as a writer. In the 1990s, her strategy of simultaneously building personal relationships and political community with those whose stories she narrated continued in her public engagement and endorsement of an exciting new Indigenous social movement, the Ejército Zapatista de Liberación Nacional. The EZLN emerged publicly during the last year of the presidency of Carlos Salinas de Gortari (1988–94).

4

Engaging with
the EZLN as a Writer
and Public Intellectual

At the end of this century, global trade and freer trade is
the way to improve the standard of living of our populations. That is why we in Mexico have proposed to the
U.S. and to Canada a free trade agreement. That is the free
movement of goods and services among sovereign nations.
For Mexico, taking this step is a very important one....
NAFTA is a job-creating agreement by increasing
competition.... NAFTA is a wage-increasing agreement
because we are committed to increasing real wages in
Mexico, more than they have increased up to today, when
NAFTA is ratified. And NAFTA is a migration-reduction
agreement, because Mexicans will not have to migrate
north, looking for jobs in this country, but they will be able
to find them in my own, which is my main commitment.
—CARLOS SALINAS DE GORTARI, May 28, 1993

THE 1990S WERE MARKED BY the further consolidation of structural ad-
justments in Mexico, with a particular focus on the signing of the North
American Free Trade Agreement (NAFTA) after years of bargaining between Mexico and the United States. During Salinas de Gortari's presidency, Mexico had twenty-four billionaires and oversaw the privatization

of a wide range of former government services and enterprises that benefited economic elites. With its emphasis on privatization, investment, international markets, and global capital, NAFTA was supposed to be the gateway for Mexico to enter the "First World."

In the years of negotiations leading up to NAFTA, something different was going on in the southern part of Mexico, building on a history of regional Indigenous organizing supported by the Catholic Church, Maoists, and other leftist organizers. The Ejército Zapatista de Liberación Nacional (EZLN) was secretly organizing in Chiapas. On January 1, 1994, Mexico awakened to news of the armed rebellion of the EZLN, formed by Tzotzil, Tzeltal, Tojolabal, Ch'ol, and Mam Indigenous people from the central highlands of Chiapas and the Lacandón Jungle bordering Guatemala. The EZLN broadcast a political platform of work, land, housing, food, health, education, independence, liberty, democracy, justice, and peace in the names of the Mexican revolutionary heroes Emiliano Zapata and Pancho Villa. Proclaiming initially that they would march to Mexico City and calling for the overthrow of the "dictator" Salinas de Gortari, their presence was flashed around the world and in Mexico through foreign reporters who were already there to report on the initiation of NAFTA. The Zapatistas occupied five county seats. After thirty-six hours, the Mexican government responded with a military confrontation that resulted in between one hundred and four hundred casualties. Zapatista militants were detained, humiliated, and tortured in the wake of the military action. Twelve days into the confrontation and in response to significant national and international pressure, the government agreed to negotiations.[1]

The vision of the EZLN was built on a legacy of struggles for land, liberation from sharecropping and servitude, recognition of cultural and political rights of Indigenous peoples, and decades of exclusion from Mexico's political and economic systems. A growing population of Indigenous migrants who moved from elsewhere to the borderlands of Chiapas with Guatemala, the Indigenous communities that came to form the core support for the EZLN, were primarily composed of subsistence farmers who eked out a living on progressively smaller plots of land. As detailed by George Collier, the government's interventions in eastern Chiapas resulted in the state taking over the role of large landowners as the enemy. This was done by establishing biospheres as off-limits, rewarding people who were loyal to the PRI, changing the law to end agrarian reform, and cutting back on vital supports for farmers.[2]

From January to June 1994, when the Zapatistas rejected the government's thirty-four-point peace plan, and afterward when they mounted a large national and international gathering in the community of Guadalupe Tepeyac, the EZLN used diverse tactics to bring its message to public attention. Interacting with public intellectuals, writers, and journalists was one way it gained publicity and connection with a wider public. Subcomandante Marcos was the primary channel for the EZLN's engagement with writers, but he also quoted Latin American writers in his own prose.[3] Poniatowska's involvement with the Zapatistas was initially mediated through her interactions with Subcomandante Marcos and those close to him. Over time, however, her connection to the Zapatistas had less to do with Marcos and much more to do with the political perspectives of Zapatista women.

Poniatowska's relationship with the EZLN was mediated by gender and the power of words—both spoken and written. In this chapter, I discuss how she came to know and then shared the voices and ideas of the EZLN as part of a public dialogue. I document Poniatowska's relationship with the EZLN, focusing on her interactions with Subcomandante Marcos, her interest in collective Indigenous rights and autonomy, her engagement with what we might call an Indigenous feminism, and her incorporation of these ideas into her thinking, speaking, and writing as a public intellectual. In this effort, both in relation to the EZLN and earlier, she contributes to a more general trend of opening up the public sphere to popular voices and bringing testimonio to the fore. In her role as a writer and an activist with the Zapatistas, she contributed to the formation of strategic emotional political community between the EZLN and the larger Mexican public, following her model of engaging with survivors of the earthquake and urban social movement activists. She traveled to Chiapas, donated thousands of books to an EZLN library, published extensive interviews with members of the EZLN, participated in campaigns and rallies in support of the EZLN, and consistently talked about the EZLN in her public appearances in the 1990s and beyond. Her publicity of and detailed writing about the conditions that Indigenous peoples lived in and their political and social marginalization supported the EZLN's attempts to pressure the Mexican government to implement accords signed in 1996. These accords would have granted Mexico's Indigenous peoples significant protections of their territories and resources, control over their own economic development plans and funds dispersed from the central government, autonomy of governance, and the ability to federate with other communities and participate in national political affairs. Like *Nada, nadie*, the strategic aim of much of her writing about the Zapatistas was to politically influence the government to reform. Her public relationship with the Zapatistas forced her to sacrifice her own privileges of class, social and political stature, and relationship to her Catholic faith for the sake of her own evolving principles, including her evolving engagement with feminism and the issue of abortion.

While her previous crónicas focused on strong women protagonists and leaders such as Rosario Ibarra, Evangelina Corona, and Jesusa (the lead character in *Here's to You, Jesusa!*), her engagement with poor, Indigenous women as powerful political actors pushed her even further in confronting her own beliefs and positioning in Mexican society. They became some of the primary protagonists she used to build out strategic emotional political community for the EZLN with her interlocutors in public speeches, journalistic writing, and public dialogues. She had a particularly strong engagement with the Zapatista leader known as Comandanta Ramona, who stayed at her house before undergoing a kidney transplant. Many of Poniatowska's public speeches and newspaper stories written about the Zapatistas included a focus on women. In 2014, when she accepted the Miguel de Cervantes Prize, the highest honor in Spanish literature, she also highlighted the gains of Zapatista women.

The Mexican State and Indigenous Peoples

The Mexican state has had a complex and fraught relationship with Indigenous people. Benito Juárez (1858–72), Mexico's first and only Indigenous president of Zapotec origin, from San Pablo Guelatao, Oaxaca, fought foreign occupation and left a legacy of constitutional reforms to create a democratic republic. As described by historian Guy Thomson, under Juárez, "Mexico moved from being a 'Catholic nation,' in which many of the social and racial hierarchies and corporate privileges of colonial rule still held sway, to becoming a secular federal republic regulated by a liberal constitution based on the sovereignty of the people and equality before the law, reducing the legal immunities and special privileges of the army and the Catholic church and establishing a single system of civil law that guaranteed a wide range of freedoms and social rights."[4] The separation of church and state is a hallmark of Juárez's legacy. While Juárez and other liberals engaged in a sweeping project of religious and civil disentailment that abolished corporate and communal property in favor of individual private property ownership, not only did the Catholic Church lose significant land holdings but so did Indigenous peoples, through removal of protections of Indigenous corporate land holdings.

While he was in his second term of the governorship of Oaxaca, Juárez implemented laws to radically reorganize rural land tenure. In 1856 a sweeping law known as the Ley Lerdo abolished the property rights of all corporate organizations and endorsed the principles of economic individualism, advocating that only individuals should own property. Under Juárez, church lands were expropriated; many corporate and communal land holdings of rural and Indigenous communities were liquidated and made available for purchase; and bishops, priests, and nuns were disenfranchised. The legacy of this liberal economic period was that in Juárez's own state of Oaxaca, for example, 53 percent of Oaxaca's territory was privatized by 1910.[5] By that same time, in eastern Chiapas (where the EZLN was born), almost all Indigenous land had been privatized and as much as 50 percent of the rural workforce was made up of indebted, landless servants.[6] Without a land base for maintaining Indigenous rural economies or political representation, the freedoms and social rights guaranteed under the liberal constitution were not attainable for many Indigenous citizens of Mexico.

In the boom decade of the 1890s, European, U.S., and Mexican investors established plantations in tropical regions of Chiapas and bordering Guatemala to extract hardwoods and to grow coffee, sugar, and cacao. This set off a process of deterritorializing Indigenous communities that culminated before the Mexican Revolution and included the privatization of large tracts of land in the Lacandón Jungle. It wasn't until long after the Mexican Revolution, in the 1930s and 1940s, that landless Indigenous laborers who had been bound through debt servitude to plantations and ranches, along with others, began to colonize the jungle and then petitioned the government for title to the land as *ejidos*—land grants from the state that were held in shared social tenancy, with use rights, but not private ownership. It is on these ejidos in areas where people had migrated that the EZLN took hold. But petitioning for land was not the only contact that Indigenous peoples in Chiapas had with the state.

The Mexican state had attempted to assimilate and organize Indigenous communities for decades through the Instituto Nacional Indigenista (INI, National Indigenist Institute), which instituted some of its first programs in the state of Chiapas due to the extreme poverty and isolation of Indigenous communities in many parts of it. The goal of the INI, according to its founding director, anthropologist Alfonso Caso, was to "make these millions of Indigenous Mexicans feel like Mexicans; to integrate them" into the nation.[7] The INI's efforts to provide access to medical services and education no doubt helped some in Chiapas's Indigenous communities through increased rates of literacy and local training and development programs while at the same time consolidating the power of INI brokers as local and regional caciques.

Historian Stephen E. Lewis offers a nuanced and complex evaluation of the outcome of decades of INI policies on Indigenous communities in Chiapas, on the anthropologists and *indigenistas* (those who were advocates of *indigenismo*) who worked for the INI, and on the Mexican state. Of interest here is his reading of the long-term impact of the INI and its cultural centers on Indigenous communities in Chiapas. Lewis notes that "while the INI failed to lift entire communities and municipalities out of poverty and extreme poverty," it did teach INI promoters how to look out for themselves and increased stratification in Indigenous communities through fostering "a small indigenous bourgeoisie."[8] The INI also inspired thousands of Indigenous men and women to become cultural promoters, nurses, teachers, agronomists, and mechanics and "instructed the indigenous about their rights as Indigenous citizens."[9] As Jan Rus notes about Indigenous Tzotziles who were forced out of San Juan Chamula by some of the Indigenous caciques that the INI perhaps helped create, "How many others have fought so persistently, and at such costs against corporatism, the PRI, and Caciquismo as the thousands of Chamula expulsados?"[10] Rus suggests, as have others, the ways in which the INI contributed to the building of an Indigenous movement in unanticipated ways that would only became apparent later. Nevertheless, Lewis concludes that the INI as a national project engaged in "an often remarkable journey from utopian dreams and innovation to a period of stagnation and neglect followed by an undeniable trend towards bureaucratization and careerism" that ultimately did little for Indigenous communities and perhaps served to ease the guilty conscience of urban intellectuals and utopian thinkers.[11] Following the establishment of the INI project in Indigenous Chiapas in the 1950s, other outreach projects began.

With the arrival of Bishop Samuel Ruiz and Marist priests in Tzeltal and Tojolabal communities in the 1960s and 1970s, who trained thousands of catechists in themes of liberation, and activists who arrived from various strands of the left, Chiapas was ripe for the first Indigenous Congress of 1974. The Congress brought together 1,230 delegates and published a wide range of demands focused on land and labor rights, language and education, Indigenous systems of healing, and access to health care. Speakers discussed ethnic autonomy and political representation in the Mexican nation.[12] Following the Congress, grassroots organizing efforts took off, with regional peasant organizations coordinating ejidos to form larger organizations, such as the Unión de Ejidos de la Selva (Union of Ejidos of the Jungle) in 1983, which political scientist Neil Harvey has called "the most important organization prior to the EZLN."[13] In 1988, the Unión de Ejidos de la Selva joined with the Asociación Rural de Interés Colectivo (Rural Collective Interest Association) to form the Asociación Rural de Interés Colectivo–Unión de Uniones (Rural Collective Interest Association–Union of Unions), which became the de facto government in the region.

During this same period, a small but dedicated group of activists began to organize secretly in Indigenous communities, focusing on women and youth in health and literacy projects.[14] This group of activists was the nucleus of the EZLN. They slowly expanded their organizing into the other important ejido and peasant organizations in the region. When the price of coffee—a main cash crop for many communities—collapsed, many people who were affiliated with the Asociación Rural de Interés Colectivo began to participate in the EZLN and received armed training. In the early 1990s, the EZLN began to build safe houses and expand its presence through an organization known by 1992 as the Alianza Nacional Campesina Independiente Emiliano Zapata (Emiliano Zapata National Independent Peasant Alliance).

In his presidential inauguration speech on December 1, 1988, Carlos Salinas de Gortari outlined his goal to modernize Mexico. This vision of modernity and neoliberal policies provided the foil for the EZLN's vision of the world. Salinas de Gortari stated, "The modernization of Mexico is essential if we are to meet the demands of the 85 million Mexicans of today.... In brief, we need to modernize politics, the economy, and society. The modernization of Mexico is, moreover, an absolute imperative. This is the only way we will be able to affirm our sovereignty in a world undergoing profound transformation."[15] Salinas de Gortari's neoliberal policies of modernization, which built on those of de la Madrid, hit rural Mexicans particularly hard and had a strong effect on many Indigenous communities. For example, Salinas de Gortari eliminated guaranteed prices for agricultural products except for corn and beans, opened the Mexican market to foreign imported agricultural products, privatized the state-owned processing companies, and cut rural credit way back for subsistence and small-scale farmers. Furthermore, a counteragrarian reform to Article 27 of the Mexican Constitution ended land redistribution. Purchasing power declined for many Mexicans under Salinas de Gortari's presidency, and 71 percent of the rural Indigenous population was considered malnourished in 1989.[16]

The end of land redistribution—first mandated after the Mexican Revolution in the 1917 Constitution and responsible for the redistribution of seventy million hectares from large estates to landless peasant beneficiaries, including in Chiapas—was devastating to people who were expecting more land. While some Indigenous communities in the Lacandón Jungle received land in the original redistribution, the increase in populations in ejidos through the 1960s, 1970s, and 1980s produced new land shortages, thus many ejidos were petitioning for the expansion of their lands.[17] When this was ruled to be no longer possible and existing ejidos were encouraged to privatize, more people were motivated to join the EZLN. The reformation of Article 27 had slammed the door on their future, and they were looking for another way out.

The Alianza Nacional Campesina Independiente Emiliano Zapata soon organized several large-scale protests against the Article 27 reform and the impending NAFTA agreement. At the end of 1992, communities working with the social organization of the EZLN voted in assemblies to give the EZLN military wing one year to prepare for war. The emergence of the Zapatistas on January 1, 1994, was in response to this vote. Upstaging the announcement of NAFTA with a takeover of towns and cities in the state of Chiapas—including Ocosingo, Las Margaritas, Huixtán, Oxchuc, Rancho Nuevo, Altamirano, and Chanal—armed Mayan insurgents of the EZLN shouted "BASTA!" (Enough!). They brought "the other Mexico" center stage, stating, "We have nothing, absolutely nothing, not even a decent roof over our heads, no land, no work, no health care, no food, no education."[18]

Strategic Communication

After they burst onto the international scene through the press, the Zapatistas began disseminating regular communiqués about issues they wanted to bring to the public and messages they wanted to communicate to the government. The Zapatistas skillfully harnessed what was initially fairly rudimentary technology—a laptop and printer hooked up to a car battery—to disseminate their communiqués. Printed and signed copies of communiqués were delivered to *El Tiempo* newspaper in San Cristóbal de las Casas and from there faxed to *La Jornada*, which dutifully published all the communiqués sent to them. Though EZLN leader Subcomandante Marcos wrote the majority of the communiqués, he insisted that he did so in the name of the EZLN. Poniatowska and other Mexican public intellectuals immediately began to engage with Subcomandante Marcos and the Zapatistas on the pages of *La Jornada*. Poniatowska stressed the importance of the press in serving as an outlet for broadcasting Zapatista voices and ideas: "*La Jornada* was essential for Marcos and the Zapatistas . . . because everything that Marcos said or did was published and praised. No one received such attention and praise, and a great deal of respect."[19]

A retinue of writers began to cover the EZLN, with reporters from the *New York Times* and *La Jornada* maintaining a regular presence in Zapatista territory to report on their activities. *La Jornada* reporters such as Blanche Petrich and Elio Henríquez provided daily coverage. Petrich and Henríquez were granted the first interview with the Comité Clandestino Revolucionario Indígena-Comandancia General (Clandestine Revolutionary Indigenous Committee of the General Command) of the EZLN (the military branch of the EZLN) in early February 1995.[20] Hermann Bellinghausen also reported for years from Zapatista territory and lived under the same conditions as the Zapatistas. He was the director of the monthly supplement *Ojarasco*, which covered literature, art, and Indigenous struggles.[21] Poniatowska also began reporting on the EZLN and became an ardent public supporter of the group early on.

Poniatowska's engagement with the Zapatistas, and specifically with Subcomandante Marcos, initially took place in print. It was a relationship of reading and writing at first. One of the ways that Marcos courted public intellectuals was by identifying the importance of their work for him. In a collective interview with reporters from *Proceso*, *El Financiero*, and the *New York Times*, Marcos referenced the books he consulted and carried around with him in the mountains. According to the interview published in *Proceso*, Marcos "says he had a lot [of books]. A good reader. Monsiváis. Poniatowska's *La Noche de Tlatelolco*. Everything from Cortázar, Fuentes, Vargas Llosa 'when he was still palatable' and García Márquez, 'who's another story, that is, special.'"[22] Poniatowska is one of very few women writers or intellectuals Marcos named as influential, and by mentioning *La noche*, he signaled not only the impact of the book on his own political formation and thinking but also his interest in her, and perhaps an identification with the hybridity of her writing.

Like Poniatowska, Marcos published in a variety of genres, including what he called "communiqués," that is, letters, essays, and stories as told through the characters of Durito and Viejo Antonio.[23] Marcos was a chronicler and testimonial writer, acting as the voice of the multiethnic Mayan EZLN leadership—a role that Poniatowska had taken on through her earlier crónicas about the student movement and massacre, the plight of the disappeared and political prisoners, and earthquake survivors. As Cynthia Steele argues in an analysis of Marcos's communiques, "He acts as a combination of scribe and cultural interpreter, lending the EZLN his university education and pedagogical experience along with his native command of Spanish and knowledge of Mexican urban culture."[24] In describing Marcos's playful communiqué postscripts, where the "Sub" engaged his readers in public dialogue, Steele highlights the mixed-genre characteristics of his prose, incorporating fiction and nonfiction. Steele finds the hybridity of fiction and nonfiction in the postscripts of Marcos's communiqués to be particularly important: "In these postscripts—in which, in postmodern fashion the 'afterward' playfully subsumes the main message—he combines political analysis with stories of the material hardships and human rewards of camp life in which he plays the role of fond but beleaguered uncle to the Zapatista children; creation myths and didactic fables from el Viejo Antonio, the elderly peasant who allegedly served as his initiator to Mayan culture; and tales of his misadventures as a bumbling squire to the rainforest beetle Don Durito de la Lacandona—that is, Sancho Panza to a subaltern Don Quixote."[25] In his experimentation with form and slippage between fiction and nonfiction, his style approaches some of the key elements of the crónicas of Poniatowska, Monsiváis, and others.[26]

Like many readers, Poniatowska followed Marcos through his communiqués that *La Jornada* published. She came to admire the literary acumen in his writing and in some of his speeches. Reading his communiqués and interviewing him and other Zapatistas was a way to communicate with him, and to a larger public for the EZLN that she and others at *La Jornada* were helping build. Probably her two most widely read pieces were an interview she conducted with Marcos in July 1994 and her coverage of the Convención Nacional Democrático (CND, National Democratic Convention) held by the EZLN in August 1994.[27] Ediciones Era published the first eight months of Zapatista communiqués in an edited volume together with crónicas from Poniatowska and Monsiváis and photographs of the Zapatistas taken by Poniatowska's daughter, Paula Haro.[28] By publishing in the same book with the EZLN, Poniatowska took an obvious public stance in solidarity with the Zapatistas.

Poniatowska credits the significant effect Marcos had inside and outside Mexico partly on his skillful, accessible writing and use of stories to connect with readers, a strategy she employs herself. In a conversation we had in 2011, she explained:

> This happened in part through the literary language of Marcos that we saw reflected in the character of Durito. He is a character who has been translated into English and has had an enormous effect, not only in Mexico. Marcos knew how to write in a language that everyone could understand and so that everyone identified with him. I know a lot of people who eagerly waited for Marcos's communiqués to be published in La Jornada—they couldn't wait to read them. They were very strongly affected by his writing.
>
> I myself have a lot of plastic supermarket bags upstairs, here in my house, that are full of clippings about the Zapatista movement from La Jornada and other newspapers. . . . I was incredibly enthusiastic about the EZLN. My mother was also very enthusiastic about the Zapatista movement, in spite of some of her other fears. . . . She read newspapers and was a wonderful and very intelligent collaborator who supported the EZLN. . . . She read [the communiqués] every afternoon and every night.[29]

Poniatowska's mother was captivated by what she saw on television and in the papers, and by what her daughter told her about her visits to Chiapas. This is just one illustration of how the EZLN harnessed the media to begin building strategic emotional political community; the outpouring of support for the Zapatistas within Mexico and from around the globe, and their ability to draw people out to the jungle to document and join their struggle, are manifestations of that.

A Visit to the EZLN

About two months after Poniatowska began to clip stories from La Jornada, Marcos sent her a letter inviting her to come and talk with him in Chiapas. Dated July 14, 1994, the invitation referred to her own royal background as a princess. The letter and communication that followed play on literary references, with Marcos fashioning himself as a humble knight such as Don Quixote to Poniatowska's princess, referencing her literary positioning and class status. Marcos had a habit of often appearing dramatically on the scene astride a horse, channeling the many national statues, photographs, and drawings of Zapata on horseback with a large sombrero and rifle—symbols of his masculine power and strength. The invitation began, "On what floor of your fair Excellency's abode? Couldn't we negotiate a ground floor?" It continued in elegant yet ironic prose: "Let my mare Rocinante approach the sill of thy window and my intrepid daring reach up to thy balcony so that I might with the awkward danger of falling to the ground ... formally invite you to condescend to place upon these rebellious and threatening lands the tender sole of thy foot. We could converse on many subjects, and more important, silence many others."[30]

Marcos suggested a tentative day, July 23, 1994, when "the stars, the moon, the tides, the military checkpoints, and the evictions" might come into "a favorable conjunction," referencing the Mexican Army's occupation of eastern Chiapas after the Zapatista rebellion and the displacement of Indigenous Mayans after the initial confrontation between the EZLN and the Mexican Army in January 1994. He suggested that Poniatowska bring a sleeping bag "because here, besides being full of dignity, our ground is hard." Marcos suggested that the place, time, and probable agenda would come from the mouths of the "kind envoys of my missive" and hinted at the looseness of EZLN appointment scheduling.[31] Poniatowska took the invitation seriously and hastily prepared to pack and bring her children with her. In an interview in 2011, Poniatowska pondered Marcos's invitation.

> I remember that Subcomandante Marcos wrote to me and asked me to go to Chiapas. I went and I remember that he treated me very well. I went with my two children, Paula and Felipe. I think it was a very good experience for them because they were at the age of wanting [things]. "Mom, I want a car. Mom, I want certain things that I don't have." This trip did a lot for them because it made them stop asking; those are the requests of children who have a lot of privileges.... Mane [her oldest son] was in France getting his doctorate in physics.[32]

Following the thread of reading and writing initiated in their exchanges, Poniatowska assembled a large load of books to bring to build the Zapatista library in Guadalupe Tepeyac. "Paula stayed there a month, fixing up and categorizing all the books that we had gathered here in this house. A huge truck left from here full of books for Zapatistas' library."[33]

Poniatowska's first published piece about Subcomandante Marcos was based on her initial trip to Chiapas in July 1994 with two of her children. Published in *La Jornada* as "Entrevista del Subcomandante Insurgente Marcos con Elena Poniatowska" (Insurgent Subcommander Marcos Interview with Elena Poniatowska), Poniatowska's first piece on Marcos and the Zapatistas incorporates detailed descriptions of her travel to Chiapas, portrayals of the Zapatistas, the long wait for Marcos, and finally the interview.[34] The article is framed like a journey, with readers accompanying her for the first time into the Lacandón Jungle and as she waits eagerly for Marcos after spending the night sleeping on the dirt floor of an empty clinic. She begins by describing what she did when Marcos's first letter arrived.

First, I received the letter, the 14th of July, Bastille Day. It didn't occur to me to publish it. Later, when I was in the Lacandón Jungle, I realized that Subcomandante Marcos would have liked that, even if it were just to show the diversity in his writing style. My reaction was to run over to the Aviacsa office [the airline serving Tuxtla Gutierrez, Chiapas] to buy four tickets to the airport of Terán [the closest airport to San Cristóbal at the time, closed in 2006 and now an air base for the Secretary of National Defense of Mexico] for me, Felipe and Paula, and my adopted son Manuel Fernández. We were very happy when we flew at 5:30 in the morning on July 22.[35]

Once they landed, Poniatowska and her children piled into a cab and began the trip up to San Cristóbal de las Casas, the gateway city to the Zapatistas. Looking out the window through the rain and mist to the green scenery, Poniatowska saw Indigenous families carrying different-sized loads of firewood: a big one for the father, a medium-sized one for the mother, and a little one for the small son. In San Cristóbal, Poniatowska and the children stayed at the Hotel Casa Vieja, owned by photographer Raúl Ortega, which had become the headquarters for a retinue of *La Jornada* writers, except Jaime Avilés and Hermann Bellinghausen, who lived in the Lacandón Jungle.

The following day, Poniatowska and her children visited an alphabet soup of nonprofits and nongovernmental organizations (NGOs) in San Cristóbal that at the time were supporting the Zapatistas. Poniatowska describes her children as sick and coughing nonstop as they visited these organizations in the rain without the protection of umbrellas. As she attempted to balance the role of being a mother with her sick children and a reporter, the journey started out with some strain. They were still a long way from Zapatista territory and had no certainty of when they would see Marcos. He liked to make people wait. Of the journey to reach Subcomandante Marcos, whom she hoped to interview, she writes:

It isn't easy to get to Subcomandante Marcos. You have to make contacts, connections, and submerge yourself in an ocean of abbreviations. They say that it is five hours from San Cristóbal to Guadalupe Tepeyac, but because it is the rainy season it takes more time, and this is only if you get the right vehicle, because only jeeps, pickup trucks, and some Volkswagen bugs [*vochos*] that are not afraid of ruts in the road can make it. And this doesn't include all the roadblocks that started as soon as we got off the plane in Tuxtla Gutierrez.[36]

Once Poniatowska and her children made the journey to Zapatista territory, the waiting began. They were put up in the Guadalupe Tepeyac "hostel" (*albergue*), part of the community hospital that had been constructed with federal funds from Salinas de Gortari's Solidarity program. After Salinas de Gortari became president of Mexico in 1988, he announced a national poverty program, Solidarity, aimed at the 48 percent of Mexico's population who were categorized as poor, but particularly the 19 percent who at the time were classified as living in extreme poverty.[37] This program was implemented to attempt to offset wage decreases and job losses resulting from structural adjustment policies and also offered funds to municipalities for local health and development projects, hence the hospital in Guadalupe Tepeyac. The Zapatistas had confiscated the hospital, and it was where journalists slept and were housed while they waited to talk with "El Sub" and other members of the EZLN. When Poniatowska arrived, many were already waiting to talk to Marcos—a reporter from the *Miami Herald*, one from *Le Monde*, three Germans, two Spaniards, a gringo, a Salvadoran, and Alejandro and Marina Calvillo (who had brought a proposal from Greenpeace). Poniatowska was in line with them all. She and her children spent the day waiting—an inversion of their social and economic position, which usually meant they were among the first to be attended to. As she describes,

You never know when a short man or woman wearing a ski mask will come in and say "now." Meanwhile about 300 feet away in a little wooden house, you can ask them to prepare rice and beans or you can buy sodas and junk food—the delights of which I am discovering. You can go over to eat, come back up to wait, or watch the basketball game on the town's court. You can pass one day, two days, or even three days like this. Until the sky opens up. Now they have come for us. Then the chosen grab their things, forgetting half their stuff, and go outside without any jacket on to jump into a pickup truck, with their hearts in their throats. This can happen in the middle of the night, in the middle of a rainstorm, at dawn, or at any hour. The twenty-third is just about over when I receive another letter.[38]

While Poniatowska waited longer to talk with "El Sub," at the very least she received a long and flowery letter from Marcos, dated July 23, 1994. The letter continued the kind of literary tone of courting and anticipation of the previous one. It also played on Poniatowska's exalted ancestry, marking the contrast between her and the Indigenous, dirt-poor Zapatistas: "The sound of thousands of trumpets resounds in alleys and ravines. Could it be the aspiring candidate from some official party of some country in some imminent election process? No! It is your arrival being announced and the cortege being formed; the sounds of the military bands may be heard, the bells are ringing."[39] As Marcos suggested in the letter, it could take "hours, perhaps days (months and years if the wind blows against us) to arrive at your side. Patience is the virtue of warriors but not of writers."[40] He explained that he must wait for the clock "at Buckingham" to strike twelve, because before that hour he would turn into a pumpkin, and he found "it doubtful that your Excellency would consider it prudent to interview a pumpkin, especially if the pumpkin is wearing a ski mask, so I beg you to wait for the improbable hour of the improbable clock, within the improbable palace of the improbable 'Buckingham' (is that the proper way to spell it?)."[41] He signed the letter with the usual "Desde las montañas del sureste mexicano o sea, muy cerquita" (from the mountains of southeastern Mexico or very nearby). Poniatowska wondered, "How did he find time to write this letter in the middle of so much work, so many requests, so many journalists waiting for him. . . . Scribbling a response to him on a page from my office lined notebook, I guard his letter at the bottom of my sleeping bag for safekeeping."[42]

Poniatowska finally interviewed Subcomandante Marcos—the meeting consolidating the literary courtship. From his perspective, the conversation was clearly seen as a preview for the CND, the Zapatistas' first mass meeting, which was scheduled to occur about two weeks later, August 6–9, 1994. For Poniatowska, it was to establish an ongoing relationship. The piece served as an important announcement and endorsement of the EZLN and the upcoming CND, demonstrating how she used her writing as a political tool. On the morning of July 24, she and her children were escorted in a pickup truck through a roadblock and into Marcos's camp, where he emerged from a tent. Seats were brought outside, and they began to talk (figures 4.1 and 4.2). All around Poniatowska there were about six hundred people working to build the infrastructure for the CND. Marcos pointed out that they were busy building a "library, three dormitories, and over there, kitchens, fourteen stoves, and private latrines. . . . As you can see, the 40 million pesos that we had for funding our war has already been spent. They can't say that we don't want peace."[43]

Not far into the conversation, Marcos launched an inquiry about the presence of leading Mexican public intellectuals at the event, a way to legitimize it and bring it publicity: "Is Krauze going to come? Will Monsiváis come? Will Fuentes? The Grupo San Ángel?" (referring to Enrique Krauze, a Mexican public intellectual and publisher who has written on the Mexican Revolution; cronista and writer Carlos Monsiváis; Carlos Fuentes, the Mexican novelist who died in 2012; and Grupo San Ángel, a group of political thinkers and politicians from different ideological viewpoints, founded in 1994 at politician and academic Jorge G. Castañeda's house). Poniatowska responded, "Why do you care so much about the intellectuals?"

"Because they are opinion leaders."
"What is their power?"
"What I said before. They affect public opinion in civil society."[44]

Marcos's recognition of the influence of intellectuals and writers in Mexico suggests one of the ways that political community is built. Through inviting a wide range of sympathetic writers to visit Chiapas and later the CND, he was able to harness them in a public dialogue with the EZLN. No doubt he was courting Poniatowska for the same purpose. Her engagement with the EZLN was in significant part tied to her position in 1994 as a leading thinker and writer who could influence public opinion, and perhaps through her writing, she could garner public support for the EZLN.

Confronting Differences and Inequality

The wide-ranging interview touched on several topics, including the EZLN's refusal of government offers, presidential politics, the possibility for lasting peace in Chiapas, the Zapatistas' vision for the future of Mexico,

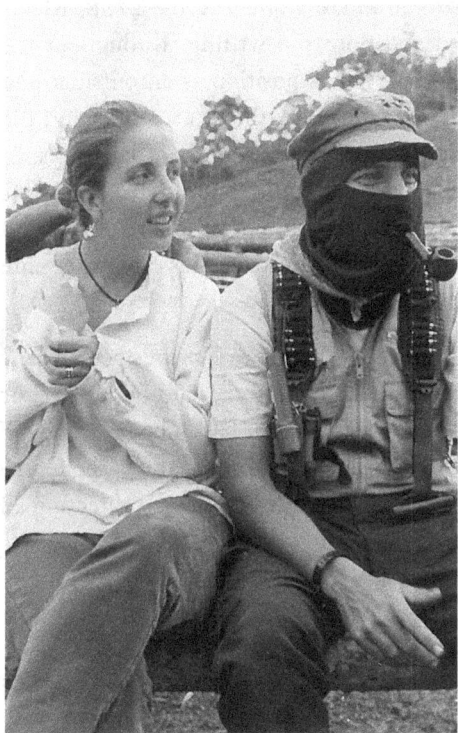

Figure 4.1 Paula Haro Poniatowska with Subcomandante Marcos, July 24, 1994. Photograph by Felipe Haro Poniatowska. Used by permission of the Fundación Elena Poniatowska Amor, Mexico City, Mexico.

Figure 4.2 Comandante Moises, Paula Haro Poniatowska, Subcomandante Marcos, Elena Poniatowska, and Felipe Haro Poniatowska, July 24, 1994. Photograph by Manuel Fernández. Used by permission of the Fundación Elena Poniatowska Amor, Mexico City, Mexico.

the decision-making structure of the EZLN, women in the EZLN, Mexican feminism and the politics of abortion, and writing. Throughout the exchange, Marcos highlighted Poniatowska's position as an outsider and suggested her lack of understanding about how the EZLN works and the many kinds of ongoing difficulties Zapatistas faced in their daily lives. In a later part of the interview, Marcos reiterated the point that Indigenous people were the force of the EZLN, responsible for its vision, policy, and decision-making, and he suggested that Poniatowska was like other elite outsiders who found it hard to believe.

> What happens is that you [plural] think that an Indigenous person can't be part of a national consciousness. This is absurd. And because he or she doesn't have a national consciousness then it has to be Marcos who stands in their place. When the government realizes that it is the Committee [referring to the CCRI] that is in charge, it will start directing all its proposals to the Committee.
>
> [Poniatowska:] But in the end, it is you.
>
> [Subcomandante Marcos:] The big decisions, the strategies, the most definitive decisions come from below. The decision to go to war, to accept government offers, the peace accords, all of this has to be consulted and decided from below.[45]

Poniatowska pushed Marcos again.

> "But by any means, Subcomandante, you are still a mestizo, here you are white. You are the one who gives the orders, you are a white person in the midst of all of this, a white who writes and who sends the communiqués. Is there some distance between you and the rest of the EZLN?"[46]
>
> [Subcomandante Marcos:] "Distance in what sense? Cultural? Wealth? I don't have better clothes than others; I am not better armed than others; I don't eat better."[47]

In the later part of the interview, Marcos commented on how Mexico discovered Chiapas on January 1, 1994, when the Zapatista uprising made international headlines, but the ongoing reality of extreme inequality, poverty, poor health, and marginalization of Chiapas's Indigenous peoples had been around for a long time. No one saw it or engaged with it, including Poniatowska. And he suggested that making Indigenous people visible elsewhere in Mexico and working to defend their rights still needed to be done. He homed in on the kind of sexual assault and violence suffered by Indigenous women. His response reflected his ideas about who he anticipated would be reading the interview. He clearly addressed not only Poniatowska but also those who would be her readers, acknowledging the critical public she reached.

We ask ourselves, will we have to repeat the first of January in Guerrero so that they discover Guerrero, Oaxaca, Yucatán, Campeche, Veracruz, Puebla, all of the parts of Mexico where there are Indigenous peoples? . . . I can't explain why people are so surprised by Chiapas, these people who you imagine are thinkers and analysts about the national situation. How is it possible that they waited until now to discover Chiapas? Chiapas has existed for a long time. Why were they so surprised about the rape of three Tzeltal women if they have always been raped and no one ever knew about it? Is it necessary to start a war for Mexicans to discover that in Chiapas they rape Indigenous women?[48]

Marcos was referring to the case of three Tzeltal sisters and their mother who were detained at a military checkpoint in the municipality of Altamirano. Separated from their mother, the sisters were repeatedly beaten and raped by soldiers. They reported the case first to local authorities, then to *La Jornada* newspaper. Later they reported their case to several local human rights organizations in San Cristóbal de las Casas, and the case was taken to the federal public prosecutor in Chiapas. A complaint was also filed with the Comisión Nacional de Derechos Humanos (National Human Rights Commission), with no result.[49] Finally, in 2001, the Inter-American Commission on Human Rights (IACHR) took up the case in Chile, and the Mexican state was held responsible for violating the human rights of the sisters and their mother. The IACHR recommended that the Mexican government conduct a complete, impartial, and effective investigation into the responsibility of all those who had committed the crimes against the four women and that reparations be paid to them for the court-established violations of their human rights.[50] Marcos's telling Poniatowska about the rape of the three women seems to be a deliberate strategy for connecting to readers and to motivate Poniatowska to act.

Published in three parts, the initial long interview between Poniatowska and Marcos reflects the engagement of two public intellectuals living in parallel worlds. Both use narrative and storytelling to translate and disseminate the experiences of marginalized Mexicans to a wider public. Both also harness testimony and storytelling to motivate readers to act, as Marcos did in telling of the rape of three Tzeltal women. In July 1994, Marcos functioned as the EZLN scribe, but slowly that role opened up to others who used spoken testimony to represent the movement's collective voice. Poniatowska was a perfect connection for Marcos; she was already well known for publishing testimony and crafting books that had influenced how traumatic events such as the 1968 assassinations of students and the 1985 earthquake were documented and remembered in Mexico. And Marcos was a perfect connection for Poniatowska as she sought to understand and share with the rest of Mexico the Zapatistas' experiences and visions for the future. Both Marcos and Poniatowska mobilized storytelling and emotion to communicate and build support for the Zapatista movement. Through the stories of the hardships, tragedies, challenges, and visions of EZLN members, both used written testimonies as a way to motivate and connect with readers—building emotional community from the page.

Performance, Community Engagement, and Political Strategy

Poniatowska also used her interview with Marcos to build anticipation and provide publicity for a large upcoming event, the CND. While she was in Chiapas interviewing Marcos in Guadalupe Tepeyac, hundreds of Zapatistas were busy building the infrastructure that would receive thousands of people. Poniatowska wrote of their efforts, "'These are good people,' 'these are good people,' 'these are good people,' the hammer says to me. It is difficult to take my eyes off the men perched on the beams above us, their muddy boots hanging in the emptiness between the boards. The sound of wood is in the air. . . . It is a forest with an immense marimba playing around us and the musicians are all playing the same note."[51]

When Poniatowska began her conversation with Marcos on July 24, the first thing they talked about was the CND. Marcos explained that there were six hundred builders who were preparing a meeting place for six thousand people. "What if it rains?" asked Poniatowska. "To prepare for the rain we are going to put up a huge tarp that is three thousand square meters," commented Marcos, "sustained by the post. Do you see it? There is a steel cable that we will connect to the hill back there. . . . There is going to be a library, these three shelters, a kitchen, stoves, and 14 latrines." Poniatowska then pondered how it was that thousands who just went to war to bring the plight of Indigenous peoples to the attention of the Mexican nation could now be building a library: "Four thousand people who just went to war and now the first thing they do is build a library? The military people here and the surveillance planes flying overhead to report on what these crazy Zapatistas are doing don't understand either that they are building a theater, a Greek-style theater, although the Sub does not like the word 'amphitheater.'"[52] The Zapatistas were portrayed by Poniatowska as a very different kind of guerrilla army, one that built theaters and cared about books.

Marcos told Poniatowska that the idea for the CND came about because "we had a lot of people from different social strata writing to us to tell us to not give up our weapons, because for them we represented a struggle and were a symbol. They said that we shouldn't give into the government's demands until we had our own demands resolved. We got all these messages and we discussed them … and we said, well, let's talk to the rest of the country, and that is how the idea was born for this National Democratic Convention. … Just as we decided on the war between all of us, we also decided on this dialogue and the invitation to the rest of the country."[53] Marcos returned to talking about the hundreds of Indigenous peoples building the structure, and by quoting him at length, Poniatowska continued building a picture of who the Zapatistas were for her reading public. They were people who wanted dialogue with civil society and were willing to come great distances and make great sacrifices to do so, according to Marcos. Poniatowska and Marcos were setting up a dramatic public dialogue in the jungle of Chiapas, which they hoped would build lasting strategic emotional political community for the EZLN at a national level. Marcos explained the motivation of all the workers.

> They are doing all this tremendous work [for the CND installations] and they aren't receiving a penny. The work they are doing is the work of peace, not of war. You wouldn't be able to convince them to come here and work if they were not sure that it is worth the effort. The people you see here [working] have walked four or five days from the deepest parts of the jungle. They come from places where there are no roads. They eat poor-quality food and sleep under a piece of plastic like this one here or they hang up their hammocks and sleep in the open air where they get stung by nasty mosquitos. It's impossible to explain how they put up with these uncomfortable positions without pay, without any money, unless they were in agreement with the decision we made by voting from the bottom up [to hold the CND]. They know what they are doing.[54]

Two weeks after her interview with Marcos, while she was attending the EZLN's convention in Chiapas, Poniatowska wrote a subsequent piece,

"La CND: De naves mayores a menores" (The CND: From ships larger to smaller), which appeared in *La Jornada* on August 16, 1994, and was later republished as part of *EZLN: Documentos y comunicados, 1° de enero/8° de agosto de 1994*. This was the first of multiple volumes of Zapatistas communiqués published by Era. By placing her chronicle prominently in the first volume, Poniatowska endorsed the EZLN.

Poniatowska participated in the convention hosted by the EZLN in the ejido of Guadalupe Tepeyac. It was a major event in Mexico and received significant press coverage—from Poniatowska herself in her first interview and from others. From the guest list, it is easy to see how the EZLN was able to harness well-known public figures to legitimate and promote its cause. The whole CND itself featured careful attention to performance, narrative, and symbol. Also attending with Poniatowska were other national artistic, political, and literary luminaries, such as Poniatowska's good friend Carlos Monsiváis; singer Eugenia León; Mexican writer, poet, and politician Eracilo Zepeda; Mexican painter Alberto Gironella; actress and performance artist Jesusa Rodríguez (a senator since 2016); photographers Mariana Yampolksy and Graciela Iturbide; Carlos Payán (then director of *La Jornada*); lawyer, sociologist, and UNAM rector Pablo González Casanova; poet Juan Gelman; and activist Rosario Ibarra of Comité ¡Eureka! (Eureka Committee).

In 1994 the Zapatistas had labored for twenty-eight days to create the new Aguascalientes convention site in La Realidad, Chiapas, named for the first constitutional convention in 1914, which Emiliano Zapata (among others) attended and which resulted in Mexico's 1917 Constitution. The site featured an amphitheater, called *el barco* (the boat), large enough for eight thousand people to sit on wooden benches. There was also a clinic, Poniatowska's library with more than three thousand volumes, long lines of carefully constructed outdoor latrines for both men and women, potable drinking water stations, eight dormitories, kitchens, and a location for the press that included outlets for computers.

I attended the CND in August 1994 and found it to be an amazing experience—full of hope and optimism for transforming Mexico. More than six thousand delegates attended, as did observers from hundreds of organizations. The convention opened with a very solemn and moving greeting from the Zapatista base communities, introduced by Comandante Tacho from the general command of the EZLN: "These are the bases of support for the EZLN. . . . They represent all the people in struggle; they are equal to all of you. These men and women, boys and girls are those who sustained us, and they kept the deepest secrets in the history of Mexico and the EZLN in hiding."[55] After the presentation of the bases, Tacho spoke and then was followed by Marcos, who introduced the combat troops of the EZLN. They marched in silence with a white piece of cloth tied over the ends of their rifles, their faces covered with bandanas and ski masks. It was a moving performance for the thousands who had journeyed from all over Mexico to meet the Zapatistas. Shortly after Marcos finished his speech, the skies opened up and a torrential rainstorm blew over the giant tarp and soaked the attendees. As we compared stories in 2011, Poniatowska recalled, "In Guadalupe Tepeyac where the first Zapatista *encuentro* [meeting] was held, it rained so much. It was a huge downpour. They had built a large boat-like structure, like Fitzcarraldo's, and it had a giant, beautiful tarp on top, like a sail. It broke and we spent the entire night in camping tents struggling to keep the water out."[56] But that did not dampen the enthusiasm of Poniatowska and many others inspired by the event, including her daughter: "It was such an amazing experience that Paula decided to stay there for a month in the jungle. She helped organize all the books that had to be unpacked. She worked really hard there. . . . I think that it was really important for her to live in the jungle. . . . It is one of the most beautiful memories in my life." Poniatowska's enthusiasm at being a part of this public dialogue and performance choreographed by the Zapatistas is evocative of the large-scale mobilizations she documented in relation to the 1968 student movement and 1985 earthquake. She worked to build personal relationships at the CND while also documenting the social movement building that was occurring there—again combining activism with writing.

The speeches and parades that were so moving at the convention, as well as people's interactions and conversations with participants in the EZLN, fueled a wave of solidarity. According to Poniatowska, "As with many of the Mexicans who participated [in the CND], everyone was excited. University students filled buses to go to Chiapas, even though the trip took two or three days. It was indeed madness. You have to realize that it was as if Che Guevara had appeared once again," in reference to Marcos. Many felt that the Zapatista uprising was going to spark a major change in Mexico in the treatment of and access to power for Indigenous peoples. Poniatowska returned from Chiapas energized and committed to the Zapatista cause; like others, she took the Zapatistas' message and worked to center it in discussions of Mexican politics and Indigenous rights. I asked her how she saw this period of Zapatismo affecting Mexico.

It was the first time that Indigenous peoples were invited to take part in political discussions and to participate at the negotiating table. Before, they were forgotten. They were, as Marcos called them, "the smallest," those who were cast aside, those who practically did not exist. In a very rich state like Chiapas, they were the ones who had no running water, no electricity, no schools, no hospitals.

The cry of the Zapatistas was essential because the North American Free Trade Agreement had been signed and President Carlos Salinas was very proud of this. He said that we were going to become a modern country, that we were going to be part of the First World and leave the Third World once and for all. That our luck would change. And suddenly the Indigenous peoples of Chiapas rose up. The poorest people. . . . The absolutely poorest Mexicans rose up in Chiapas armed with pretend wooden guns and said, "What about us?" "What are you going to do with us?" "We are ten million people. Are you going to kill us?" "Did you forget that we exist?" They were clearly speaking to those who signed the North American Free Trade Agreement.

They had been waiting for years in the jungle. And suddenly this extraordinary man, Rafael Guillén Vicente from Tampico, stood up and shouted. The CIA had already revealed his real name, but he deserved the name he gave himself: Subcomandante Marcos. He was a man who we all respected.[57]

Poniatowska identified Marcos's project of storytelling, of sharing testimonies, and of disseminating them to a larger public as revolutionary—perhaps reflecting her own aspirations.

Beyond the importance of sharing the experiences of the Mayan peoples of Chiapas, Poniatowska also expressed a commitment to their demands for Indigenous autonomy. In 1995 she wrote an accessible summary that appeared in English of what Indigenous autonomy meant at that time for the EZLN. The book that contained this piece, *Distant Relations/Cercanías Distantes/Clann I Gcéin: Chicano, Irish, Mexican Art and Critical Writing*, was edited by Trisha Ziff.

They asked that all Indigenous languages be declared official Mexican languages, and that all the teaching of these be required in primary, secondary, and high schools as well as in universities; they also asked that their rights and dignity as Indigenous peoples be respected, and that their cultures and traditions be taken into consideration. They want the discrimination and contempt they have suffered for centuries to stop. They demand the right to organize and to govern themselves autonomously, because they do not want to be subject to the will of powerful Mexicans and foreigners. They want their justice to be administered by the Indigenous people themselves, according to their customs and traditions, without intervention from illegitimate, corrupt governments.[58]

Through this chapter placed to reach readers outside Mexico, and, in comparison with Irish and Chicano writing and movements, Poniatowska moved the Zapatista message to a wider public.

More than two decades later, these same ideas continue to be fought for and carried out throughout Mexico in a wide range of Indigenous communities, from Chiapas, to Oaxaca, to Guerrero, to Puebla, to Baja California. For Poniatowska, her face-to-face engagements with the Zapatistas in Chiapas were crucial to her writing about them, and she also met many people through these encounters who were part of a national support network for the EZLN. She became particularly inspired by the courage and radical vision of Zapatista women. Some women who were important leaders in the EZLN became public figures after the CND.

Zapatista Gender Politics

The proposals contained in the Ley Revolucionaria de Mujeres (Women's Revolutionary Law) were the most radical and difficult part of the Zapatista agenda to achieve on the local level and still stand as a challenge for gender equality in Indigenous and other communities throughout the Americas. In the wake of the "Me Too" campaign in 2017 and 2018, and the fact that in Mexico an estimated seven women were killed every day in 2016, these demands remain painfully relevant.[59] They not only focus on sexual violence and forced marriage but also outline a wide range of rights that Poniatowska and many other women in Mexico are still fighting for: the right to participate in political struggle in any way determined by their desire and capacity, regardless of their race, creed, color or political affiliation; to work and receive a fair wage; to decide the number of children they have; to participate in community matters and hold elected positions of authority; to health and nutrition; to an education; to choose their romantic partner and not be forced into marriage; to not be beaten or physically mistreated by family members or strangers, with severe punishment for rape and attempted rape; and to occupy positions of leadership and hold military ranks in the revolutionary armed forces.[60] Zapatista women came from a completely different experience of life from Poniatowska's and often had very different ways of thinking about their roles as women. But Poniatowska's ongoing interactions with them, writing about their ideas and experiences, became a central part of her activism in relation to the EZLN. She became a champion for the ideas of Zapatista women and helped connect them to her readers. Some of the most difficult topics EZLN women engaged with, such as sexual assault and abortion, were also difficult subjects for Poniatowska herself.

In an interview with journalists Matilde Pérez and Laura Castellanos, published as part of an article in *La Jornada*'s supplement for International Women's Day in March 1994, Comandanta Ramona and Major Ana María fielded questions about the Women's Revolutionary Law. The journalists brought up the topic of abortion.

"Ramona, you went to the communities and talked with the women. Didn't you discuss the issue of abortion?"

"No, no."

"Why not?"

Both women look at each other, and it's Major Ana María who replies.

"It didn't occur to them. It's that there's a belief among Indigenous people that there shouldn't be abortion."

"Nevertheless, there are women who die from badly performed abortions."

"Oh, yes, of course. There are young women this happens to."

"Would that be challenging a tradition?"

"Well, I don't know." Ana María turns to look at Javier [Comandante Javier, translator of Tzotzil to Spanish] for help. "You, comrade, what opinion do you have about this belief, of what happens in the villages. . . ."

"Well," Javier says, "there hasn't been a lot of agreement about this situation. In these same villages there is a tradition about how to care for women."

"But this tradition carries risks for the health and lives of women," interrupts the journalist.

"Many times," Javier continues, "they really do run risks because there are no doctors to attend to them. But the women have their own customs for how they are cared for."

In response to the reporter's insistence on whether Indigenous women would go to a clinic to receive a safe abortion—in the event that there should ever be such a service—Ana María interrupts Javier to say:

> When we talk about there being a tradition, this doesn't imply continuing it. But in many communities a punishment is applied if the woman doesn't report that she's pregnant and wants to have an abortion.
>
> Because many times this happens, the young woman goes to a midwife or a *curandera* [healer] and asks for an abortion for fear that her family will mistreat or punish her. In the communities I know, a man is fined or detained if he gets a woman pregnant, and he is imprisoned for a few days, or he is expected to pay for the woman's medical attention.

Regarding the use of contraceptives, Major Ana María says, "They don't exist. They're unknown in any of the communities. And pregnancy happens infrequently because parents take great care that their daughters do not get pregnant. Fearing their parents, the young women don't talk to men. If they do become pregnant, many of them give birth to the children because it's very difficult to get an abortion and, even if they get one, many die."[61]

This exchange underlines the difficult conditions under which young Mayan women lived in Chiapas in the 1990s. It also illustrates important political work that these Zapatista women are doing through their communications with journalists to shed light on their situation. They were very much under their parents' control, often not free to leave the house unaccompanied, and strictly forbidden to have contact with young men. Any sexual relationship they developed was kept a secret, and they knew nothing about their bodies and sexual reproduction. If they became pregnant, it created a terrible dilemma. In the communities that Ana María and Ramona came from, most people did not believe in abortion, but some women did get them, and many who got clandestine abortions died. Yet at the same time, there were curanderas and midwives with the knowledge of how to induce an abortion. And most communities knew nothing about contraceptives.

These realities and the dire consequences of not having access to reproductive health care and other rights were behind the process that led to Ramona and Ana María, working with other women, to create the Women's Revolutionary Law in 1993, the year before the Zapatista movement went public. Ana María explained, "They'd given us the right to participate in the assemblies and in study groups, but there was no law about women.

And so we protested, and that's how the law for women came about. We all formulated it and presented it in an assembly of all the towns. Men and women voted on it. There were no problems. Throughout the process, women's opinions were sought in all the towns."[62]

Zapatista women, along with the women from within their communities, engaged in a radical act as they worked to pass the Women's Revolutionary Law. Their demands were borne from the material, psychological, and physical conditions they experienced day to day in a state where racism against the Indigenous was institutionalized. From literally being expected to sit at the back of the bus or move off the sidewalk every time a non-Indigenous person passed them, to waiting in endless lines at clinics and government offices, should they manage to get there, Indigenous women were at the bottom of the social strata. The scope of their demands came from their life experience, not through formal systems of education or through engagement with urban social movements and politics.

A woman's right to access abortion and determine if she wants children, and how many, would become topics of intense public discussion between Zapatistas and others. To some, it appeared that the EZLN had taken a stance against abortion. To understand this assumption and concern, we have to step back in time for a brief political history of the topic. In 1936, when Ofelia Domínguez Navarro participated in a convention dedicated to creating uniformity throughout Mexico's postrevolutionary penal code, she proposed that the state control and regulate the practice of abortion during the first three months of pregnancy.[63] The proposal was not adopted, but in the 1970s feminists took up the issue again by proposing "voluntary motherhood," which included a program of widespread sexual education, access to birth control, and, as a last resort, abortion. They also advocated against involuntary sterilization.[64] In 1990 the state legislature of Chiapas quietly revised its abortion law to permit first-trimester abortions within a broad set of circumstances.[65] When these revisions to the law were made public in December 1990, feminist advocates for abortion along with the Catholic Church and church-linked organizations reacted strongly.

Within two weeks of the announcement, the Chiapas state legislature suspended the process and the federal government kicked the issue to the Comisión Nacional de Derechos Humanos, which avoided ruling on the law.[66] It remained on the books but was not implemented. Feminists in Mexico City along with sixty-two unions, NGOs, and a large feminist coalition founded the Frente Nacional por la Maternidad Voluntaria y la

Despenalización del Aborto (National Front for Voluntary Motherhood and Decriminalization of Abortion) in 1991. The Frente Nacional got the PRD to put the decriminalization of abortion on the party platform. In 1992 the group carried out a survey, engaged in public actions, and continued to make connections with the United Nations and other spaces where abortion was being debated.

In Chiapas in 1994, the interim governor, Javier López Morena, proposed a discussion of thirteen new state initiatives that were supposed to be in response to demands put forward by the EZLN. On April 12, 1994, *La Jornada* published an article by Candelaria Rodríguez titled "They Will Repenalize Abortion in Chiapas," which suggested that the Chiapas state government, acting in response to an EZLN petition, was recriminalizing abortion in the only state in Mexico where state legislative reform had legalized it.[67] Responding to this article and the suggestion that the EZLN was pushing for the recriminalization of abortion, Mexico City feminist, intellectual, and pro–reproductive rights activist Marta Lamas published an article in *La Jornada* later that month titled "The EZLN, the Vatican, Abortion and the Mexican State." Lamas wrote that there was an apparent contradiction between the third point of the Women's Revolutionary Law (women should have the right to determine how many children they have and care for) and "the actual demand of the EZLN: criminalization of abortion."[68] Subcomandante Marcos responded in a letter addressed to Lamas and sent to *La Jornada* on May 5, 1994: "The EZLN has never demanded the criminalization of abortion, nor have we presented any kind of project for legal reform to the state Penal Code, nor have we participated in any discussion about the reforms that are in process. . . . With respect to the Penal Code of Chiapas [we ask] that the Penal Code be eliminated because it only allows for us to organize with weapons, because the legal and peaceful ways to fight are punished and repressed."[69] Marcos was suggesting that Indigenous peoples did not have access to the legal system and were not represented in formal systems of governance, and that the Chiapas state penal code was primarily used to criminalize and imprison Indigenous people. Because legal protest was repressed and people were put in prison for peaceful forms of protest, their only recourse was to use weapons. Eliminating the penal code completely, he suggested, was the best solution.

Marcos ended his letter, including his characteristic postscripts, with two strong messages: "For sure, Indigenous women abort here and not by their own choosing. 'Chronic malnutrition' is the reason according to the statistics. . . . The *compañeras* say they have not asked for abortion clinics because they don't even have clinics in which women can give birth. Also, penal codes don't take into account the toll it takes [for pregnant women] to climb up big hills carrying a large load of firewood [and perhaps induce abortion]."[70]

In her July 1994 interview with Marcos published prior to the CND, Poniatowska asked Marcos about this exchange with Lamas, which took place in April and May 1994. In her article, Lamas suggested that the new discussion of recriminalizing abortion in a new Penal Code was related to the influences of the Catholic Church over the EZLN and the intractable position of the bishop against abortion: "Although the EZLN shares ten points in its Women's Revolutionary Law that offer a glimpse into what seemed to be an interesting process—the struggle for the specific demands of the Indigenous women within the EZLN—these points have been ignored due to the strengthening of the traditional position of the Catholic Church."[71] Poniatowska asked Marcos, "What do you think about the answer that Marta Lamas gave you in the name of the feminists, published in *La Jornada*?"[72] Marcos responded strongly, referring to the difficult conditions in which women were living.

> One of the *compañeras* here just died of an abortion. This article by Marta Lamas comes out, and I wasn't there in Mexico [City] to explain to her that the conditions are different here, that here in the mountains of the southeast we have a law that is maintained and it doesn't have anything to do with devotees of the Church with respect to the use of condoms or contraceptives or the interruptions of pregnancies or abortions. . . .
>
> We have had to deny this [the original news article stating that the EZLN wanted to recriminalize abortion and is influenced by the Catholic Church] and other things and then [Lamas's] article comes out and . . . we feel like it's against Zapatista women. We feel the opposite. We belong to the women, they are not "our women," we belong to them and they have control over their bodies and their lives.[73]

Their conversation about the issue continued. Poniatowska explained that because Chiapas was the first state to legalize abortion, it seemed as if the law had been thwarted because of political pressure from the government, from the PRI, and from Samuel Ruiz, the Catholic bishop in Chiapas at the time. Marcos said the EZLN never asked that they reform the state legal code and suggested that Lamas got it wrong. Then Poniatowska's son Felipe, who was present and taking photographs during the interview, joined in with a question for Marcos about his personal opinion on abortion. Marcos's response was somewhat satirical, and he ended with a sexist phrase that put Poniatowska on edge: "Personally, I think that a woman can turn her body into a windmill if she wants it that way. We in the EZLN . . . can't say anything, neither that women should abort or that they shouldn't. That is their decision. *Es una decisión de viejas* [that's a decision for broads to make]."[74] Poniatowska responded, "*Las viejas?* [Broads?]. . . . You sound like Fernández de Cevallos. . . . *Qué horror!* [Come on!]," suggesting that the comment was out of line and sounded like something Partido Acción Nacional (PAN, National Action Party) presidential candidate Diego Fernández de Cevallos would say.

Poniatowska's long interview with Subcomandante Marcos and her subsequent writing on the topic further exposed the complexity of the experiences and perspectives of Zapatista women in Chiapas, especially when it came to the question of having control over the number of children they had and with whom. Their perspective was very different from that of middle-class women in the capital but not completely different. Multiple feminisms, and even the definitions of women's rights and how to situate them in relation to Indigenous rights and collective and individual rights, were at the center of a complex set of conversations and positions in Mexico in the 1990s and later.[75] In her ongoing writing about the Zapatistas, Poniatowska kept a spotlight on Indigenous women's ideas about their rights.

In 2008 Mexico's Supreme Court upheld Mexico City's abortion law making abortion legal in the first trimester. In September 2019, the state of Oaxaca decriminalized abortion up to twelve weeks of pregnancy, making it the second place in Mexico where abortion is legal. Across Mexico, women continue to militate for abortion rights but most recently for the right to be free from violence. In the spring of 2020, millions took to the streets to protest against feminicide and gender violence, beginning on Valentine's Day. Women continue to be the backbone of multiple antiviolence movements and in many states are also leading movements to find the disappeared. During the COVID-19 pandemic, women were being killed and harmed at increasing rates, but Mexican president López Obrador dismissed the scale of the problem, upsetting many feminists and activists.[76] The Zapatista women's movement that Poniatowska accompanied continued to advocate for women to be free from violence.

Connections across Difference

Poniatowska had been raised a devout Catholic, and her Catholic education as an adolescent and young woman left a strong mark on her. In *La herida de Paulina*, a crónica focusing on the case of a thirteen-year-old Oaxacan girl who was raped and then denied an abortion, Poniatowska writes in the introduction:

> Like many feminists, I have suffered abortion. Like many Catholics for Free Choice, I was also a girl in a convent of nuns where I received communion every day for seven years. The Church has dogmas of faith that I accepted without question. I was a Child of Mary, a blue ribbon [an award or medal]. I thought that because I had earned the medal [blue ribbon award], when my final hour arrived, the Virgin would come to pull me up to heaven hung from her like an effigy. When I returned from the Convent of the Sacred Heart in Torresdale, Pennsylvania, I taught catechism, prepared children for their First Communion. . . .
>
> As the years went by, I realized that although the pope prohibits birth control methods, Catholics use them. They go to confession and then they continue to use them. Their consciences are tormented, and I suppose that they live with a divided soul. Surely in the privacy of many women, there in the dark, in the deepest part, where the most painful thoughts exist, there is an abortion. Inside of me there is one.
>
> The interruption of a pregnancy is part of women's choice. My evolution on this topic has been slow.[77]

Choosing when, how, and how many children to have as suggested in the Zapatista Women's Revolutionary Law is a topic Poniatowska struggled deeply with as a young woman. At age eighty-seven, with the release of her book *El amante polaco* (The Polish lover), Poniatowska revealed a closely guarded secret she and her family held from public scrutiny for more than six decades. The Mexican writer Juan José Arreola sexually assaulted her and left her pregnant, and she raised her eldest son as a single mother for fifteen years.[78] During our first interview over several days in 2011, Poniatowska discussed the circumstances of Mane's birth and how agonizing the entire episode was for her. She stated at the time that this was not something that could be published. Later, when I shared the transcript of the interview with her, she stated that this part of the transcript was something even her children didn't know about. It would be best, she commented in 2011, "for me to be able to tell this as part of a novel so that

I can understand it. But I don't know how to do that. I have never known how to write about this, because it is something that is still really terrible for me."[79] Eight years after our conversation, Poniatowska did just this through publishing a thinly disguised account of the sexual assault, her pregnancy, giving birth to Emanuel (Mane) in a convent, and the great pain she felt when she agreed to let him be taken back to Mexico to be raised by a relative. In her 2019 novel, *El amante polaco*, Poniatowska weaves together two strands of history: that of the life of her relative Stanisław Poniatowski, born in 1732 and king of Poland from 1764 to 1795; and of her parents, siblings, and herself in Mexico. The book brings together the lives of Stanisław Poniatowski and Elena Poniatowska, born two hundred years apart, beginning when each is a child. In narrating her own life through the first-person narrative, Poniatowska tells her own story.

In the novel, a figure she calls "El Maestro" cultivates her friendship and asks, during their first meeting, if she has "any other text" that isn't journalistic. From this first encounter in his fifth-floor apartment in the Colonia Cuauhtémoc where El Maestro paints, Poniatowska writes, "From this moment . . . I came once a week. I went up the stairs two at a time."[80] When El Maestro invites her to accompany him to give a talk, she is ecstatic: "What a privilege. What a gift! Oh my God! A girl on her knees in front of the altar who receives the privileges of being companion and driver [to Arreola]. What an amazing day."[81] Changing her voice to the present, she writes later in the same chapter, "Now that I am old, I am afraid of what I was; a piece of tissue paper on the rooftop."[82]

Poniatowska accompanies El Maestro to his lecture, where many people take notes. Some days later, when she is halfway through a class with him, he assaults her: "El Maestro stands threateningly, thin, his hair standing on end, with an erection [*palo*] inside his pants. 'You are a peacock who has come to strut in a chicken coop,' he spits out."[83] His body, his expression, became distorted, she writes. He was "absolutely distinct from the person who I had admired days ago. I don't know if he screamed; he walked like a caged animal. I approached the door. 'Oh, no, it's not that easy,' he threatened. I pay for going up the steps with such haste. . . . I pay for the rooftop and for each step because now he is coming down full speed toward the door and afterward, when I am in the street, I don't understand. I only know that, like him, the rooftop with its sheet spread out on it has slapped me."[84]

Afterward, Poniatowska writes about lying in bed in pain, asking, "Is this love? If it is, why is it so different from what I have seen in the movies? . . . Until last night, in the solitude of my bedroom I had never suffered,

I had no idea of why I was in so much pain; but I woke up a different person. The world was different. . . . Nobody realizes what they don't know."[85] In what has become one of the most quoted lines from the book, Poniatowska writes about how she felt after the assault: "I am alone. I don't know what love is. What happened to me, the cot, the threat, the attack doesn't have anything to do with what I read about in books or saw at the movie theater Vanguardias."[86]

At the age of twenty-two, Poniatowska met Mexican writer Juan José Arreola, who a friend recommended to her as a writing coach.[87] She shared some of her newspaper stories and interviews with him. In 1952 Arreola had published the successful novel *Confabulario*, and he also worked as an editor and was interested in promoting young writers. Poniatowska shared the manuscript from her first novel, *Lilus Kikus*, with him. The book is written from a child's point of view and provides heavy hints of Poniatowska's own Catholic upbringing, spirituality, and the expectations for girls to get married and behave properly as well as Poniatowska's own independent inclinations as a young woman. The book was published in 1954 with Los Presentes Press, which Arreola ran and served as editor for. In Arreola's memoir, first published in 1999 and resulting from a series of conversations with his son Orso, Arreola states that for two years he had a romantic relationship with Poniatowska and it resulted in a son.[88] When *El amante polaco* was published in December 2019, the press focused almost exclusively on the part of the book describing her sexual assault by Arreola. His family denounced her version of the story and stated that it was a consensual relationship.[89] Poniatowska stuck to her version of events, stating, in response to accusations by Arreola's family that she was disrespectful, "The respectful person has been me. I never asked for anything. The person who never saw him again was me. The person who kept silent was me. Arreola never saw my son, never knew him, and never supported him."[90]

Until 2019, Poniatowska did not talk publicly about Arreola. In our conversations, after an intense and difficult narration of her pregnancy and devastation when her son was taken away from her in Rome, she focused on her joy at the birth of Mane and how his arrival changed her life but also how very difficult and painful this time in her life was. Mane was born in Italy in a convent where Poniatowska went to give birth. She had been in Europe working as a reporter, already pregnant when she left Mexico. Throwing herself into her work, she conducted "thousands of interviews," as she recalled. She was strongly pressured to give up her son. She was told that she didn't have anything to offer to the baby. As no one knew she was pregnant, she should give him up for someone else to raise. But Poniatowska would not accept that. As she told me, Mane's birth was "the most important moment in my life. The one that marked me the most."[91] She affirms this in *El amante polaco*, which was read and commented on by Mane and to whom she dedicates the book, along with close friend Marta Lamas.[92] In the depth of her pain and confusion about the sexual assault she describes in *El amante polaco*, she asks, "What is going to happen? What is my destiny?"[93] Although she didn't know it at the time, with the passage of many years, she now knows: "My destiny is to write. You, write. Go, write, go on, write."[94]

Poniatowska returned to Mexico City, where Mane lived with her grandparents, who lived next door to her parents. Poniatowska's insistence that she raise and support Mane was an act of rebellion in her family and in upper-class Mexican society at the time. As a single mother who worked in public as a reporter, Poniatowska was not seen as having the proper home or lifestyle to raise a child. As she explained in 2012, "I raised him at a time when there was great social rejection of single mothers. I worked to keep him and have him with me."[95] Our conversation in 2011, when she was almost eighty years old, suggested that this judgment had followed her throughout her life. Her act of rebellion and insistence on being a single, working mother meant she paid a high price in her social world. "The pressure in my social environment was strong, terribly strong," she told me.[96]

Marked as a single mother, Poniatowska had crossed a line into the territory of marginalized women. But thanks to her high social and class status, she was able to continue her career and struggle to be taken seriously as a writer in the 1950s. The experience of being socially judged produced not only guilt in her but also a deep well of empathy for other women, as well as for men, who transgressed social norms and pushed for change. While a more dramatic contrast could not be imagined in comparing the life of Poniatowska and the impoverished women she came to know, they did have several things in common. They were often raised with little to no information about how the female body becomes pregnant, they had little to no knowledge about female sexuality and desire, and they all had little understanding about a woman's rights over her body. In Poniatowska's case, her lack of such knowledge was a result of her protective Catholic upbringing. As she wrote in *La herida de Paulina*, "In the 1950s, neither my sister nor I had information about this thing called our body.

One time I asked my mother about my birth and she told me that she had gone hunting."[97]

Poniatowska's experience as a single mother who had a child that was the result of a sexual assault that she kept secret provided her with an opening to relate to the narratives of EZLN women. Her own experience, albeit within entirely different material circumstances, drew her to what the Zapatista women had accomplished and what they had risked in order to establish the Women's Revolutionary Law. In our conversations, she repeatedly mentioned her admiration for what the EZLN women were doing and would mention her own difficulties as a female journalist when she was younger. Like the Zapatista women, Poniatowska came into her own brand of feminism through her engagement with social movements.

In 2001 Poniatowska published the essay "Women, Mexico, and Chiapas," which summarized some of her key thoughts regarding women's activism, women's rights, the Catholic Church, patriarchy, and the importance of her work with activists, at the time culminating with Zapatista women.

> Women in Mexico live under the weight of an age-old patriarchy and under a much heavier burden still, that of the Catholic Church.... Contemporary Mexican women, following the example of the seamstresses, are also saying good-bye to their parents, their bosses, their husbands, their confessors, or any form of authority; and privileged women have much to learn from the classes they so despise. The new Mexico (now in crisis) has grown from roots in its poorest states. And now men, women, and children have begun to fight for their rights, with the intelligence and efforts of women like the seamstresses, who come from the streets, or EZLN guerrillas, who come from the fields of Chiapas.[98]

Poniatowska's engagement with women activists solidified through her experience with Evangelina Corona and the Mexico City textile workers, and it continued with her advocacy and support for the compañeras of the EZLN.

Zapatista Women in the National Imagination

In the 1990s, Zapatista women were quite successful in capturing widespread media attention and in engaging a wide range of people in the country, including Poniatowska, who supported them in public political events, through hosting Comandanta Ramona in her home before surgery, and in print. Comandanta Ramona was the first of several iconic Zapatista women who had a national platform in the 1990s. Her legacy continued in 2018 through the candidacy of María de Jesús Patricio Martínez, also known as Marichuy, who ran as an independent candidate for president of Mexico with Poniatowska's political support. "When they rape, disappear, jail or assassinate a woman, it is as if all the community, the neighborhood, the community or the family has been raped," said the Mexican Mep'ha (Indigenous activist) Marichuy at a rally against gender violence in Mexico City in 2017.[99]

In Marichuy's analysis, if violence against one woman is violence committed against a collective group of people—Indigenous women and men—in a society that dehumanizes that same group, then such crimes call for more than simply sending the abuser to prison. They call for a punishment that implicates the community and the abuser, and tries to heal them both.

Comandanta Ramona first gained recognition as the woman commander behind the EZLN's strategic takeover of San Cristóbal de las Casas on January 1, 1994. Prior to that, she and Major Ana María worked tirelessly in consultation with many EZLN communities to craft the Women's Revolutionary Law. Ramona was one of a few EZLN women who participated in the first round of peace talks with Manuel Camacho Solís, a Mexican government negotiator, in the cathedral in San Cristóbal de las Casas. Ramona also attended the CND in 1994, appearing with many other Zapatista women and as part of the Comité Clandestino Revolucionario Indígena-Comandancia General. In 1995 the federal government under Ernesto Zedillo sent in the Mexican Army to arrest Marcos (which didn't happen). Zapatista communities were ransacked, and the army began its long-term armed presence in the regions. Ramona made a special appeal to women by video, saying, "I want all the women to wake up and to plant in their hearts the necessity of organizing themselves, because with our arms crossed we will never build the free and just Mexico we all want."[100]

In October 1996, Ramona made a highly publicized trip from the Lacandón Jungle in Chiapas to Mexico City, where she represented the EZLN at the founding of the Congreso Nacional Indígena (National Indigenous Congress). The event took place at the auditorium of UNAM's Medical School in the historic center of Mexico City. The trip's timing was important for both Ramona and the EZLN. The talks focused on passing legislation to implement the Acuerdos de San Andrés sobre Derechos y

Cultura Indígena (San Andrés Accords on Indigenous Rights and Culture) that the Mexican government had signed with the EZLN. At the time, the government did not allow the Zapatistas to leave the EZLN conflict zone in Chiapas.

The San Andrés Accords on Indigenous Rights and Culture lay the groundwork for significant changes in the areas of Indigenous rights, political participation, and cultural autonomy in Mexico. Most important, the accords recognized the existence of political subjects called *pueblos indios* (Indigenous peoples/towns/communities) and gave conceptual validation to the terms *self-determination* and *autonomy* by using them in the signed accords.[101] The EZLN and the Mexican government signed them on February 16, 1996, in San Andrés Larráinzar, Chiapas. In the fall of 1996, the EZLN was working to pressure the government to pass legislation to implement the accords (they never did).[102]

Before Ramona and the rest of the EZLN came to Mexico City in the fall of 1996, Poniatowska was one of a group of twelve artists, writers, and public intellectuals who used their public positions to support the EZLN visit. An article in *La Jornada* highlighted their enthusiasm for the EZLN and the visit. Poniatowska was quoted extensively in the article, endorsing the visit. Having public intellectuals comment in the press about their support for the presence of the EZLN in Mexico City was a strategy to help protect the Zapatistas during their visit. Poniatowska stated in the press before their arrival:

It seems like a splendid idea, it makes me very happy, it would be a day of celebration. I hope with all my soul that they are received here the way we were received in the jungle: with open arms, attending to each one of us personally. I would love to see the women, Maribel, Ana María, Doña Trini; I hope all of them are allowed to come. It would be very smart if there were a greater number of women; that way the government would be less brutal with the Zapatistas [thinking that detaining, beating, and imprisoning women might look bad]. Ramona has all my admiration, I hope she comes.[103]

In 1996, accompanied by Subcomandante Marcos, Ramona said a very public good-bye from Chiapas, and many Zapatistas kicked off her trip in La Realidad. She stopped in San Cristóbal de las Casas for a press conference before moving on to Mexico City. First, she spoke at the Congreso Nacional Indígena and also at a large rally in the Zócalo of Mexico City. After those appearances, she was hospitalized and had a kidney transplant, donated by her brother. She spent about a week in Poniatowska's home before the surgery. Poniatowska knew that it was a safe and secure environment where Ramona was unlikely to be pursued. Ramona's stay further solidified Poniatowska's feelings of connection to Zapatista women and also subtly demonstrated her ongoing support for the EZLN. Her circle of friends and family knew that Ramona was staying at her house. In conversation, Poniatowska expressed a great deal of affection for Ramona and concern for her health and fragility. Unable to communicate much with Ramona due to her inability to speak Tzotzil and Ramona's limited Spanish, she nonetheless felt a connection—perhaps because of her understanding of Ramona's politically and physically vulnerable position.

> She lived here and slept here. I first saw her where she was being taken care of in a place on the big avenue called Patriotismo, and then she came here to live for a while. . . . She was already sick and she had a serious kidney problem. She had to have dialysis. She was very pretty, very small, and she would go out the back door there to sit on a bench and embroider in the sun. All of them [Zapatista women] are able to embroider in an extraordinary manner. Ramona was like a little flower who would sit so that she could turn her face toward the sun. She could talk, but not much. There was not a lot of verbal communication. We communicated with our eyes, with smile, with affection.[104]

Following Ramona's visit to Mexico City in 1996, the EZLN organized a caravan of 1,111 Zapatistas who traveled from Chiapas to Mexico City, passing through Oaxaca, Puebla, and Morelos, following the route Emiliano Zapata took in 1914. They timed their arrival in Mexico City to coincide with Mexican Independence Day. The Zapatistas' tour and their meetings with political leaders, community members, students, peasants, and Indigenous peoples with thousands of admirers en route were meant to draw support for Indigenous rights and autonomy as outlined in the San Andrés Accords.

In addition to the trips and the caravan to Mexico City, the EZLN hosted a series of "encuentros" (meetings/encounters) in the 1990s, such as the Primer Encuentro Intercontinental por la Humanidad y contra el Neoliberalismo (First Zapatista Intercontinental Encuentro for Humanity and against Neoliberalism). In 1999 the EZLN organized a national consultation on Indigenous rights and sent Zapatista representatives out to every municipality in Mexico. In 2000 Vicente Fox of the conservative PAN defeated the PRI at the polls; Fox promised to implement the San Andrés

Accords and demilitarize Chiapas. The Mexican government withdrew troops from two of seven military bases, but by 2001 the talks were faltering again. The Zapatistas decided to come to Mexico City again in what came to be known as the Zapatour in Mexico. They stopped in many states on the way to the capital, where a crowd of about 100,000 supporters welcomed Subcomandante Marcos and twenty-three other comandantes in the Zócalo on March 11, 2001.[105] Poniatowska was among them.

The following day, Poniatowska—along with fellow intellectuals Carlos Monsiváis, Portuguese novelist José Saramago (who won the Nobel Prize for literature in 1998 and visited Chiapas and wrote about the EZLN), French sociologist Alain Touraine, Mexican novelist and poet Carlos Montemayor, and others—participated in a public meeting with Marcos held at the Stadium of the Olympic Village in Mexico City.[106] Poniatowska's remarks at that large public event with Marcos were published the next day as a column in *La Jornada*. In this set of activities, she publicly endorsed the Zapatistas and their push to have the San Andrés Accords legislated, and as she often did, she called out the importance of Zapatista women. Her strategy of publicly engaging with activists, sharing a public platform with them, and then publishing a column praising their initiatives builds on the great enthusiasm generated for the EZLN and channels that response to build strategic emotional political community both face-to-face and through her published texts.

She centered the activities of the EZLN in the core institutions of the Mexican nation: "The Zapatistas have come here to test our institutions. They didn't come to sign peace accords, but to open a dialogue, to be listened to and to listen, to be respected and to show respect. Their beautiful presence [in Mexico City] has inverted the concept of democracy and is showing us how decisions should be made from below" and not from above.[107] She went on to mention novels and books about Indigenous peoples but stated, "Now it is Indigenous peoples themselves who have come to share with us information about themselves. It is Indigenous peoples now who come to speak directly to us [not others for or about them] and to teach us. And the women!"[108]

It is the Indigenous women, wrote Poniatowska, who will confront Mexican senators. It is Indigenous women who "will speak to the congress. It is the women who know that peace [in Chiapas] is in the hands of the congress. . . . Today, we the Women of Mexico City pay homage to the Zapatistas and to the Indigenous women . . . who with all of our help, are proposing to build a new social relationship between all of us and our way of being."[109] Poniatowska reiterated the long list of rights that Zapatista women called for and emphasized their importance to the public. Her speech and its publication in *La Jornada* were aimed at trying to build public support for the EZLN's visit to the Mexican Congress later in the month.

On March 28, 2001, after a very warm welcome, four members of the EZLN spoke to the Mexican Congress, urging them to pass the languishing San Andrés Accords. Comandanta Esther spoke first, and although her speech has remained one of the most powerful and influential from the EZLN, it did not have the desired result in terms of passing legislation to implement the accords. Instead, the Mexican Senate implemented constitutional amendments for Articles 1, 2, 3, 18, and 115 in a legislative package officially known as La Reforma Constitucional sobre Derechos y Cultura Indígena (The Constitutional Reform for Indigenous Rights and Culture); Indigenous leaders called the legislation "San Andrés lite" because the package fell far short of much of what was proposed in the San Andrés Accords.

Nevertheless, Comandanta Esther's remarks broke an important barrier in terms of an Indigenous woman addressing the Mexican Congress, and her powerful speech resonated with many people. Her words sketched a vision for an alternative and inclusive Mexico. Two huge flags framed Comandanta Esther as she stood at the podium speaking to hundreds of people inside the Congress. Photographers were taking photos, and dozens of video cameras were filming her. The leaders of the Mexican Congress were seated at the podium with her. Hundreds of people lined the walls and filled the seats, and the event was broadcast.[110] Many longtime supporters of the EZLN were there to listen. For Poniatowska, Esther's speech was a high point for the EZLN and its presence in the capital in 2001. "When the Zapatistas came to Mexico City, the person who moved me was Comandanta Esther, when she went to our Chamber of Deputies [Congress] and gave a splendid speech," Poniatowska told me in 2011.[111]

At different times in her columns in *La Jornada*, Poniatowska has made reference to the importance of the speech that Esther gave in the Mexican Congress. In 2016 she wrote, "I remember the significance it had for all of us to hear [Esther] in the Chamber of Deputies [where she said]: 'I am an Indigenous woman and a Zapatista. Not only are hundreds of millions of Zapatistas speaking through me, but also millions of Indigenous peoples in the whole country. . . . I have come to ask for justice, liberty and democracy for the Indigenous peoples. . . . I demand constitutional acknowledgement of our rights and our culture.'"[112]

Poniatowska continued in her own voice, painting a vivid picture for her readers of what an Indigenous woman president would do for Mexico, based in part on what Zapatista women advocated for: "I don't believe that any Indigenous woman [in charge of the country] would sell out our oil to transnational companies and privatize everything. . . . An Indigenous woman would ask to have the number of children she chooses to have and can maintain; she would take care of the countryside and the forests, and for the sake of her children, she would conserve water, and ask, as the Zapatistas have, for education and health for all."[113]

Both Ramona's and Esther's presence in Mexico City, and an Indigenous leader addressing the Mexican Congress, indeed represented a symbolic change in the treatment of Indigenous women. Comandanta Esther's steadfast insistence that Indigenous women's rights had to be considered part and parcel of Indigenous autonomy and collective rights set out very clear signposts for what might be called a kind of Indigenous feminism. Indigenous women's insistence that they want to struggle "simultaneously for their communities' collective right to define themselves and determine their own future or change within the community to meet their gender demands as individual women" rendered moot the dichotomy between individual versus collective rights on which the government and many others insisted.[114] At a larger level, the actions of Zapatista women, such as Ramona, Esther, and many others, also helped "denaturalize violence and female exclusion" in Mexico, and EZLN women succeeded in moving their demands from the Lacandón Jungle of Chiapas to a central place in contemporary Mexican rights discourses, including to this day.[115] Poniatowska's ongoing public advocacy for Zapatista women was part of what helped keep their contributions in the limelight in Mexico.

Long-Term Impact

Before the United States sought to swallow the entire continent, the Indigenous resistance lifted golden shields and headdresses of Quetzal feathers. And these were lifted very high when the women of Chiapas, previously humiliated and furtive, declared in 1994 that they wanted to choose their own husbands, look them in the eyes, decide the number of children they wanted, and they did not want to be traded for a jug of alcohol. They wanted the same rights as men.
—ELENA PONIATOWSKA, April 23, 2014

Elena Poniatowska spoke these words in Madrid, Spain, when she received the Miguel de Cervantes Prize, the highest honor in Spanish literature.[116] It is telling that Poniatowska chose to cite the Women's Revolutionary Law, which, although it was published in 1994, was debated earlier in Zapatista communities such as the ejidos of Guadalupe Tepeyac and La Realidad.[117] In delivering her acceptance speech highlighting the Zapatista movement, Poniatowska was also making a strong public statement about the importance of Mexico's Indigenous peoples—particularly women—in a space symbolizing the longue durée and continued presence of Spanish colonialism in Mexico. The Cervantes prize is awarded by the king of Spain at the University of Alcalá, near the birthplace of Miguel de Cervantes (1547–1616), author of *Don Quijote de la Mancha*. The prize selection process is supported by the Spanish Royal Academy (founded in 1713 and charged with safeguarding the correct use of the Spanish language) and all the National Academies of the Spanish language in the different Spanish-speaking countries (twenty-three in total).[118] The Zapatistas brought Indigenous peoples, their language, and their quest for rights and autonomy to the attention of the world. And they also proposed key changes for women.

Poniatowska followed the public appearances of all the Zapatista women in Mexico City and elsewhere. And her long-term admiration of Mayan Zapatista women, who insisted on exercising their collective rights as Indigenous women fighting for autonomy and equity with men, endures. In my interviews with her, and as seen in her dedication in Spain when she received the Cervantes prize, she chose to focus on the Zapatista women, among others. The prize and its setting are steeped in Spanish colonialism and language. Profiling Indigenous peoples and their languages sent a particular message, one that Poniatowska articulated in conversation as well. In addition to an acceptance, her speech was a public performance embracing Mexico's Indigenous peoples and speaking back to Spanish colonialism and its inheritance, a position she took often on the public stage.

In one of our conversations, Poniatowska emphasized the lasting impact of the Zapatista movement:

The most important inheritance has been to insert Indigenous peoples into national political life. As I said before, they are now present at the table for discussions. I think before [the Zapatista movement], many people treated Indigenous people just as artisans—weavers or potters or servants if they came to Mexico City. There was a huge distance between them and the rest of the country—including for reasons of social class. This is also true in Chiapas on the part of the people of San Cristóbal de las Casas known as Coletos—who despised them [the Zapatistas].[119]

According to Poniatowska, the Zapatistas have confronted and forced others to confront a long history of racism and colonialism. Her own embrace and public advocacy for the Zapatistas in person and in print, even when accepting a literature prize, marks her continued and consistent embrace of activism as a part of writing. As she told me,

> Mexico is a racist country—racist against itself. There is racism in all thirty-two states of the republic. If you look at it, there are very few Indigenous people who have been in power. After Benito Juárez, there was one Indigenous person in power in Oaxaca, who was Heladio Ramírez [governor of Oaxaca from 1986 to 1992 and a senator from 1996 to 2012], but in general, all those who come to occupy positions of power are *criollos*—of Spanish descent. They are people who feel they are Spanish—including José López Portillo, who one time declared that he wanted to be buried in Caparrosa in Spain because his origins are not Indigenous but European. So they all want to be recognized as Spanish or presumed to have Spanish blood.[120]

She went on to talk about the ongoing colonialism of the Spanish language in the world of writers. She commented on how Mexican writers want their works translated into English but not into any of the sixty-six Indigenous languages of Mexico, to reach more Mexican readers.

> And I can say that about [well-known] writers as well. Writers are not interested in having their work translated into Indigenous languages. People, artists of all kinds, they want to become known in the United States because that is where they can make money. If you tell a writer that their work is going to be translated into Tzotzil, they couldn't care less. They wouldn't find that important at all. If you tell them, however, that their work is going to be translated into English—then, wow. That matters. A writer would consider being published in English to be an accomplishment and the path to success.[121]

It is, however, primarily through the language of Spanish that Poniatowska endorsed and promoted the ideas and accomplishments of Zapatista women to a critical Mexican public, often through her column in *La*

Jornada. Poniatowska believes that perhaps women experienced the greatest changes from the Zapatista movement. She optimistically states that the ideas of the Zapatista women changed the lives not only of Indigenous women but of all women, and men too.

> I think that the situation of many Indigenous people has changed—especially the situation of women. . . . When Indigenous women claimed their rights and said, "We want to choose the man we love . . ." "We want to look into the eyes of the man we love, that we want to choose." "We want to choose the number of children we want to have and can have." This was a huge step forward. They also said they wanted all the rights, the rights to health, the right to control the birth rate. They said, "And we want to drive a car, to drive a car just like men." This was a huge step. . . . This changed the mentality of many women. And of many men as well, I hope.[122]

Poniatowska's engagement with the Zapatistas over the long haul and her continued endorsement of their demands for Indigenous autonomy, for the rights of Indigenous women, and by extension for all women reflects the lasting effect that the Zapatista movement has had on her. The key underlying demands of the Zapatistas continue to be alive in Indigenous and non-Indigenous communities throughout Mexico. As organized crime has extended its grip into significant parts of Mexican national territory, the struggles for Indigenous autonomy, control of natural resources, governance, and justice continue. Zapatista women's demands to be free of violence and sexual assault have appeared in many other Indigenous communities in Guerrero, Oaxaca, Michoacán, and elsewhere. And their interest in political representation took off at the national level.

Marichuy's political candidacy for president in 2018, which the Congreso Nacional Indígena (initiated by the Zapatistas in 1996) promoted, animated Indigenous organizing at local, regional, state, and national levels. She focused her campaign on defending Indigenous territories from extractive mining, logging, and other industries, and called for a broader program of Indigenous rights and autonomy. Marichuy received extensive and daily press coverage in the months before the 2018 election. Her very presence as an Indigenous, female candidate for president changed the symbolic landscape of Mexican politics as she declared that there will "never be a Mexico without us, Indigenous peoples."[123] While Marichuy did not receive enough signatures to make it onto the formal ballot as a presidential candidate, she did receive almost 300,000 of the 866,593 signatures required. Poniatowska and her daughter, Paula, went out and collected signatures to help get Marichuy on the ballot. In one of her columns for *La Jornada* in 2016, Poniatowska endorsed Marichuy as the first Indigenous woman presidential candidate, leveraging her position as a public intellectual to try to influence her readers and honor the legacy and message of the EZLN. She used the memory of Comandanta Ramona to connect the 1990s to 2016: "Commander Ramona, who died of kidney cancer [in 2006], asked us to walk with her. I still remember her embroidering flowers of mutual respect on blouses and scarves. Hopefully, the new and welcome Zapatista candidate will embroider our brains."[124]

Poniatowska has used her newspaper columns and appearances as a political tool. In choosing to side with the EZLN, she was strongly motivated by the message of Indigenous women's rights that Zapatista women delivered. She commented on it several times in our conversations. She understood the importance of public support for the Zapatistas and their legal strategies in their efforts to gain more rights and change the Mexican Constitution to include the agreements outlined by the San Andrés Accords. When this failed and the accords were not implemented, backing an Indigenous female candidate for president in her effort to gain sufficient signatures to be on the ballot was an extension of Poniatowska's earlier efforts. The Zapatistas were not the only political cause she openly advocated for in the 1990s and the following decade. In 2005 she was approached by Andrés Manuel López Obrador, then mayor of Mexico City, to work with him on his first presidential campaign.

Amanecer en el Zócalo

Crónica, Diary, and
Gendered Political Analysis

PONIATOWSKA'S ACTIVISM FOR THE ZAPATISTAS in the 1990s and into the following decade often placed her at public events in support of this and other social movements. At the same time, she was remarkably productive as a writer and received international recognition for her work. She continued writing columns for *La Jornada*, and between 1994 and 2006 she published four long essays, three novels, one crónica, a book of oral histories and photos, a collection of short stories, and a book of photos with an essay. Her writing and literary production continued at a staggering pace, as did her public appearances. The prizes, her publications, and her ongoing activism kept her in the limelight. Her writing came together with her active performance of politics—a Mexican tradition consolidated in leftist politics in Mexico City, where artists and intellectuals are concentrated along with relatively autonomous institutions of public education. This chapter highlights the ways in which left creative performative politics occupy their own particular space in the critical public sphere. In addition, the chapter highlights how political protests, sit-ins, public space occupations, and mass demonstrations "have often been enacted through ritualized performances in public space."[1]

In 2000 Mexico experienced an important transition in electoral politics. For the first time since the Mexican Revolution, an opposition candidate for president won. Vicente Fox of the Partido Acción Nacional (PAN), representing the larger Alliance for Change, won the election with 42.52 percent of the vote. The PRI candidate, Francisco Labastida Ochoa, who had been predicted to win, came in second with 26.11 percent of the vote. Cuauhtémoc Cárdenas, the first head of the independent government of Mexico City (known then as the Distrito Federal) from 1997 to 1999, and head of the Partido de la Revolución Democrática (PRD) from 1989 to 1993, came in third on his third attempt to win the presidency.[2] The big news was that the seventy-year rule of the PRI had been overturned.

During the Fox administration (2000–2006), Poniatowska continued to make public appearances, including a lecture she gave in 2003 on the political importance of testimonial literature and crónicas at Casa Lamm, a cultural center in Mexico City.[3] In 2000 Colombia and Chile gave Poniatowska their highest writing awards. The following year she received the José Fuentes Mares National Prize for Literature in Mexico as well as the annual prize for best novel by the Spanish publishing house Alfaguara for *La piel del cielo* (The skin of heaven). In 2006 she received the Lifetime Achievement Award from the International Women's Media Foundation for her work. By then she was approaching the pinnacle of her national and international recognition as a writer and public intellectual, and she was widely recognized as a very important cultural and activist figure in Mexico.

It is not surprising, then, that in 2005, when he was planning a presidential run from the platform of mayor of Mexico City, Andrés Manuel López Obrador (AMLO) came to ask for her help. It took some time for Poniatowska to develop a relationship with AMLO and his campaign. Her most intensive involvement with him and his organization came before and after the elections of 2006 when the PRD occupied the Zócalo and Paseo de la Reforma in Mexico City from July 29 through September 13, 2006. López Obrador and the PRD alleged that there had been major voting irregularities. After they lost the preliminary vote count, AMLO and his supporters took to the streets and set up a long-running occupancy of Mexico City's Zócalo.

On July 29, 2006, López Obrador told Poniatowska; her daughter, Paula; and Jesusa Rodríguez, "I have thought about it. We are going to stay. We are going to set up and settle into encampments until the Tribunal Electoral del Poder Judicial de la Federación [Electoral Tribunal of the Judicial Power of the Federation] orders a recount of all of the votes in all of the ballot boxes."[4]

Figure 5.1 Elena Poniatowska with Andrés Manuel López Obrador in Mexico City. Used by permission of the Fundación Elena Poniatowska Amor, Mexico City, Mexico.

Deciding to work with AMLO was another significant turning point in her career. It also, ironically, pushed her away from writing. She spent many hours traveling, giving talks, meeting people, and attending events for AMLO's campaign. Like other choices she made to prioritize activism, this resulted in a sacrifice.

> Writing is a great solitary adventure at your desk and if you are answering the phone, and if you are going to the corner, and if you are going to a bunch of meetings, there comes a point when you no longer have a relationship with your work and, sometimes, not even with yourself. And you think that you are being useful because you do twenty thousand things per day, and you come and go and never stop. And in the end, it is simply a terrifying scattering of oneself. You are like a whirling tornado. . . . I thought, "I am deceiving myself." I should not continue with this.[5]

She sacrificed writing time but also some of her public, judging by the popularity of her crónica *Amanecer en el Zócalo* (Waking up in the Zócalo), about her experiences in AMLO's 2006 campaign and the subsequent fifty-day occupation of Mexico City's Zócalo (figure 5.1). She has often noted that it has sold the lowest number of copies of all her books.

Despite its apparently narrow reach, *Amanecer en el Zócalo* is a crucial crónica in Poniatowska's oeuvre. As both a crónica and a sort of personal diary, it inserts Poniatowska as a major protagonist and thinker into Mexican politics. As longtime Poniatowska analyst Beth Jörgensen argues, *Amanecer* is a book "with its own unique double personality . . . one that combines a chronicle of contemporary political events with an autobiographical narrative in the form of the diary. Politics and self-portrait come together."[6] The book offers readers an intimate look at the people in the *plantón* (sit-in); their personal, political, and daily-life engagements; and their diversity, hopes, dreams, and challenges—an intimacy consistent with her other analyses of social movements from the 1968 student movement to the civil society movement sparked by the 1985 earthquake to the Zapatistas. *Amanecer* weaves the plantón in the Zócalo into the historical continuity of these prior movements. This chapter seeks to illustrate two different dimensions to the construction of strategic emotional political community in relation to the plantón. One dimension is the spatially restricted face-to-face strategic emotional political community that emerged during the occupation of the Zócalo by thousands of people that Poniatowska herself participated in. Political and theatrical performances at the Zócalo emphasize performative politics and serve in the moment as a way to bring the disparate groups of people living in the Zócalo together. In addition to her daily participation there, Poniatowska also strategically writes about this community, seeking to connect it to readers, many of whom were likely not directly involved in the plantón on a daily basis. The performative politics of the plantón is also reported on by many media sources, some of which Poniatowska also reproduces and comments on in her book. Both in person and in the writing of *Amanecer*, Poniatowska tries to link the strategic emotional political community that emerged in the physical space of the Zócalo to the organizing of a larger political movement that eventually carried López Obrador to electoral victory in the 2018 presidential elections. It is here where the limits to this strategic emotional political community are revealed, both for her and ultimately for readers as reflected in the low sales of the book. Her descriptions of the day-to-day life of the plantón emerge as the most genuine expression of this community. Later in the book, she expresses some doubt about the seemingly ritualized political performance of a massive *consulta* (consultation) carried out in one day with no real discussion or process with the movement supporting López Obrador that takes place in the same public space after the plantón has been dismantled. As a personal narrative, it offers a rich and honest picture of Poniatowska's direct engagement with electoral and party politics as she learned and navigated the many requests made of her to support López Obrador and the PRD from April 2005 until mid-September 2006.

Amanecer also tells the story of contemporary Mexican politics through the analysis, friendship, and collaboration of two women: Poniatowska and her close friend and compatriot Jesusa Rodríguez, an actress, director, playwright, performance artist, social activist, and improvisational theater producer who was elected to the Senate in July 2018 through the MORENA coalition. Rodríguez and Poniatowska most likely met in the late 1980s during Friday lunches at the home of mutual friend and feminist Marta Lamas. During the period covered in *Amanecer*, Poniatowska and Rodríguez saw each other constantly; shared the experience of the plantón on a daily basis; observed López Obrador and his team plan their strategies and speak in public every day; and shared information, questions, and analysis. Both Rodríguez and Poniatowska were familiar public figures on the left, and they had long used art and culture (particularly public performances) to make political statements and as political strategies.

The story of their friendship and collaboration in the plantón reveals how they applied the lessons they learned from being social movement activists to the more formal sphere of electoral and party politics and together worked with others face-to-face to build strategic emotional political community in the Zócalo and beyond. Poniatowska portrays Rodríguez as one of the key protagonists in the plantón who provided the organization, inspiration, and an unending stream of cultural and intellectual activities to occupy and engage the thousands of men, women, and children who were camped out there. In centering her work, the book suggests a broader definition of "politics" to include not only formal political rallies but all the cultural and social work done to sustain them and the occupation. As such, it illustrates how Mexican politics can move on a continuum from social movements and different kinds of activism into more formal electoral and party politics. Rodríguez remained committed to AMLO and, like him in July 2018, became a part of the formally elected government that they both had criticized for so long.

While Andrés Manuel López Obrador is a significant character in *Amanecer*, he is not the main character; it is the plantón itself and its people. For Poniatowska and all the people she describes, the Zócalo's meaning transformed and changed through its long-term occupation by people from throughout Mexico. Thirty-one encampments were set up, representing the different states that made up the entire nation of Mexico.

The plantón came to function as a local community that Poniatowska, Rodríguez, and thousands of others participated in on a daily basis, with twenty kitchens, a wide range of stages, day-care centers, spaces to show movies, bathrooms, a church, a market, a hospital, and other installations. Poniatowska highlights the people who maintained the plantón, the backbone of the resistance to what they believed was a fraudulent election that had discounted their votes and the issues important to them, erasing what were supposed to be democratic processes. This is the most direct manifestation of strategic emotional political community the book documents.

Thus, while Poniatowska's book is a partial portrayal of AMLO, it also works as a critical analysis of Mexico's political processes and parties. It provides ongoing documentation and critical commentary of politics itself—that is, the way that the strategy team and PRD politicians functioned—and she continually contrasted this with those who were not at the top of the political hierarchy: women in small communities who engaged in debate, students, the daily discussions on the Zócalo, and more. As in her other crónicas, the description of the plantón in *Amanecer* is gendered in that it pays careful attention to and validates the many contributions women made in work that often remained invisible in chronicles of protest and politics. Women really were the glue that held the encampment together, hauling water, cooking and serving food for thousands, watching children and keeping them entertained day and night, and adapting to the extreme weather. This might be seen as a binary gender analysis of politics itself with men as formal leaders and women as their support, but it's more complex. Rather than seeking to establish AMLO as the center of the movement she is documenting and participating in, she opts to move other figures to the center and to interrogate politics itself.

Through Poniatowska's analysis, we can see the determination, stamina, and hope of those in the plantón and the 1,125,000 people who pledged to work for AMLO into the future. The strategic emotional political community Poniatowska helped create on the ground through her public presence and on the page through her documentation of the plantón is consciously represented as continuous with similar communities in the past, such as the student movement of 1968, the civil society movement of 1985, the movement that founded the PRD and worked with Cárdenas's campaign in 1988, and the Zapatistas in 1994 and into the current century. Poniatowska's own involvement and the text that grew out of it thus work to connect the plantón and the people behind it with strategic emotional and political communities that her work had helped articulate in the past and continued to create in the future. *Amanecer* strategically links and represents Ponia-towska's written work and her public political activism.

Joining the Team

López Obrador caught Poniatowska's attention as early as 1991, when he was part of a PAN, PRD, and Partido Demócrata Mexicano (Mexican Democratic Party) coalition supporting Dr. Salvador Nava Martínez as a candidate for governor in San Luis Potosí.[7] When Nava lost the election due to what many believed to be electoral fraud (echoing the 1988 national elections), López Obrador participated in the Marcha de la Dignidad (March for Dignity) on September 27, 1991, which Nava led.[8] After Nava died of cancer in May 1992, seven months after the protest, his widow, Conchita Calvillo de Nava, continued her husband's democratization movement. López Obrador was a part of that legacy.[9] The Marcha de la Dignidad was part of a series of ongoing actions that López Obrador participated in from the early 1990s through his third presidential campaign to democratize the formal electoral system in Mexico and push back on suspected fraud attempts.

Poniatowska first met López Obrador in person when he showed up at her house in early April 2005 to ask for her help.[10] This was the first of two visits that month. At that time, he was the *jefe de gobierno* (head of government, equivalent to mayor, from December 5, 2000, to July 29, 2005) of Mexico City and fighting an effort to revoke his state immunity from prosecution, referred to as *fuero*, which elected officials in Mexico enjoy while in office. He was also privately contemplating being a presidential candidate for the PRD. Losing this immunity is a process known as *desafuero*.

López Obrador had gotten caught up in a lawsuit that predated his tenure but impacted him nonetheless; his predecessor had expropriated land for a private hospital, leading the landowner to sue the government in 2001. A federal judicial order called for construction to be halted until the matter was resolved. López Obrador, however, did not follow the order, and work on building a road to the hospital continued. When the Attorney General of Mexico, Rafael Macedo de la Concha, called for desafuero to be applied to López Obrador in May 2004, it was the beginning of a two-year process that raised important issues related to democracy, including the uneven application of the law to large financial scandals involving members of PAN, Fox's growing weakness as president and his inability to deliver on his campaign promises, and AMLO's great popularity. López Obrador would have to go before the Chamber of Deputies, which would vote on whether to strip him of his immunity. If the Chamber of Deputies voted in favor, then by law he would lose his office immediately and be required to step down as head of Mexico City's government.

If AMLO did become a public candidate for the presidency, he would also need to cut short his term as the head of the Mexico City government. In September 2005, he was nominated by the PRD as a pre-candidate for president in the general elections for 2006. Internal polls of the PRD showed he had widespread support within the party. When he approached Poniatowska twice in April 2005, he was recruiting her as an extremely well-known public intellectual to advocate for him, for his honesty, and for his ideas, much as she had done for Subcomandante Marcos and the EZLN. At the time he first approached her, he was likely thinking of her ability to defend him not only in the process of the desafuero but also for the long term, as a key participant in his future presidential campaign team. She was at the peak of her fame and popular with many people, particularly from the Mexican left, from social movements, and from the urban popular classes.

After AMLO's first visit, when he requested that she defend him as an honest and effective mayor of Mexico City, Poniatowska began to speak out on his behalf. On April 18, 2005, she and writer Paco Ignacio Taibo went on the television program *Democracy Now!* with Amy Goodman to defend AMLO. Goodman asked Poniatowska to explain what was going on in Mexican politics. Poniatowska responded, "I was just asked by Andres Manuel López Obrador, who suddenly arrived at my house. I hadn't even—I think I had seen him twice in my life, and he asked me to help him. And I was so indignant at what was happening [referring to the desafuero effort] that, of course, I said yes."[11] Poniatowska and Taibo both make it clear that the attempt to remove AMLO from his Mexico City office was also perceived as a way to prevent him from being a formal presidential candidate. Poniatowska's defense of him clearly works not only to discredit the accusations levied at him by the Fox administration through the desafuero process but also to help position him as a popular candidate for president, even if he was not yet formally declared as a candidate at that point in time. Goodman summarized the situation for listeners: "A crisis as the leading presidential candidate, the Mayor of Mexico City, López Obrador, has been accused by the ruling party of breaking the law years ago in allowing the construction of a ramp onto a highway, something that people have not quite figured out yet exactly what it is that he was charged with, tremendous reaction in the Mexican population. Last week, a protest of perhaps a third of a million people in the streets of Mexico City."[12] Earlier in the conversation, Poniatowska described this protest and what AMLO had done for the city: "Yes. 350,000 people now march, because maybe he's a different kind of a politician. . . . He is a man who speaks like you and me and Paco. He makes mistakes. He has another voice. His voice is different from the voice of the political men we are used to. I think that's very important. Besides, people love him. He has given money for the first time in the history of Mexico to all the men and women. He has built a university. He has built schools. He has built hospitals."[13]

Before he was even a formal candidate, Poniatowska was using her connections and network to organize support for him. Poniatowska suspected that AMLO came to her based on the books she had written and their political and social influence and content: "Maybe he looked me up because of my book *La noche de Tlatelolco* or . . . *Fuerte es el silencio*, which speaks about the forced disappearance of political activists."[14] When we first talked in 2011, her face suggested real curiosity about why AMLO initially came to her. She was still puzzled about what he saw in her in terms of her ability to contribute to a political campaign team, which was his request on his second visit to her house in April 2005.

Poniatowska explained, "He sat there on the same yellow sofa you're sitting on now and told me that he wanted me to help him. I was very surprised; I responded that I didn't have any [political] experience. But then I started to work a lot. I stopped doing everything else, even writing" to work on his campaign.[15] In *Amanecer*, Poniatowska shared the specific request AMLO made of her to serve as a campaign adviser: "When I was sitting by the bougainvillea creating the first pages of a novel, Andrés Manuel returned to my house [a few weeks after his initial visit] in his white [vw] Jetta." He made a specific request: "I want you to be my adviser, I want you to create proposals for me and talk with everyone in the world of literature, art, and science to put together a cultural project/platform" for the campaign.[16] During some of the first meetings of the campaign, Poniatowska was given the task of amassing a massive amount of data on a wide range of topics in every state in Mexico. López Obrador was speaking to thousands of people on a daily basis as he campaigned in every municipality in Mexico. As AMLO wound his way through dozens of isolated towns in the far corners of Mexico, Poniatowska was put to work helping prepare him for all these visits. She used her literary and social activism connections to help smooth the way for his arrival in many places. She put the multiple strategic emotional political communities she had helped forge since 1968 through her activism and publishing in the service of AMLO's campaign. This was an extremely valuable resource for him and his team. According to Poniatowska:

> He was going to travel to all the states in the Republic, so political analyst Ignacio Marván [who worked for AMLO] asked me to find distinguished people in each state in the sciences and culture, etcetera, and write about them for him to mention, and also write about the histories of the buildings, monuments, and churches. . . . He wanted to know about the culture of each state, including the food. So I also did that. . . . More than anything else, I went to many rallies, spoke in meetings, wrote speeches. It frightened me to have to speak like that all the time. It was also gratifying for me because it meant being closer to the people.[17]

Poniatowska's work for the campaign also entailed appearing in a set of television advertising spots to bolster AMLO in April 2006, less than three months shy of election day. The ads were made to counter negative campaigning by PAN. In order to undermine AMLO's candidacy, a series of ads paid for by PAN stated the same message, repeatedly: "López Obrador is a danger for Mexico." Poniatowska was featured in one TV ad defending AMLO from charges made in the PAN ads, including that he had indebted Mexico City while he was mayor and that he was linked to Hugo Chávez, the president of Venezuela at the time. In the commercials, she stated that AMLO had led Mexico City with honesty, had achieved savings, and had led with good government. At the end of the ad, she said, "Play cleanly, don't defame."[18]

Reactions to the ad were swift. Carlos Monsiváis defended her, as did other intellectuals on the left, but some family, friends, and fellow journalists were condemning. Some responses were clearly sexist and tried to diminish Poniatowska's ability and her right to comment on politics as a literary figure. One even questioned AMLO's masculinity. Amon Ra of the newspaper *Universal* wrote, "Mrs. Poniatowska wasn't that prudent when she lent her image to defend the ideas of AMLO, who, by the way, seems to need someone with the appearance of a grandmother to come out and defend him. Does he have no balls?"[19] The response to Poniatowska as a public political figure was severe. Her experience supporting AMLO in 2006 cost her friends and likely some family connections, and put her in danger.

López Obrador ran a well-disciplined campaign. There were wide expectations that he would win, probably by a large proportion of votes. With a historic turnout of forty-two million voters, many were positive that he had, including Poniatowska. As she recounts in *Amanecer*,

After the elections of July 2, the IFE [Instituto Federal Electoral, Federal Electoral Institute] declared Felipe Calderón the winner. Andrés Manuel López Obrador was stunned. He couldn't believe it. He had never even considered the possibility of defeat, and as the political scientists say, he didn't have a plan B. A lot of us Mexicans felt like we had been beaten over the head with a stick. . . . I thought that despite all the dirty campaigning that went on, the fear mongering, the campaign [against AMLO] led by businessmen, [and] the enormous amount of money spent to beat it into people's heads over the radio and television that AMLO was a danger to Mexico, and the difference between one candidate and another was 0.57 percent. . . . I thought after all of this that Andrés Manuel had to be the winner.[20]

To demonstrate the depth of despair and discontent his supporters and he felt, AMLO declared that they were going to occupy the Zócalo in the center of Mexico City and demand a recount of the votes. After AMLO decided to occupy the Zócalo, Poniatowska; her daughter, Paula; and her friend Jesusa Rodríguez bought a tent to serve as their base in the Zócalo. They gathered all their yellow clothes, to match the color of the PRD's Aztec yellow symbol, to wear every day. They drove to the Zócalo, where thousands of people were gathering and distributing free food, including *tortas de mole* (chicken mole sandwiches). Poniatowska's son Felipe was always present at meetings and traveled with López Obrador.

Poniatowska was delighted with the scene at the Zócalo, where she recognized the same feeling of community and support she had experienced in earlier critical moments of Mexican history. As she recounts early on in *Amanecer*, "¡La solidaridad es le reina de la fiesta! [Solidarity is the queen of the party!]. I remember the solidarity after the earthquakes of 1985. 'I'll help you out. Here, I will pitch in and dig with my shovel.' It was the people on the street who got the survivors out of the wreckage."[21] Connecting the plantón experience to the mass organizing of civil society in 1985 links the base of López Obrador's campaign operation to this transformative event in Mexican politics, which eventually launched what became the PRD through the electoral campaign of Cuauhtémoc Cárdenas. It also creates a link between the memory of the strategic emotional political community that emerged in 1985 with the growing plantón community that gathered in the Zócalo in 2006. Delegations began to pour in from the states of Guerrero, Hidalgo, Puebla, Quintana Roo, Sonora, Sinaloa, and from around the country, turning the Zócalo into a truly national space.

Soon after he announced the plantón, López Obrador asked Poniatowska to address the crowd of two million people gathered in the Zócalo, which she eventually agreed to do, but with fear and trepidation. Poniatowska followed Evangelina Corona, who spoke for the seamstresses, and Rosario Ibarra, who addressed the issue of political prisoners and the disappeared, including her son Jesús Piedra Ibarra, who vanished in 1975. Having Poniatowska speak after these figures whom she had written about and their associated movements allowed the audience to connect the importance of AMLO's Zócalo occupation and the PRD with these previous movements. It was a powerful performative political beginning for the occupation of the Zócalo.

Poniatowska's speech, quoted in her book, pulled together some of the historical figures she had written about in other crónicas as well as highlighted ordinary people. This performance is another way that she used her public stature and fame as a writer to advance AMLO's cause and to justify the plantón. It also reflects AMLO's strategic use of the networks and connections that Poniatowska had forged through time. Her testimony on the stage, with her daughter and granddaughter, Luna, by her side, worked to bring together multiple generations of social movement heroes with the cultural and political figures who have acted in resistance throughout Mexican history. In channeling them, she channeled Mexican history and her credibility as a Mexican public intellectual, and political leader. Her presence and words also linked AMLO to these histories, perhaps suggesting that they were on that day making Mexican history. By reproducing her speech in her crónica later, she moved this timeline of resistance into a fixed medium that can be read, discussed, and interpreted. The speech and its reproduction were part of a conscious effort to build out the strategic emotional political community that was coming together in the plantón with a wider critical public.

We resist today because we will be resisting tomorrow, and because in each one of us the roots of civil and peaceful resistance, the foundation of our history, can be found. Morelos, Hidalgo, Guadalupe Victoria, Juárez, Madero, Zapata, Villa, Lázaro Cárdenas existed just as Demetrio Vallejo, Valentín Campa, Othón Salazar, Frida Kahlo, Rosario Ibarra, Evangelina Corona, Rubén Jaramillo, Florencio el Güero Medrano, Tere the juice vendor who has sent us fruit and has given us water, the Río Blanco and Nueva Rosita strikers, the Pasta de Conchos miners, and the seamstresses who survived the earthquakes of 1985 have existed. Our resistance is open, legal, transparent, and we practice it in plain sight and under the open sky. . . .

Here are the blood and bones of our grandparents. Mexico is ours by our own right; we are not orphans, we are Mexicans and, today more than ever, Mexico belongs to us in this great party of resistance.[22]

The Story of the Plantón

The Zócalo, saturated with history, is located close to the Mexica (Aztec) ceremonial site of Templo Mayor, dedicated to Huitzilopochtli, the god of war, and Tláloc, the god of rain. The Spanish destroyed Templo Mayor to make way for a cathedral in 1521. The Zócalo itself has served through both colonial and modern times as a major staging area for proclamations, ceremonies, parades, religious celebrations, protests, and the swearing in of viceroys and presidents. In Poniatowska's *Amanecer*, the Zócalo and the plantón occupation become important protagonists. Much as James Joyce's *Ulysses* is set in Dublin; Gabriel García's Márquez's *Love in the Time of Cholera* invokes Cartagena, Colombia; and Zadie Smith's books *White Teeth* and *NW* are set in London, the ever-changing daily life of the plantón in the middle of Mexico City emerges as a major character in Poniatowska's book and is one she cares for and admires.

The entry for July 31, one of the longest in the book, discusses the Zócalo and the plantón in great detail. "At twelve p.m., the transformation of the Zócalo is a great surprise. Is it the Zócalo or is it a popular fair?"[23] The mayor of Mexico City in 2006 who followed AMLO in the post after his term ended at the end of July 2005, Alejandro Encinas Rodríguez of the PRD, ordered that a series of large white tents with windows and zippers be installed to accommodate the people from his party. Each representative of the PRD would have their own encampment in a large tent that they paid for in part. López Obrador's tent became the political meeting room for AMLO's strategic teams. Apart from these somewhat luxurious accommodations for politicians, those who decided to stay set up tents and slept on mattresses, blankets, or just cardboard on the ground. The rainy season provided an ongoing challenge. Poniatowska described the Zócalo as extremely wet and full of puddles, "but it smells of coffee, of bread, of onions, it is a huge market like the one that Diego Rivera attributed to the great Tenochtitlán and painted celestially. Here, at the corner, a woman who sells quesadillas fries the potato quesadillas, the *chicharrón* [pork rind] ones, the *huitlacoche* [corn smut or fungus] ones, and she distributes water. Over there, the *atole* [drink made of corn flour] is boiling. How were they able to get supplies so fast?"[24]

Ordinary people had disrupted their lives and come to live in the Zócalo. Poniatowska profiled María de la Luz Mendoza de Chapela, who was eighty-seven years old and had eleven children and twenty-five grandchildren. She said she could stay and live in the Zócalo because she had the advantage of being old: "Now all my children have gone their own way and I can make use of my own time. When I have to go home, I take the metro, which is very comfortable."[25] Another person, Luchita, whose husband was a PAN activist, had moved to Mexico City, where she saw López Obrador close up and was converted. He was, she said, "an authentic man."[26] Then there was ninety-four-year-old Anastasia Flores Moreno, diminutive, with her white hair plaited into four braids; she wore a prosthetic leg and still liked to dance. Or Doña Herminia, from San Fernando in the state of Mexico, who got up at 5 a.m. to plant herself in the Zócalo with hopes of getting a hug from AMLO. The women Poniatowska describes were the heart of the life of the Zócalo: they cleaned, they made the coffee, they organized everything. They arrived from Coyoacán, Tlalpan, Xochimilco, and other places in the city with cooked food—rice, beans, and tortillas—for those who were camped out. They were the workers behind the amazing daily activity in the plantón. These portraits illustrate how Poniatowska endears readers to her characters and through these connections strategically describes and represents the people in the plantón on the page.

Poniatowska's writing suggests that the efficiency with which everything was carried out in the giant encampment came from the older people who knew how to survive and move forward in what were often difficult daily lives. Fourteen large water tanks were set up for everyone to use, electricity was "stolen through the '*diablitos*'" (unauthorized connections to the power supply), as was done in the poor *colonias* (neighborhoods) around Mexico City. The Mexico City government provided latrines. There was a workshop that taught men how to put on a condom, as well as dances to different kinds of music, and activities until one in the morning. People continued to pour in, like the one thousand people from Sinaloa who arrived on buses and had to park very far away because the Zócalo and surrounding area were already full. What amazed Poniatowska the most was the diversity and cooperation that existed across so many differences: "There are children, elderly people and women to feed. Here, social divisions have lost any meaning; there is a common task: Surviving. There is no hostility and, if there is, I don't perceive it. Social power is built by all of us and, while this grows, the individual disappears."[27] Here she is building a narrative of community in the plantón that also connects to readers.

The Zócalo had become "Andrés Manuel López Obrador's living room," and millions of people were excited and motivated to occupy the city and stay with him at great sacrifice, in the rain and in the cold. They listened to his speeches every night at 7 p.m. and tried to get as close to him as possible. Poniatowska saw the social body of people who formed the Zócalo community as strong but also as vulnerable.

Throughout the almost two-month period that the plantón endured, the weather was terrible. It rained on a daily basis, and on August 3, a major hailstorm destroyed tents and walls, soaking through sleeping bags and blankets and in general turning the encampment upside down. Ever vigilant and extremely dedicated, Jesusa Rodríguez grabbed the microphone and said, "Nobody is leaving here. The hail came down with such strength that it went right through the plastic and all our things got wet; but we will remain here until the election is cleaned up."[28] People swept up the hailstones, doing their best to dry out their tents and things and go to sleep. The next day their signs were displayed in the Paseo de la Reforma, proclaiming, "No to Fraud, not a step backward. We are all López Obrador."[29] The collective character of the plantón, as illustrated in Poniatowska's *Amanecer*, was firm and resilient in the face of ongoing challenges.

One of the measures of the plantón's effectiveness was the strong reaction to it in Mexico City. Many of Poniatowska's friends and relatives thought that her participation in the plantón was insane. Beyond her own circle, many in the city—including Poniatowska's dear friend, Carlos Monsiváis—were against the plantón and said so in published comments. The Confederación Patronal de la República Mexicana (Employers' Confederation of the Mexican Republic) stated that at least 25 hundred million pesos (US$125 million in 2018) were wasted thanks to the presence of the plantón.[30] Poniatowska described newspaper stories that suggested it was costing hotel operators 2 million pesos per day and that it left 100,000 people in the city without access to public transportation. Because of the plantón, it took them three hours longer to get to work.[31] An Associated Press report suggested that tourists were afraid to go to Mexico City, costing it US$23 million per day, and that many families were losing income.[32] *Amanecer* highlights the many critiques made on both sides of the political spectrum and provides a wide selection of opinions about the plantón and its impact on the city, both positive and negative.

Poniatowska also documents the racism people in the plantón endured from those who opposed it. People passing by shouted insults, calling them "a bunch of *nacos*, Indians without mothers, outcasts, and thieves who now have the opportunity to make a mark."[33] While Poniatowska documents the insults that were hurled on a daily basis at those camped out in the plantón, she also describes the ongoing personal criticism she endured from friends and family for the public role she played in AMLO's campaign and her support of and presence in the plantón. She paid a high cost. *Amanecer* recounts calls from Poniatowska's sister, Kitzia, who tried periodically to convince her to abandon AMLO's team. Her sister worried about her: "Do you think you are Joan of Arc or did you hit your head? You are completely crazy. You have never been grounded in reality, but now, even less. Get out, sister, get out. Those people don't deserve you. . . . Sister, get out, it will end badly for you, you are scaring me. I don't want anything to happen to you."[34] Later, Kitzia suggests that Poniatowska's political work for AMLO is negatively impacting her family, something that Poniatowska partially validates. On a phone call, her sister asks, "'Don't you realize that you are hurting your children horribly, and also mine? Santiago had been working for a year on a house project for Roberto Hernández, and he has canceled it . . . and Santiago is only your nephew. What will happen to your own kids?' . . . It is true, my family, my children—except Mane who is at UAM [Universidad Autónoma Metropolitana]—my daughter-in-law are all suffering the consequences of my support for AMLO."[35]

She documented several death threats called into her home phone in the middle of the night during the period of the plantón, for example, "Stupid ass whore, we are fed up with you and we'll finish you off. Fucking bitch, we're going to kill you."[36] The phone call that most upset her was not a death threat but someone who called in the middle of the night to tell her that someone was in her garden. What disconcerted her most was the realization of the intense hatred the caller felt. This contrasted profoundly with the love she felt daily among all the people in the plantón: "At 2:40 a.m. the phone rings and I look at the clock. A very beautiful masculine voice tells me as if in a friendly way: Elena, a man just went into your garden. Call the police. . . . Among all the aggressions that I have received, this is the worst because, for the first time, I experienced something I had just been guessing before: Hate."[37] The call reveals the high levels of animosity toward the plantón, AMLO, and ultimately the existence of another political community galvanized against the PRD and her personally.

Through documenting the contradictory and complex nature of this sustained political protest and her part in it, Poniatowska draws her readers into a personal, emotional relationship. Being able to experience the daily life in the plantón through the eyes of Poniatowska not only as an observer but as a participant makes this crónica unique. The emotional connection for readers is further strengthened through the foregrounding she gives to her friendship and political collaboration with Jesusa Rodríguez.

Politics through the Lens of Friendship

The friendship between Elena Poniatowska and Jesusa Rodríguez serves as an important lens for the underlying analysis of politics that permeates *Amanecer*. It also provides insight into the ways that public performances and performative culture are important parts of creating strategic emotional political community and consistent with the long history of performative politics in Mexico. After Poniatowska agreed to help out AMLO following his visit to her home in 2005, she immediately recruited Rodríguez to work with her. Rodríguez was active in social movements and critical popular culture before she took on coordinating the stage, entertainment, and cultural activities at the plantón. She had decades of experience in performance, political satire, theater, and creative commentary on Mexican society. Her experience creating *espectáculos* (performances) on topics ranging from the Conquest according to Malinche to a mock trial of former Mexican president Carlos Salinas de Gortari prepared her well for the role she took on in the 2006 plantón and related protests. Rodríguez and her spouse, singer Liliana Felipe, opened up a political cabaret called El Hábito in Mexico City in 1990 in a house that had belonged to Salvador Novo, the well-known poet, essayist, chronicler, and historian of Mexico.

By the time Rodríguez and Felipe opened the performance space known as La Capilla in the former Novo house, Rodríguez recalls that she and Poniatowska were good friends: "We would see each other every Friday; we would see each other often. We would go to the movies, we would travel. . . . Elena always had me dazzled. . . . I was completely in love with Elena and happy to have her nearby."[38] Like Poniatowska, Rodríguez came to politics through culture and through listening to a wide range of voices, particularly of those who were not in power. She approached politics as an observer and then translated her observations into theater and performance. In an interview with me in 2015, she explained, "I never had any political education through a political party. I never belonged to a political party. So for me everything was about reading, listening, listening in the streets, reading the newspaper, reading everything I could, and trying to guess what was happening in the country in order to create daily performances."[39] Rodríguez traveled to Chiapas with Poniatowska for the CND of the Zapatistas in 1994 and ended up in charge of the microphone in front of 100,000 people. She organized a massive clean-up and reorganization of the CND space after a major thunderstorm abruptly ended the inaugural ceremony and dispersed people far and wide.

As two women who listened to the voices of those on the streets, who read widely from a variety of viewpoints, and who looked for ways to communicate about politics to a broad public, Poniatowska and Rodríguez had much in common. When Poniatowska approached Rodríguez about working with her to support AMLO in his campaign, and then AMLO asked Rodríguez to take charge of the stage in the Zócalo plantón, their friendship entered an intense phase. Their lives changed from the moment on July 29, 2006, that AMLO announced that his supporters were going to remain in the Zócalo and then asked the two friends to come and see him.

Rodríguez told me that she didn't know what it would really mean to close down the Paseo de la Reforma, a major thoroughfare that runs through the heart of Mexico City. Many of Mexico City's tallest buildings are on Reforma as well as important national monuments such as the Ángel de la Independencia (Angel of Independence), built to mark the one hundredth anniversary of Mexico's independence, and the Monumento a la Revolución (Monument to the Revolution). Both monuments contain tombs bearing the remains of heroes of both Mexican independence and the Mexican Revolution. Paseo de la Reforma runs into the Plaza de las Tres Culturas in Tlatelolco, heavy with the history of the massacre. The other end of Reforma runs into Chapultepec Castle. It is "the" route for protests and marches, and because of its location and engagement with historical buildings and monuments, it bears much symbolic weight. The permanent occupation of Reforma, the streets of Madero and Juárez, and the Zócalo effected a historic alteration of the space in central Mexico City. Rodríguez recalled:

Paula, Elena's daughter, Elena, and I went to see Andrés Manuel. And Andrés said something very heavy, "I am going to ask the two million people who will be standing there to stay." "And what does this imply?" he says to Elena. "It implies that maybe I won't be the president of the Republic, but it does not matter, because what I want is a true democracy, that has been my dream, I have lived for that. And maybe, because of the mere fact of living in a tent in the Zócalo, this country won't ever forgive me and I won't make it to the presidency." Elena cried. It is one of the few times that I have ever seen her cry for political reasons, because I have seen her cry very little, but only because of the illness of a grandkid or something like that. But this time she cried, her tears were falling in front of that incredible man that is Andrés, who was telling her, "I don't care, I will gamble everything for democracy." We left there very moved and in a hurry because we had to start organizing like crazy.

I went to buy a laptop, a tent, to help get the plantón started. I lived there, because I had to organize many performances all the time on the stage in the Zócalo. I went to political meetings where Andrés would meet with politicians and to work out strategy, which I loved, because I was very interested in seeing how politics functioned from the inside.[40]

Once she had agreed to become part of the plantón's organizational team, Rodríguez learned about politics from the inside. Her tent was next to López Obrador's, and because of her ongoing and daily presence, she knew from one moment to the next what the strategies of AMLO and his team would be.

Many of the passages of *Amanecer* centered on Rodríguez are reflections on the politics of resistance and cultural and political strategies for engagement with the larger public, aside from the continuous occupation of the Zócalo. Rodríguez discussed Henry David Thoreau's ideas justifying civil disobedience and resistance. She also talked about the importance of expanding protest activities to other sites of encounter, such as supermarkets, chain stores, and banks. One of the most important rules of engagement for Rodríguez was that citizen initiatives should not be deprived of their creativity. "No boring the people. You can be '*insumiso*' and seduce the family," wrote Poniatowska, quoting Rodríguez.[41] When asked what she meant by *insumisa*, which roughly translated as unsubmissive, Rodríguez responded with a flood of examples, such as not paying taxes to the government when the funds are used to purchase arms; hunger strikes; surprise occupations of public or private entities; informative brigades that distribute information and operate in airports, hospitals, bus terminals, shopping centers, churches, schools, and public transport; and collective surprise visits to radio and TV stations.[42]

Rodríguez had a history of creative engagements with the state, the Catholic Church, and others that provided her with a repertoire of performance techniques, ideas, and even definitions of audiences. As "Mexico's most outrageous and powerful cabaret/performance artist," according to Diana Taylor, Rodríguez found endless ways to extend the venues from the plantón and to call out those who supported PAN presidential candidate Felipe Calderón.[43] With a group called Resistencia Creativa (Creative Resistance), Rodríguez took on a wide range of commercial targets, including Sabritas, Jumex, Banamex, Mexicana de Aviación, La Bolsa Mexicana de Valores, and more.[44]

While some questioned the work of Resistencia Creativa as it entered many venues outside the plantón, and perhaps even suggested that the type of creative confrontation Rodríguez and others orchestrated might be "illegal," Rodríguez would respond with ideas from Thoreau. Rodríguez said Thoreau believed that resistance is part of civil and political rights and should be considered as an ethical imperative. "If you refuse to follow an unjust law for motives of consciousness, that is your right. The conscientious objectors had that right. The strongest cannot impose his law," Poniatowska quoted her as saying.[45]

While Poniatowska learned much from watching Rodríguez work and through their interactions, she also signaled the stress Rodríguez was operating under continually and how it affected their interactions: "I think a lot about Jesusa's heroism, every day in the Zócalo, on the front lines. Not only does she say valuable things to people, but she also kills herself physically. She imposes order in the tent, picks up money and puts it inside a locked metal box, sweeps, puts up with the rain, tolerates our human stupidity and the many nonsensical proposals that we make to her. She does not sleep."[46] Watching the 24/7 intensity of Rodríguez's unstoppable projects and energy appeared to take a toll not only on Rodríguez herself but sometimes on her relationship with Poniatowska and perhaps with others: "When will Jesusa laugh again? She looks straight ahead, impatient, she no longer looks at me. . . . Jesusa is the owner of the Zócalo."[47] Ironically, Poniatowska was able to articulate the toll that running the cultural activities took on Jesusa but not on herself.

In one of the most important political moments described in *Amanecer*, on September 5, Rodríguez called Poniatowska on the phone from the plantón to tell her that the Tribunal Federal Electoral (TRIFE, Federal Electoral Tribunal) had declared Calderón the winner of the election. "What a *chingadazo* [fucking blow]!" Rodríguez cried into the phone. Then she related that the first chingadazo was that the TRIFE had only recounted 9 percent of the votes in response to AMLO and the PRD's demand that all votes be recounted. According to Rodríguez, "Here [at the Zócalo], people are crying. At the moment, AMLO has rejected the TRIFE's decision and is not recognizing Calderón."[48] The event behind the phone call marks the moment when AMLO and those with him disengaged from formal electoral institutions and decided to hold their own Convención Nacional Democrático (CND) in the spirit of the Soberana Convención Revolucionaria de Aguascalientes (Sovereign Revolutionary Convention of Aguascalientes) in 1914 that brought together different factions and leaders of the Mexican Revolution, but to take place in 2006 with followers of AMLO. The presidency of Calderón was not recognized by AMLO and his followers and, ultimately, after the convention, AMLO was declared to be *presidente legítimo* (legitimate president) by the crowd present at the convention. It was also a moment when the social movement supporters of the PRD triumphed over the more traditional politicians. This set the stage for creating a set of parallel institutions as part of a strategy to symbolically disregard the Mexican state. The PRD used the form of an alternative constitution convention, following the model of the EZLN in 1994. While Poniatowska went along with the plan, she also wrote a critique of it in *Amanecer*.

Supporting and Decentering AMLO

The relationship between Rodríguez and Poniatowska is a focal point for viewing the unfolding strategies and politics coming from AMLO's team and the PRD. It also is a lens for Poniatowska's ongoing reflection about her own relationship to politics and what politics mean to her and others. My reading of *Amanecer* does not focus on the persona of AMLO, nor does, I believe, Poniatowska's book. Through her reproduction of his nightly addresses to the people in the plantón, AMLO is a daily presence in the book. There is a speech for every dated entry in her *crónica*. Occasionally she comments on what he said. She often characterizes him through the words of others and through her descriptions of him interacting with a wide range of people, as well as quoting him, as Jörgensen notes.[49] Jörgensen's analysis of *Amanecer* quotes one of the few places where Poniatowska directly describes AMLO's personal qualities: "His shirt is white, his hair, salt and pepper. Nobody smiles like he does. Poor people see him as the remedy to all their ailments. Doña Luchita gets excited: 'I love him more than Pope John Paul.' AMLO hugs each person as if they are treasures. He is right, the Zócalo is his treasure."[50]

In the second section of Poniatowska's book, "Llamado a mi puerta," in which she describes how she became involved with AMLO, she reflects on the great enthusiasm that women showed for AMLO, "who saw in him the fact that he was reviving so much hope."[51] Poniatowska then asks, "What did I see in him?" She notes honestly that of course one of the reasons that she believes in him is that he personally came and asked for her support. She describes his inclusive language, modesty, equal treatment of everyone, and concern for the poor as major reasons why she decided to work for him: "He speaks like you and I; he worries about those who have nothing and treats them like the rest of the candidates treat bankers and businessmen. He has not taken advantage of his political offices to profit, he lives in a modest apartment and, for a long time, he drove his well-known white Tsuru. Above all, poor people have been first in his life, and this has always called my attention."[52]

Poniatowska highlights his deep and engaged connections with a wide range of people: his use of the familiar *tú* to address everyone, his equal treatment of people, his ability to listen to people, and his unending concern for the poor. It is precisely his everyday qualities and down-to-earth ability to engage with people that she believes made him successful.

In a move to decenter AMLO, and formal political leadership, Poniatowska highlights the vast diversity of people who are involved in making the plantón function. Her description of the performance, public engagement, and dialogues fostered by Rodríguez's Resistencia Creativa points to the broad space of the social movement of the plantón. As Lessie Jo Frazier and Deborah Cohen suggest in their analysis of women's participation in the 1968 student movement, analyzing women's stories of participation reveals how involved women were in different ways in the movement, and their accounts of interactions in the streets, home, and markets highlight connections between the movement and the rest of Mexican society.[53] Poniatowska's reading of the plantón and its activities follows in this model of profiling the participation of women and at the same time highlighting the breadth of the movement; through the work of Rodríguez and others, she critiques "authoritarianism in the formal political sphere" but also in the open public "domestic sphere" on display in the Zócalo.[54] Poniatowska's emphasis on the great variety of people in the plantón and who she meets on the campaign trail should not be mistaken for a homogeneous reading of "the people," versus "the state," where "the people" are feminized and "the state" is represented by masculine leadership who will save "the people." As Frazier and Cohen argue, it is important to unpack the assumed gendering of Mexican political culture. Through Poniatowska's detailed analysis of the great diversity of those who are in the base, but also to some degree those in the leadership of the plantón (through the figure of Rodríguez), and her deliberate decentering of AMLO, *Amanecer en el Zócalo* contributes to this project.

Interrogating Politics

More important than Poniatowska's descriptions and interpretation of AMLO as a person in *Amanecer* is her ongoing critical reflection about formal politics and the processes and forms of rapid and mass decision-making reflected in the PRD's convention and that party's declaration of AMLO as the "Legitimate President." On a trip to Quintana Roo to promote AMLO for the PRD, Poniatowska reflects on "what is politics?" and through this question links the plantón and protest in 2006 to the student movement of 1968 and the earthquake of 1985. In this way, she connects to the memories of strategic emotional political communities documented in her earlier works while continuing her prior project of broadening the definition of politics to include the importance of social movements. She is clearly interested in how social movements both depart from yet also connect with electoral politics and political parties.

> I stayed out on the streets for four months after the earthquakes of 1985, listening to the victims. In 1968, after the student massacre of October 2, I went to Lecumberri, the preventative detention facility, almost every Sunday for a whole year to interview the students. If this is politics, then, I am political! Now, I am at the plantón in the Zócalo, side by side with many other Mexicans who don't accept fraud; and from what I have seen since the month of April 2005 (with the desafuero), what politicians do the most is talk and talk. . . . Is this politics?"[55]

Later in the trip, while in a small town after visiting the city of Felipe Carrillo Puerto, some young women came out to meet her and to talk to her about AMLO and the plantón. They shared an engaged and lively exchange, and Poniatowska came away convinced that the power of politics could be found in the people. The people illuminated the best of what politics could be with engagement, intelligent exchanges, and excitement—not authoritarian leadership styles that center men talking at people: "They interrupt each other and say profound and intelligent things. Their warmth goes through me and to a place inside me that has to do with life; this is politics as it should be. . . . Democracy is about these enlightened and participative minds, this hair, these intense eyes, this political behavior under the midday sun. This is my country that in the middle of a highway offers up human flowers that straighten me out and they have nothing to do with factious rage or with untrusting indifference" usually found in politics.[56]

Poniatowska reveled in the trip. She met more motivated young people at a talk she gave at the Universidad de Quintana Roo (University of Quintana Roo) in Chetumal. After her return to Mexico City, she described sitting in on a strategy meeting with Rodríguez, José Agustín Ortiz Pinchetti, Dante Delgado, Porfirio Muñoz Ledo, Rafael Hernández Estrada, and perhaps others. She took notes and at one point wrote down that the people in the meeting were "frankly bored or half asleep."[57] In an illuminating passage, she asks, "What is the politicians' job?" In striking prose, she provides an analysis of class in terms of the day-to-day work that is done by many different kinds of people in the plantón in contrast to the politicians who show up in their chauffeured cars at 7 p.m. to stay only for a while.

> For me, to work is to sweep, to carry, to write, to teach, to sew, to paint, but I suppose that they [the politicians] are preparing the country for the future, and have in their hands the key to its well-being. In the case of the plantón, those who keep it alive are the ones who are out there, the quesadilla lady, the tamal lady, the one who brings the water bottles from Monclova, the one who comes here with big pots of stew, the one who has a bike as his only vehicle, Luchita, Doña Ceferina, Don Sebastián. Instead, the politicians come at 7 p.m. in their bulletproof cars, with their chauffeurs, and then they leave; but now they are the ones who dictate the steps to take.[58]

This reflection of contrast between those who maintained the plantón day in and day out and the politicians who arrived in the evening, like insects briefly alighting on a plant or person, offers a backdrop for Poniatowska's discussion regarding a letter she received from PRD founder Cuauhtémoc

Cárdenas and the questions she raised about the political process that was carried out at a major PRD event.

Using Her Platform

After the TRIFE declared Felipe Calderón the winner of the 2006 elections, AMLO and his team began to prepare plans to hold a CND in the Zócalo to decide how they should respond. The legitimacy of the convention, as AMLO and others articulated it, emanates from Article 39 of the 1917 Mexican Constitution, which states, "The national sovereignty resides essentially and originally in the people. All public power originates in the people and is instituted for their benefit. The people at all times have the inalienable right to alter or modify their form of government."[59] The CND was promoted through the plantón and the press, and more than a million people signed up to attend as delegates. Every day, AMLO announced the increasing number of people who would be coming.

On September 13, three days before the CND was to take place, Poniatowska received a long letter from Cuauhtémoc Cárdenas. The entire text takes up many pages in *Amanecer*, making it the longest direct text quoted in the book. She writes that she admires Cárdenas, as does her mother, and she describes in detail the two meals she shared with him. The letter was obviously important to her. Poniatowska brings it to the plantón in the Zócalo and tries to get Rodríguez to read it, but she does not have time and brushes her aside. Poniatowska then tries to go to see AMLO with the letter in her hand, and that isn't possible either. Given the prominence of the episode and her detailed description of it, Poniatowska is emphasizing how shocking it was that neither Rodríguez nor AMLO wanted to read the letter. Cárdenas was the most recognized political figure from the PRD; he had served as a senator from and governor of the PRD, was elected head of government of Mexico City, and was the president of the PRD from 1989 to 1993. He ran for president under the PRD in 1994 and 2000, coming in third each time. He was a major political figure in Mexico. To ignore his letter seemed unthinkable, but instead of reading the letter, Rodríguez told Poniatowska that AMLO wanted her to deliver the inaugural address at the CND. After this, on the following day the plantón was dismantled.

In his letter to Poniatowska, Cárdenas enumerates his differences with AMLO and states that AMLO doesn't have clear positions on defending Mexican sovereignty in relation to Petróleos Mexicanos (Mexican Petroleum), defending national resources, illegal extraditions of Mexican citizens to the United States, and on defending the rights of Mexicans in relation to the proposed Sensenbrenner bill in the United States.[60] In addition, the letter notes that AMLO had people in his circle who perpetrated electoral fraud in 1988 when Cárdenas ran for president. Other critiques include the fact that AMLO did not put electoral reform and reducing campaign costs into his official 2006 platform. But the harshest criticisms in the letter are about AMLO's political style: "I am deeply worried about the intolerance and demonizing, the dogmatic attitude found in Andrés Manuel's circle for those of us who do not accept his proposals unconditionally and who question his points of view and decisions. With him, the fundamental principles of democracy are contradicted."[61] Finally, in his letter to Poniatowska, Cárdenas refers directly to the CND that was to take place on September 16 (three days after the letter was dated), where the party "is likely to declare AMLO as 'legitimate president' of Mexico." Cárdenas wonders why AMLO would then wait until November 20 to assume this position if he considered the government illegitimate.

> If he believes that the current government has broken the constitutional order, why wait until November 20, or December 1? Why not begin by not acknowledging the current administration? . . . I do not think that we should proceed in that way. Doing that would be a gross mistake with a very high cost for the PRD and the democratic movement as a whole. Instead, I agree with Luis Villoro's good judgment and wisdom, who states recently that the discussion of a new project for the nation requires time for its debate and cannot be approved in a statement given during an event at the Zócalo, in the heat of that discourse, since, at least, a consultation and the consent of delegates from around the Republic are needed.[62]

At the end of the letter, Cárdenas proposes a longer process, a new electoral law, new legislation for Indigenous rights, resistance to the privatization of natural resources, and steps to combat inequality. While Poniatowska was not successful in getting others to read Cárdenas's letter at the time, its content appears to have influenced her, as reflected in her own speech at the CND and her description of the event, following the "Grito de Dolores" (Cry of/from Dolores, reference to the small town where independence hero and priest Miguel Hidalgo is from and where his parishioners first took up arms) to mark Mexican independence. She chose to use the platform of her public speech to present some of Cárdenas's observations.

At midnight during the first minute of September 16, 2006, Alejandro Encinas Rodríguez, mayor of Mexico City, gave the Grito de Resistencia (Cry of Resistance) in the Zócalo, which was packed with AMLO supporters.[63] This was the lead-up event for the convention that took place later that day. As described in *Amanecer*, on September 16, a downpour in the Zócalo drenched the people waiting for the CND to begin, including delegates from all over Mexico.[64] According to Rafael Hernández, national coordinator of the convention, the CND event in the Zócalo was "preceded by 10,728 people's assemblies and 168 debate forums, in which more than 1.5 million people around the country participated."[65] Poniatowska reported that there were 1,025,724 delegates in the Zócalo that day.[66]

Dante Delgado opened the convention and then turned over the microphone to Poniatowska. Her inaugural address focuses first on the decrease of democracy since the end of Lázaro Cárdenas's term in 1940, the high rates of poverty in Mexico, and the struggle of ten million Indigenous peoples who had been displaced from their lands. Poniatowska then states that those who have followed López Obrador are "free men and women. The slogan 'either you are with me or you are my enemy' doesn't apply here."[67] She then discusses the importance of being self-critical: "Maybe this is the moment to look at ourselves with critical eyes. Being critical of oneself is key for being critical of a situation—be that personal or political—and we all know that the personal is political. Our critical capacity is what strengthens and makes us free. Fanaticism is limiting, it makes us unyielding and takes us into the abyss."[68] At the end of her remarks, Poniatowska mentions her letter from Cárdenas: "Cuauhtémoc Cárdenas honored me by writing me this letter (in this moment there is a burst of whistling [in protest] that takes me by surprise).... I am grateful because listening to others makes you grow and contributes to the dialogue, but I keep thinking that the election was unjust and fraudulent."[69] Then she reminds the crowd again that they are free beings and need to think for themselves: "As sheep, we are not useful at all to Andrés Manuel López Obrador, as people who think, yes."[70]

Amanecer goes on to chronicle the various speakers that day and includes AMLO's speech. Poniatowska recounts what he said "we won't accept" and his vision for what a new republic would look like. López Obrador announced a new political front, Frente Amplio Progresista (Broad Progressive Front), which included the PRD and the small Convergencia (Convergence) party and the Partido del Trabajo (Labor Party) in the Coalición por el Bien de Todos (Coalition for the Good of All).

Poniatowska details the naming of commissions and who was appointed to them and includes a detailed ethnographic description of the mass decision-making process at the convention.

There are nine questions broadcast over the loudspeaker: Do you agree to recognize the usurper Felipe Calderón as president? Do you agree in rejecting a simulated Republic and declaring the abolition of the regime of corruption and privilege? Do you agree with the victory of López Obrador in the elections? Do you agree that Andrés López Obrador should be declared president of Mexico? Do you agree that Andrés Manuel López Obrador should create a cabinet and collect his own funds if he is recognized as president? If he is recognized as president should he take power on November 20 or on December 1, 2006? Do you agree with the realization of a plebiscite to start a new constitutional process? Do you agree with the integration of the commissions appointed here at the Convention? Do you agree that the next meeting of the CND should be March 7, 2007?[71]

Poniatowska then raises a series of questions about the process, illustrating her commitment to dialogue and open political processes. Clearly, she was unhappy with what she was witnessing.

Everybody raises a hand; there is not a single dissident voice in the unison choir, and this troubles me and unsettles me. Was it the rain? Why don't people want to elect a coordinator in chief of the resistance, instead of a president? Why this offensive unanimity? Is this a convention?

Or, are there too many of us and no time for discussion? Where will our real power be? I ask myself. Everybody says yes to the proposals. Was the Aguascalientes Convention [in 1914] like this? I had been persuaded that things would be discussed; that different points of view would be presented. I am naive; how can a million men and women have a discussion in a public plaza? What kind of mechanism would allow it? Nevertheless, a way should be found so that their voices are heard.[72]

Here Poniatowska signals a lack of exchange and discussion that would allow and highlight differences. The most thrilling part of the campaign for her had been the interactions, the exchange of ideas, the back-and-forth, the discussions and debates. She highlighted this in the plantón and in her trips on the campaign trail. The CND was hollow by contrast with everything done by acclamation, not dialogue and exchange. The culmination of the plantón and of the campaign was the CND. López Obrador was declared the "legitimate president of Mexico" and would take possession on November 20, 2006, in the Zócalo. The Frente Amplio Progresista became the primary vehicle for AMLO to continue his work and permanent campaigning that lasted until July 1, 2018, when he finally was recognized as the winner of an election; he won by twenty percentage points.

In the closing pages of *Amanecer*, Poniatowska returns to the people who were the foundation of the plantón for fifty days and, in my reading, the primary point of engagement for her on a daily basis. She wondered who would thank them, take care of them. Many were far from home. The passage marks a sadness at the dismantling of the face-to-face community that she had participated in, accompanied, and documented. The sadness may also signal her knowledge of its limitations and fragility.

> In the end, when the twilight sets in, we disperse. Will the supporters of López Obrador here have a roof over their head, a room, a shower with hot water and food? I am sure that Ortiz Pinchetti will go home to get a nice shower. But for those at the bottom of the stage [those on the margins], who will offer support to them if the plantón is over? Where are the shelters? . . . Hundreds of men, women, elders, and children are walking in groups through the streets; entire families coming from different states of the country. Who will look after them? Who will thank them? Many of them lived at the Zócalo for fifty days and nights and bore the epic hailstorm, the almost daily storms. . . . Some who are addicted to the plantón have been there for over a month and a half, far from their hometowns, far from their families, from their regular life, from their routines.[73]

In the end, thousands of men, women, and children built the community of the plantón, occupied Mexico City day in and day out, and provided the backbone for López Obrador's long-term protest. They, Poniatowska suggests, should get most of the credit and are who she most identifies with: "The plaza was our refuge; here we met, the ugly, the beautiful, the children, the *pejeviejitos* [López Obrador's older supporters], here on these stones centuries have passed and our footsteps will also pass on from here. There is no longer a plantón, the huge love of the plantón has been dismantled, everyone has already taken their tents down."[74]

On Independence

Amanecer en el Zócalo offers key insights into the passion and the ethical, personal, strategic, and emotional connections that many participants felt—including Poniatowska herself. The book also documents how Poniatowska mobilized her networks and the strategic emotional political communities and networks she built as both an activist and a writer who chronicled key historical moments and social movements for AMLO's campaign. She documents how one dimension of community was built through face-to-face shared collective action in the plantón. And through publishing this account with intimate details of the people there, she also builds a strategy for forging connections with her readers as a part of that community. Her commitment to be simultaneously an activist and a chronicler is front and center in this book.

The hybrid form of *Amanecer* as a crónica/diary offers us a unique opportunity not only to read a wonderfully written description of a major political event and time in the history of Mexico but also to see the mind of Elena Poniatowska at work as a political thinker and commentator. Her insights into the strengths and weaknesses of AMLO's campaign and the social movement behind it in the Coalición por el Bien de Todos offer important clues to populism and the political shadows that accompany it. Her detailed accounting of how the people in the plantón, and those who worked with Rodríguez outside the Zócalo, connected the movement with the city broadens the sense of engagement and suggests how the strategic emotional political community centered in the Zócalo attempted to extend beyond the plantón and connect outward with others in the city. On the flip side, she also documents the severe criticism and dislike that many felt for the plantón as it tied up traffic and forced many people to alter their daily routines. This suggests the ways in which the community was not able to extend beyond the plantón and alienated as well as embraced people. And through her emphasis on the women, as well as the men, who made the plantón function every day, she decenters male authoritarian leadership and suggests the importance of the many contributions of the movement's diverse participants.

Importantly, throughout *Amanecer*, Poniatowska reflects on the formal political process, the importance of dialogue, engagement, and inclusion through not only party leaders but young people and others organized in myriad ways that relate to formal politics and to social movement politics. At a larger level, this contrast also suggests the difference in how a shared strategic emotional political community can be built, versus dyadic relationships between powerful charismatic leaders and individual campaign workers and voters. In her own mind, the idea of independence of thought and action is important. After watching the Grito de Resistencia, she writes, "I walk through Brazil Street, repeating el Grito like the Lord's prayer and I understand it for the first time: it is the independence of my country, the independence from all prejudices that have overwhelmed me, the independence from all ties, the independence of my children and grandchildren whom I want to be free, the independence of all children in Mexico, the independence that I should practice in the last years of my life."[75]

As a writer, Poniatowska took a risk in publishing *Amanecer en el Zócalo*. She directly exposed herself and her own thoughts and processes not through fiction but through a diary, documenting even the death threats and insults she received. *Amanecer en el Zócalo* is Elena Poniatowska's declaration of independence and confirmation of her dual commitment to activism and writing. Her pattern of activist public performance and dialogue paired with using her newspaper column as a way to build community and call attention to injustice became even more pronounced when forty-three student teachers from the Ayotzinapa Teachers' College were forcibly abducted and disappeared in September 2014. Another six people, including several students, were killed at this time.

¡Regrésenlos!

The Forty-Three Disappeared
Students from Ayotzinapa

ON DECEMBER 6, 2014, during an event known as "Una hora con la Poni" (An hour with Poniatowska) at the Feria Internacional del Libro (International Book Fair) in Guadalajara, Elena Poniatowska invited onto the stage two students from the Escuela Normal Rural Raúl Isidro Burgos (Ayotzinapa Rural Normal School Raúl Isidro Burgos, known as Escuela Normal Rural de Ayotzinapa) as well as a brother and father of one of the forty-three students who had disappeared in Iguala, Guerrero, on September 26, 2014. As the crowd began to count aloud from one to forty-three (a chant done throughout Mexico in public spaces), three young men and one older man sprang onto the stage. Once the counting was completed, Poniatowska, the four guests, and two others led the crowd in a chant of "Justicia. Vivos se los llevaron, Vivos los Queremos. Vivos se los llevaron, Vivos los Queremos."[1] "Justice! They were taken alive, we want them returned alive" was a chant adopted from the Argentine Madres de Plaza de Mayo as they demanded the return of their disappeared children in the 1970s and 1980s when the military regime disappeared thousands of students, young professionals, union workers, activists, and others.

In leading this chant at the book fair, Poniatowska used her credibility and reputation as a spokesperson for justice to call attention to the missing students and their families. In reciting the names and numbers of the students, publicly sharing their biographies, and representing them as impoverished, rural, and Indigenous young people who are struggling to be legible in an exclusionary nation and history, Poniatowska continues to use public performance to construct strategic emotional political community. She self-consciously harnesses her role as a public intellectual and writer to turn her platform into a space for activism. This provides access to the public and the media that people such as the parents of the forty-three disappeared students may not always have. During the book fair, the stage was filled with the stories, suffering, anger, and frustration of the parents and built on what had become an on-the-hour reminder of the disappeared students, making them present and acknowledging each of them individually but also collectively as a group. Poniatowska recalled how emotional the event on stage was that day and why it was important.

> There was a brother who started to cry right there and touched the one thousand people in the auditorium. What was very moving was that these people spoke in front of so many, and about something as painful as the death of a family member. . . .
>
> We used the hour and the room they had assigned me so that the people from Ayotzinapa could speak. . . . At every hour, somebody would start counting "one, two . . ." and then you'd hear a choir of voices who would then count up to number forty-three; and this would happen, easily, eight times a day. And all the visitors would stop, those who were buying books, and would start counting "one, two, three . . ." I think that this counting really shook the foundations of Mexico; and those who had no social consciousness got it at that moment.[2]

Six weeks earlier, on October 26, 2014 (one month after the forty-three students from the Normal Rural School in Iguala disappeared, and three students and three civilians had been murdered), Poniatowska spoke before a large MORENA rally in the Zócalo of Mexico City. Her talk was titled "Regrésenlos" (Bring them back).[3] In her speech, she cited the work of journalist Paris Martínez, a writer for *Animal Político*, who covered the disappearances and the efforts of the students' parents to pressure the government to act. Through talking with their friends and families, Martínez developed biographies of the forty-three students who had disappeared.

By providing rich verbal descriptions of each student, Poniatowska's presentation in the Zócalo dovetailed with the strategy of the students' parents and others to display in public large, detailed facial photographs of the students both individually and collectively. Her public discourse on October 24 drew on the cultural and political capital of her earlier crónicas and public appearances. Her embodied performance in the Zócalo in front of thousands of people, which was captured on video and published as a text in multiple sources, invokes the massacre of Tlatelolco in 1968, the earthquake of 1985, and the occupation of the Zócalo in 2006. Press coverage of the event focused on her message but also on her as a person and as a cultural icon.[4] The event was covered by a wide range of media outlets such as *La Jornada*, *Animal Político* (a political magazine), *Excélsior* newspaper, Televisa, and several radio stations. When all was said and done, her performance, combined with where she performed it, invoked past events and political messages, reinscribing them together with the Ayotzinapa tragedy in public memory. This and Poniatowska's public performance during the 2014 Feria Internacional del Libro illustrate two principal points: how the use of numbers, counting, and individual biographies rendered visible the victims of state violence and kept them visible through time; and how the cumulative power of Poniatowska's presence as a public intellectual was leveraged through her performances to build strategic emotional political community for the families of the disappeared students.

Context

The disappearance of students from the Escuela Normal Rural de Ayotzinapa and the deaths of six to eight people—including up to six students, a taxi passenger, a bus driver, and a soccer player—on September 26, 2014, are part of a tragic story that still has no widely agreed-upon explanation. The number of deaths perhaps grew from six to eight when DNA remains of two of the missing students were identified by a high-tech laboratory at the University of Innsbruck in Austria that has a reputation for handling the most difficult cases.[5] But families of the students were warned by the Equipo Argentino de Antropología Forense (Argentine Forensic Anthropology Team) that the genetic overlap between the mitochondrial DNA remains that were used to identify one of the students, Jhosivani Guerrero de la Cruz, and those of his mother were very low, placing Guerrero de la Cruz's identification in doubt.[6] The bone fragments were only a partial match. The ongoing uncertainty is characteristic of the unsettling narratives that surround the case of Ayotzinapa. Disagreements between different forensic anthropologists are just the beginning.

The changing version of events put forward by the Mexican government continues to be challenged by journalists, international commissions, eyewitnesses, scientists, and the family members of the disappeared students. There is no universally accepted narrative. More than six years after the students disappeared, as I finalize this book in 2021, it is clear that the investigation that the government of President Enrique Peña Nieto carried out and then declared closed had serious procedural and investigative problems. Confessions were procured from local men who stated that they were members of a drug-trafficking gang and that they burned all forty-three bodies on the instructions of local police. International and national investigative bodies, however, say the wrong people were arrested, confessions were obtained through torture, and there is no physical evidence to support the version of events the government proclaimed as "the historic truth." Importantly, when the families of the missing students and finally the Mexican authorities began searching for the bodies, they found 184 clandestine burial sites and 184 bodies—none of which belonged to the students. Furthermore, the students are part of a much larger group of at least 77,178 people officially registered as disappeared in Mexico from 2006 until late 2020, and that figure doesn't include 27,000 unidentified bodies.[7] The case of Ayotzinapa is part of a larger gruesome story of murder and disappearance with impunity.

Poniatowska's activism along with that of many others to keep the case of the missing students alive and to demand justice and a competent investigation has been important in applying continued pressure on President López Obrador to open a new investigation. Upon taking office, AMLO did reopen the case and appoint a special commission to handle the investigation. As of September 2019, of the 142 people originally arrested, half had been freed, and no one had been convicted. Allegations of torture and lack of respect for the suspects' human rights have resulted in highly problematic legal cases.[8] In July 2020, Mexico's foreign minister, Marcelo Abrard, announced that the chief investigator of the Ayotzinapa murders and disappearances, Tomás Zerón, had fled to Canada after a video surfaced that showed him interrogating a suspect and threatening torture. Mexican authorities have sought his extradition.[9]

On September 26, 2014, a group of students enrolled in the Escuela Normal Rural de Ayotzinapa set out to commandeer passenger buses with the intention of returning with them to Ayotzinapa. As was customary, they intended to use the buses to transport their classmates to Mexico City to a rally and other events that were commemorating the 1968 Tlatelolco massacre. Unable to secure buses in the bus station of Chilpancingo, because it was surrounded by army troops and state police officers, they returned to Ayotzinapa. There they decided to try again to obtain buses by going to Iguala. They were traveling in two Estrella de Oro buses numbered 1568 and 1531, with roughly one hundred students combined. Once they arrived in Iguala, ten students decided to take over another bus. They waited until they arrived at the bus station in Iguala to commandeer the bus. The driver let them onto the bus but he then locked them inside. Panicked, the students called their classmates in Ayotzinapa for help. Student leaders told them to hold tight and take more buses. After some time, they were able to disembark from the first bus they boarded and proceeded to take over three other buses. The students had gained control of a total of five buses. From this point, there are varying versions of the story with different details, but eyewitness accounts suggest that the students were attacked by a combination of police—most likely municipal—and civilians, identified by Mexican reporter Sergio Ocampo Arista as *pistoleros* (armed men). Ocampo Arista was one of the first reporters on the scene and published an account on September 28, 2014.[10]

During the night and early morning of September 26 and 27, there were five separate attacks on the students. The first occurred in Iguala at about 9:30 p.m. when gunfire, involving local police and other men with a "military-like" appearance, erupted in two locations.[11] No one was hurt in this attack. The second attack in Iguala involved heavy gunfire aimed at the Estrella de Oro bus number 1568, which the students had occupied. Two students were shot and injured. Another injured student, Fernando Marín, was removed from the bus; he later said he had seen twenty classmates in police custody lying on the sidewalk.[12] At the same time, a third attack took place in front of the state courthouse where the Estrella de Oro bus number 1531 and an Estrella Roja bus had stopped. Federal police officers threw canisters of tear gas at the buses and forced the students to exit the bus. Extremely frightened, the students desperately called their classmates in Ayotzinapa and asked for help. A group of students left the Ayotzinapa campus, heading for Iguala.[13] Ocampo Arista reports that two hours of persecution ensued on the part of municipal, state, and federal police.[14]

As journalist Anabel Hernández documented, the students traveling in the two Estrella de Oro buses disappeared. A driver of the Estrella de Oro bus number 1531 later testified that "federal police, as well as Iguala and Huitzuco local police, were present at the moment of the disappearance in front of the state courthouse."[15] A fourth attack occurred on a bus in which the Avispones soccer team was traveling. The players were pulled off the bus, and one student soccer player and the bus driver were killed as was a passenger of a nearby taxi.[16] After midnight, when the students who had been called to provide aid arrived and held a press conference, a fifth attack took place in Iguala. Armed men fired into the crowd at the press conference. Two students were wounded.[17]

As these events wound down, there were initially six dead, up to forty-three students missing, and twenty-four to forty people wounded, depending on the source. State prosecutors immediately began to arrest local police from Iguala and another nearby town, implying that the mayor and local police chief had been involved and were possibly linked to a local organized crime group, Los Guerreros Unidos (Warriors United). On October 22, 2014, an arrest warrant was issued for Iguala mayor José Luis Abarca and his wife, charging them with orchestrating the attack, based on their belief that the students had planned to disrupt a public event featuring the accomplishments of Abarca's wife, First Lady María de Los Ángeles Pineda Villa. Abarca and Pineda Villa were indicted as the masterminds of the attacks and disappearances, though further information indicated that they were not involved, and they were subsequently freed.[18] In October, other arrests included supposed drug cartel members and dozens of local police.

Shortly after the attacks and disappearances, the parents of the students began to organize and hundreds of thousands of people began to protest around the country. Students led the first large-scale demonstration in Mexico City. On October 10, 2014, the missing students' parents had their first meeting with Miguel Ángel Osorio Chong, Mexico's interior minister. Protesters and the parents began to accuse the state of being the intellectual author of the disappearances, chanting, "Fue el Estado!" (It was the State!). Two important human rights centers, Tlachinollan in Guerrero and the Centro Prodh in Mexico City, were working with and representing the missing students' parents. The parents accused the 27th Infantry Battalion of the Mexican Army of participating in the attacks and were upset that the government had waited until October 5 to step in and begin its own investigation.[19] At the end of the meeting with Osorio Chong, the parents demanded to meet with President Peña Nieto. While searching for the students in the vicinity of Iguala, investigators found at least twelve mass graves containing unidentified bodies. None of those were the students.[20] On October 22, demonstrations continued throughout Mexico. In Iguala, teachers set fire to the City Hall after Osorio Chong announced that the mayor of Iguala had been formally accused of ordering the attacks and disappearances. The following day, the governor of Guerrero, Ángel Aguirre Rivero, resigned under political pressure. On October 26, one month after the killings and disappearances, MORENA and López Obrador organized a massive rally in the Zócalo in Mexico City, where Poniatowska engaged with the public in an emotional performance.

López Obrador was the first to speak at the rally. He needed to distance himself from Abarca, the mayor of Iguala, because the mayor had been elected under the banner of the PRD, the same party with which AMLO was affiliated. At the same time, AMLO needed to signal his absolute support for the parents of the missing students from Ayotzinapa. In his speech, he said it was urgent that the government immediately "look for and find alive the forty-three students from Ayotzinapa and stop, with all possible methods, impunity and punish the intellectual and material authors and the authorities who were responsible" for the crimes of homicide and disappearance. He further proposed "the immediate creation of a truth commission with truly independent citizens with impeccable honesty . . . such as Elenita," a reference to Poniatowska.[21]

Performance

Poniatowska's speech followed AMLO's at the October 24 rally. Into bright sunlight, she walked out onto the stage to stand in front of thousands of people shouting, "Elena, Elena, Elena." She wore a long black dress to signify mourning for the students. When the shouts of "Elena" subsided, she moved right into her speech.[22] Gesturing to the blue sky overhead, Poniatowska suggested to the crowd that "here in the center of the country, in the capital of Mexico . . . we shout to the open sky, 'Bring them back.'"[23] In this moment, Poniatowska had positioned herself, along with the thousands of people with her in the Zócalo, in the historical heart of Mexico, which extended back through time to the Conquest, to colonialism. Before saying the name and providing a description of each student, one by one, she reminded people about the living conditions of the poor, rural students who were enrolled in the Ayotzinapa Rural Teachers' College. There, education is free, and for many rural families, having a teacher in the family helps elevate family income. It can be a source of hope. Poniatowska provided a very concrete example of the extent of the students' poverty: "When one of them was given milk, he exclaimed that it was the first time he had seen it and smiled as he said that he liked it. Besides milk, there are many other foods that the youngsters don't know. Their shirts, their backpacks, their sweaters hung on the walls of their empty rooms, their plastic cooking utensils . . . all are testament to their poverty."[24] Here she depicted the students as coming from extremely poor backgrounds and wanting to use their education to become teachers and serve other rural, poor, and Indigenous students. The press coverage of the students has often emphasized the extreme poverty of many of their families. The picture of poverty, eagerness to contribute, and youth created an innocent victim deserving of sympathy whose rights have been violated. The very detailed descriptions of each disappeared student also created sympathy and emotional connection with each of the students for the thousands present, for those who watched videos, heard it on the radio, or read the text in newspapers or online. She was building strategic emotional political community through this performance.

As the speech continued, Poniatowska described the most recent large march in Mexico City, emphasizing the size of the crowd and the fact that it had not been organized by a political party but by a wide range of groups. She said, "Citizens organized themselves and carried out an exemplary protest, an absolute one of a kind. The protest was five times bigger than was reported by the media: 350,000 people, a river of people, flowed into and packed the streets adjacent to the Zócalo until it was bursting at the seams. The crowd protested against the crime of Ayotzinapa, a crime against humanity."[25] She reminded the crowd that the students had been hunted, subjected to torture until death, and that the attacks involved forced disappearances. She called the Iguala case "an atrocious stain on the official and political life of our country, which was already sinking in the mud."[26] Then Poniatowska began to read a brief profile of each student, citing information from journalist Paris Martínez. She requested that the crowd shout "bring him back" in unison as she finished each bio. I recommend viewing the video of Poniatowska's performance to understand its full effect.[27] Poniatowska's speech was also published in *La Jornada*.[28] The names and bios Poniatowska read that day include the following.

1. Jhosivani Guerrero de la Cruz [the student inconclusively identified], 20 from Omeapa; skinny, with a slender face, slanted eyes, nicknamed Korean. He walks 4 kilometers [2.5 miles] to the highway to

catch the bus and four kilometers back because he wants to be an elementary school teacher in Omeapa, his hometown.

2. Luis Ángel Abarca Carrillo, 21, of Costa Chica, San Antonio, municipality of Cuautepec, they nicknamed him Amiltzingo. Very affectionate, he is a member of the "Activist House" in which the students can register to receive political training. The name of Lucio Cabañas resonates inside there. The rich people of Guerrero consider Cabañas to be a disruptive influence on normal school students, because they are always seeking to emulate the guerrillero Lucio Cabañas, who was also a teacher.

3. Marco Antonio Gómez Molina, 20 years old, nicknamed Tuntún, of Tixtla. He loves rock bands and particularly likes "Saratoga," "Extravaganza" and "Los Ángeles del Infierno." He is also the classmate who always makes the others laugh in Activist House.

4. Saúl Bruno García, 18 years old, known as Chicharrón (Pork Rind), he's a complete "disaster," one of the students who tries to make you laugh until you cry, a big, friendly joker. He's from Tecuanapa and is missing the ring finger on his left hand because it was chopped off at the mill when he was making tortillas. Saúl Bruno García shaved off everyone's hair in the Activist House. A classmate had photos from the "shaving" on his cell phone but the police took it from him. . . .

16. Christian Tomás Colón Garnica, 18 years old, from Tlacolula de Matamoros, Oaxaca. His father traveled as soon as the abduction of the forty-three students was reported [and said], "I am a day laborer, I make 600 pesos a week maximum and that's when there is work because sometimes there is none. My boy wants to be a teacher, that's the profession that he wants but they put a brake on it, they stopped it. What will we do?" . . .

25. Marcial Pablo Baranda, 20 years old. He speaks an Indigenous language and wants to be a bilingual teacher alongside other bilingual teachers that come from the poorest towns. He's short, good-natured, cousin of Jorge Luis and Doriam, and his friends call him "Magallón," because his family has a tropical-beat musical group with that name that sings songs from his homelands, the Costa Chica. He spends his free time singing *cumbias* [Colombian music style popular in Mexico] and playing the trumpet and drums. . . .

39. Christian Alfonso Rodríguez, 21 years old, from Tixtla, longs to be a teacher and likes folkloric dance. He is called "Hugo" because he always wears Hugo Boss T-shirts. His cousin, during the march on Wednesday the 22nd, grew hoarse from explaining so many times that "he's not just my cousin, he's my friend . . . he's a very diligent person, very dedicated to his studies and dance and it is unjust that someone who gives so much of himself and makes such an effort should suffer such tragic consequences at the hands of the government."

40. José Ángel Navarrete González, 18 years old. He shares a room inside the school with two other young students in which there is not one piece of furniture, not even beds, just frayed sheets of rubber foam.

41. Carlos Iván Ramírez Villarreal, 20 years old. He is called "The Little Devil." The truth is that he is good, doesn't interfere with anybody, is calm, he wants to be someone, but not the clown.

42. José Ángel Campos Cantor, 33 years old from Tixtla is the oldest of the forty-three disappeared students. Although he's older he never takes advantage of the others. On the contrary he supports them in everything, he's everybody's friend.

43. Israel Caballero Sánchez, originally from Atliaca, a small town halfway along the road between Tixtla and Apango. He's called "Aguirrito" because he is chubby. He's preparing himself to be a teacher in Indigenous communities, and when his classmates call him Aguirrito he complains, "Don't be assholes, don't call me that stupid name."[29]

The bios Poniatowska read made each student's individual personality shine through but also positioned them collectively as rural, poor, partially Indigenous, and activists. They are linked to the legacy of Lucio Cabañas—a schoolteacher turned revolutionary who had also attended the Ayotzinapa Rural Teachers' College. In 1968 Cabañas fled the school and joined a guerrilla group led by Genaro Vásquez in the mountains of Guerrero. When Vásquez died in 1972, Cabañas led his own guerrilla group, known as the Brigada Campesina de Ajusticiamiento (Peasants' Justice Brigade), which was affiliated with the left-wing political movement known as the Partido de los Pobres (Party of the Poor). In 1974 Cabañas and others kidnapped Ruben Figueroa, a senator from Guerrero. Many believe that when the Mexican Army came to rescue Figueroa, Cabañas was killed. His legacy at the school in Ayotzinapa was to fight for the rights of the rural poor, linking his struggle to the legacy of Emiliano Zapata.

Poniatowska appeared to be straining as she read the last few names and biographies. When she finished reading the last one, Israel Caballero Sánchez, she turned to Jesusa Rodríguez and said, "Creo que ya" (I think that's it). A young woman wearing a black T-shirt escorted her off the stage. Poniatowska was walking somewhat unsteadily. Rodríguez returned to the stage and reported, "Since she came here in the morning, Elena told me that she could not cope with what is happening. She was extremely emotional. . . . Viva Elena Poniatowska!"[30]

Poniatowska commented later in an interview with me about the presentation:

It was terrible at that time. It all happened very quickly and we didn't know hardly anything about them [the disappeared students]. A journalist named Paris started to collect details about the life and character of each one of them. If one of them wore a particular kind of shirt, if the other one played the guitar. This moved me very much. But at the time I didn't get to finish speaking because I felt weak. I didn't sleep the night before. It would have been terrible to faint there right in front of the whole world. I was feeling sad when I got there. I was dressed in all black and black captures the sun's rays. This protest rally was very impactful for me.[31]

Although she wasn't able to read the end of her own speech—Rodríguez did instead—Poniatowska's words were a call to action:

Ayotzinapa is devastated. Mexico is devastated. The students of the Escuela Normal Rural de Ayotzinapa keep the broken sneakers of their classmates, their clothes, even the cardboard that they used as beds. They wait for their return despite the extraordinary priest Alejandro Solalinde . . . who was told by several witnesses that said that the students had been murdered, dismembered and thrown into a pit, which was set on fire. There is no adequate response to such a heinous crime. . . . Mexico is bleeding. The international community is shocked and now considers Mexico the most dangerous, non war-zone country for young people. . . . In the face of terror all that is left is the unity of the people who rise up and shout as they have done for days: "They were taken alive, we want them alive."[32]

While Poniatowska was not able to deliver these final words herself in the Zócalo, they were published in *La Jornada*, translated into English, and disseminated through a variety of social media.[33] The speech itself, videos of it, and publication of the words amplified the performance. Poniatowska's fame as a writer, winner of the Cervantes prize for Spanish literature, and many connections all helped build support for the families of the disappeared students. Advocating for the students was part and parcel of her performance and writing.

Stories and Statistics

The cumulative effect of Poniatowska's reading the name of each student and including a biography for each person combined two strategies for keeping the missing students present instead of forgotten: the use of statistics (that is, stressing the number of the forty-three students who had disappeared) and the use of individual biographies. At many events and rallies in Mexico, including at the Feria Internacional del Libro in Guadalajara, the numbers one through forty-three were counted in sequence as a public performance strategy to embody each of the missing students, one at a time. The aggregation of these numbers into a statistic of "forty-three disappeared" served to make the larger point of just how many students were gone and to hold the Mexican state accountable for finding them.

Diane Nelson has written elegantly about the role of numbers in making genocide visible and "count," in the sense of opening the doors for legal acknowledgment of genocide and reparation in Guatemala: "Number's unconcealing is a weapon against forgetting, circumventing the murders of witnesses, the clandestine cemeteries and the stifling aftereffects of a terror state's stranglehold. . . . Rather than dehumanize, it helps reinforce the relations between singularity and plurality, one to many, our relations of juxtaposition. . . . Numbers . . . made death and suffering count in ways that earlier recountings were not able to, opening the doors to efforts at rectification and reparation."[34] In Guatemala as well as in the context of the Ayotzinapa killings and forced disappearances, we have to keep "counting" so that when the political context changes, such numbers can "count" for significant legal and reparation actions.

Within a new political context, numbers may open the door for some relief for the families of the massacred and missing, those who have carried the burden of the individual death of a loved one with them over time. Thus, repeatedly counting and deploying the statistics of murder, disappearance, and other forms of violence is an important tool for long-term advocacy and securing justice. In the case of the missing students from Ayotzinapa and the subsequent suspected government cover-up, strategies of enumeration and counting have been important in maintaining the visibility of the parents' campaign to hold the Mexican government accountable in providing answers about what happened to their children and where.

Counting has also been important for multiple institutions and organizations in rebutting the numbers and inconsistencies in the accounts that the government of Enrique Peña Nieto revealed in press conferences organized by Jesús Murillo Karam, then head of the Procuraduría General de la República (Attorney General's Office of the Republic). In its attempt to quickly close the investigation of the Ayotzinapa murders and disappearances, the Mexican state used the mantle of forensic science and much data—counting and sharing different evidence based on experts, arrests, and reports—to build its case and try to present it as airtight. It also presented its own version of what happened, which many still contest.

Competing Accounts

In a press conference on November 7, 2014, Murillo Karam identified three suspects who he said had confessed to killing the students. He showed a video of the confession, which also included footage of calcified human remains, suggesting that they belonged to the students. But, because the bones were supposedly burned beyond the possibility of DNA recognition, they could not be identified.[35] This quantifiable evidence labeled as "calcified bone fragments" in the video shown was acknowledged by Murillo Karam to be difficult to extract DNA from for the purposes of identification. "Nevertheless," he commented, "we won't give up or discard this evidence [the bones] until we have exhausted all scientific and technical possibilities" for trying to identify who the bone fragments belong to.[36] At that point in time, the state said it would send the bone fragments to the best forensic anthropology lab in the world in Innsbruck, Austria, to be analyzed.[37] One student was later positively identified with this evidence and another partially, but far from beyond doubt, according to forensic anthropologists.[38]

In January 2015, Murillo Karam, joined by Tomás Zerón de Lucio, then head of Mexico's Agencia de Investigación Criminal de la Procuraduría General de la República (Criminal Investigations Agency of the Attorney General's Office), held a follow-up press conference to present the results of their investigation. This included an analysis of those calcified bone fragments presented in November 2014. They provided a new video with a more complete "story" produced by the Ministerio Público Federal (Federal Attorney General's Office). This video reconstructed their version of the events, which Murillo Karam said was "la verdad histórica" (the historic truth).[39] With this information, the Mexican government hoped to declare the case closed and to sentence the ninety-nine people they had detained and who were supposedly all involved in the disappearances. In its presentation of results, the PGR put forth numbers to try to convince the Mexican public of the objective and scientific nature of its investigation. For example, the PGR said the investigation involved "39 confessions, 487 expert reports, 386 declarations, 153 ministerial inspections, all of which were connected and consistent and would ratify the official version of the account of what happened."[40] Although these Mexican officials claimed to be telling the historic truth, their claim would continuously be challenged with counternarratives and truths.

The Interdisciplinary Group of Independent Experts (IGIE), which investigated the Ayotzinapa case, suggested that it was impossible that the forty-three students had been burned on the same night that they had been killed, and it also suggested that the official "historical truth" version of events was based on testimonies of people who had been tortured.[41] In June 2018, the Inter-American Commission on Human Rights (IACHR), through its Mecanismo Especial de Seguimiento al Asunto Ayotzinapa (MESA, Special Follow-Up Mechanism for the Ayotzinapa Case), evaluated mechanisms adopted by the Mexican state that were supposed to contribute to finding the missing students. The report released notes suggesting that the investigation remained fragmented, that many of the proceedings were left incomplete, dismissed, or were not actively pursued.[42] The MESA report further noted "that the degree of involvement in these events of the federal police, the army, municipal police forces and state authorities is yet to be established" and "the IACHR will continue to monitor investigations on the serious allegations of torture, on allegations of concealing evidence and on an alleged attempt to damage—using malware—computers belonging to several human rights defenders linked to this case."[43]

The 2018 MESA report contains one more important finding: information confirming the existence of cross-border drug trafficking using buses in the area where the events occurred. This was significant because the students could have commandeered at least one bus that was likely being used to traffic cocaine and heroin into the United States, and thus they were targeted because they took that particular bus. The IGIE mentioned this possibility as a central hypothesis in the case, despite the fact that a number of investigators denied the existence of such information at the time. Evidence received through international legal assistance from the United States as well as a statement by a member of Guerreros Unidos taken in 2017 support that hypothesis. The IACHR notes that the state has recognized that drugs are trafficked from Guerrero to the United States on buses: "The IACHR believes this information to be of the utmost importance as it reveals various aspects that had been highlighted by the IGIE, such as cross-border drug trafficking using buses and Guerreros Unidos' connections in both the United States and Mexico. All of the foregoing helps to understand various aspects of the investigation and the possible link to the events in September 2014. In the opinion of the IACHR, this information provides additional elements on several open lines of inquiry that need to be pursued."[44]

On April 12, 2018, an article published by the Mexican newspaper *Reforma* described a series of text messages between Mexican drug traffickers based in Chicago and their partners in Guerrero. According to Kate Doyle, analyst at the U.S.-based National Security Archive, "the messages contain new details about the events, including the names of gang members involved, the demands of the Chicago bosses that municipal police from neighboring towns participate, and their orders that the Guerrero prosecutor and other state officials intervene to support them."[45] Doyle, the IGIE, and MESA all have elements of their analyses that suggest, without knowing it, that the students commandeered at least one bus that was likely being used to traffic cocaine and heroin into the United States and were targeted for disappearance and death. What remains unclear is who targeted the students and in what combination, including local police, federal police, the army, and officials, as the events of September 26–27 and what appears to be a subsequent cover-up unfolded.

Cultural Production of Counternarratives

While Paris Martínez and Poniatowska were compiling the stories of the individual students, drawing from their lives, experiences, and everyday activities, and as Poniatowska continued to talk about the missing students in the media and in public presentations, many other groups were doing the same. The families of the disappeared students, others from the school, and a wide range of social movements, particularly those linked to education and human rights, engaged in other counternarrative strategies to contest the government's account. Some were textual, but others were visual and performative.

Photographs and illustrations of the students, painted on walls and hung in windows, began to appear at protests all over Mexico to the point where many people became familiar with their names and images. In the small city of Tlacolula, Oaxaca, home to Christian Tomás Colón Garnica, one of the forty-three missing students, local middle school students painted a mural of portraits of all the students on a public wall. A local artists' collective, known as Los Tlacolulokos, painted references to the forty-three students in various public places in Tlacolula, Oaxaca, and elsewhere in 2014.

Another collective, known as the Asamblea de Artistas Revolucionarios de Oaxaca (Assembly of Revolutionary Artists of Oaxaca), featured woodblock portraits of all forty-three students, including Colón Garnica from Tlacolula, in downtown Oaxaca in 2016. The faces and names of the forty-three students were also part of protests in the United States and in Europe. Protesters would take photographs holding images of the forty-three individual students and post them to Facebook. Slogans such as "vivos los llevaron, vivos los queremos" (they took them away alive, we want them back alive) would accompany these photographs. I participated in several such events where I live in Eugene, Oregon.

And the parents of the disappeared students held their own press conferences and gave speeches, touring around the United States, Mexico, and Europe. Telling their own stories and giving detailed, rich descriptions of their children were important strategies for humanizing the students individually and collectively—for making them "count" in the minds of Mexicans and others around the world. Images used by the parents also emphasized each student as an individual, but their collective presence counted too, as evident in an image and message for justice and for the return of their children that the parents sent during the 2015 Christmas season.

Persistence

In Poniatowska's other writings, particularly in *La noche de Tlatelolco* and *Nada, nadie*, she emphasized the testimonies of survivors of trauma and how they are impacted by tragic events. The parents of the students of Ayotzinapa have given their testimonies. In Poniatowska's public reading and the subsequent publication of her speech on Ayotzinapa, the students are present through their biographies. The dead and the disappeared cannot speak.

It is up to others—their families, friends, and writers like Poniatowska—to keep their memory alive and visible. Public performances, like Poniatowska's in the Zócalo in October 2014, work to build face-to-face strategic emotional political community, and through their reproduction they become part of a larger cultural archive that works with social media, public art, and in-person demonstrations. For the parents and family members of the disappeared students, this archive becomes an important resource for their continued efforts to find out what happened to the students.

After AMLO was elected president of Mexico in July 2018 and took office in December of that same year, the parents of the missing students, their classmates, and others who suffered the events of that terrible night in Iguala, and who also believed the Peña Nieto government orchestrated a cover-up, tried again to engage with the Mexican political system.[46] The social movement and strategic emotional political community they built with many people and organizations provided a platform for their new engagement with the state. On January 15, 2019, the Mexican government of López Obrador announced the formation of the Comisión para la Verdad y Acceso a la Justicia en el Caso Ayotzinapa (Commission for Truth and Access to Justice for the Ayotzinapa Case). Parents of the disappeared students attended this announcement. They tried to be hopeful, again, after years of despair. One of them, Emiliano Navarrete, commented, "As a father, I thank you all for this commission that this new government has displayed to uncover the truth. . . . I ask for your commitment and seriousness in this effort."[47]

Three days later, one of the principal actors in the 2014–15 government investigation of the murders and disappearances of the Ayotzinapa students became a target of the newly created truth commission. Alejandro Encinas, Undersecretary of Human Rights of the Secretaría de Gobernación (Ministry of the Interior), announced that the commission would investigate Tomás Zerón de Lucio, the former head of the Agencia de Investigación Criminal (Criminal Investigation Agency) of the PGR. Zerón de Lucio was a key actor behind the crafting of the "historical truth" video and the material evidence that the government displayed to convince the public that the students had been detained and kidnapped by local police and then turned over to local organized crime bosses, who killed them and incinerated their bodies beyond recognition. In September 2019, Encinas added that the attorney general would begin investigating all officials who had been in charge of the Ayotzinapa case in the previous administration. So far, AMLO's government has been very slow to investigate involvement by the military, despite the belief of the IGIE and journalists such as Anabel Hernández that there is some evidence of involvement. Members of the IGIE returned to Mexico close to the fifth anniversary of the students' disappearances to support the work of the commission AMLO appointed in January 2019. After six years, it is still unclear where the students are, and naming all the perpetrators and bringing them to justice—including the intellectual authors—has not occurred. On September 26, 2019, Encinas announced a substantial reward for new information about where the students could be found. In a press conference, he stated, "In the case of Ayotzinapa, the only clear truth is that until now there is no truth."[48] And he added that the case is now classified as a forced disappearance committed by agents of the Mexican state.[49]

On September 24, 2019, the parents of the students and thousands of others marched through downtown Mexico City carrying a Mexican flag spattered with blood and chanting, "Ayotzinapa vive" (Ayotzinapa lives).[50] They held pictures of their children and marched as they have every month on the twenty-sixth, the day their children disappeared in September 2014. They are still marching.

In July 2020, the remains of Christian Alfonso Rodríguez Telumbre were identified by the Mexican government. The identification was based on six pieces of remains at a laboratory at the University of Innsbruck in Austria.[51] The remains were found about eight hundred yards from where the government of Peña Nieto had claimed that the students were burned. For the parents of the other forty-two students who still have no answers, the identification provided fresh hope that they may still find out what happened and that a new serious investigation is underway. On the sixth anniversary of the disappearances, September 24, 2020, AMLO revealed that arrest warrants "are going to be executed" against members of the military. He promised that there would not be impunity.[52] In November 2020, Captain José Martínez Crespo was arrested. In January 2021, a newspaper published leaked testimony from a local boss of the Guerreros Unidos organized crime group that linked the military, state police, and Guerreros Unidos members in detaining, interrogating, killing, and disposing of the bodies of the forty-three students and as many as thirty other people. According to the witness, the students were mixed in with members of a rival gang who owed Guerreros Unidos money. The witness detailed how the detained students and others were interrogated in three groups, one on an army base, another by state police, and a third by Guerreros Unidos and how Guerreros Unidos killed these people and disposed of their bodies. He also shared that state police who worked with Guerreros Unidos planted evidence including ashes of cremated remains at the Cocula dump to support the government's "historical truth."[53] The Peña Nieto government's original explanation is thus unraveling as more arrests occur and new evidence comes to light.

Strategic Emotional Political Community and Justice

Keeping alive the memory of the forty-three missing students and pressuring the government to conduct a credible investigation has required constant vigilance on the part of their parents and the human rights organizations that represent them. Poniatowska's public performance, activism, and writing in support of the parents in their quest for justice is one small part of a larger cultural, legal, journalistic, and political effort, one that involves thousands of people around Mexico and the world, to make the forty-three students "count." By using her cultural and political public capital, Poniatowska has been able to work as an activist to support the families and keep the story of the students' disappearances in the public eye. Through continued public dialogues, press appearances, and on CNN in 2018 comparing the crime of the students' disappearances with the massacre in Tlatelolco, Poniatowska has continued to use the different strands of strategic emotional political community built through her crónicas, activism, and performances to bring attention not only to the disappeared students but also to the larger issue of forced disappearances in Mexico.[54]

Conclusion

Telling Stories, Making History

TODAY IS JANUARY 22, 2021. More than 550,000 people have died from the COVID-19 pandemic in Mexico and the United States. The year 2020 was marked by mass protests all over the United States and even in Mexico City, denouncing the murder of Black people at the hands of police. Weeks and months of lockdowns to prevent the spread of COVID-19 have produced catastrophic health, economic, and social consequences for populations of color and the poor in the United States, Mexico, and other parts of the world. The pandemic has magnified existing inequalities and highlighted a centuries-old system of white supremacy and institutional anti-Black and other forms of racism and xenophobia.

Historical moments when the status quo is cracked open, when people take to the streets and demand change, when another future seems possible, are the moments when gifted writers and artists step up. The ways that pandemics, massacres, earthquakes, and broad social movements for change are represented and documented can determine their place in history. As Ariel Dorfman explains, "Some of humanity's greatest writing has been born in times of turmoil. In an effort to make sense of painful encounters with death and loss, authors have always tried to turn their sorrow and confusion . . . into masterpieces that stubbornly surface in the wake of natural and man-made catastrophes, wars, civil strife, revolutions and political and economic upheaval."[1] Dorfman's words capture the great potential writers have to influence the historical record through emotive writing for readers and to illuminate human connections. Material, social, and political factors are important in the creation of strategic emotional political communities that emerge from the COVID-19 pandemic and the Black Lives Matter movement and other similar movements and events, but so are the interventions that writers, intellectuals, and artists make. How we will see this moment and other historical moments—who matters, what the turning points are, what behaviors are construed as ethical or not, and what must change and how—is also shaped in real time by the people who write and document.

Compelling writing and other forms of expression and performance are central to political life. Writing involves strategies of representation that in the hands of writers such as Elena Poniatowska can become political tools for influencing change. Emotion channeled through in-depth testimonies and stories on the page and in person creates connection between people that may be intense or muted, that endures or fades with time. Emotional connection is forged on the ground and can result in the creation of emotional and political community in the moment. The strategic writing involved in documenting and representing such connections and communities may also result in the building of an emotional political community among those who read such accounts and through their reproduction and memorialization. Political performances are also strategies that build strategic emotional political community in the moment and through time.

Elena Poniatowska was drawn to documenting already existing or evolving strategic emotional political communities as well as helping foster them through her writing and political performances. Strategic emotional political community as used in this book is a flexible concept with multiple dimensions that include (1) on-the-ground, face-to-face networks and community building; (2) the representation of such communities in texts; and (3) the possibility of communities of readers. Strategic emotional political communities are not fixed and necessarily stable through time. People may move in and out of them; they ebb and flow. At a larger level, writers such as Poniatowska and others actively worked to create, preserve, and expand what we might call a strategic emotional political community of the left in Mexico that was a guiding light for oppositional politics for decades. This has been an important contribution to supporting a broad critical public and processes of democratization in Mexico.

Through straddling the line between activism and journalism, writing and action, Poniatowska has been an important public intellectual and political figure in modern Mexico. Poniatowska's most compelling crónica writing links the experiences of particular individuals to larger political movements and events. Individual oral testimonies that recount a particular experience or event are further developed with rich descriptions that flesh out who the person is—how they dress, how they smile, how they sit—and then move directly to how they feel, what kinds of emotions they are experiencing. For example, in *Nada, nadie*, Salomón Reyes, who "will keep on walking in hope of finding my little Ricardo," is introduced by Poniatowska with these words: "With his black puffy cap with the English word *captain* written across the visor, his arms snug against his chest as if to hold back the emotion, Salomón Reyes begins his tale."[2]

The narrative continues simultaneously detailing Reyes's own terror as buildings fall down around him and his fears about the fates of his wife and children.

From parking space z-650 at the corner of the Nuevo León Building, I saw the tremor unleashed, and the first thought I had was of my children, my wife Jose, because I thought she was up there, but she had gone to fetch milk at Conasupo [a government-subsidized store]. I saw as clear as day how the building fell over, but what can you do? Turn into Superman and stop it? My children were waiting for breakfast to go to school: the oldest, Gloria Leticia, seventeen; Miguel Angel, fifteen; Guadalupe Adriana, eleven; Mayito, Mario, whom I found dead in the Cuauhtémoc Delegation [neighborhood], ten; Ricardo, five; Alma Celia, three. The first thing I thought was, "My children, my children, God of mine!" And the building came down, nothing but a screech, and when it hit the ground as if yanked out from the roots, it raised black smoke, really black smoke that spread all over Reforma [Avenue]. I sprinted like everyone, going to look for their family, their loved ones, their relatives, their acquaintances.[3]

This one oral testimony presents us to Reyes, gives us a snapshot of what he looks like, and immediately plunges us into his experience of watching a building fall over as he thinks about his wife, three daughters, and three sons, one of whom we learn died. We feel the devastation, the smoke, and we imagine terrified people running through the streets of Mexico City desperately seeking those they loved. We are connected to one person but also to the experiences of dozens of others going through the same thing as Reyes. Poniatowska succeeds in engaging readers directly and emotionally. She captures the richness of individual people but embeds their experiences in a set of larger relationships and structures. The story of Reyes becomes a building block in documenting the strategic emotional communities that emerged in the wake of the earthquake. The juxtaposition of dozens of stories like Reyes's documents connections to others, strategically representing existing networks, connections, and movements, and those that emerged after the quake. For readers, these stories may forge emotional connections with Reyes and the many others in the book. Such connections may fade or intensify at another point in time when the earthquake and the social movements it spawned are memorialized.

In another example, student leader José Luis Becerra Guerrero gives a detailed account in *La noche de Tlatelolco* of his beating and torture while detained in Lecumberri Prison after the student massacre. Poniatowska uses his words to craft an intimate, detailed account that directly connects to readers.

"The floor was covered with puddles of vomit where we'd thrown up after being tortured. . . .

They told me to shut my trap, hit me in the arms and legs with truncheons, boxed my ears, punched me in the stomach, and said, 'So you think you're pretty tough, do you? Well, we'll see whether you are as tough as you think you are.'"[4]

As this experience is textualized in the book and then read, the suffering and courage of Becerra Guerrero expand beyond the story of an individual victim to connect with the other students, the larger movement, and widespread government repression. Josefina, someone who read this book decades after it was written, shared with me that she was moved by the many student testimonies she read, and through her reading and reflection, her connection to the book also became political: "The descriptions of the repression, violation, and detention of the students affected me very strongly. . . . I think if I had not been exposed to [Poniatowska's] book . . . that my sympathies toward the students would have been very different, considering the dominant discourse . . . about student movements."[5] The detailed and very personalized testimonies she read about in *La noche de*

Tlatelolco seemed to have changed her perspective on student movements and helped her feel personally connected to others.

Beyond Josefina's individual experience reading *La noche*, encountering the book in school gave it additional meaning. Taught as a part of some school curriculums in Mexico, *La noche* is potentially influencing multiple generations of readers. Such readers might become linked to the larger project of building a strategic emotional political community of the left in Mexico or at least become part of a broad critical public in which such a project is legible.

Poniatowska's cumulative production as a writer, activist, and political performer for more than five decades has resulted in significant interpersonal networks linked to a wide range of writers, artists, intellectuals, political figures, activists, and political movements. Public performances and dialogues and exhibits that repeatedly memorialize the 1968 student massacre, the 1985 earthquake, the Zapatistas movement, and the disappeared students from Ayotzinapa provide annual opportunities for the memorialization. Poniatowska's decision to wed activism and writing allows her to serve as an iconic figure in these rituals of memorialization. For example, on October 1, 2018, one day before the fiftieth anniversary of the Tlatelolco massacre, she was interviewed on Televisa. She chose to focus her comments on the disappeared students from Ayotzinapa who at that point were missing for four years rather than focus back on the events of 1968. She was actively using her public speaking invitations to push the government of Enrique Peña Nieto to provide real answers to the families of the disappeared students. As she explained, "Ultimately [what happened to the students from Ayotzinapa] was much worse than 1968 because there were 43 young student teachers disappeared in one night. And afterward there was not a single response from the government."[6]

Historians have noted the particular ways politics in the public arena have been performative in Mexico beginning with its Indigenous states. From Mixtec Codices read in front of public audiences to confirm the rights of ruling lineages, to Aztec pictorial histories read aloud to an audience, to ceremonies carried out during the colonial period that included the participation of all social groups in big events incorporating color, fragrance, sound, and movement as a part of vice-regal entry processions or other events, performative politics has been a uniquely Mexican form of political expression.[7] The use of music, theater, dance, and fireworks in patriotic events such as celebrations of independence in Mexico City's

Figure C.1 Lynn Stephen and Elena Poniatowska, 2019. Photograph by author.

Alameda, and more recently hip-hop cultural elements as well as social media in protests and commemorations, suggests the ways that multimedia performative politics continue to this day in Mexico.[8]

An exploration of Poniatowska's career reveals how public performances and dialogues can augment the force of writers and their personas in the eyes of their public. Since the 1980s, Poniatowska has combined public activism with writing crónicas to bring attention to the issues she writes about, herself as a public figure, and the impact of her books. She has, for example, strategically used invitations to speak at book fairs on her own writing as launching pads for public discussion about political events and causes. While at the Feria Internacional del Libro in Guadalajara in December 2019 presenting her latest novel, *El amante polaco*, she commented on the climate of violence in Mexico and the danger for journalists.[9] At the 2017 Feria Internacional del Libro, Poniatowska engaged in an open dialogue with one thousand young people. When one young woman asked Poniatowska what people could do so that events such as the massacre of Tlatelolco and the disappearance of the students from Ayotzinapa would not be forgotten, Poniatowska responded, "You can keep asking what happened!" At the same event, she stated that it was unacceptable that forty-three people had disappeared without explanation and complained that the government investigation to that point had not had any results.[10] In December 2014, while Poniatowska was presenting the book of short stories *Hojas de papel volando* (Flying sheets of paper), she again used the book fair platform to push for a response from the government to the disappearance of the forty-three students. A newspaper report about her comments noted that she has also done that in "every public event she has appeared in over the past 12 months."[11] "It is impossible to not mention them [the students] every morning, afternoon, and evening. . . . It is intolerable to us that [President] Enrique Peña Nieto says that he is Ayotzinapa," stated Poniatowska at the 2014 book fair.[12]

While many writers like Poniatowska do not think of themselves as political actors, engaged writing and public speaking influence politics and thus result in writers having an impact in public politics. Poniatowska is one of many writers in Mexico who have commented on politics through cultural venues and through writing. By January 2021, at age eighty-eight, Poniatowska is one of the most recognized public intellectuals in Mexico, and through her crónicas, performances, and public dialogues she has documented and commented on some of the most important political events in modern Mexican history.[13] As she told me in May 2019, "I have situated myself in Mexican social and political life. I have dedicated myself to this. But I never thought of myself as doing political work in the formal sense. I am a reporter, a chronicler—not someone who takes the reins—in the political sense as someone who is in charge or has a political position of authority. . . . But . . . I have had the life of an activist without me ever taking that part of myself seriously. I never looked at myself in that way."[14] Few observers, however, would debate whether Poniatowska is an activist. She is. That and her engaged writing are how she has influenced Mexican politics and historical narrative. Talking with her over the past ten years, often in her living room (figure C.1), has allowed me to document this.

Poniatowska has devoted much of her writing to telling the stories of the people of Mexico. Her crónicas highlight the trauma, drama, anguish, hope, brilliance, tenacity, and resilience of Mexicans as they have lived through government repression and massacres, earthquakes, social and political movements, major political battles, and forced disappearances. Through telling stories, Poniatowska is making history (figures C.2 and C.3).

Figure C.2 Elena Poniatowska after receiving the 2013 Miguel de Cervantes Prize in Madrid, April 2014. Photograph by Felipe Haro Poniatowska. Used by permission of the Fundación Elena Poniatowska Amor, Mexico City, Mexico.

Figure C.3 Elena Poniatowska in La Universidad del Claustro de Sor Juana Inés de la Cruz, Mexico City, 2014. Photograph by Alan Flores Vargas. Used by permission of the Fundación Elena Poniatowska Amor, Mexico City, Mexico.

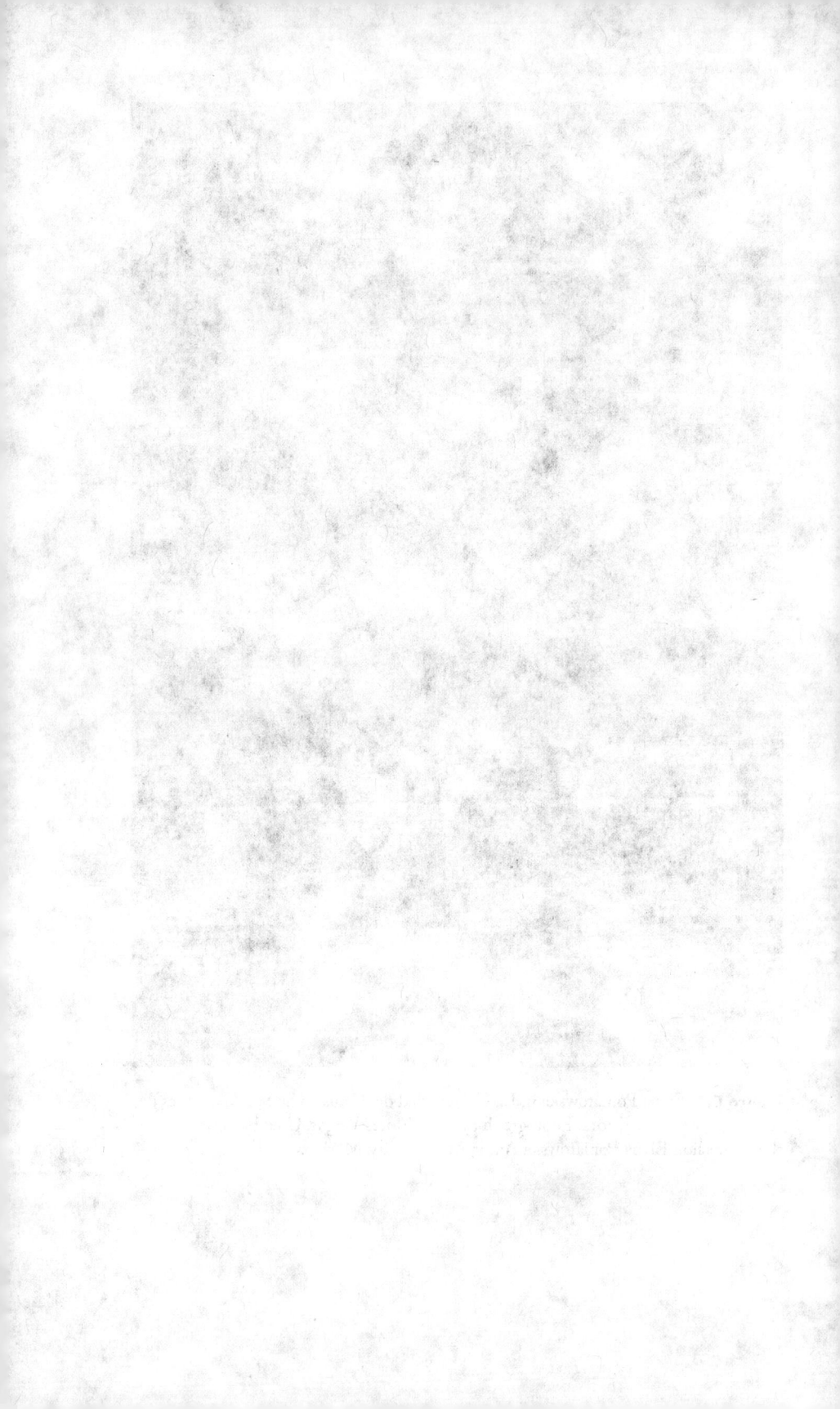

Notes

Introduction

1. See Egan, *Carlos Monsiváis*; and Wood, Review. Mark Anderson refers to *La noche de Tlatelolco* as Poniatowska's pioneering "collective testimonials." He also suggests that Poniatowska's and Monsiváis's crónicas of the 1985 earthquake were likely published and timed deliberately to have an impact on the 1988 elections. M. Anderson, *Disaster Writing*, 179, 172.

2. Meyer and Olivera de Bonfil, "La historia oral," 381. As I noted in the acknowledgments, all translations of quotes from my interviews of Poniatowska and untranslated works of hers and of other sources in Spanish were done by Sylvia Escarcega in chapters 1, 2, 5, and 6. All translations of quotes from my interviews with Poniatowska, as well as untranslated works of hers and of other Spanish sources in the introduction, chapters 3 and 4, and the conclusion, are mine.

3. Meyer and Olivera de Bonfil, "La historia oral," 381.

4. Stephen, *We Are the Face of Oaxaca*, 109–10.

5. Felman and Laub, *Testimony*, 7.

6. For a good summary, see Beverly, *Testimonio*.

7. Rabasa, *History*, 234; Stephen, *We Are the Face of Oaxaca*, 12.

8. Monsiváis, "De la Santa Doctrina."

9. Jörgensen, "Chronicle and Diary," 8.

10. Jimeno, Varela, and Castillo, *Después de la masacre*; Stephen, *We Are the Face of Oaxaca*.

11. Poniatowska interview by the author, June 19, 2015. Sylvia Escarcega worked with me on some of the translations from interviews I carried out with Poniatowska. I edited all final versions.

12. Poniatowska's *Nada, nadie* appeared in English in 1995 as *Nothing, Nobody*, translated by Aurora Camacho de Schmidt and Arthur Schmidt.

13. Poniatowska interview by the author, June 19, 2015.

14. Poniatowska interview by the author, June 19, 2015.

15. Poniatowska interview by the author, July 27–29, 2011.

16. Poniatowska interview by the author, June 19, 2015. "Crónicas de las Indias" refers to chronicles of the conquest period, which as a group are narratives from a Spanish point of view that document the colonization of the American continent.

17. Poniatowska interview by the author, June 19, 2015.

18. Boone and Mignolo, *Writing without Words*; Flannery and Marcus, *Cloud People*; Terraciano, *Mixtecs of Colonial Oaxaca*.

19. Monsiváis, "Prologo," 13.

20. Monsiváis, "Prologo," 13.

21. Añón, "Women 'Cronistas' in Colonial Latin America."

22. Añón, "Women 'Cronistas' in Colonial Latin America," 69–70; Lopreto, "Isabela de Guevara."

23. Añón, "Women 'Cronistas' in Colonial Latin America," 71.

24. Johnson, "Review of McKinley."

25. Añón, "Women 'Cronistas' in Colonial Latin America," 67.

26. Mahieux, *Urban Chroniclers in Modern Latin America*, 97.

27. Mahieux, *Urban Chroniclers in Modern Latin America*, 97.

28. Mahieux, *Urban Chroniclers in Modern Latin America*, 140.

29. Mahieux, *Urban Chroniclers in Modern Latin America*, 153.

30. Mahieux, *Urban Chroniclers in Modern Latin America*, 153.

31. Monsiváis, "De la Santa Doctrina," 753.

32. Corona and Jörgensen, *Contemporary Mexican Chronicle*.

33. Jörgensen, *Documents in Crisis*, 5.

34. Jörgensen, *Documents in Crisis*, 13.

35. Jörgensen, *Documents in Crisis*, 13.

36. Jörgensen, *Documents in Crisis*, 12, 15.

37. Jörgensen, *Documents in Crisis*, 15–16.

38. Poniatowska, *Nothing, Nobody*, 82.

39. Poniatowska, *Nothing, Nobody*, 83.

40. Egan, *Carlos Monsiváis*, 84.

41. Egan, *Carlos Monsiváis*, 84.

42. Monsiváis, "De la Santa Doctrina," 755.

43. Egan, *Carlos Monsiváis*, 84.

44. Jörgensen, *Documents in Crisis*, 143.

45. Jörgensen, *Documents in Crisis*, 141.

46. Jörgensen, *Documents in Crisis*, 143.

47. Egan, *Carlos Monsiváis*, 88.

48. On the Nahua, see Maffie, *Aztec Philosophy*; on the Maya, see León-Portilla, *Time and Reality*; on the Nasa, see Rappaport, *Politics of Memory*; and Rappaport, *Intercultural Utopias*; on the Mixtec, see Terraciano, *Mixtecs of Colonial Oaxaca*; and on the Kahnawake Mohawks, see Simpson, *Mohawk Interruptus*.

49. Jimeno, "Emoções e política"; Jimeno interview by Macleod; Jimeno, Castillo, and Varela, "Violencia, Comunidades Emocionales," 212–14.

50. Spivak, *Other Asias*, 260.

51. B. Anderson, *Imagined Communities*, 6.

52. B. Anderson, *Imagined Communities*, 7.

53. Jimeno, "Emoções e política"; Jimeno interview by Macleod.

54. Jimeno interview by Macleod.

55. Poniatowska, *Massacre in Mexico*, 223.

56. See Stephen, *Women and Social Movements*; and Stephen, *Zapata Lives!*, respectively.

57. See Stephen, *Transborder Lives*, 321–25; Hale and Stephen, introduction; and Stephen, *We Are the Face of Oaxaca*, 17–27.

58. See Hale, *Engaging Contradictions*; and Lassiter, "Collaborative Ethnography."

59. Robles Lomeli and Rappaport, "Imagining Latin American Social Science." See also Rappaport, *Cowards Don't Make History*.

Chapter One. Mexico City's Growing Critical Public

1. CNN en Español, "Elena Poniatowska recuerda."

2. CNN en Español, "Elena Poniatowska recuerda."

3. CNN en Español, "Elena Poniatowska recuerda."

4. Vaughan, *Portrait of a Young Painter*, 13.

5. Vaughan, *Portrait of a Young Painter*, 13.

6. The concept of a critical public is a variation on Jürgen Habermas's bourgeois public sphere. See Habermas, *Structural Transformation of the Public Sphere*; and Vaughan, *Portrait of a Young Painter*, 12–28. On the political effervescence sparked by the Cuban Revolution and the formation of the Movimiento de Liberación Nacional (MLN, Movement of National Liberation), see Zolov, *Last Good Neighbor*. On UNAM as a center of political and artistic critique, see Monsiváis, *Historia mínima*, 355–68. See also Volpi, *La imaginación y el poder*.

7. Freije, *Citizens of Scandal*, 4.

8. See Rubin, *Decentering the Regime*, on the "perfect dictatorship." On opposition journalism, see Freije, *Citizens of Scandal*; and Vaughan, *Portrait of a Young Painter*. On regional papers and investigative journalism, see Smith, *Mexican Press*; and Gillingham, Lettieri, and Smith, *Journalism, Satire, and Censorship in Mexico*. And on crime news and other popular media, see Piccato, "Murders of Nota Roja"; and Picatto, *History of Infamy*.

9. Zolov, *Last Good Neighbor*, 8.

10. Zolov, *Last Good Neighbor*, 8.

11. Zolov, *Refried Elvis*.

12. Harrison, *Changing Habits*, 25.

13. Boggs, "Sanctuary or Prison?," 39.

14. The niece of Eduardo Correo, the editor of the Social Events Section of the paper, recommended her for the job, according to Bautista, "Todo comenzó en Excélsior." Unless otherwise noted, all background information and quotations

in this chapter come from the author's three-day interview with Poniatowska, July 27–29, 2011.

15. Bautista, "Todo comenzó en Excélsior."

16. Benítez, "Una historia de suplementos."

17. Quoted in Schuessler, *Elena Poniatowska*, 55.

18. Quoted in Schuessler, *Elena Poniatowska*, 55.

19. Smith, *Mexican Press*, 46.

20. Smith, *Mexican Press*, 46.

21. Smith, *Mexican Press*, 47.

22. Smith, *Mexican Press*, 48.

23. Smith, *Mexican Press*, 48.

24. Vaughan, *Portrait of a Young Painter*, 22.

25. Vaughan, *Portrait of a Young Painter*, 24.

26. Solares, "La Revista de la Universidad," 82.

27. Solares, "La Revista de la Universidad," 82; see also Vaughan, *Portrait of a Young Painter*, 24.

28. King, *Role of Mexico's Plural*, 26.

29. Benítez, "Una historia de suplementos."

30. Benítez, "Una historia de suplementos."

31. King, *Role of Mexico's Plural*, 26.

32. Freije, *Citizens of Scandal*, 7.

33. Piccato, "Notes for a History," 50.

34. See, for example, Freije, *Citizens of Scandal*; and Piccato, *History of Infamy*.

35. Piccato, "Notes for a History," 49.

36. Piccato, "Notes for a History," 49.

37. Piccato, "Notes for a History," 50.

38. Piccato, "Notes for a History," 50.

39. Piccato, "Notes for a History," 50.

40. Lawson, *Building the Fourth Estate*, 61–62.

41. Smith, *Mexican Press*, 14.

42. Freije, *Citizens of Scandal*, 5.

43. Freije, *Citizens of Scandal*, 5; Smith, *Mexican Press*, 14–15.

44. See O. Lewis, *Los hijos de Sánchez*; and Vélez-Ibañez, *Rituals of Marginality*.

45. Smith, *Mexican Press*, 27.

46. Smith, *Mexican Press*, 27.

47. According to surveys done by the U.S. State Department in 1940 and 1954. Smith, *Mexican Press*, 28.

48. Smith, *Mexican Press*, 28.

49. Nolasco Armas, *Cuatro ciudades*, 227.

50. Piccato, "Murders of Nota Roja," 196.

51. Piccato, "Murders of Nota Roja," 197.

52. Piccato, "Murders of Nota Roja," 195.

53. Piccato, "Murders of Nota Roja," 204.

54. Piccato, "Murders of Nota Roja," 210.

55. Piccato, "Murders of Nota Roja," 206.

56. Piccato, "Murders of Nota Roja," 208.

57. Piccato, "Murders of Nota Roja," 209.

58. Piccato, *History of Infamy*, 64.

59. Piccato, *History of Infamy*, 73.

60. Piccato, *History of Infamy*, 74.

61. Gillingham, Lettieri, and Smith, "Journalism, Satire, and Censorship in Mexico," 8–9.

62. Piccato, *History of Infamy*, 102.

63. Piccato, *History of Infamy*, 103.

64. Fondo de la Cultura Económica, "8210 títulos."

65. *Enciclopedia de la literatura en México*, "Arnaldo Orfila Reynal."

66. Zolov, *Last Good Neighbor*.

67. Freije, *Citizens of Scandal*, 40.

68. Zolov, *Last Good Neighbor*, 28.

69. Lomnitz, "Prólogo."

70. Walker, *Waking from the Dream*, 8.

71. Walker, *Waking from the Dream*, 9.

72. Lomnitz, "Prólogo," location 86.

73. Lomnitz, "Prólogo," location 86.

74. Lomnitz, "Prólogo," location 317.

75. Freije, *Citizens of Scandal*, 42.

76. Freije, *Citizens of Scandal*, 43.

77. Freije, *Citizens of Scandal*, 43.

78. There, Haro made important astronomical discoveries, including many planetary nebulae and recent star formations called Herbi-Haro objects. He also uncovered flare stars in the Orion nebula region.

79. Poniatowska, *El universo o nada*, 172.

80. Poniatowska, *El universo o nada*, 190.

81. Poniatowska, *El universo o nada*, 191.

82. Poniatowska, *El universo o nada*, 208.

83. Poniatowska, *El universo o nada*, 212–14.

84. Monsiváis, "En el centenario."

85. For a list of her works, see Ediciones Era, "Elena Poniatowska."

86. Gray, "Spanish Diaspora," 71. On their influence in cultural fields, see Fagen, *Exiles and Citizens*.

87. García Hernández, "Editorial Era."

88. Quoted in García Hernández, "Editorial Era."

89. *Estandarte*, "Muere Joaquín Díez-Canedo.

90. Grupo Planeta, "Editorial Joaquín Mortiz."

91. Schuessler, *Elena Poniatowska*, 121.

92. Caballero, "Demetrio Vallejo fue un hombre."

93. Poniatowska, *Here's to You, Jesusa!*, xiii.

94. Poniatowska, *Here's to You, Jesusa!*, xix.

95. Schuessler, *Elena Poniatowska*, 142.

96. *Soldaderas* or *adelitas* were women who played a lot of different roles during the Mexican Revolution, from commanding posts to helping out in the camps, not only by taking care of others but also by preparing the weapons, tasks that were mostly unpaid. They usually came from the lower classes and were Indigenous or mestizas.

97. Smith, *Mexican Press*, 115.

98. Smith, *Mexican Press*, 114.

99. Smith, *Mexican Press*, 138.

100. Smith, *Mexican Press*, 147.

101. Smith, *Mexican Press*, 152.

102. Smith, *Mexican Press*, 153.

103. Freije, "Censorship in the Headlines," 244.

104. Freije, "Censorship in the Headlines," 244.

105. Freije, "Censorship in the Headlines," 248.

106. Lawson, *Building the Fourth Estate*, 68.

107. Lawson, *Building the Fourth Estate*, 68.

108. Lawson, *Building the Fourth Estate*, 68–69.

109. Poniatowska, "Llanto por Julio Scherer García."

110. Martínez Ahrens, "Poniatowska se enfrenta a los informes secretos."

111. Hernández and Villa Caña, "'A mis espias les llevaba café y galletas.'"

112. Piccato, "Notes for a History of the Press," 56.

Chapter Two. The 1968 Student Movement and Massacre

1. *Rojo amanecer* was finished in 1989 but not released until 1990. This fictional film portrays October 2, 1968, from the perspective of a middle-class family living in one of the apartment buildings on the Plaza de la Tres Culturas where the massacre took place. Carlos Salinas de Gortari decided that scenes involving the army had to be cut, thus delaying the film's release.

2. Poniatowska, *Massacre in Mexico*, 328.

3. Poniatowska interview by the author, July 27–29, 2011.

4. Schuessler, "Mexico's Tlatelolco Massacre."

5. Schuessler, "Mexico's Tlatelolco Massacre."

6. Aguayo, *México 68*.

7. Pensado, "Rise of a 'National Student Problem,'" 365.

8. Pensado, "Rise of a 'National Student Problem,'" 366–67.

9. Pensado, "Rise of a 'National Student Problem,'" 370–71. Historians of the 1960s have often referred to the period as the long 1960s, extending their analysis of student movements of 1968 from its roots in the 1950s to its continuation in the 1970s. See Pensado, *Rebel Mexico*. They have also called for a broader focus on the range of politics that influenced the 1960s, particularly in relation to global events and international relations. See Zolov, *Last Good Neighbor*.

10. See Pensado, *Rebel Mexico*; and Pensado, "Rise of a 'National Student Problem.'"

11. See Escudero, "El liberalismo del movimiento estudiantil de 1968."

12. Doyle, "Tlatelolco Massacre," October 2, 1998; Doyle, "Tlatelolco Massacre," October 10, 2003; Doyle, "Dead of Tlatelolco."

13. Malkin, "50 Years after a Student Massacre."

14. Noticieros Televisa, "2 de octubre."

15. Noticieros Televisa, "2 de octubre."

16. Aristegui Noticias, "Los muertos de Tlatelolco."

17. Aristegui Noticias, "Los muertos de Tlatelolco."

18. Aristegui Noticias, "Los muertos de Tlatelolco."

19. Rodda, "Trapped at Gunpoint."

20. Paz, *Posdata*, 38.

21. Aristegui Noticias, "Los muertos de Tlatelolco."

22. Poniatowska, *Massacre in Mexico*, 199.

23. See De Marinis and Macleod, "Resisting Violence," 1, 4, 5.

24. Poniatowska, *Massacre in Mexico*, 5.

25. De Marinis and Macleod, "Resisting Violence," 5; with reference to Jimeno, *Crimen pasional*.

26. See Abu-Lughod, *Veiled Sentiments*; Lutz, "Emotion, Thought and Estrangement"; Lutz and White, "Anthropology of Emotions"; and Lutz and Abu-Lughod, *Language and the Politics of Emotion*.

27. Jimeno, Castillo, and Varela, "Violencia, Comunidades Emocionales y Acción Política," 213–14; and Stephen, *We Are the Face of Oaxaca*.

28. Jimeno interview by Macleod, 2014.

29. Jimeno interview by Macleod, 2014; De Marinis and Macleod, "Resisting Violence," 5.

30. De Marinis and Macleod, "Resisting Violence," 6.

31. Vega, "Celebra 20 años."

32. Schuessler, "Mexico's Tlatelolco Massacre."

33. I do not propose this as a statistical or scientific demonstration of the effect that this book has had on the Mexican people's understanding of this event in history or as evidence of the book's influence. Rather, I offer this as a reflection on how Poniatowska's book may have affected these different generations of educated readers—but not all readers.

34. I have given them pseudonyms to protect their privacy.

35. This refers to the controversy raised by Luis González de Alba, where he stated that part of what Poniatowska included in the original Spanish version was taken from a book he published.

36. Brewster, "Mexico 1968," 164.

37. Brewster, "Mexico 1968," 164.

38. See, for example, Noticias Milenio, "Marcha a 50 años."

39. Excélsior TV, "Conmemoran 50 aniversario."

40. Monsiváis, "A veinte años."

41. Aranda Luna, "*La noche de Tlatelolco*"; Montero, "La noche de Tlatelolco"; Poniatowska, "Solo la muerte."

42. Noticieros Televisa, "2 de octubre."

43. Tomlinson, *Masacre en Tlatelolco.*

44. Sorensen, *Turbulent Decade Remembered*, 77.

45. *La noche de Tlatelolco* has been corrected by its publisher, Ediciones Era, in response to an article published by one of the student leaders most cited in the text, Luis González de Alba. In a 1997 article published in *Nexos*, González de Alba identified thirty paragraphs where, he stated, Poniatowska used material without attribution from his own 1971 book, titled *Los días y los años*, his account of the student movement and Tlatelolco published shortly before Poniatowska's book. In the *Nexos* article, González de Alba stated that Poniatowska asked permission to use excerpts from his manuscript while she was interviewing him and others in Lecumberri Prison. Her use of those excerpts, he wrote, lacked attribution to him and were sometimes attributed to other student leaders when they came from him: "Elena wishes to use my narration, given the more than 30 paragraphs that are included in *La noche de Tlatelolco*. She should have quoted González de Alba on more than 30 occasions, because he is the narrator." González de Alba, "Para limpiar la memoria." González de Alba asked that she publish a corrected edition, which Era did in time for the thirtieth anniversary of the Tlatelolco massacre in 1998. This edition includes more attributions to González de Alba. Harris, "Remembering 1968," 493. All Spanish editions of Poniatowska's book since 1998 have been corrected. The English translation, published in 1975 and based on Poniatowska's original 1971 publication, as well as subsequent editions do not appear to have these corrections. (The quotations for this chapter are from the 1975 English translation read against the second corrected Spanish edition of 1998.) González de Alba ended his own life on October 2, 2016, on the forty-eighth anniversary of the Tlatelolco massacre. He had continued to criticize Poniatowska even after the corrected edition of the book was published in 1998. In an article in *Aristegui Noticias* in 2016, Poniatowska explained that Ediciones Era had undertaken the task of revising the book and deleting the testimony of González de Alba: "But he kept after me for my whole life. He turned against me and I never answered him and I certainly am not thinking of doing it now." Castellanos, "'El odio de González de Alba.'"

46. Sorensen, *Turbulent Decade Remembered*, 5.

47. Sorensen, *Turbulent Decade Remembered*, 6.

48. Zolov, "Culture in Mexico."

49. Zolov, *Refried Elvis.*

50. Zolov, "Culture in Mexico."

51. Zolov, "Culture in Mexico."

52. Zolov, "Culture in Mexico."

53. Zolov, "Culture in Mexico."

54. Poniatowska, *Massacre in Mexico*, 20–21.

55. Through the work of historians such as Vaughan, Zolov, and others, we can see the creative dimensions of the movement that permeated the daily lives of people in Mexico City during 1968. See Vaughan, *Portrait of a Young Painter*, Zolov, *Refried Elvis*, and Zolov, "Culture in Mexico."

56. Museo Universitario Arte Contemporaneo, *Gráfica del 68*.

57. Museo Universitario Arte Contemporaneo, *Gráfica del 68*.

58. Vázquez Mantecón, "The '68 Impact."

59. Vázquez Mantecón, "The '68 Impact."

60. Poniatowska, *Massacre in Mexico*, 187, 188, 192, 192, 198.

61. Literary scholars such as Sorensen (*Turbulent Decade Remembered*), Brewster (*Responding to Crisis in Contemporary Mexico*), Jörgensen (*Writing of Elena Poniatowska*), Franco (*Plotting Women*), and others have commented on the creative and nonconventional form of *La noche de Tlatelolco*. Sorensen focuses on Poniatowska's use of photography and the importance of the authority of photographic proof—an element that builds on photographic journalism of the time. "Before even starting to read—indeed, before the title page—the primacy of vision elicits spectatorial engagement while at the same time affirming the irrefutable proof of the existence of the crowds and armed *granaderos* (riot policemen) sent to repress them. . . . Vision and knowledge validate each other as distances are controlled by the freezing of time. The photographic representational system produces a kind of photographic memory . . . and multiply the ensuing *testimonios de historia oral*." Sorensen, *Turbulent Decade Remembered*, 75.

62. Jörgensen, *Writing of Elena Poniatowska*, 90.

63. Jörgensen, *Writing of Elena Poniatowska*, 92.

64. Sorensen, *Turbulent Decade Remembered*, 75.

65. Poniatowska, *Massacre in Mexico*, 63.

66. Poniatowska, *Massacre in Mexico*, 64.

67. Poniatowska, *Massacre in Mexico*, 63.

68. Poniatowska, *Massacre in Mexico*, 22.

69. Poniatowska, *Massacre in Mexico*, 115–16.

70. Poniatowska, *Massacre in Mexico*, 117.

71. Poniatowska, *Massacre in Mexico*, 117.

72. Poniatowska, *Massacre in Mexico*, 118.

73. Poniatowska, *Massacre in Mexico*, 118.

74. Pensado, "Rise of a 'National Student Problem,'" 372.

75. Pensado, "Rise of a 'National Student Problem,'" 372.

76. Poniatowska, *Massacre in Mexico*, 328.

77. Poniatowska, *Massacre in Mexico*, 332.

78. Poniatowska, *Massacre in Mexico*, 41.

79. The quotes in this paragraph are from Poniatowska, *Massacre in Mexico*, 178–79.

80. Poniatowska, *La noche de Tlatelolco* (1998 corrected version, my translation), 49.

81. Zolov, *Refried Elvis*, 126.

82. Zolov, *Refried Elvis*, 127.

83. Poniatowska, *Massacre in Mexico*, 145.

84. Poniatowska, *Massacre in Mexico*, 304–5.

85. Brewster, "Student Movement of 1968," 175.

86. Poniatowska, *Massacre in Mexico*, 55.

87. Brewster, "Latin America's First Olympics," 434.

88. Poniatowska, *Massacre in Mexico*, 332.

89. Poniatowska, *Massacre in Mexico*, 79.

90. Poniatowska, *Massacre in Mexico*, 81.

91. Poniatowska, *Massacre in Mexico*, 81.

92. Poniatowska, *Massacre in Mexico*, 80–81.

93. Poniatowska, *Massacre in Mexico*, 82–83.

94. Brewster, "Student Movement of 1968," 176.

95. Brewster, "Student Movement of 1968," 177; López Naváez, "Manifestación permanente."

96. Brewster, "Student Movement of 1968," 178.

97. Brewster, "Student Movement of 1968," 178.

98. Brewster, "Student Movement of 1968," 178.

99. See Poniatowska, "Posición frente a los problemas nacionales"; and Poniatowska, "7 días del mundo."

100. Pensado, "Rise of a 'National Student Problem,'" 363–64.

101. Pensado, "Rise of a 'National Student Problem,'" 372.

102. Carey, *Plaza of Sacrifices*, 63.

103. Carey, *Plaza of Sacrifices*, 63.

104. Carey, *Plaza of Sacrifices*, 64, 209n83.

105. Carey, *Plaza of Sacrifices*, 64.

106. Carey, *Plaza of Sacrifices*, 64.

107. Poniatowska, *Massacre in Mexico*, 26–27.

108. Poniatowska, *Massacre in Mexico*, 92–93.

109. Universidad Autónoma de México (UNAM), "Anuario estadístico 1968 UNAM," 19.

110. For more analysis on gender in 1968 not only in Mexico but also around the world, see Frazier and Cohen, *Gender and Sexuality in 1968*.

111. Poniatowska, *Massacre in Mexico*, 89.

112. Poniatowska, *Massacre in Mexico*, 89–90.

113. Poniatowska, *Massacre in Mexico*, 90.

114. Poniatowska, *Massacre in Mexico*, 90.

115. Poniatowska, *Massacre in Mexico*, 60–61.

116. Quoted in Castro, "La patria que no cambió." A *grillo* in Mexico is a political activist who often acts in a dishonest way.

117. Castro, "La patria que no cambió."

118. Vázquez Delgado, "Entrevista a Ana Ignacia 'La Nacha' Rodríguez."

119. For an interview with Nacha in which she details her detentions, see Panorama68, "Tercer fragmento de entrevista a Ana Ignacio

Rodriguez, 'Nacha,'" October 26, 2020, https://m.facebook.com/watch/?v
=791072104785552&_rdr.

120. Poniatowska, *Massacre in Mexico*, 68–69.

121. Poniatowska, *Massacre in Mexico*, 218.

122. Poniatowska, *Massacre in Mexico*, 216.

123. Poniatowska, *Massacre in Mexico*, 216.

124. Poniatowska, *Massacre in Mexico*, 217.

125. López, "Guerrilleras, abogadas y artistas"; *Proceso*, "Historias del 68."

126. Poniatowska, *Massacre in Mexico*, 125–27.

127. *Proceso*, "Historias del 68."

128. Poniatowska, *Massacre in Mexico*, 148.

129. Carey, *Plaza of Sacrifices*, 160–61.

130. *Proceso*, "Historias del 68," 4.

131. *Proceso*, "Historias del 68," 3.

132. Carey, *Plaza of Sacrifices*; Draper, *1968 Mexico*.

133. Poniatowska, *Massacre in Mexico*, 199.

134. *Proceso*, "Historias del 68," 2.

135. Poniatowska, *Massacre in Mexico*, 221–22.

136. Poniatowska, *Massacre in Mexico*, 251.

137. Poniatowska, *Massacre in Mexico*, 285.

138. Poniatowska, *Massacre in Mexico*, 213–14.

139. Poniatowska, *Massacre in Mexico*, 229–30.

140. Poniatowska, *Massacre in Mexico*, 235.

141. Poniatowska, *Massacre in Mexico*, 222–23.

142. Poniatowska, *Massacre in Mexico*, 222–23.

143. Brewster, "Student Movement of 1968," 181–82; Poniatowska, *Massacre in Mexico*, 200.

144. Brewster, "Student Movement of 1968," 182.

145. All headlines are quoted from Poniatowska, *Massacre in Mexico*, 200–201.

146. Poniatowska, *Massacre in Mexico*, 238.

147. Poniatowska, *Massacre in Mexico*, 225.

148. Poniatowska, *Massacre in Mexico*, 237.

149. Poniatowska, *Massacre in Mexico*, 253–56.

150. Poniatowska, *Massacre in Mexico*, 207.

151. Poniatowska, *Massacre in Mexico*, 207.

152. Kahn, "What's Changed since Mexico's Bloody Crackdown?"

153. Poniatowska, *Massacre in Mexico*, 288–89.

154. Poniatowska, *Massacre in Mexico*, 293.

155. Poniatowska, *Massacre in Mexico*, 304.

156. Poniatowska, *Massacre in Mexico*, 298–99.

157. Poniatowska, *Massacre in Mexico*, 298.

158. These included Carlos Madrazo (former president of the executive committee of the PRI), Humberto Romero (former secretary of López Mateos), Victor Urquidi (director of the Colegio de México), and Braulio Maldonado (former governor of Baja California).

159. Carey, *Plaza of Sacrifices*, 142–44; Secretaría de Gobernación, "Problema estudantil."

160. Secretaría de Gobernación, "Problema estudantil"; Carey, *Plaza of Sacrifices*, 243; *Proceso*, "Sócrates, 'delator' del movimiento."

161. Poniatowska, *Massacre in Mexico*, 113, 115, 116, 118, 134.

162. Poniatowska, *Massacre in Mexico*, 115.

163. Poniatowska, *Massacre in Mexico*, 116–17.

164. Poniatowska, *Massacre in Mexico*, 257.

165. Poniatowska, *Massacre in Mexico*, 257.

166. Poniatowska, *Massacre in Mexico*, 314.

167. Poniatowska, *Massacre in Mexico*, 317.

168. *La Jornada Maya*, "Masacre del 2 de octubre."

169. *La Jornada Maya*, "Masacre del 2 de octubre."

170. Poniatowska, "Alaíde Foppa" (1990).

171. Fundación de Antropología Forense de Guatemala, "Entrevista Julio Solórzano Foppa." Poniatowska puts the date as December 19, 1980, in Poniatowska, "Alaíde Foppa" (1990). In a later piece published in 2012, she puts the date as December 19, 1981. See Poniatowska, "Alaíde Foppa: 31 años depués."

172. Fundación de Antropología Forense de Guatemala, "Entrevista a Julio Solórzano Foppa."

Chapter Three. A History We Cannot Forget

1. Beginning in 1985, diverse organizations formed to deal with the problems stemming from extensive damage to the twelve thousand apartments in the Tlatelolco complex known as Unidad Habitacional Tlatelolco. The Coordinadora de Organizaciones Residentes de Tlatelolco brought together various neighborhood associations to act as a large political power bloc and voice. It then changed its name to Coordinadora de Residentes de Tlatelolco. The organization is still active and is known as Tlatelolco Unido on its Facebook page, https://www.facebook.com/TlatelolcoUnido/. See Sandoval Ramírez, "Unidad Tlatelolco."

2. The Comité 19 de Septiembre 1985 sponsored a series of public events and discussions around memories of the 1985 earthquake and reconstruction, and it continues sponsoring community events. It was formed in 2015, thirty years after the earthquake. See its Facebook page, https://www.facebook.com /Comit%C3%A9-19-de-septiembre-1985-1664812610413805/.

3. See Brewster, *Responding to Crisis*, 105–11; and Steele, "Entrevista," 101.

4. *Labor Research Review*, "Costureras' Struggle Continues."

5. Brewster, *Responding to Crisis*, 117.

6. Brewster, *Responding to Crisis*, 117.

7. Poniatowska interview by the author, June 19, 2015.

8. Cornelius, "Political Economy of Mexico," 87.

9. Escobar Latapí and González de la Rocha, "Crisis, Restructuring and Urban Poverty," 57–58.

10. Escobar Latapí and González de la Rocha, "Crisis, Restructuring and Urban Poverty," 59.

11. Carlsen, "Grassroots Social Movements in Mexico," 36. See also Stephen, "Women in Mexico's Popular Movements."

12. Hernández Laos, *Crecimiento económico y pobreza*.

13. Instituto National de Estadística, Geografía e Informática (INEGI), "VIII General Population Census 1960"; Instituto National de Estadística, Geografía e Informática (INEGI), "X General Population and Housing Census 1980."

14. Vera, *La economía subterránea en México*, 81.

15. Davis, *Urban Leviathan*, 277.

16. Nuccio and Ornelas, "Mexico's Environment and the United States," 39.

17. Mexico's urban social movements didn't all begin in Mexico City, with significant popular movements consolidating in the early 1970s in Chihuahua, Nuevo León, Durango, and Oaxaca. Most of these movements were formed during the presidential administration of Luis Echeverría (1970–76).

18. Bennett, "Evolution of Urban Popular Movements," 248.

19. Moctezuma, "Breve semblanza," 7.

20. Stephen, *Women and Social Movements*, 11.

21. Watt, "Mexico's Secret Dirty War," 15. "Se murmuraba pero había un enorme indiferencia. Se murmuraba que había cárceles clandestinas, se murmuraba que se torturaba a la gente pero no se sabía de cierto. Una ignorancia, una indiferencia. Había presión para guardar silencio."

22. Watt, "Mexico's Secret Dirty War," 17.

23. Echeverría appointed Rosario Castellanos as ambassador to Israel, and Carlos Fuentes became ambassador to France.

24. Mary Kay Vaughan, personal communication, April 23, 2020.

25. Poniatowska, *Nothing, Nobody*, 15.

26. Steele, "Entrevista," 101.

27. Steele, "Entrevista," 101.

28. Steele, "Entrevista," 102. See also Brewster, *Responding to Crisis in Contemporary Mexico*, 108–9.

29. Poniatowska, *Nothing, Nobody*, 83–84.

30. Poniatowska, "Nuestro peor enemigo es el olvido," 9.

31. Ortiz de Zárate, "Miguel de la Madrid Hurtado."

32. Monsiváis, *"No sin nosostros,"* 85.

33. Monsiváis, *"No sin nosostros,"* 9.

34. Ramírez Cuevas, "Repercusiones sociales y políticas."

35. Poniatowska interview by the author, July 27–29, 2011.

36. Poniatowska interview by the author, July 27–29, 2011.

37. *El Informador*, "Poniatowska describe como 'guerra.'"

38. Steele, "Entrevista," 103.

39. Poniatowska interview by the author, June 19, 2015.

40. *El Informador*, "Poniatowska describe como 'guerra.'"

41. Poniatowska interview by the author, May 1, 2019.

42. Steele, "Entrevista," 104.

43. Poniatowska interview by the author, July 27–29, 2011.

44. Poniatowska interview by the author, July 27–29, 2011.

45. Poniatowska, *Nothing, Nobody*, 224.

46. Poniatowska, *Nothing, Nobody*, 184.

47. Poniatowska, *Nothing, Nobody*, 89–90.

48. De la Madrid, *Cambio de Rumbo*, 474.

49. Poniatowska, *Nothing, Nobody*, 92–93.

50. Poniatowska, *Nothing, Nobody*, 92.

51. Poniatowska, *Nothing, Nobody*, 92.

52. Poniatowska, *Nothing, Nobody*, 95.

53. Poniatowska, *Nothing, Nobody*, 96.

54. Poniatowska, *Nothing, Nobody*, 96.

55. De la Madrid, *Cambio de rumbo*, 473.

56. De la Madrid, *Cambio de rumbo*, 473.

57. De la Madrid, *Cambio de rumbo*, 473.

58. De la Madrid, *Cambio de rumbo*, 473.

59. Poniatowska, *Nothing, Nobody*, 96–97.

60. Poniatowska, *Nothing, Nobody*, 97–98.

61. De la Madrid, *Cambio de rumbo*, 473.

62. De la Madrid, *Cambio de rumbo*, 473.

63. Poniatowska, *Nothing, Nobody*, 223.

64. Poniatowska, *Nothing, Nobody*, 224.

65. Poniatowska, *Nothing, Nobody*, 224

66. Poniatowska, *Nothing, Nobody*, 227–28.

67. Poniatowska, *Nothing, Nobody*, 228.

68. Poniatowska, *Nothing, Nobody*, 228–99.

69. De la Madrid, *Cambio de rumbo*, 482.

70. De la Madrid, *Cambio de rumbo*, 483.

71. De la Madrid, *Cambio de rumbo*, 483.

72. Meneses, "Costureras del 85"; Monsiváis *"No sin nosotros,"* 143.

73. De la Madrid, *Cambio de rumbo*, 484.

74. De la Madrid, *Cambio de rumbo*, 484.

75. De la Madrid, *Cambio de rumbo*, 484.

76. De la Madrid, *Cambio de rumbo*, 487.

77. De la Madrid, *Cambio de rumbo*, 488.

78. Fonseca, "Cuauhtémoc Abarca."

79. Poniatowska, *Nothing, Nobody*, 257.

80. Poniatowska, *Nothing, Nobody*, 258–59.

81. Altamirano, "Lo que el sismo reveló."

82. Altamirano, "Lo que el sismo reveló."

83. Poniatowska, *Nothing, Nobody*, 259.

84. Poniatowska, *Nothing, Nobody*, 259–60.

85. Altamirano, "Lo que el sismo reveló."

86. Coordinadora Única de Damnificados (CUD), "Carta al Presidente Miguel de La Madrid."

87. Coordinadora Única de Damnificados (CUD), "Carta al Presidente Miguel de La Madrid."

88. Poniatowska, *Nothing, Nobody*, 263–69.

89. Poniatowska, *Nothing, Nobody*, 264.

90. Poniatowska, *Nothing, Nobody*, 268. There is a translation error in this passage in English. It says "I want to express my condolences to the Sr. Presidente" but should read "from the Sr. Presidente." The original reads, "porque quiero expresarles en primer lugar, y antes de nada, el pésame del señor Presidente, que esta muy dolido por lo que les ha sucedido a ustedes." Poniatowska, *Nada, nadie*, 265.

91. Poniatowska, *Nothing, Nobody*, 268.

92. Poniatowska, *Nothing, Nobody*, 268–69.

93. Preston and Dillon, *Opening Mexico*, 115.

94. Poniatowska, "Nuestro peor enemigo es el olvido," 14.

95. Poniatowska, "Las memorias de una costurera."

96. Poniatowska, *Nothing, Nobody*, 143.

97. Transcription and translation of Poniatowska's recorded remarks from event on July 28, 2015. Audio recording done by author and Spanish audio and transcript in possession of author. The quotes from her in the remainder of this chapter at the same event are from this same source.

98. Translation from my audio recording and transcription of this exchange. Spanish audio and transcript in possession of author.

99. Poniatowska, *Nothing, Nobody*, 249.

100. De la Madrid, *Cambio de rumbo*, 816.

101. De la Madrid, *Cambio de rumbo*, 816.

102. De la Madrid, *Cambio de rumbo*, 818.

103. Poniatowska interview by the author, October 11, 2015.

Chapter Four. Engaging with the EZLN as a Writer and Public Intellectual

1. Information consolidated from Stephen, *Zapata Lives!*, preface and introduction. See also Eliás, "200 muertos en la guerra."

2. Collier, *Basta!*, 53.

3. Franco, *Decline and Fall of the Lettered City*, 7.

4. Thomson, "Benito Juárez and Liberalism," 1.

5. Stephen, *Zapata Lives!*, 229.

6. Harvey, *Chiapas Rebellion*, 59.

7. S. Lewis, *Rethinking Mexican Indigenismo*, 7.

8. S. Lewis, *Rethinking Mexican Indigenismo*, 269.

9. S. Lewis, *Rethinking Mexican Indigenismo*, 270.

10. Rus, "Struggle against Indigenous Caciques," 171.

11. S. Lewis, *Rethinking Mexican Indigenismo*, 278.

12. Stephen, *Zapata Lives!*, 115–19.

13. Harvey, *Chiapas Rebellion*, 193.

14. Stephen, *Zapata Lives!*, 134–35.

15. Salinas de Gortari, "Discurso de Toma de Posesión."

16. Fox, "Targeting the Poorest"; Teichman, "Neoliberalism and the Transformation of Mexican Authoritarianism," 4.

17. See Stephen, *Zapata Lives!*, 109–11, 113–15.

18. General Command of the EZLN, "Declaration of War."

19. Poniatowska interview by the author, July 27–29, 2011.

20. *Zapatistas! Documents of the New Mexican Revolution*, chapter 4.

21. Caicedo Flórez, "Tourism in Chiapas."

22. Leñero, "Interview with Marcos," 201.

23. Marcos has also written children's stories. See Subcomandante Marcos, *The Story of Colors/La Historia de los Colores*; and Subcomandante Marcos, *Questions and Swords: Folktales from the Zapatista Revolution*.

24. Steele, "Rainforest Chronicles," 248. Steele confirms that the Mexican government identified Marcos in February 1995 as Rafael Sebastián Guillén Vicente, who studied at UNAM. Guillén Vicente earned two degrees from UNAM, a bachelor's and a master's in philosophy. In 1981 he was one of five students from UNAM's Department of Philosophy and Letters to receive a national medal of excellence from President José López Portillo. His undergraduate thesis was on discursive and ideological practices in elementary school textbooks—hence his penchant for writing critically about mainstream accounts of Mexican history, culture, and politics. After graduating, the "Sub" then taught communications for several years at UNAM.

25. Steele, "Rainforest Chronicles," 248.

26. Jörgensen, "Matters of Fact"; Jörgensen, *Documents in Crisis*; Egan, *Carlos Monsiváis*.

27. Poniatowska, "Entrevista del Subcomandante Marcos"; Poniatowska, "La CND." Translations are mine.

28. Ejército Zapatista de Liberación Nacional (EZLN), *EZLN: Documentos y comunicados*, vol. 1.

29. Poniatowska interview by the author, July 27–29, 2011.

30. Schuessler, *Elena Poniatowska*, 219.

31. Schuessler, *Elena Poniatowska*, 219–20.

32. Poniatowska interview by the author, July 27–29, 2011.

33. Poniatowska interview by the author, July 27–29, 2011.

34. Poniatowska, "Entrevista del Subcomandante Marcos."

35. Poniatowska, "Entrevista del Subcomandante Marcos."

36. Poniatowska, "Entrevista del Subcomandante Marcos."

37. Moguel, "Salinas' Failed War on Poverty."

38. Poniatowska, "Entrevista del Subcomandante Marcos."

39. Schuessler, *Elena Poniatowska*, 221.

40. Schuessler, *Elena Poniatowska*, 232.

41. Schuessler, *Elena Poniatowska*, 223.

42. Poniatowska, "Entrevista del Subcomandante Marcos."

43. Poniatowska, "Entrevista del Subcomandante Marcos."

44. Poniatowska, "Entrevista del Subcomandante Marcos."

45. Poniatowska, "Entrevista del Subcomandante Marcos."

46. Poniatowska, "Entrevista del Subcomandante Marcos."

47. Poniatowska, "Entrevista del Subcomandante Marcos."

48. Poniatowska, "Entrevista del Subcomandante Marcos."

49. Lovera, "Tzeltales violadas," 114–15.

50. Comisión Interamericana de Derechos Humanos, "Informe No. 53/01 Caso 11.565, Ana, Beatriz y Celia González Pérez."

51. Poniatowska, "La CND."

52. Poniatowska, "Entrevista del Subcomandante Marcos."

53. Poniatowska, "Entrevista del Subcomandante Marcos."

54. Poniatowska, "Entrevista del Subcomandante Marcos."

55. *Enlace Zapatista*, "CND, discurso del Comandante Tacho." See also Canal GEAVIDEO, "La larga marcha."

56. Poniatowska interview by the author, July 27–29, 2011. Peruvian rubber baron Carlos Fermín Fitzcarraldo organized the transport of a steamer over an isthmus from one river to another in Peru. The story was made famous in the 1982 movie *Fitzcarraldo*, directed by Werner Herzog. The film depicted the effort to move a three-story 320-ton steamship over a hill from one river to another. The giant structure that the EZLN built for the 1994 CND in the middle of the Lacandón Jungle appeared to resemble a ship with a giant sail, thus Poniatowska's reference to Fitzcarraldo from the 1982 film.

57. Poniatowska interview by the author, July 27–29, 2011.

58. Poniatowska, "Communiqué," 221.

59. UN Women, "Long Road to Justice."

60. Speed, Hernández Castillo, and Stephen, *Dissident Women*, 3–4.

61. Pérez y Castellaños, "Major Ana María y Comandanta Ramona." All quotes from this interview are my translation from Spanish to English.

62. Pérez y Castellaños, "Major Ana María y Comandanta Ramona." See also Rovira, *Women of Maize*.

63. Lamas, "La despenalización del aborto," 156.

64. Lamas, "La despenalización del aborto," 157.

65. Kulczycki, "Abortion Debate in Mexico," 55.

66. Kulczycki, "Abortion Debate in Mexico," 55.

67. Rodríguez, "Se repenaliza en Chiapas el aborto."

68. Lamas, "El EZLN, el Vaticano."

69. Subcomandante Marcos, "Comunicado de Prensa."

70. Subcomandante Marcos, "Comunicado de Prensa."

71. Lamas, "El EZLN, el Vaticano."

72. Poniatowska, "Subcomandante Marcos."

73. Poniatowska, "Subcomandante Marcos."

74. Poniatowska, "Subcomandante Marcos."

75. Hernández Castillo, *Multiple Injustices*; Stephen, "Rural Women's Activism."

76. Gallón, "Women Are Being Killed."

77. Poniatowska, *La herida de Paulina*, 10–11.

78. Salinas and Aguilar, "Elena Poniatowska desvela."

79. Poniatowska interview by the author, July 27, 2011.

80. Poniatowska, *El amante polaco*, 307.

81. Poniatowska, *El amante polaco*, 308.

82. Poniatowska, *El amante polaco*, 309.

83. Poniatowska, *El amante polaco*, 333.

84. Poniatowska, *El amante polaco*, 333.

85. Poniatowska, *El amante polaco*, 349–50.

86. Poniatowska, *El amante polaco*, 364.

87. Cherem, "Celebra Poniatowska 80 años."

88. Arreola, *El último juglar*, 446.

89. Chávez and Sánchez, "Familia de Arreola pide disculpa pública."

90. Salinas and Aguilar, "Elena Poniatowska desvela."

91. Poniatowska interview by the author, July 27, 2011.

92. Poniatowska, *El amante polaco*, 25.

93. Poniatowska, *El amante polaco*, 350.

94. Poniatowska, *El amante polaco*, 350.

95. Cherem, "Celebra Poniatowska 80 años."

96. Poniatowska interview by the author, July 27–29, 2011.

97. Poniatowska, *La herida de Paulina*, 10–11. My translation.

98. Poniatowska, "Women, Mexico, and Chiapas," 100, 102. By "seamstresses," she is referring to the female garment workers who organized after the 1985 earthquake (see chapter 3).

99. Congreso Nacional Indígena, "Palabra de Marichuy en Neza."

100. Muñoz Ramírez, "Ramona, comandanta."

101. The accords emphasized that the Mexican government would take responsibility not only for reinforcing the political representation of Indigenous peoples and their participation in legislatures but also for guaranteeing the validity of internal forms of Indigenous government. They further noted that the government promised to create national legislation guaranteeing Indigenous communities the right to (1) freely associate themselves with municipalities that are primarily Indigenous in population, (2) form associations between communities, and (3) coordinate their actions as Indigenous peoples. In addition, the accords stated that it is up to the legislatures of individual states to determine the best criteria for self-determination and autonomy. See Aubry, "Autonomy in the San Andrés Accords."

102. Stephen, "Asserting Indigeneity," 248–49.

103. *La Jornada,* "Tiene derecho a venir al congreso." "Me parece espléndido, es una gran alegría, me parece que será un día de fiesta. Espero con toda mi alma que ellos sean recibidos como nos han recibido en la selva: con los brazos abiertos, atendiendo a cada uno de nosotros personalmente. Me fascinaría ver a las mujeres, a Maribel, a Ana María, a doña Trini; ojalá que a todas ellas se les permita venir. Sería muy inteligente que hubiera un mayor número de mujeres, así se ensañaría menos el gobierno con los zapatistas. Ramona tiene toda mi admiración, ojalá que venga."

104. Poniatowska interview by the author, July 27–29, 2011.

105. Thompson and Weiner, "Zapatista Rebels Rally in Mexico City."

106. *Enlace Zapatista,* "Villa Olímpica."

107. Poniatowska, "¡Que viva la marcha INDIGENA!"

108. Poniatowska, "¡Que viva la marcha INDIGENA!"

109. Poniatowska, "¡Que viva la marcha INDIGENA!"

110. See Canal GEAVIDEO, "La larga marcha," 26:42–32:38.

111. Poniatowska interview by the author, July 27–29, 2011.

112. Poniatowska, "La postulación de una mujer indígena."

113. Poniatowska, "La postulación de una mujer indígena."

114. Hernández Castillo, Stephen, and Speed, introduction, 52.

115. Hernández Castillo, *Multiple Injustices,* 82.

116. Poniatowska, "Discurso de Elena Poniatowska en el Cervantes."

117. Stephen, "Rural Women's Activism," 165; Speed, Hernández Castillo, and Stephen, *Dissident Women,* 3–4.

118. Europeancollections, "Cervantes Prize."

119. Poniatowska interview by the author, July 27–29, 2011.

120. Poniatowska interview by the author, July 27–29, 2011.

121. Poniatowska interview by the author, July 27–29, 2011.

122. Poniatowska interview by the author, July 27–29, 2011.

123. Radio Zapatista, "Discurso de Marichuy."

124. Poniatowska, "La postulación de una mujer indígena."

Chapter Five. *Amanecer en el Zócalo*

1. Vaughan, "Cultural Approaches to Peasant Politics," 295; see also Lomnitz, "Ritual, Rumor, and Corruption."

2. As noted in chapter 3, many believe he won in the 1988 elections.

3. Jiménez, "Elena Poniatowska reivindica el papel."

4. Poniatowska, *Amanecer en el Zócalo,* 15.

5. Poniatowska interview by the author, July 27–29, 2011.

6. Jörgensen, "Chronicle and Diary," 8.

7. *El Mañana de Nuevo Laredo,* "Elena Poniatowska responde."

8. Cuauhtémoc Cárdenas was declared the loser in the presidential elections of 1988 when the government vote-counting system shut down—*se cayó*

el sistema—and when it was restored, PRI candidate Carlos Salinas de Gortari was declared the winner. See chapter 3.

9. Poniatowska interviewed Salvador Nava's brother, Manuel Nava, in San Luis Potosí in 1953, when he was the head of the University of San Luis Potosí. Poniatowska, "Los 100 años."

10. Poniatowska, *Amanecer en el Zócalo*, 139–43.

11. *Democracy Now!*, "An Hour with Mexican Writers."

12. *Democracy Now!*, "An Hour with Mexican Writers."

13. *Democracy Now!*, "An Hour with Mexican Writers."

14. Poniatowska interview by the author, July 27–29, 2011. I first spoke with Poniatowska about her work for López Obrador during our July 2011 interview, and we discussed her involvement with him again in August 2012 and June 2018. Rosario Ibarra is a political activist whose son, Jesús Piedra Ibarra, disappeared in April 1975. He was accused of being a member of the Liga Comunista 23 de Septiembre, a political-military organization. After Ibarra's efforts to get the government to investigate her son's disappearance fell on deaf ears, she formed what became known as the Comité ¡*Eureka*! in 1977 with about one hundred other women. She went on several hunger strikes in the 1970s to draw attention to the plight of political prisoners and those who had disappeared. Poniatowska's book *Fuerte es el silencio*, published in 1980, documented disappearances and the existence of political prisoners, focusing on the work of Ibarra and others who were trying to hold the Mexican government accountable for at least four hundred disappearances in the 1970s. See also chapter 3.

15. Poniatowska interview by the author, July 27–29, 2011.

16. Poniatowska, *Amanecer en el Zócalo*, 141.

17. Poniatowska interview by the author, August 28, 2012.

18. See YoAMLO, "AMLO Spot–NO CALUMNIEN."

19. Poniatowska, *Amanecer en el Zócalo*, 149.

20. Poniatowska, *Amanecer en el Zócalo*, 17–18.

21. Poniatowska, *Amanecer en el Zócalo*, 21.

22. Poniatowska, *Amanecer en el Zócalo*, 25.

23. Poniatowska, *Amanecer en el Zócalo*, 30.

24. Poniatowska, *Amanecer en el Zócalo*, 31.

25. Poniatowska, *Amanecer en el Zócalo*, 31–32.

26. Poniatowska, *Amanecer en el Zócalo*, 33.

27. Poniatowska, *Amanecer en el Zócalo*, 38.

28. Poniatowska, *Amanecer en el Zócalo*, 94.

29. Poniatowska, *Amanecer en el Zócalo*, 95

30. Poniatowska, *Amanecer en el Zócalo*, 99.

31. Poniatowska, *Amanecer en el Zócalo*, 100.

32. Poniatowska, *Amanecer en el Zócalo*, 100.

33. Poniatowska, *Amanecer en el Zócalo*, 110. The word *naco* likely originated as a contraction for *Totonacos* and is used to insult people as low class, poor, and of Indigenous origin, lacking "culture" in the sense of high culture.

34. Poniatowska, *Amanecer en el Zócalo*, 170.

35. Poniatowska, *Amanecer en el Zócalo*, 200.

36. Poniatowska, *Amanecer en el Zócalo*, 189.

37. Poniatowska, *Amanecer en el Zócalo*, 323. In Mexico's cities, big and sturdy fences, concrete, or brick walls enclose most houses and their gardens; thus, going into somebody's garden without permission is like invading someone's intimate space.

38. J. Rodríguez interview by the author, October 12, 2015.

39. J. Rodríguez interview by the author.

40. J. Rodríguez interview by the author.

41. Poniatowska, *Amanecer en el Zócalo*, 262.

42. Poniatowska, *Amanecer en el Zócalo*, 262.

43. Taylor, *Archive and the Repertoire*, 1.

44. Poniatowska, *Amanecer en el Zócalo*, 247.

45. Poniatowska, *Amanecer en el Zócalo*, 262.

46. Poniatowska, *Amanecer en el Zócalo*, 159.

47. Poniatowska, *Amanecer en el Zócalo*, 237.

48. Poniatowska, *Amanecer en el Zócalo*, 290.

49. Jörgensen, "Chronicle and Diary," 12.

50. Jörgensen, "Chronicle and Diary," 12, quoting Poniatowska, *Amanecer en el Zócalo*, 23.

51. Poniatowska, *Amanecer en el Zócalo*, 156.

52. Poniatowska, *Amanecer en el Zócalo*, 156.

53. Frazier and Cohen, "Defining the Space of Mexico '68," 658.

54. Frazier and Cohen, "Defining the Space of Mexico '68," 658.

55. Poniatowska, *Amanecer en el Zócalo*, 210.

56. Poniatowska, *Amanecer en el Zócalo*, 220.

57. Poniatowska, *Amanecer en el Zócalo*, 229.

58. Poniatowska, *Amanecer en el Zócalo*, 229–30.

59. Organization of American States (OAS), "Political Constitution of the United Mexican States."

60. The Sensenbrenner bill, which was passed by the U.S. House of Representatives but not the Senate in 2005, would have criminalized unlawful presence; increased penalties for a variety of immigration-related crimes; expanded expedited removal; broadened the definition of alien smuggling to include churches, employers, family members, and immigrant advocates; expanded the definition of aggravated felony; created new grounds of deportability and inadmissibility; increased mandatory detention; further militarized the border; and placed limitations on eligibility for naturalization. It also proposed building a wall. While it did not pass, many parts of the bill are now effectively parts of the anti-immigrant agenda in the United States with strong supporters, most recently under the presidency of Donald Trump.

61. Poniatowska, *Amanecer en el Zócalo*, 249.

62. Poniatowska, *Amanecer en el Zócalo*, 350–51.

63. The Grito en Resistencia was not broadcast by the mainstream TV stations such as Televisa and TV Azteca. A posted video documents part of

the event. "Grito en Resistencia," YouTube, September 15, 2007, https://www
.youtube.com/watch?v=vfaJ4Bx6BEQ.

64. Poniatowska, *Amanecer en el Zócalo*, 386.

65. Cevallos, "MEXICO."

66. Poniatowska, *Amanecer en el Zócalo*, 386.

67. Poniatowska, *Amanecer en el Zócalo*, 371.

68. Poniatowska, *Amanecer en el Zócalo*, 371.

69. Poniatowska, *Amanecer en el Zócalo*, 372.

70. Poniatowska, *Amanecer en el Zócalo*, 373.

71. Poniatowska, *Amanecer en el Zócalo*, 385.

72. Poniatowska, *Amanecer en el Zócalo*, 386.

73. Poniatowska, *Amanecer en el Zócalo*, 387. Ortiz Pinchetti is a Mexican
politician affiliated with the PRD.

74. Poniatowska, *Amanecer en el Zócalo*, 355.

75. Poniatowska, *Amanecer en el Zócalo*, 365.

Chapter Six. *¡Regrésenlos!*

1. Poniatowska, "Elena Poniatowska recuerda."

2. Poniatowska interview by the author, June 19, 2015.

3. Poniatowska, "'Regrésenlos' (discurso de Elena Poniatowska)."

4. See, for example, Baranda, "Caso Iguala."

5. Archibald and Villegas, "Remains of Student"; Vela, "Identifican restos de
otro normalista."

6. Aristegui Noticias, "EAAF 'discrepa profundamente.'"

7. Tribune News Service, "México cifra 77,178 desaparecidos"; Wattenbarger,
"For Mexico's President"; Wilkinson, "Los otros desaparecidos."

8. Associated Press, "Mexico Finds Rumors, Bodies."

9. *El Universal*, "Ayotzinapa."

10. Ocampo Arista, "Policías balean a normalistas."

11. A. Hernández, *Massacre in Mexico*, 365–36.

12. A. Hernández and Fisher, "Iguala"; A. Hernández, *Massacre in Mexico*,
270–71, 277.

13. Hernández, *Massacre in Mexico*, 367.

14. Ocampo Arista, "Policías balean a normalistas."

15. A. Hernández, *Massacre in Mexico*, 368.

16. Ocampo Arista, "Policías balean a normalistas."

17. A. Hernández, *Massacre in Mexico*, 368.

18. A. Hernández, *Massacre in Mexico*, 149.

19. A. Hernández, *Massacre in Mexico*, 153.

20. Alfred, "Mexico Is Looking."

21. López Obrador, "Cambiar política."

22. Poniatowska, "Intervención de Elena Poniatowska."

23. Poniatowska, "Intervención de Elena Poniatowska."

24. Poniatowska, "Intervención de Elena Poniatowska."

25. Poniatowska, "Intervención de Elena Poniatowska."

26. Poniatowska, "Intervención de Elena Poniatowska."

27. Poniatowska, "Intervención de Elena Poniatowska."

28. Poniatowska, "'Regrésenlos' (discurso de Elena Poniatowska)."

29. Poniatowska, "'Regrésenlos' (discurso de la escritora Elena Poniatowska)."

30. Poniatowska, "Intervención de Elena Poniatowska."

31. Poniatowska, interview by the author, June 19, 2015.

32. Poniatowska, "'Regrésenlos' (discurso de Elena Poniatowska)."

33. Poniatowska, "'Regrésenlos' (discurso de Elena Poniatowska)."

34. Nelson, *Who Counts?*, 81.

35. Presidencia Enrique Peña Nieto, "Conferencia de Prensa del Procurador," 15:43–26:00.

36. Presidencia Enrique Peña Nieto, "Conferencia de Prensa del Procurador," 22:34–22:52.

37. Presidencia Enrique Peña Nieto, "Conferencia de Prensa del Procurador," 15:43–26:00.

38. *Aristegui Noticias*, "EAAF 'discrepa profundamente.'"

39. Vicenteño, "Oficialmente muertos"; Fiscalía General de la República, "Video que explica."

40. Vicenteño, "Oficialmente muertos"; Fiscalía General de la República, "Video que explica."

41. *La Opinión*, "Tomás Zerón."

42. Inter-American Commission on Human Rights (IACHR), "IACHR Presents Performance Report"; Inter-American Commission on Human Rights (IACHR), "Special Follow-Up Mechanism."

43. Inter-American Commission on Human Rights (IACHR), "IACHR Presents Performance Report." For a detailed discussion, see Inter-American Commission for Human Rights (IACHR), "Special Follow-Up Mechanism."

44. Inter-American Commission for Human Rights (IACHR), "Special Follow-Up Mechanism," 28–29.

45. Doyle, "Transcripts of Intercepted Cell Phones."

46. See A. Hernández, *Massacre in Mexico*.

47. Martínez and Olivares, "Instalan comisión por Ayotzinapa."

48. Casasola, "A 5 años de Ayotzinapa."

49. Casasola, "A 5 años de Ayotzinapa."

50. Wattenbarger, "For Mexico's President."

51. Gallón, "Remains Identified."

52. Aristegui Noticias, "Se ejecutarán órdenes de aprehensión contra militares por caso Ayotzinapa."

53. *La Reforma*, "Militares y narcos." See also *Mexico News Daily*, "Leaked Testimony."

54. R. Rodríguez, "Elena Poniatowska sobre la violencia."

Conclusion

1. Dorfman, "Writers of the Past."
2. Poniatowska, *Nothing, Nobody*, 48.
3. Poniatowska, *Nothing, Nobody*, 48.
4. Poniatowska, *Massacre in Mexico*, 111–12.
5. Response to reader survey and interview, May 2019.
6. Noticieros Televisa, "Poniatowska."
7. Monaghan, "Performance and the Structure of the Mixtec Codices"; Monaghan, "Performance and the Structure of the Mixtec Codices"; Cañeque, *King's Living Image*.
8. Beezley, *Mexican National Identity*; Magaña, *Cartographies of Youth Resistance*.
9. Ávila, "'Ha sido un año difícil.'"
10. *La República*, "Elena Poniatowska pide a los jóvenes."
11. *El Comercio*, "Elena Poniatowska muestra su lado más sencillo."
12. *El Comercio*, "Elena Poniatowska muestra su lado más sencillo."
13. Poniatowska's 2019 novel, *El amante polaco*, is perhaps the most intimate she has written for the way it is interwoven with her own personal and family history. There, she applies the rich human and emotional engagements that characterize her crónicas in the lives of two parallel characters who live two hundred years apart: the "I" of the book, who is Poniatowska herself (as amply acknowledged in interviews), and Stanislav Augusto Poniatowska II, last king of independent Poland, who lived from 1732 to 1798. Stanislav the king is a figure who cares about some of the same kinds of people and causes that Poniatowska has championed herself: peasants, the poor, young people, the needy, democracy, autonomy, and the need to improve government services. In the parallel story, Poniatowska narrates her own life, from a young girl in France to her arrival and life in Mexico. The book serves, in many ways, as her own oral testimony—albeit it in the form of a novel with names changed, but with details and places very close to what she remembers about her own life and career. *El amante polaco* positions Poniatowska's family in the life of Mexican history.
14. Poniatowska interview by the author, May 1, 2019.

Bibliography

Abu-Lughod, Lila. *Veiled Sentiments: Honor and Poetry in a Bedouin Society.* Berkeley: University of California Press, 1986.

Aguayo, Sergio. *México 68: The Students, the President and the CIA.* Translated by Tanya Huntington. N.p.: Gandhi Pública, 2018.

Alfred, Charlotte. "Mexico Is Looking for 43 Missing Students: What Has Been Found Is Truly Terrifying." *Huffington Post,* October 30, 2014. https://www.huffingtonpost.com/2014/10/30/mexico-missing-students_n _6069706.html.

Altamirano, Claudia. "Lo que el sismo reveló." *Nexos,* September 1, 2015. http:// www.nexos.com.mx/?p=26145.

Anderson, Benedict. *Imagined Communities: Reflections on the Origin and Spread of Nationalism.* London: Verso, 1983.

Anderson, Mark D. *Disaster Writing: The Cultural Politics of Catastrophe in Latin America.* Charlottesville: University of Virginia Press, 2011.

Añón, Valeria. "Women 'Cronistas' in Colonial Latin America." In *The Cambridge History of Latin American Women's Literature,* edited by Ileana Rodriguez and Monica Szurmuk, 66–80. New York: Cambridge University Press, 2016.

Aranda Luna, Javier. "*La noche de Tlatelolco* y el dolor en el país van de la mano: Poniatowska." *La Jornada,* October 2, 2018.

Archibald, Randal C., and Paulina Villegas. "Remains of Student in Mexico Identified." *New York Times,* December 6, 2014.

Aristegui Noticias. "Los muertos de Tlatelolco, ¿cuántos fueron?" *Aristegui Noticias,* October 1, 2013. https://aristeguinoticias.com/0110/mexico/los -muertos-de-tlatelolco-cuantos-fueron/.

Aristegui Noticias. "EAAF 'discrepa profundamente' con partes del informe de la CNDH sobre Ayotzinapa." *Aristegui Noticias,* November 29, 2018. https://aristeguinoticias.com/2911/mexico/eaaf-discrepa-profundamente -con-partes-del-informe-de-la-cndh-sobre-ayotzinapa/.

Aristegui Noticias. "Se ejecutarán órdenes de aprehensión contra militares por caso Ayotzinapa." *Aristegui Noticias*. September 26, 2020. https://aristeguinoticias.com/2609/mexico/se-ejecutaran-ordenes-de -aprehension-contra-militares-por-caso-ayotzinapa-amlo/.

Arreola, Orso. *El último juglar: Memorias de Juan José Arreola*. Barcelona: Jus, 2015.

Associated Press. "Mexico Finds Rumors, Bodies, but Not 43 Missing Students." September 26, 2019.

Aubry, Andrés. "Autonomy in the San Andrés Accords: Expression and Fulfillment of a New Federal Pact." In *Mayan Lives, Mayan Utopias: The Indigenous Peoples of Chiapas and the Zapatista Rebellion*, edited by Jan Rus, Rosalva Aída Hernández Castillo, and Shannan Mattiace, 219–42. Lanham, MD: Rowan and Littlefield, 2003.

Ávila, Sonia. "'Ha sido un año difícil'; afirma Elena Poniatowska." *El Heraldo de México*, December 3, 2019. https://heraldodemexico.com.mx/cultura /2019/12/3/ha-sido-un-ano-dificil-afirma-elena-poniatowska-136751.html.

Baranda, Antonio. "Caso Iguala, mancha atroz—Poniatowska." *El Norte*, October 26, 2014. https://www.elnorte.com/aplicacioneslibre/articulo/default .aspx?id=376926&md5=a51e014fbbd33272dbae4828a8d53de7&ta=0dfdbac11 765226904c16cb9ad1b2efe.

Bautista, Virginia. "Todo comenzó en Excélsior; Elena Poniatowska." *Excelsior*, May 19, 2017. https://www.excelsior.com.mx/expresiones/2017/05/19 /1164421.

Beezley, William H. *Mexican National Identity: Memory, Innuendo, and Popular Culture*. Tucson: University of Arizona Press, 2008.

Benítez, Fernando. *La batalla de Cuba*. Mexico City: Ediciones Era, 1960.

Benítez, Fernando. "Una historia de suplementos." *La Jornada Semanal*, February 27, 2000. https://www.jornada.com.mx/2000/02/27/sem-benitez.html.

Bennett, Vivienne. "The Evolution of Urban Popular Movements in Mexico between 1968 and 1988." In *The Making of Social Movements in Latin America: Identity, Strategy, and Democracy*, edited by Arturo Escobar and Sonia E. Alvarez, 240–50. Boulder, CO: Westview, 1992.

Beverly, John. *Testimonio: On the Politics of Truth*. Minneapolis: University of Minnesota Press, 2004.

Boggs Sigmund, Barbara. "Sanctuary or Prison?" *New York Times Book Review*, May 7, 1989, 39.

Boone, Elizabeth, and Walter D. Mignolo. *Writing without Words*. Durham, NC: Duke University Press, 1994.

Brewster, Claire. "Latin America's First Olympics: Mexico 1968." In *Routledge Handbook of Sport and Politics*, edited by Alan Bairner, John Kelly, and Jung Woo Lee, 429–39. Abingdon, Oxon: Routledge, 2016.

Brewster, Claire. "Mexico 1968: A Crisis of National Identity." In *Memories of 1968: International Perspectives*, edited by Ingo Cornils and Sarah Water, 149–78. New York: Peter Lang, 2010.

Brewster, Claire. *Responding to Crisis in Contemporary Mexico: The Political Writings of Paz, Fuentes, Monsiváis, and Poniatowska.* Tucson: University of Arizona Press, 2005.

Brewster, Claire. "The Student Movement of 1968 and the Mexican Press: The Cases of *Excélsior* and *Siempre!" Bulletin of Latin American Research* 21, no. 2 (2002): 171–90.

Caballero, Jorge. "Demetrio Vallejo fue un hombre fuera de serie, inteligente y coqueto, dijo Poniatowska." *La Jornada*, May 28, 2009. https://www.jornada.com.mx/2009/05/28/espectaculos/a11n1esp.

Caicedo Flórez, Karolina. "Tourism in Chiapas: A Conversation with Hermann Bellinghausen." *Upside Down World*, April 2, 2013. http://upsidedownworld.org/archives/mexico/tourism-in-chiapas-a-conversation-with-hermann-bellinghausen/.

Canal GEAVIDEO. "La larga marcha de los indios del México Profundo." YouTube, March 27, 2014. https://www.youtube.com/watch?v=GKlLDbUpliE.

Cañeque, Alejandro. *The King's Living Image: The Culture and Politics of Viceregal Power in Colonial Mexico.* New York: Routledge, 2004.

Carey, Elaine. *Plaza of Sacrifices: Gender, Power, and Terror in 1968 Mexico.* Albuquerque: University of New Mexico Press, 2005.

Carlsen, Laura. "Grassroots Social Movements in Mexico." *Radical America* 22 (July–August 1988): 35–52.

Casasola, Tania. "A 5 años de Ayotzinapa, gobierno ofrece recompensa por información sobre los 43 normalistas." *Animal Político*, September 26, 2019. https://www.animalpolitico.com/2019/09/5-anos-43-normalistas-desaparecidos-ayotzinapa-recompensa/.

Castellanos C., Juan Carlos. "'El odio de González de Alba me persiguió toda la vida': Poniatowska." *Aristegui Noticias*, October 24, 2016. https://aristeguinoticias.com/2410/kiosko/el-odio-de-gonzalez-de-alba-me-persiguio-toda-la-vida-poniatowska/.

Castro, Hermenegildo. "La patria que no cambió, entrevista con Roberta Avendaño." *Nexos*, January 1, 1988. https://www.nexos.com.mx/?p=5018.

Cevallos, Diego. "MEXICO: National Democratic Convention Faces Uncertain Future." *Inter Press Service*, September 25, 2006. http://www.ipsnews.net/2006/09/mexico-national-democratic-convention-faces-uncertain-future/.

Chávez, Victor, and Carmen Sánchez. "Familia de Arreola pide disculpa pública a Elena Poniatowska." *El Sol de Mexico*, December 9, 2019. https://www.elsoldemexico.com.mx/cultura/familia-de-arreola-pide-disculpa-publica-a-elena-poniatowska-4566409.html.

Cherem, Silvia. "Celebra Poniatowska 80 años." *Enlace Judio*, May 15, 2012. https://www.enlacejudio.com/2012/05/15/celebra-poniatowska-80-anos/.

CNN en Español. "Elena Poniatowska recuerda lo que vio en Tlatelolco tras la masacre del 68." YouTube, October 2, 2018. https://www.youtube.com/watch?v=A28fsY4qnZE&feature=emb_rel_pause.

Collier, George A., with Elizabeth Lowery Quaratiello. *Basta! Land and the Zapatista Rebellion in Chiapas*. Oakland, CA: Institute for Food and Development Policy, 1994.

Comisión Interamericana de Derechos Humanos. "Informe No. 53/01 Caso 11.565, Ana, Beatriz y Celia González Pérez, México." April 4, 2001. http://www.alertadegenerochiapas.org.mx/agenero/Normateca/107.pdf.

Congreso Nacional Indígena. "Palabra de Marichuy en Neza: Sobre las mujeres y los feminicidios." November 27, 2017. http://www.congresonacional indigena.org/2017/11/27/palabra-marichuy-neza-las-mujeres-los -feminicidios.

Coordinadora Única de Damnificados (CUD). "Carta al Presidente Miguel de La Madrid Hurtado por la Coordinadora Única de Damnificados de los sismos de 1985." October 26, 1985. Reprinted as "1985 Demandas de la Coordinadora Única de Damnificados al presidente Miguel de la Madrid." Memoria Política de México. Accessed January 26, 2021. https://www .memoriapoliticademexico.org/Textos/7CRumbo/1985-DCUD-MMH .html.

Corona Cadena, Evangelina. *Contar las cosas como fueron*. Mexico City: Documentación y Estudios de Mujeres, A.C., 2007.

Corona, Ignacio, and Beth E. Jörgensen, eds. *The Contemporary Mexican Chronicle: Theoretical Perspectives on the Liminal Genre*. Albany: State University of New York Press, 2002.

Cornelius, Wayne. "The Political Economy of Mexico under De la Madrid: Austerity, Routinized Crisis, and Nascent Recovery." *Mexican Studies/ Estudios Mexicanos* 1, no. 1 (Winter 1985): 83–124.

Davis, Diane E. *Urban Leviathan: Mexico City in the Twentieth Century*. Philadelphia: Temple University Press, 1994.

de la Madrid, Miguel. *Cambio de rumbo: Testimonio de una presidencia, 1982– 1988*. Mexico City: Fondo de la Cultura Económica, 2004.

De Marinis, Natalia, and Morna Mcleod. "Resisting Violence: Emotional Communities in Latin America." In *Resisting Violence: Emotional Communities in Latin America*, edited by Morna Macleod and Natalia De Marinis, 1–22. Cham, Switzerland: Palgrave Macmillan, 2018.

Democracy Now! "An Hour with Mexican Writers Elena Poniatowska and Paco Ignacio Taibo on the Mexican Elections, the Zapatistas and President Bush." *Democracy Now!*, April 18, 2005. https://www.democracynow.org /2005/4/18/an_hour_with_mexican_writers_elena.

Díaz del Castillo, Bernal. *Historia verdadera de la conquista de la Nueva España*. 1568. Mexico City: Editorial Pedro Robredo, 1944.

Dorfman, Ariel. "Writers of the Past Turned Suffering into Literary Masterpieces. They Might Help Us Understand How to Meet the Challenges of Our Day." *Washington Post*, June 3, 2020.

Doyle, Kate. "The Dead of Tlatelolco: Using the Archives to Exhume the Past." National Security Archive, George Washington University, October 1, 2006. https://nsarchive2.gwu.edu/NSAEBB/NSAEBB201/index.htm.

Doyle, Kate. "Tlatelolco Massacre: Declassified U.S. Documents on Mexico and the Events of 1968." National Security Archive, George Washington University, October 2, 1998. https://nsarchive2.gwu.edu/NSAEBB /NSAEBB10/intro.htm.

Doyle, Kate. "Tlatelolco Massacre: U.S. Documents on Mexico and the Events of 1968." National Security Archive, George Washington University, October 10, 2003. https://nsarchive2.gwu.edu/NSAEBB/NSAEBB99/.

Doyle, Kate. 2018. "Transcripts of Intercepted Cell Phones Open New Lines of Investigation in Ayotzinapa Case." *Unredacted*, April 16, 2018. https:// unredacted.com/2018/04/16/transcripts-of-intercepted-cell-phones-open -new-lines-of-investigation-in-ayotzinapa-case/.

Draper, Susan. *1968 Mexico: Constellations of Freedom and Democracy.* Durham, NC: Duke University Press, 2018.

Durán, Diego. "Historia de las Indias de Nueva España e islas de la tierra firme." Manuscript, 1579. Biblioteca Nacional de España. http://bdh-rd .bne.es/viewer.vm?id=0000169486&page=1.

Ediciones Era. "Elena Poniatowska." Accessed January 24, 2021. https://www .edicionesera.com.mx/autor/elena-poniatowska/.

Egan, Linda. *Carlos Monsiváis: Culture and Chronicle in Contemporary Mexico.* Tucson: University of Arizona Press, 2001.

Ejército Zapatista de Liberación Nacional (EZLN). *EZLN: Documentos y comunicados.* Vol. 1. Mexico City: Ediciones Era, 1994.

Eliás, José. "200 muertos en la guerra abierta en el sur de México." *El País*, January 5, 1994. https://elpais.com/diario/1994/01/05/internacional /757724411_850215.html.

El Comercio. "Elena Poniatowska muestra su lado más sencillo en nuevo volumen de cuentos." *El Comercio*, December 4, 2014. https://www.elcomercio.com /tendencias/elenaponiatowska-libro-cuentos-feriadellibrodeguadalajara -mexico.html.

El Informador. "Poniatowska describe como 'guerra' lo que vivió en sismo del 85." *El Informador*, September 14, 2015. http://www.informador.com.mx /cultura/2015/614315/6/poniatowska-describe-como-guerra-lo-que-vivio -en-sismo-del-85.htmt/.

El Mañana de Nuevo Laredo. "Elena Poniatowska responde sobre su apoyo AMLO." YouTube, March 28, 2017. https://www.youtube.com/watch?v =7Rj4MboqMf4.

El Universal. "Ayotzinapa: Video Shows Tomás Zerón Conducting an Interrogation." *El Universal*, July 15, 2020. https://www.eluniversal.com.mx /english/ayotzinapa-video-shows-tomas-zeron-conducting-interrogation.

Enciclopedia de la literatura en México. "Arnaldo Orfila Reynal." Fundación para las Letras Mexicanas. April 22, 2019. http://www.elem.mx/autor/datos/14918.

Enlace Zapatista. "CND, discurso del Comandante Tacho: Nosotros queremos decirles que aquí estamos levantados en armas, esto es territorio zapatista, que quiere decir territorio rebelde contra el mal gobierno." *Enlace Zapatista* (Aguascalientes, Chiapas), August 3, 1994. https://enlacezapatista

.ezln.org.mx/1994/08/03/cnd-discurso-del-comandante-tacho-nosotros
-queremos-decirles-que-aqui-estamos-levantados-en-armas-esto-es
-territorio-zapatista-que-quiere-decir-territorio-rebelde-contra-el-mal
-gobierno/.

Enlace Zapatista. "Villa Olímpica. Subcomandante Marcos: El otro jugador."
Texto presentado por el Subcomandante Insurgente Marcos. *Enlace
Zapatista,* March 12, 2001. https://enlacezapatista.ezln.org.mx/2001/03/12
/villa-olimpica-subcomandante-marcos-el-otro-jugador/.

Escobar Lapatí, Agustín, and Mercedes González de la Rocha. "Crisis, Restructuring and Urban Poverty in Mexico." *Environment and Urbaniza-
tion* 7, no. 1 (1995): 57–76.

Escudero, Roberto. "El liberalismo del movimiento estudiantil de 1968." *Este
País,* October 2008. http://www.abcuniversidades.com/Tema/50/El
_liberalismo_del_movimiento_estudiantil_de_1968.html.

Estandarte. "Muere Joaquín Díez-Canedo." *Estandarte,* July 6, 1999. https://
www.estandarte.com/noticias/editoriales/muere-el-editor-espaol-joaqun
-dezcanedo-en-mxico_160.html.

Europeancollections. "The Cervantes Prize, the Most Important Spanish Literary Award." Cambridge University Library, *European Languages across
Borders,* May 4, 2017. https://europeancollections.wordpress.com/2017/05
/04/the-cervantes-prize-the-most-important-spanish-literary-award/.

Excélsior TV. "Conmemoran 50 aniversario de la masacre en Tlatelolco." October 2, 2018. https://www.youtube.com/watch?v=ZrJt54xLaoE.

Fagen, Patricia W. *Exiles and Citizens: Spanish Republicans in Mexico.* Austin:
University of Texas Press, 1973.

Felman, Shoshana, and Dori Laub. *Testimony: Crises in Witnessing in Literature, Psychoanalysis, and History.* New York: Routledge, 1992.

Fiscalía General de la República. "Video que explica hechos en caso Iguala."
YouTube, January 27, 2015. https://www.youtube.com/watch?v
=vaBxcRx5Qlo.

Flannery, Ken V., and Joyce Marcus. *The Cloud People.* New York: Academic
Press, 1983.

Fondo de la Cultura Económica. "8210 títulos para 'Fondo De Cultura Eco-
nomica.'"TodosTusLibros.Com. Accessed January 24, 2021. https://www
.todostuslibros.com/editorial/fondo-de-cultura-economica.

Fonseca, Antonio. "Cuauhtémoc Abarca: 'Dos sismos han marcado mi vida
uno en 1985 y otro en 2010.'" *Vivir en Tlatelolco: Periodismo Comunitario,*
September 21, 2010. https://vivirtlatelolco.blogspot.com/2010/09/blog
-post.html.

Fox, Jonathan. "Targeting the Poorest: The Role of the National Indigenous
Institute in Mexico's Solidarity Program." In *Transforming State Society
Relations in Mexico,* edited by Wayne A. Cornelius, Ann L. Craig, and
Jonathan Fox, 179–216. San Diego: Center for U.S.-Mexican Studies,
University of California, 1994.

Franco, Jean. *The Decline and Fall of the Lettered City: Latin America in the Cold War*. Cambridge, MA: Harvard University Press, 2002.

Franco, Jean. *Plotting Women: Gender and Representation in Mexico*. New York: Columbia University Press, 1989.

Frazier, Lessie Jo, and Deborah Cohen. "Defining the Space of Mexico '68: Heroic Masculinity in the Prison and 'Women' in the Streets." *Hispanic American Historical Review* 83, no. 4 (2003): 617–60.

Frazier, Lessie Jo, and Deborah Cohen. *Gender and Sexuality in 1968: Transformative Politics in the Cultural Imagination*. New York: Palgrave Macmillan, 2009.

Freije, Vanessa. "Censorship in the Headlines: National News and the Contradictions of Mexico City's Press Opening in the 1970s." In *Journalism, Satire, and Censorship in Mexico*, edited by Paul Gillingham, Michael Lettieri, and Benjamin T. Smith, 237–63. Albuquerque: University of New Mexico Press, 2018.

Freije, Vanessa. *Citizens of Scandal: Journalism, Secrecy, and the Politics of Reckoning in Mexico*. Durham, NC: Duke University Press, 2020.

Fuentes, Carlos. *La muerte de Artemio Cruz*. Mexico City: Fondo de la Cultural Económica, 1962.

Fuentes, Carlos. *La región más transparente*. Mexico City: Fondo de la Cultural Económica, 1958.

Fundación de Antropología Forense de Guatemala. "Entrevista a Julio Solórzano Foppa." 2009. https://web.archive.org/web/20140101191747/http://www.fafg.org/entrevistas/EntrevistaFoppa.html.

Gallón, Natalie. "Remains Identified of One of 43 Students Who Went Missing More than Five Years Ago." CNN World, July 8, 2020. https://www.cnn.com/2020/07/07/americas/identified-remains-missing-mexico-students/index.html.

Gallón, Natalie. "Women Are Being Killed in Mexico at Record Rates, but the President Says Most Emergency Calls Are 'False.'" CNN World, July 16, 2020. https://www.cnn.com/2020/06/05/americas/mexico-femicide-coronavirus-lopez-obrador-intl/index.html.

Gárcia Hernández, Arturo. "Editorial Era, 50 años de independencia." *La Jornada*, December 21, 2009.

General Command of the EZLN. "Declaration of War." December 31, 1993. In *Zapatistas! Documents of the New Mexican Revolution*, 49–51. Brooklyn, NY: Autonomedia, 1994.

Gillingham, Paul, Michael Lettieri, and Benjamin T. Smith, eds. *Journalism, Satire, and Censorship in Mexico*. Albuquerque: University of New Mexico Press, 2018.

Gillingham, Paul, Michael Lettieri, and Benjamin T. Smith. "Introduction: Journalism, Satire, and Censorship in Mexico." In *Journalism, Satire, and Censorship in Mexico*, edited by Paul Gillingham, Michael Lettieri, and Benjamin T. Smith, 1–32. Albuquerque: University of New Mexico Press, 2018.

González de Alba, Luis. *Los días y los años*. Mexico City: Ediciones Era, 1971.

González de Alba, Luis. "Para limpiar la memoria." *Nexos*, October 1, 1997. https://www.nexos.com.mx/?p=8565.

Gray, Rockwell. "Spanish Diaspora: A Culture in Exile." *Salmagundi*, no. 76/77 (Fall 1987–Winter 1988): 53–83.

Grupo Planeta. "Editorial Joaquín Mortiz." Accessed January 24, 2021. https://www.planeta.es/en/editorial-joaquín-mortiz.

Habermas, Jürgen. *The Structural Transformation of the Public Sphere: An Inquiry into a Category of Bourgeoise Society*. Translated by Thomas Burger and Frederick Lawrence. Cambridge, MA: MIT Press, 1962.

Hale, Charles R., ed. *Engaging Contradictions: Theory, Politics, and Methods of Activist Scholarship*. Berkeley: University of California Press, 2008.

Hale, Charles R., and Lynn Stephen. Introduction to *Otros Saberes: Collaborative Research on Indigenous and Afro-Descendent Politics*, edited by Charles R. Hale and Lynn Stephen, 1–29. Santa Fe, NM: School for Advanced Research Press, 2013.

Harris, Christopher. "Remembering 1968 in Mexico: Elena Poniatowska's *La noche de Tlatelolco* as Documentary Narrative." *Bulletin of Latin American Research* 24, no. 4 (2005): 481–95.

Harrison, V. V. *Changing Habits: A Memoir of the Society of the Sacred Heart*. New York: Doubleday, 1988.

Harvey, Neil. *The Chiapas Rebellion: The Struggle for Land and Democracy*. Durham, NC: Duke University Press, 1998.

Hernández, Anabel. *A Massacre in Mexico: The True Story behind the Missing Forty-Three Students*. Translated by John Washington. New York: Verso, 2018.

Hernández, Anabel, and Steve Fisher. "Iguala: Las horas del exterminio de los estudiantes mexicanos de Ayotzinapa." *Tercera Información—Artículos de Opinión*, January 11, 2015.

Hernández, Cristina, and Pedro Villa Caña. "'A mis espias les llevaba café y galletas, dice Elena Poniatowska." *El Universal*, March 16, 2019. https://www.eluniversal.com.mx/nacion/mis-espias-les-llevaba-cafe-y-galletas-dice-elena-poniatowska.

Hernández Castillo, R. Aída. *Multiple Injustices: Indigenous Women, Law, and Political Struggle in Latin America*. Tucson: University of Arizona Press, 2016.

Hernández Castillo, R. Aída, Lynn Stephen, and Shannon Speed. Introduction to *Dissident Women: Gender and Cultural Politics in Chiapas*, edited by Shannon Speed, R. Aída Hernández Castillo, and Lynn Stephen, 33–53. Austin: University of Texas Press, 2006.

Hernández Laos, Enrique. *Crecimiento económico y pobreza en México: Una agenda para la investigación*. Mexico City: Universidad Autónoma de México, Centro de Investigaciones Interdisciplinarias en Humanidades, 1992.

Hill Boone, Elizabeth. "Aztec Pictoral Histories: Record without Words." In *Writing without Words: Alternative Literacies in Mesoamerica and the Andes*, edited by Elizabeth Hill Boone and Walter D. Mignolo, 50–76. Durham, NC: Duke University Press, 1994.

Instituto National de Estadística, Geografía e Informática (INEGI). "X General Population and Housing Census 1980." https://en.www.inegi.org.mx /programas/ccpv/1980/.

Instituto National de Estadística, Geografía e Informática (INEGI). "VIII General Population Census 1960." https://en.www.inegi.org.mx /programas/ccpv/1960/.

Inter-American Commission on Human Rights (IACHR). "IACHR Presents Performance Report on the Special Follow-Up Mechanism for Ayotzinapa, Mexico, One Year into Its Work." Organization of American States, press release, June 6, 2018. https://www.oas.org/en/iachr/media _center/PReleases/2018/126.asp.

Inter-American Commission on Human Rights (IACHR). "Special Follow-Up Mechanism to the Ayotzinapa Case of the IACHR." Inter-American Commission on Human Rights, situation report, 2018. https://www.oas .org/en/iachr/docs/Mesa/ReportAyotzinapa.pdf.

Jimeno, Myriam. *Crimen pasional: Contribución a una antropología de las emociones*. Bogotá: Universidad Nacional de Colombia, 2004.

Jimeno, Myriam. "Emoções e política: A vítima e a construção de comunidades emocionais." *Mana: Estudos de Antropologia Social* 16, no. 1 (2010): 99–121.

Jimeno, Myriam. Interview by Morna Macleod, 2014. https://mornamacleod .net/.

Jimeno, Myriam, Ángeles Castillo, and Daniel Varela. "Violencia, comunidades emocionales y acción política en Colombia." *Abya Yala* 2, no. 1 (2018): 212–42.

Jimeno, Myriam, Daniel Varela, and Ángeles Castillo. *Después de la masacre: Emociones y política en el cauca indio*. Bogotá: Instituto Colombiano de Antropología e Historia, Centro de Estudios Sociales, Universidad Nacional de Colombia, 2015.

Jiménez, Arturo. "Elena Poniatowska reivindica el papel de la literatura testimonial." *La Jornada*, July 3, 2003.

Johnson, Lyman. Review of Michelle A. McKinley, *Fractional Freedoms: Slavery, Intimacy, and Legal Mobilization in Colonial Lima, 1600–1700*. H-Law, H-Net Reviews, December 2017. http://www.h-net.org/reviews /showrev.php?id=49605.

Jörgensen, Beth E. 2012. "Chronicle and Diary, Politics and Self-Portrait in Elena Poniatowska's 'Amanecer en el Zócalo.'" *Textos Híbridos: Revista de Estudios Sobre Crónica Latinoamericana* 2, no. 1 (2012): 4–21.

Jörgensen, Beth E. *Documents in Crisis: Nonfiction Literatures in Twentieth-Century Mexico*. Albany: State University of New York Press, 2011.

Jörgensen, Beth E. "Matters of Fact: The Contemporary Mexican Chronicle and/as Nonfiction Narrative." In *The Contemporary Mexican Chronicle: Theoretical Perspectives on the Liminal Genre,* edited by Ignacio Corona and Beth E. Jörgensen, 71–94. Albany: State University of New York Press, 2002.

Jörgensen, Beth E. *The Writing of Elena Poniatowska.* Austin: University of Texas Press, 1994.

Kahn, Carrie. "What's Changed since Mexico's Bloody Crackdown on 1968 Student Protests?" *National Public Radio,* October 2, 2018. https://www.npr.org/2018/10/02/653779935/whats-changed-in-mexico-since-the-1968-student-protests.

King, John. *The Role of Mexico's Plural in Latin American Literary and Political Culture: From Tlatelolco to "Philanthropic Ogre."* New York: Palgrave Macmillan, 2007.

Kulczycki, Andrzej. "The Abortion Debate in Mexico: Realities and Stalled Policy Reform." *Bulletin of Latin American Research* 26, no. 1 (2007): 50–58.

Labor Research Review. "Costureras' Struggle Continues: Feminizing Unions." *Labor Research Review* 1, no. 11 (1988).

La Jornada. "Tiene derecho a venir al congreso coinciden intelectuales y artistas." *La Jornada,* October 5, 1996.

La Jornada Maya. "Masacre del 2 de octubre, crimen de Estado: Jaime Rochín 'No debe haber perdón ni olvido, consideró el titular de la CEAV.'" *La Jornada Maya,* October 2, 2018.

Lamas, Marta. "El EZLN, el Vaticano, el aborto y el estado Mexicano." In *Chiapas, ¿y las mujeres qué?,* edited by María Rosa García Rojas, 1:139–42. Mexico City: Ediciones La Correa Feminista, 1994.

Lamas, Marta. "La despenalización del aborto en México." *Nueva Sociedad,* no. 220 (2009): 154–72.

La Opinión. "México: Tomás Zerón, un protegido de EPN, será indagado por la desaparición de Los 43." *La Opinión,* January 16, 2019. https://laopinion.com/2019/01/16/mexico-tomas-zeron-un-protegido-de-epn-sera-indagado-por-la-desaparicion-de-los-43/.

La Opinión. "Tomás Zerón: El verdadero hombre detrás de la 'verdad histórica.'" *La Opinión,* May 16, 2016. https://laopinion.com/2016/05/16/tomas-zeron-el-verdadero-hombre-detras-de-la-verdad-historica/.

La Reforma. "Militares y narcos detienen a los 43." *La Reforma,* January 20 2021. https://www.reforma.com/aplicacioneslibre/preacceso/articulo/default.aspx?__rval=1&urlredirect=https://www.reforma.com/militares-y-narcos-detienen-a-los-43/ar2108936?referer=---7d616165662f3a3a6262623b727a7a7279703b767a783a--.

La República. "Elena Poniatowska pide a los jóvenes mexicanos que no se 'desestimen.'" *La República,* November 28, 2017. https://www.larepublica.ec/blog/2017/11/28/elenaponiatowska-pide-a-los-jovenes-mexicanos-que-no-se-desestimen/.

Lassiter, Luke. "Collaborative Ethnography and Public Anthropology." *Current Anthropology* 46, no. 1 (2015): 83–106.

Lawson, Chappell H. *Building the Fourth Estate: Democratization and the Rise of a Free Press in Mexico*. Berkeley: University of California Press, 2002.

Leñero, Vicente. "Interview with Marcos before the Dialogue." In *Zapatistas! Documents of the New Mexican Revolution*, 196–210. Brooklyn, NY: Autonomedia, 1994.

León Portilla, Miguel. *Time and Reality in the Thought of the Maya*. Norman: University of Oklahoma Press, 1990.

Lewis, Oscar. *The Children of Sánchez: Autobiography of a Mexican Family*. London: Secker and Warburg, 1961.

Lewis, Oscar. *Five Families: Mexican Case Studies of the Culture of Poverty*. New York: Science Edition, 1962.

Lewis, Oscar. *Los hijos de Sánchez*. Mexico City: Fondo de la Cultura Económica, 1965.

Lewis, Stephen. *Rethinking Mexican Indigenismo: The INI's Coordinating Center in Highland Chiapas and the Fate of a Utopian Project*. Albuquerque: University of New Mexico Press, 2018.

Lomnitz, Claudio. "Prólogo." In *Los hijos de Sánchez/Una muerte en la familia Sánchez*, by Oscar Lewis. Electronic ed. Mexico City: Fondo de la Cultura Económica, 2012.

Lomnitz, Claudio. "Ritual, Rumor, and Corruption in the Constitution of Polity in Modern Mexico." *Journal of Latin American Anthropology* 1 (1995): 20–47.

López, Paulina. "Guerrilleras, abogadas y artistas: 8 mujeres del 68." *Vice México*, October 2, 2018. https://www.vice.com/es_latam/article/vbnzxx /guerrilleras-abogadas-y-artistas-8-mujeres-del-68.

López Naváez, F. M. "Manifestación permanente: Ratificación de demandas." *Excélsior*, August 28, 1968, 7.

López Obrador, Andrés Manuel. "Cambiar política y al presidente propone López Obrador a los ciudadanos en el Zócalo del D.F." *AMLO* (blog), October 26, 2014. https://lopezobrador.org.mx/2014/10/26/cambio-de -politica-y-de-presidente-propone-lopez-obrador-a-los-ciudadanos-al -zocalo-del-df/.

Lopreto, Gladys. "Isabela de Guevara, la primera feminista." *Todo Es Historia*, no. 285 (March 1991): 43–49.

Lovera, Sara. "Tzeltales violadas: Cronología de otra impunidad." In *Chiapas, ¿y las mujeres qué?*, edited by María Rosa García Rojas, 1:114–17. Mexico City: Ediciones La Correa Feminista, 1994.

Lutz, Catherine. "Emotion, Thought and Estrangement: Emotion as a Cultural Category." *Cultural Anthropology* 1, no. 3 (1986): 287–309.

Lutz, Catherine, and Lila Abu-Lughod. *Language and the Politics of Emotion*. Cambridge: Cambridge University Press, 1990.

Lutz, Catherine, and Geoffrey White. "The Anthropology of Emotions." *Annual Review of Anthropology* 15 (1986): 405–36.

Maffie, James. *Aztec Philosophy: Understanding a World in Motion*. Denver: University Press of Colorado, 2014.

Magaña, Maurice. *Cartographies of Youth Resistance: Hip-Hop, Punk, and Urban Autonomy in Mexico*. Oakland: University of California Press, 2020.

Mahieux, Viviane. *Urban Chroniclers in Modern Latin America: The Shared Intimacy of Everyday Life*. Austin: University of Texas Press, 2011.

Malkin, Elisabeth. "50 Years after a Student Massacre, Mexico Reflects on Democracy." *New York Times*, October 1, 2018.

Martínez, Fabiola, and Emir Olivares. "Instalan comisión por Ayotzinapa; padres reclaman 'la verdad.'" *La Jornada*, January 15, 2019. https://media .jornada.com.mx/ultimas/2019/01/15/instalan-comision-por-ayotzinapa -padres-reclaman-la-verdad-6190.html.

Martínez Ahrens, Jan. 2016. "Poniatowska se enfrenta a los informes secretos del régimen priísta sobre ella." *El País*, October 23, 2016. https://elpais .com/cultura/2016/10/21/actualidad/1477070699_702419.html.

McKinley, Michelle. *Fractional Freedoms: Slavery, Intimacy, and Legal Mobilization in Colonial Lima, 1600–1700*. New York: Cambridge University Press, 2016.

Menchú, Rigoberta. *I, Rigoberta Menchú: An Indian Woman in Guatemala*. Edited by Elisabeth Burgos-De Bray. Translated by Ann Wright. London: Verso, 1984.

Meneses, Natyelly. "Costureras del 85: La lucha sindical que surgió tras la tragedia." *Milenio*, September 18, 2015. https://www.milenio.com/estados /costureras-85-lucha-sindical-surgio-tragedia.

Mexico News Daily, "Leaked Testimony Links Military with Disappearance of 43 Ayotzinapa Students." *Mexico News Daily*, January 21, 2021. https://mexiconewsdaily.com/news/leaked-testimony-links-military-with -disappearance-of-43-ayotzinapa-students/.

Meyer, Eugenia, and Alicia Olivera de Bonfil. "La historia oral: Origen, metodología, desarrollo y perspectivas." *Historia Mexicana* 21, no. 2 (1970): 372–87.

Mills, C. Wright. *Escucha yanqui: La revolución en Cuba*. Mexico City: Fondo de la Cultura Económica, 1961.

Mills, C. Wright. *Listen Yankee: The Revolution in Cuba*. New York: McGraw Hill, 1960.

Moctezuma, Pedro. "Breve semblanza del movimiento urbano popular y la CONAMUP." *Testimonios* 1, no. 1 (1983): 5–17.

Moguel, Julio. "Salinas' Failed War on Poverty." *North American Congress on Latin America*, September 25, 2007.

Monaghan, John. "Performance and the Structure of the Mixtec Codices." *Ancient Mesoamerica* 1 (1990): 133–40.

Monsiváis, Carlos. "Prologo." In *A ustedes les consta: Antología de la crónica en México*, edited by Carlos Monsiváis, 13–130. 2nd ed. Mexico City: Ediciones Era, 2006.

Monsiváis, Carlos. "A veinte años de *La noche de Tlatelolco*." *La Jornada Semanal*, October 13, 1991.

Monsiváis, Carlos. "De la Santa Doctrina al Espíritu Público (Sobre las funciones de la crónica en México)." *Nueva Revista de Filología Hispánica 35*, no. 2 (1987): 753–71.

Monsiváis, Carlos. "En el centenario de Arnaldo Orfila Reynal." *Proceso*, July 19, 1997.

Monsiváis, Carlos. *Historia mínima: La cultura mexicana en el siglo XX*. Mexico City: Universidad Nacional Autónoma de México, 2012.

Monsiváis, Carlos. *"No sin nosotros": Los dias del terremoto, 1985–2005*. Santiago de Chile: Ediciones Trilce; Mexico City: Ediciones Era, 2005.

Montero, Jorge. "La noche de Tlatelolco." *El Furgón*, October 2, 2018. Accessed December 15, 2018. http://elfurgon.com.ar/2018/10/02/la-noche-de-tlatelolco/.

Muñoz Ramírez, Gloria. "Ramona, comandanta." *La Jornada*, January 2006. https://www.jornada.com.mx/2006/01/16/oja105-gloria.html.

Museo Universitario Arte Contemporaneo. *Gráfica del 68*. Exhibition, September 1–December 30, 2018. https://muac.unam.mx/exposicion/grafica-del-68.

Nelson, Diane. *Who Counts? The Mathematics of Death and Life after Genocide*. Durham, NC: Duke University Press, 2015.

Nolasco Armas, Margarita. *Cuatro ciudades: El proceso de urbanización dependiente*. Mexico City: Instituto Nacional de Antropología e Historia, 1981.

Noticias Milenio. "Marcha a 50 años de la matanza de Tlatelolco." YouTube, October 2, 2018. https://www.youtube.com/watch?v=1TmsqnJnwXI.

Noticieros Televisa. "2 de octubre: El testimonio de La Noche de Tlatelolco." Noticieros Televisa, October 2, 2020. https://noticieros.televisa.com/especiales/2-octubre-testimonio-noche-tlatelolco-elena-poniatowska/.

Noticieros Televisa. "Poniatowska: Ayotzinapa, peor que masacre de Tlatelolco." Noticieros Televisa, October 1, 2018. https://noticieros.televisa.com/ultimas-noticias/poniatowska-ayotzinapa-peor-que-masacre-tlatelolco/.

Nuccio, Richard A., and Angelina M. Ornelas. "Mexico's Environment and the United States." In *The U.S. Interest: Resources, Growth, and Security in the Developing World*, edited by Janet Welsh Brown, 19–58. Boulder, CO: Westview, 1990.

Ocampo Arista, Sergio. "Policías balean a normalistas de Ayotzinapa en Iguala; 5 muertos." *La Jornada*, September 28, 2014. https://www.jornada.com.mx/2014/09/28/politica/005n1pol.

Olivera de Bonfil, Alicia. *Mi pueblo durante la Revolución*. Mexico City: Instituto Nacional de Antropología e Historia, 1985.

Organization of American States (OAS). "Political Constitution of the United Mexican States." Last review, October 2, 2003. http://www.oas.org/juridico/Spanish/mex_res3.pdf.

Ortiz de Zárate, Roberto. "Miguel de la Madrid Hurtado." Barcelona Centre for International Affairs (CIDOB), July 2, 2018. https://www.cidob.org

/biografias_lideres_politicos/america_del_norte/mexico/miguel_de_la
_madrid_hurtado.

Paz, Octavio. *Posdata*. Mexico City: Siglo XXI, 1970.

Pensado, Jaime. *Rebel Mexico. Student Unrest and Authoritarian Political Culture during the Long Sixties*. Palo Alto: Stanford University Press, 2013.

Pensado, Jaime. "The Rise of a 'National Student Problem' in 1956." In *Dictablanda: Politics, Work, and Culture in Mexico, 1938–1968*, edited by Paul Gillingham and Benjamin T. Smith, 360–78. Durham, NC: Duke University Press, 2014.

Pérez, Matilde, and Laura Castellanos. "Major Ana María y Comandanta Ramona: No nos dejen solas." *Doble Jornada*, March 7, 1994.

Piccato, Pablo. *A History of Infamy: Crime, Truth, and Justice in Mexico*. Oakland: University of California Press, 2017.

Piccato, Pablo. "Murders of Nota Roja: Truth and Justice in Mexican Crime News." *Past and Present* 223, no. 1 (2014): 195–231.

Piccato, Pablo. "Notes for a History of the Press in Mexico." In *Journalism, Satire, and Censorship in Mexico*, edited by Paul Gillingham, Michael Lettieri, and Benjamin T. Smith, 33–59. Albuquerque: University of New Mexico Press, 2018.

Poniatowska, Elena. "Alaíde Foppa." *Debate Feminista* 2 (September 1990): 4–15.

Poniatowska, Elena. "Alaíde Foppa: 31 años depués." *La Jornada*, October 21, 2012. https://www.jornada.com.mx/2012/10/21/cultura/a03a1cul.

Poniatowska, Elena. *Amanecer en el Zócalo: Los 50 días que confrontaron a México*. Mexico City: Editorial Planeta, 2007.

Poniatowska, Elena. "Bring Them Back—Speech by Elena Poniatowska (Translation)." *Latin America Focus*, October 29, 2014. https://peter wdavies.com/2014/10/29/bring-them-back-speech-by-elena-poniatowska -translation/.

Poniatowska, Elena. "Communiqué: Voices from the Jungle, Subcomandante Marcos and Culture." In *Distant Relations/Cercanias Distantes/Clann I gCéin: Chicano, Irish, Mexican Art and Critical Writing*, edited by Trisha Ziff, 214–25. New York: Smart Art Press, 1995.

Poniatowska, Elena. "Diez años después: El rumor de las manifestaciones." *Proceso*, September 30, 1978. https://www.proceso.com.mx/124437/diez -anos-despues.

Poniatowska, Elena. "Discurso Elena Poniatowska, Premio Cervantes 2013." Premios Cervantes en el Archivo de RTVE, Spain, April 23, 2014. http:// www.rtve.es/alacarta/videos/premios-cervantes-en-el-archivo-de-rtve /discurso-integro-elena-poniatowska-recoger-premio-cervantes/2526024/.

Poniatowska, Elena. *El amante polaco*. Libro 1. Mexico City: Seix Barral, 2019.

Poniatowska, Elena. "Elena Poniatowska recuerda a estudiantes de Ayotzinapa en FIL Guadalajara." YouTube, December 5, 2014. https://www.youtube .com/watch?v=qAZNvQq-Muk.

Poniatowska, Elena. *El universo o nada*. Mexico City: Planeta, 2013.

Poniatowska, Elena. "Entrevista del Subcomandante Marcos con Elena Poniatowska." *Enlace Zapatista*, July 24, 1994. http://enlacezapatista .ezln.org.mx/1994/07/24/subcomandante-marcos-entrevista-con-elena -poniatowska-las-decisiones-grandes-las-estrategicas-las-mas-definitivas -vienen-de-abajo/.

Poniatowska, Elena. *Fuerte es el silencio*. Mexico City: Ediciones Era, 1980.

Poniatowska, Elena. *Hasta no verte, Jesús mío*. Mexico City: Ediciones Era, 1969.

Poniatowska, Elena. *Here's to You, Jesusa!* Translated by Deanna Heikkinen. New York: Farrar, Straus and Giroux, 2001.

Poniatowska, Elena. *Hojas de Papel Volando*. Mexico City: Ediciones Era, 2014.

Poniatowska, Elena. "Intervención de Elena Poniatowska en Zócalo." YouTube, October 26, 2014. https://www.youtube.com/watch?v=tKsj6UQk_Fk.

Poniatowska, Elena. Interview by the author, July 27–29, 2011, Mexico City. Audio and transcript in possession of author.

Poniatowska, Elena. Interview by the author, August 28, 2012, Mexico City. Audio and transcript in possession of author.

Poniatowska, Elena. Interview by the author, June 19, 2015, Mexico City. Audio and transcript in possession of author.

Poniatowska, Elena. Interview by the author, June 30, 2018, Mexico City. Audio and transcript in possession of author.

Poniatowska, Elena. Interview by the author, May 1, 2019, Mexico City. Audio and transcript in possession of author.

Poniatowska, Elena. "La CND: De naves mayores a menores." In *EZLN: Documentos y comunicados, 1° de enero/8° de agosto de 1994*, 324–28. Mexico City: Ediciones Era, 1994.

Poniatowska, Elena. *La herida de Paulina: Crónica del embarazo de una niña violada*. Mexico City: Editorial Planeta Mexicana, 2007.

Poniatowska, Elena. *La noche de Tlatelolco*. Mexico City: Ediciones Era, 1971.

Poniatowska, Elena. *La noche de Tlatelolco*. 2nd corrected ed. Mexico City: Ediciones Era, 1998.

Poniatowska, Elena. *La piel del cielo*. Mexico City: Alfaguara, 2001.

Poniatowska, Elena. "La postulación de una mujer indígena a la presidencia de México." *La Jornada*, November 2, 2016. https://www.jornada.com.mx /2016/11/02/opinion/015a1pol.

Poniatowska, Elena. "Las memorias de una costurera: Evangelina Corona." *La Jornada*, May 11, 2008. https://www.jornada.com.mx/2008/05/11/index .php?section=cultura&article=a06a1cul.

Poniatowska, Elena. *Lilus Kikus*. Mexico City: Los Presentes, 1954.

Poniatowska, Elena. "Llanto por Julio Scherer García, Elena Poniatowska." *La Jornada*, January 8, 2015. https://www.jornada.com.mx/2015/01/08 /opinion/004a1pol.

Poniatowska, Elena. "Los 100 años de Doña Conchita Calvillo de Nava." *La Jornada*, December 10, 2017. http://www.jornada.unam.mx/2017/12/10 /opinion/a03a1cul.

Poniatowska, Elena. *Massacre in Mexico*. Translated by Helen R. Lane. Columbia: University of Missouri Press, 1975.

Poniatowska, Elena. *Nada, nadie: Las voces del temblor*. Mexico City: Ediciones Era, 1988.

Poniatowska, Elena. *Nothing, Nobody: The Voices of the Mexico City Earthquake*. Translated by Aurora Camacho de Schmidt and Arthur Schmidt. Philadelphia: Temple University Press, 1995.

Poniatowska, Elena. "Nuestro peor enemigo es el olvido: El septiembre negro de 1985, Terremoto." *Proceso*, no. 51 (September 2015), 8–18.

Poniatowska, Elena. *Palabras cruzadas*. Mexico City: Ediciones Era, 1961.

Poniatowska, Elena. "Posición frente a los problemas nacionales." *Siempre!* 793 (September 2, 1968): 60–62.

Poniatowska, Elena. "¡Que viva la marcha INDIGENA!" *La Jornada*, March 13, 2001. https://www.jornada.com.mx/2001/03/13/per-indigenas.html.

Poniatowska, Elena. "'Regrésenlos' (discurso de Elena Poniatowska en el Zócalo)." Universidad, October 29, 2014. http://www.unidiversidad.com.ar/regresenlos-discurso-de-elena-poniatowska-en-el-zocalo.

Poniatowska, Elena. "'Regrésenlos,' el discurso íntegro de Elena Poniatowska en el Zócalo." *Animal Político*, October 27, 2014. https://www.animalpolitico.com/2014/10/regresenlos-discurso-de-elena-poniatowska-en-el-zocalo/.

Poniatowska, Elena. "Regrésenlos" (discurso de la escritora Elena Poniatowska en el Zócalo de México). Resumen Latinoamericano, October 27, 2014. https://www.resumenlatinoamericano.org/2014/10/27/regresenlos-discurso-de-la-escritora-elena-poniatowska-en-el-zocalo-de-mexico/.

Poniatowska, Elena. "7 días del mundo." *Siempre!* 794 (September 11, 1968): 44.

Poniatowska, Elena. "Solo la muerte doma a los estudiantes." *El País*, October 4, 2018. https://elpais.com/deportes/2018/10/02/actualidad/1538504768_865568.html.

Poniatowska, Elena. *Todo empezó el domingo*. Mexico City: Fondo de la Cultura Económica, 1963.

Poniatowska, Elena. "Women, Mexico, and Chiapas." In *First World, Ha Ha Ha! The Zapatista Challenge*, edited by Elaine Katzenberger, 99–108. San Francisco: City Lights, 2001.

Presidencia Enrique Peña Nieto. "Conferencia de Prensa del Procurador, Jesús Murillo Karam (Ayotzinapa)." YouTube, November 7, 2014. https://www.youtube.com/watch?v=QNcfdHUiP8c.

Preston, Julia, and Samuel Dillon. *Opening Mexico: The Making of a Democracy*. New York: Farrar, Straus and Giroux, 2004.

Proceso. "Sócrates, 'delator' del movimiento." *Proceso*, September 30, 1978. https://www.proceso.com.mx/124433/socrates-delator-del-movimiento.

Proceso. "Historias del 68: La Nacha Rodríguez, un privilegio seguir viva." *Proceso*, October 2, 2008. https://www.proceso.com.mx/202172/historias-del-68-la-nacha-rodriguez-un-privilegio-seguir-viva.

Rabasa, José. *History: Subaltern Studies, the Zapatista Insurgency, and the Specter of History.* Pittsburgh: University of Pittsburgh Press, 2010.

Radio Zapatista. "Discurso de Marichuy, vocera del CIG, en el recinto de la Guardia Tradicional de Vicam, Cabecera de los 8 Pueblos de la Tribu Yaqui." Radio Zapatista, January 12, 2018. https://radiozapatista.org/?p =25356&lang=en.

Ramírez Cuevas, Jesús. "Repercusiones sociales y políticas del temblor de 1985: Cuando los ciudadanos tomaron la ciudad en sus manos." *La Jornada,* September 11, 2005. https://www.jornada.com.mx/2005/09/11/mas-jesus .html.

Rappaport, Joanne. *Cowards Don't Make History: Orlando Fals Borda and the Origins of Participatory Action Research.* Durham, NC: Duke University Press, 2020.

Rappaport, Joanne. *Intercultural Utopias: Public Intellectuals, Cultural Experimentation, and Ethnic Pluralism in Colombia.* Durham, NC: Duke University Press, 2005.

Rappaport, Joanne. *The Politics of Memory: Native Historical Interpretation in the Colombian Andes.* Durham, NC: Duke University Press, 1998.

Robles Lomeli, Jafte Dilean, and Joanne Rappaport. "Imagining Latin American Social Science from the Global South: Orlando Fals Borda and Participatory Action Research." *Latin American Research Review* 53, no. 3 (2018): 597–612.

Rodda, John. "Trapped at Gunpoint in the Middle of Fighting." *The Guardian,* October 4, 1968, 1, 2.

Rodríguez, Candelaria. 1994. "Se repenaliza en Chiapas el aborto." *La Jornada,* April 12, 1994. Reprinted in *Chiapas, ¿y las mujeres qué?,* edited by María Rosa García Rojas, 1:135–38. Mexico City: Ediciones La Correa Feminista.

Rodríguez, Jesusa. Interview by the author, October 12, 2015. Audio file and transcript in possession of author.

Rodríguez, Rey. 2019. "Elena Poniatowska sobre la violencia actual en México: El caso Ayotzinapa es peor que la masacre del 68." *CNN,* October 2, 2018. https://cnnespanol.cnn.com/video/ayotzinapa-43-peor-que-tlatelolco-2 -octubre-68-sot-elena-poniatowska-perspectivas-mexico/.

Rovira, Giomar. *Women of Maize: Indigenous Women and the Zapatista Rebellion.* London: Latin American Bureau, 2001.

Rubin, Jeffrey. *Decentering the Regime: Ethnicity, Radicalism, and Democracy in Juchitán, Mexico.* Durham, NC: Duke University Press, 1997.

Rus, Jan. "The Struggle against Indigenous Caciques in Highland Chiapas: Dissent, Religion and Exile in Chamula, 1965–1977." In *Caciquismo in Twentieth-Century Mexico,* edited by Alan Knight and Wil Pansters, 169–200. London: Institute for the Study of the Americas, 2005.

Salinas, Carlos, and Andrea Aguilar. "Elena Poniatowska desvela que el escritor Juan José Arreola la violó y la dejó embarazada." *El País,* December 13,

2019. https://elpais.com/cultura/2019/12/12/actualidad/1576168249_013446
.html.

Salinas de Gortari, Carlos. "Discurso de Toma de Posesión de Carlos Salinas
de Gortari como Presidente Constitucional de Los Estados Unidos Mexicanos." *500 años de México en documentos*, December 1, 1988. http://www
.biblioteca.tv/artman2/publish/1988_67/Discurso_de_Toma_de_Posesi_n
_de_Carlos_Salinas_de__74.shtml.

Salinas de Gortari, Carlos. "1993 MIT Commencement Address." May 28,
1993. YouTube, January 20, 2016. https://www.youtube.com/watch?v
=XstC7SuLotE.

Sandoval Ramírez, Denisse. "Unidad Tlatelolco: Entre la historia y el aban-
dono." *El Universal*, September 29, 2014. https://aniversario.eluniversal
.com.mx/unidad-tlatelolco-entre-la-historia-y-el-abandono/.

Schuessler, Michael K. *Elena Poniatowska: An Intimate Biography*. Tucson:
University of Arizona Press, 2007.

Schuessler, Michael K. "Mexico's Tlatelolco Massacre, and Its Echoes Today."
The Nation, August 3, 2018. https://www.thenation.com/article/mexicos
-tlatelolco-massacre-echoes-today/.

Secretaría de Gobernación. "Problema estudantil." 1968. Secretaría de Gober-
nación, Dirección Federal de Seguridad, Galería 2, IPS, Caja 1459-A,
F. 13–18. Archivo General de la Nación. https://nsarchive2.gwu.edu
/NSAEBB/NSAEBB201/Documento%205.13-18.pdf.

Simpson, Audra. *Mohawk Interruptus: Political Life across the Borders of Settler
States*. Durham, NC: Duke University Press, 2014.

Smith, Benjamin T. *The Mexican Press and Civil Society: 1940–1976*. Chapel
Hill: University of North Carolina Press, 2018.

Solares, Ignacio. "La Revista de la Universidad." *La Revista de la Universidad de México* 79, no. 3 (September 2010): 81–85.https://www
.revistadelauniversidad.mx/articles/4256d9b7-e443-422a-ab23
-ado812b20bod/la-revista-de-la-universidad.

Sorensen, Diana. *A Turbulent Decade Remembered: Scenes from the Latin American Sixties*. Palo Alto: Stanford University Press, 2007.

Speed, Shannon, Rosalva Aída Hernández Castillo, and Lynn Stephen. *Dissident Women: Gender and Cultural Politics in Chiapas*. Austin: University
of Texas Press, 2006.

Spivak, Gayatri Chakravorty. *Other Asias*. Malden, MA: Blackwell, 2008.

Steele, Cynthia. "Entrevista: Elena Poniatowska." *Hispamérica* 18, nos. 53/54
(August–December 1989): 89–105.

Steele, Cynthia. 2002. "The Rainforest Chronicles of Subcomandante Mar-
cos." In *The Contemporary Mexican Chronicle: Theoretical Perspectives on the
Liminal Genre*, edited by Ignacio Corona and Beth E. Jörgensen, 245–55.
Albany: State University of New York Press, 2002.

Stephen, Lynn. "Asserting Indigeneity in Contemporary Mexico and Central
America: Autonomy, Rights, and Confronting Nation-States." In *Hemispheric

Indigeneities: Native Identity and Agency in Mesoamerica, the Andes, and Canada, edited by Meléna Santoro and Erick Lange, 245–88. Lincoln: University of Nebraska Press, 2018.

Stephen, Lynn. "Rural Women's Activism, 1980–2000: Reframing the Nation from Below." In *Sex in Revolution: Gender, Politics, and Power in Modern Mexico*, edited by Jocelyn Olcott, Mary Kay Vaughn, and Gabriela Cano, 241–60. Durham, NC: Duke University Press, 2006.

Stephen, Lynn. *Transborder Lives: Indigenous Oaxacans in Mexico, California, and Oregon*. Durham, NC: Duke University Press, 2007.

Stephen, Lynn. *We Are the Face of Oaxaca: Testimony and Social Movements*. Durham, NC: Duke University Press, 2013.

Stephen, Lynn. *Women and Social Movements in Latin America: Power from Below*. Austin: University of Texas Press, 1997.

Stephen, Lynn. "Women in Mexico's Popular Movements: Survival Strategies for Ecological and Economic Impoverishment." *Latin American Perspectives* 10, no. 1 (1992): 73–96.

Stephen, Lynn. *Zapata Lives! Histories and Cultural Politics in Southern Mexico*. Berkeley: University of California Press, 2002.

Stoll, David. *Rigoberta Menchú and the Story of All Poor Guatemalans*. Boulder, CO: Westview, 1999.

Subcomandante Marcos. "Comunicado de Prensa del Subcomandante Marcos, a Marta Lamas." *Bibliotecas Virtuales de México*, May 5, 1994. https://www .bibliotecas.tv/chiapas/may94/05may94.html.

Subcomandante Marcos. *Questions and Swords: Folktales from the Zapatista Revolution*. El Paso: Cinco Puntos Press, 2001.

Subcomandante Marcos. *The Story of Colors/La Historia de los Colores: A Bilingual Folktale from the Jungles of Chiapas*. El Paso: Cinco Puntos Press, 2003.

Taylor, Diana. *The Archive and the Repertoire: Performing Cultural Memory in the Americas*. Durham, NC: Duke University Press, 2003.

Teichman, Judith. "Neoliberalism and the Transformation of Mexican Authoritarianism." Centre for Research on Latin America and the Caribbean, York University. January 1996. https://cerlac.info.yorku.ca/files/2016 /09/Teichman.pdf?x98575.

Terracino, Kevin. *The Mixtecs of Colonial Oaxaca*. Palo Alto: Stanford University Press, 2001.

Thompson, Ginger, and Tim Weiner. "Zapatista Rebels Rally in Mexico City." *New York Times*, March 12, 2001.

Thomson, Guy. "Benito Juárez and Liberalism." In *The Oxford Research Encyclopedia of Latin American History*, 1–45. March 28, 2018. https://doi.org/10 .1093/acrefore/9780199366439.013.461.

Tomlinson, Alan, dir. *Masacre en Tlatelolco, 2 octubre 1968*. May 26, 2012. https:// www.youtube.com/watch?v=Tw2KsKXrF50.

Tribune News Service. "México cifra en 77,178 los desaparecidos desde 2006." October 7, 2020. https://www.chicagotribune.com/espanol/sns-es-mexico

-cifra-77000-desaparecidos-20201007-bxyf2qeisnbz5hcrj2p73gmbeu-story
.html.

Universidad Autónoma de México (UNAM). "Anuario estadístico 1968 UNAM."
Universidad Autónoma de México, 1972. http://agendas.planeacion.unam
.mx/pdf/Anuario-1968.pdf.

UN Women. "The Long Road to Justice, Prosecuting Femicide in Mexico."
UN Women, November 29, 2017. http://www.unwomen.org/en/news
/stories/2017/11/feature-prosecuting-femicide-in-mexico.

Vaughan, Mary Kay. "Cultural Approaches to Peasant Politics in the Mexican
Revolution." *Hispanic American Cultural Review* 79, no. 2 (1997): 269–305.

Vaughan, Mary Kay. *Portrait of a Young Painter: Pepe Zúñiga and Mexico City's
Rebel Generation*. Durham, NC: Duke University Press, 2014.

Vázquez Delgado, Mónica. "Entrevista a Ana Ignacia 'La Nacha' Rodríguez:
Estudiante partícipe y presa política del 2 de Octubre de 1968." *Megáfono
de palabras*, March 25, 2013. https://megafonodepalabras.blogspot.com
/2013/03/entrevista-ana-ignacia-la-nacha.html.

Vázquez Mantecón, Álvaro. "The '68 Impact on the Visual Arts." In 68 + 50,
edited by Ana Xanic López, 50–59. Mexico City: Museo Universitario
Arte Contemporáneo, Universidad Nacional Autónoma de México, 2018.

Vega, Patricia. "Celebra 20 años la primera edición de *La noche de Tlatelolco*."
La Jornada, August 27, 1991, 40, 41.

Vela, David Saúl. "Identifican restos de otro normalista de Ayotzinapa." *El Financiero*, September 16, 2015. https://www.elfinanciero.com.mx/nacional
/identifican-a-otro-normalista-de-ayotzinapa.html.

Vélez-Ibañez, Carlos G. *Rituals of Marginality: Politics, Process, and Culture
Change in Urban Central Mexico, 1969–1974*. Berkeley: University of California Press, 1983.

Vera, Oscar. *La economía subterránea en México*. Mexico City: Editorial Diana,
1987.

Vicenteño, David. "Oficialmente muertos; reporte de la PGR sobre el caso
Ayotzinapa." *Excélsior*, January 28, 2015. https://www.excelsior.com.mx
/nacional/2015/01/28/1004994.

Volpi, Jorge. *La imaginación y el poder: Una historia intelectual de 1968*. Mexico
City: Ediciones Era, 1998.

Walker, Louise. *Waking from the Dream: Mexico's Middle Class after 1968*. Palo
Alto: Stanford University Press, 2013.

Watt, Peter. "Mexico's Secret Dirty War." University of Guadalajara, Sincronía,
Summer 2010. http://sincronia.cucsh.udg.mx/wattsummer2010.htm.

Wattenbarger, Madeline. "For Mexico's President, Forced Disappearances
Could Make or Break the Justice System." *Foreign Policy*, October 4,
2019. https://foreignpolicy.com/2019/10/04/ayotzinapa-anniversary-amlo
-mexico-impunity-security-forced-disappearance-justice/.

Wilkinson, Daniel. "Los otros desaparecidos." *El Universal*, January 14, 2019.
https://www.eluniversal.com.mx/articulo/daniel-wilkinson/nacion/los
-otros-desaparecidos.

Wood, Andrew G. Review of *Carlos Monsiváis: Culture and Chronicle in Contemporary Mexico*, by Linda Egan. *Hispanic American Historical Review* 83, no. 3 (2003): 588–89.

YoAMLO. "AMLO Spot—NO CALUMNIEN." Featuring Elena Poniatowska. YouTube, June 5, 2006. https://www.youtube.com/watch?v=MjPju -mPyMQ.

Zapatistas! Documents of the New Mexican Revolution. Brooklyn, NY: Autonomedia, 1994.

Zolov, Eric. "Culture in Mexico during the Miracle and Beyond, 1946–1982." In *Oxford Research Encyclopedia of Latin American History*. May 9, 2016. https://doi.org/10.1093/acrefore/9780199366439.013.25.

Zolov, Eric. *The Last Good Neighbor: Mexico in the Global Sixties*. Durham, NC: Duke University Press, 2020.

Zolov, Eric. *Refried Elvis: The Rise of Mexican Counterculture*. Berkeley: University of California Press, 1999.

Index

Corona, Evangelina, 119, 124, 131–35, 140–41, 208
Cortázar, Julio, 159
Cortés, Hernán, 9
Cosío Villegas, Daniel, 45
counternarratives, 242–43
COVID-19 pandemic, 18, 181, 247
crime news, 43–44
critical public, 31–59, 249, 251; earthquake victims and, 112, 130, 135; EZLN and, 169; Habermas and, 259n6; historical narratives and, 3–4, 24–26; student activism and, 65–66, 78; Zócalo sit-in and, 197, 208. *See also* public sphere
crónicas, 4–10, 13–16, 24–25; Egan on, 15–17; gender politics and, 10–13; of Indigenous people, 10, 15, 17, 251; Jörgensen on, 6, 13–16; Monsiváis on, 6, 10, 13, 15; novels versus, 9, 13; of Novo, 11; oral histories and, 8; of Spanish Conquest, 4, 9, 258n16; strategic emotional political communities and, 7, 18–22; of Subcomandante Marcos, 160; of Zócalo sit-in, 200, 226
Cuban Revolution (1959), 32, 34; Mexican press and, 38–39; C. Wright Mills on, 45–46

Davis, Diane, 115
de la Madrid, Miguel, 115; Abarca and, 135–41; autobiography of, 130–31; Corona on, 132–35; earthquake response of, 117, 119–21, 124, 129–30; on Salinas de Gortari's election, 148–49
del Río, Dolores, 36
Delgado, Dante, 220, 223
Departamento de Investigaciones Históricas, 5
Díaz del Castillo, Bernal, 9
Díaz Ordaz, Gustavo, 11, 34, 65–66; criticism of, 44, 46; student movement and, 85–87
Díez-Canedo, Joaquín, 51
Dirección Federal de Seguidad (DFS), 58

Dirty War: in Argentina, 228; in Mexico, 3, 6, 27, 107–9, 115–16 (See also *Fuerte es el silencio*)
domestic violence, 168–69, 175–76, 181, 187. *See also* gender politics
Domínguez Navarro, Ofelia, 178
Dorfman, Ariel, 247–248
Doyle, Kate, 67, 98, 242
Duby, Gertrudes, 36
Durán, Diego, 4

earthquake of 1985 (Mexico City), 20, 27, 117–50, 207; casualties of, 117, 126; Monsiváis on, 27; photographs of, *119*; thirtieth anniversary of, 110–12, *111*, 120–21; Zócalo sit-in and, 219. See also *Nothing, Nobody*
Echeverría, Luis, 33, 57, 116
Ediciones ERA, 50–52, 160, 172, 264n45
Editorial Joaquín Mortiz, 51
Egan, Linda, 15–17
Ejército Guerrillero de los Pobres, 108
Ejército Zapatista de Liberación Nacional (EZLN), 3, 9, 27, 151–54; on abortion, 179; communiqués of, 158–60; Convención Nacional Democrática of, 160, 165–66, 170–73; emergence of, 158; formation of, 152–54; government accords of 1996 with, 153–54; as strategic emotional political community, 161. *See also* Zapatistas
ejidos (communal land grants), 155, 158, 193
"emotional communities" (Jimeno), 7, 18–22, 68–70. *See also* strategic emotional political communities
Encinas, Alejandro, 244
Encinas Rodríguez, Alejandro, 209, 223
Equipo Argentino de Antropología Forense, 230
Erro Soler, Luis Enrique, 48
Escarcega, Sylvia, 257n2
Escoto, Alejandro, 146
Escoto, Andrés, 145–49, *147*

Habermas, Jürgen, 259n6
Haro, Guillermo, 48–49, *108*, 261n78
Haro Poniatowska, Emmanuel "Mane,"
108, 162, 182–85, 212
Haro Poniatowska, Felipe, 32, 63, *64*, *108*;
EZLN visit of, 162–63, *167*, 181; López
Obrador and, 207
Haro Poniatowska, Paula, *64*, *108*, 196;
EZLN visit of, 160–63, *167*, 173; Zócalo
sit-in and, 198, 207, 215
Harrison, V. V., 35
Harvey, Neil, 157
Hasta no verte, Jesús mío (Poniatowska),
53–55, *54*, 63
Henríquez, Elio, 159
La herida de Paulina (Poniatowska), 182,
185–86
Hernández, Anabel, 232–33, 245
Hernández Estrada, Rafael, 220
Hernández Gamundi, Félix Lucio,
73–74, 100
Hernández Posadas, Mario, 127
Herzog, Werner, 173, 273n56
Hojas de papel volando (Poniatowska),
253

Ibarra de Piedra, Rosario, 107, 116, 172,
208, 276n14
Iguala. *See* Ayotzinapa students'
disappearances
Indigenous Congress (1974), 156–57
Indigenous peoples, 154–58; abortion
issues among, 176–81; autonomy
of, 153–54, 174, 188, 195; of Chiapas,
152–58, 174; chronicles of, 10, 15, 17, 251;
feminism among, 153–54; land reforms
and, 155; languages of, 174, 194, 236;
malnutrition among, 158, 179; middle-
class, 156; rights of, 152–55, 188, 192,
195; Subcomandante Marcos on,
168–69
Instituto Federal Electoral, 207
Instituto Nacional de Antropología e
Historia, 5
Instituto Nacional de Estudios Históricos de la Revolución Mexicana, 67

Instituto Nacional Indigenista (INI),
155–56
Instituto Politécnico Nacional (IPN), 34,
65, 68, 84, 89
Inter-American Commission on
Human Rights (IACHR), 169, 241
Interdisciplinary Group of Independent
Experts (IGIE), 241–42, 245
International Monetary Fund (IMF),
114, 151–52, 164
Isabel, Margarita, 78, 91
Iturbide, Graciela, 172

Jiménez Moreno, Winberto, 5
Jimeno, Myriam, 7, 18–22, 69–70
Jörgensen, Beth, 6, 13–16; on *Amanecer
en el Zócalo*, 200, 217–18; on *Massacre
in Mexico*, 80
La Jornada (newspaper), 39, 40, 44,
58–59; Ayotzinapa students' disappearances and, 235–36, 238–39; earthquake of 1985 in, 121–23, 141–46, *143*,
147; founding of, 57, 121; Subcomandante Marcos and, 159, 161, 163, 169
Juárez, Benito, 154–55, 194

Kiejman, Claude, 97, 105
King, John, 40
Krauze, Enrique, 166

Labastida Ochoa, Francisco, 198
Lacandón Jungle, 152, 155, 158, 163
Lamas, Marta, 109, 119, 179, 180, 185, 201
land reforms: of Juárez, 154–55; of Sali-
nas de Gotari, 152, 158
Lane, Helen R., 61
Lawson, Chappell H., 41–42, 57
Lecumberri Prison, 51, 53, 55, 250
León, Eugenia, 172
Lewis, Oscar, 42, 46–49, 53, 55
Lewis, Stephen E., 156
Ley Lerdo (1856), 155
Ley Revolucionaria de Mujeres, 175–82,
186–87, 193
Liga Comunista 23 de Septiembre, 116
Lilus Kikus (Poniatowska), 184

Spanish Conquest, 4, 9, 213, 258n16
Spivak, Gayatri Chakravorty, 18
Steele, Cynthia, 118, 160, 272n24
sterilization, involuntary, 178
Stoll, David, 6
storytelling, 16–17, 170, 174; counternarratives and, 242–43; Jörgensen on, 14;
statistics and, 239–40
"strategic emotional political communities" (Stephen), 2, 106–9, 244, 246;
crónicas and, 7, 18–22; definition of,
18–19; earthquake of 1985 and, 141–48;
EZLN as, 161. *See also* "emotional
communities"
"strategic essentialism" (Spivak), 18
structural adjustment policies (SAPs),
113–15, 151–52, 164
student disappearances. *See* Ayotzinapa
students' disappearances
student movements, 20–22, 26–27, 65–68,
75–84; action committees of, 90;
Bórquez on, 250–51; class awareness
in, 89–91; gender politics of, 91–96;
slogans of, 89; Zócalo sit-in and,
200, 202, 218, 219. *See also* Tlatelolco
massacre
Subcomandante Marcos. *See* Marcos,
Subcomandante

tabloid press, 43–44, 56
Tacho, Comandante, 172–73
Taibo, Paco Ignacio, 204, 205
Taller de Gráfica Popular, 52
Taylor, Diana, 216
testimonials, 6–7, 17–18; "collective,"
257n1; of earthquake survivors, 15;
of slave women, 11; storytelling and,
174
Thoreau, Henry David, 215, 216
Tlacolulokos (artists' collective), 243
Tlatelolco massacre (1968): anniversa-
ries of, 29, 32, 251; film about, 60, 71,
262n1; maps of, *99*. *See also Massacre
in Mexico*
Tlatelolco Unido, 268n1
Tojolabal people, 152, 156

Torrecillas, Sóstenes, 104
Touraine, Alain, 190
Tovar García, Jesús, 101, 102
Tribunal Electoral del Poder Judicial de
la Federación, 198
Tribunal Federal Electoral (TRIFE), 217
Tzeltal people, 152, 169
Tzotzil people, 152, 156, 194

UNAM. *See* Universidad Autónoma de
México
Unión de Costureras en Lucha, 133–34
Unión de Ejidos de la Selva, 157
El Universal Ilustrado (magazine), 12, 42
Universidad Autónoma de Chihuahua,
90, 104
Universidad Autónoma de México
(UNAM), 32–34; Escuela Nacional
de Artes Plásticas of, 52; Instituto
de Astronomía at, 49; Law School
of, 92–93; Museo Universitario Arte
Contemporáneo at, 74; publications
of, 39
Universidad Autónoma de Puebla, 90
El universo o nada (Poniatowska), 48, 49
Unomásuno (newspaper), 39, 44, 57–59
urban social movements, 115, 148, 153,
269n17
Urquidi, Víctor, 267n158

Valadez Capistrán, Marcos, 88
Valle Espinoza, Eduardo, 91–92, 103, 104
Vallejo, Demetrio, 53
Vargas Llosa, Mario, 159
Vásquez, Genaro, 237
Vaughan, Mary Kay, 32
Vega, David, 98
Vélez de Aguilera, Perla, 106
Villa, Pancho, 152
Villoro, Luis, 222

Walker, Louise, 47
White, Francis, 35–36
Women's Revolutionary Law, 175–82,
186–87, 193. *See also* gender politics
World Bank, 114, 151–52, 164

Yampolksy, Mariana, 172

Zabludowsky, Jacobo, 144
Zaid, Gabriel, 40
Zapata, Emiliano, 85, 152, 157, 172, 189;
Cabañas and, 238; Subcomandante
Marcos and, 162
Zapatistas, 3, 27, 72, 151–54; class issues
with, 168, 171; gender politics of,
153–54, 175–96. *See also* Ejército
Zapatista de Liberación Nacional
(EZLN)
Zapotec people, 154
Zavalla, Susana, 67
Zedillo, Ernesto, 187
Zepeda, Eracilo, 172

Zerón, Tomás, 231
Zerón de Lucio, Tomás, 240–41, 244
Ziff, Trisha, 174
Zócalo, 86, 209, 214; Ayotzinapa students' rally in, 234–39, 244; Zapatista
march in, 190
Zócalo AMLO sit-in (2006), 3, 28–29,
198–209; background of, 209–13;
Convención Nacional Democrática
during, 214, 217, 223; economic impact
of, 211; gender politics of, 202; legacy
of, 226–27; performative culture at,
213–17; student movement of 1968
and, 200, 202
Zolov, Eric, 34, 77, 86
Zúñiga, Pepe, 32

www.ingramcontent.com/pod-product-compliance
Lightning Source LLC
Chambersburg PA
CBHW071731270326
41928CB00013B/2633

* 9 7 8 1 4 7 8 0 1 4 6 4 5 *